MY LIFE

*Richard Wagner about 1872
by Lenbach
Original in the possession of Frau Cosima Wagner*

MY LIFE

BY

RICHARD WAGNER

IN TWO VOLUMES

VOL. II

AUTHORIZED TRANSLATION FROM THE GERMAN

NEW YORK
DODD, MEAD AND COMPANY
1911

CONTENTS

PART III. 1850–1861

PART IV. 1861–1864

▼

MY LIFE

PART III

1850–1861

MINNA had been lucky enough to find quarters near Zürich which corresponded very closely with the wishes I had so emphatically expressed before leaving. The house was situated in the parish of Enge, a good fifteen minutes' walk from the town, on a site overlooking the lake, and was an old-fashioned hostelry called 'Zum Abendstern,' belonging to a certain Frau Hirel, who was a pleasant old lady. The second floor, which was quite self-contained and very quiet, offered us humble but adequate accommodations for a modest rent.

I arrived early in the morning and found Minna still in bed. She was anxious to know whether I had returned simply out of pity; but I quickly succeeded in obtaining her promise that she would never again refer to what had taken place. She was soon quite herself again when she began to show me the progress she had made in arranging the rooms.

Our position had for some years been growing more comfortable, in spite of the fact that at this time various difficulties again arose, and our domestic happiness seemed tolerably secure. Yet I could never quite master a restless inclination to deviate from anything that was regarded as conventional.

Our two pets, Peps and Papo, largely helped to make our lodgings homelike; both were very fond of me, and were sometimes even too obtrusive in showing their affection. Peps would always lie behind me in the armchair while I was working, and Papo, after repeatedly calling out 'Richard' in vain, would often come fluttering into my study if I stayed away from the sitting-room too long. He would then settle down on my desk and vigorously shuffle about the papers and pens. He was so well trained that he never uttered the ordinary cry of a bird, but expressed his sentiments only by talking or singing. As soon as he heard my step on the staircase he would begin whistling a tune, as, for instance, the great march in the finale of the Symphony in C minor, the beginning of the Eighth Symphony in F major, or even a bright bit out of the *Rienzi* Overture. Peps, our little dog, on the other hand, was a highly sensitive and nervous creature. My friends used to call him 'Peps the petulant,' and there were times when we could not speak to him even in the friendliest way without bringing on paroxysms of howls and sobs. These two pets of course helped very much to increase the mutual understanding between myself and my wife.

Unfortunately, there was one perpetual source of quarrel, arising from my wife's behaviour towards poor Nathalie. Until her death she shamefully withheld from the girl the fact that she was her mother. Nathalie, therefore, always believed that she was Minna's sister, and consequently could not understand why she should not have the same rights as my wife, who always treated her in an authoritative way, as a strict mother would do, and seemed to think herself justified in complaining of Nathalie's behaviour. Apparently the latter had been much neglected and spoiled just at the critical age, and deprived of any proper training. She was short in stature and inclined to become stout, her manners were awkward and her opinions narrow. Minna's hasty temper and continual jeering made the girl, who was naturally very good-natured, stubborn and spiteful, so that the behaviour of the 'sisters' often caused the most hateful scenes in our quiet home. I never lost my patience at these incidents, however, but remained completely indifferent to everything going on around me.

The arrival of my young friend Karl was a pleasant diversion in our small household. He occupied a tiny attic above our rooms and shared our meals. Sometimes he would accompany me on my walks, and for a time seemed quite satisfied.

But I soon noticed in him a growing restlessness. He had not been slow to recognise, by the unpleasant scenes that again became daily occurrences in our married life, at what point the shoe pinched that I had good-naturedly put on again at his request. However, when one day I reminded him that in coming back to Zürich I had other objects in view besides the longing for a quiet domestic life, he remained silent. But I saw that there was another peculiar reason for his uneasiness; he took to coming in late for meals, and even then he had no appetite. At first I was anxious at this, fearing he might have taken a dislike to our simple fare, but I soon discovered that my young friend was so passionately addicted to sweets that I feared he might eventually ruin his health by trying to live on large quantities of confectionery. My remarks seemed to annoy him, as his absences from the house became more frequent, I thought that probably his small room did not afford him the comfort he required, and I therefore made no objection when he left us and took a room in town.

As his state of uneasiness still seemed to increase and he did not appear at all happy in Zürich, I was glad to be able to suggest a little change for him, and persuade him to go for a holiday to Weimar, where the first performance of *Lohengrin* was to take place about the end of August.

About the same time I induced Minna to go with me for our first ascent of the Righi, a feat we both accomplished very energetically on foot. I was very much grieved on this occasion to discover that my wife had symptoms of heart disease, which continued to develop subsequently. We spent the evening of the 28th of August, while the first performance of *Lohengrin* was taking place at Weimar, in Lucerne, at the Schwan inn, watching the clock as the hands went round, and marking the various times at which the performance presumably began, developed, and came to a close.

I always felt somewhat distressed, uncomfortable, and ill at ease whenever I tried to pass a few pleasant hours in the society of my wife.

The reports received of that first performance gave me no clear or reassuring impression of it. Karl Ritter soon came back to Zürich, and told me of deficiencies in staging and of the unfortunate choice of a singer for the leading part, but remarked that on the whole it had gone fairly well. The reports sent me by Liszt were the most encouraging. He did not seem to think it worth while to allude to the inadequacy of the means at his command for such a bold undertaking, but preferred to dwell on the sympathetic spirit that prevailed in the company and the effect it produced on the influential personages he had invited to be present.

Although everything in connection with this important enterprise eventually assumed a bright aspect, the direct result on my position at the time was very slight. I was more interested in the future of the young friend who had been entrusted to my care than in anything else. At the time of his visit to Weimar he had been to stay with his family in Dresden, and after his return expressed an anxious wish to become a musician, and possibly to secure a position as a musical director at a theatre. I had never had an opportunity of judging of his gifts in this line. He had always refused to play the piano in my presence, but I had seen his setting of an alliterative poem of his own, *Die Walküre,* which, though rather awkwardly put together, struck me by its precise and skilful compliance with the rules of composition.

He proved himself to be the worthy pupil of his master, Robert Schumann, who, long before, had told me that Karl possessed great musical gifts, and that he could not remember ever having had any other pupil endowed with such a keen ear and such a ready facility for assimilation. Consequently I had no reason to discourage the young man's confidence in his capacity for the career of a musical director. As the winter season was approaching, I asked the manager of the theatre for the address of Herr Kramer, who was coming for the season, and learned that he was still engaged at Winterthur.

Sulzer, who was always ready when help or advice was needed, arranged for a meeting with Herr Kramer at a dinner at the 'Wilden Mann' in Winterthur. At this meeting it was decided, on my recommendation, that Karl Ritter should be appointed musical director at the theatre for the ensuing winter, starting from October, and the remuneration he was to receive was really a very fair one. As my protégé was admittedly a beginner, I had to guarantee his capacity by undertaking to perform his duties in the event of any trouble arising at the theatre on the ground of his inefficiency. Karl seemed delighted. As October drew near and the opening of the theatre was announced to take place 'under exceptional artistic auspices,' I thought it advisable to see what Karl's views were.

By way of a début I had selected *Der Freischütz,* so that he might open his career with a well-known opera. Karl did not entertain the slightest doubt of being able to master such a simple score, but when he had to overcome his reserve in playing the piano before me, as I wanted to go through the whole opera with him, I was amazed at seeing that he had no idea of accompaniment. He played the arrangement for the pianoforte with the characteristic carelessness of an amateur who attaches no importance to lengthening a bar by incorrect fingering. He knew nothing whatever about rhythmic precision or tempo, the very essentials of a conductor's career. I felt completely nonplussed and was absolutely at a loss what to say. However, I still hoped the young man's talent might suddenly break out, and I looked forward to an orchestral rehearsal, for which I provided him with a pair of large spectacles. I had never noticed before that he was so shortsighted, but when reading he had to keep his face so close to the music that it would have been impossible for him to control both orchestra and singers. When I saw him, hitherto so confident, standing at the conductor's desk staring hard at the score, in spite of his spectacles, and making meaningless signs in the air like one in a trance, I at once realised that the time for carrying out my guarantee had arrived.

It was, nevertheless, a somewhat difficult and trying task to make young Ritter understand that I should be compelled to take his place; but there was no help for it, and it was I who had to inaugurate Kramer's winter season under such 'exceptional artistic auspices.' The success of *Der Freischütz* placed me in a peculiar position as regards both the company and the public, but it was quite out of the question to suppose that Karl could continue to act as musical director at the theatre by himself.

Strange to say, this trying experience coincided with an important change in the life of another young friend of mine, Hans von Bülow, whom I had known in Dresden. I had met his father at Zürich in the previous year just after his second marriage. He afterwards settled down at Lake Constance,

and it was from this place that Hans wrote to me expressing
his regret that he was unable to pay his long-desired visit to
Zürich, as he had previously promised to do.

As far as I could make out, his mother, who had been divorced
from his father, did all in her power to restrain him from
embracing the career of an artist, and tried to persuade him to
enter the civil or the diplomatic service, as he had studied law.
But his inclinations and talents impelled him to a musical
career. It seemed that his mother, when giving him permission to go to visit his father, had particularly urged him to
avoid any meeting with me. When I afterwards heard that he
had been advised by his father also not to come to Zürich, I
felt sure that the latter, although he had been on friendly terms
with me, was anxious to act in accordance with his first wife's
wishes in this serious matter of his son's future, so as to avoid
any further disputes after the friction of the divorce had barely
been allayed. Later on I learned that these statements, which
roused a strong feeling of resentment in me against Eduard von
Bülow, were unfounded; but the despairing tone of Hans's
letter, clearly showing that any other career would be repugnant
to him and would be a constant source of misery, seemed to be
ample reason for my interference. This was one of the occasions
when my easily excited indignation roused me to activity. I
replied very fully, and eloquently pointed out to him the vital
importance of this moment in his life. The desperate tone of
his letter justified me in telling him very plainly that this was
not a case in which he could deal hastily with his views as to the
future, but that it was a matter profoundly affecting his whole
heart and soul. I told him what I myself would do in his case,
that is to say, if he really felt an overwhelming and irresistible
impulse to become an artist, and would prefer to endure the
greatest hardships and trials rather than be forced into a course
he felt was a wrong one, he ought, in defiance of everything, to
make up his mind to accept the helping hand I was holding out
to him at once. If, in spite of his father's prohibition, he still
wished to come to me, he ought not to hesitate, but should
carry out his wishes immediately on the receipt of my letter.

Karl Ritter was pleased when I entrusted him with the duty
of delivering the letter personally at Bülow's country villa.

When he arrived he asked to see his friend at the door, and went for a stroll with him, during which he gave him my letter. Thereupon Hans, who like Karl had no money, at once decided, in spite of storm and rain, to accompany Karl back to Zürich on foot. So one day they turned up absolutely tired out, and came into my room looking like a couple of tramps, with visible signs about them of their mad expedition. Karl beamed with joy over this feat, while young Bülow was quite overcome with emotion.

I at once realised that I had taken a very serious responsibility on my shoulders, yet I sympathised deeply with the overwrought youth, and my conduct towards him was guided by all that had occurred for a long time afterwards.

At first we had to console him, and stimulate his confidence by our cheerfulness. His appointment was soon arranged. He was to share Karl's contract at the theatre, and enjoy the same rights; both were to receive a small salary, and I was to continue to act as surety for their capabilities.

At this time they happened to be rehearsing a musical comedy, and Hans, without any knowledge of the subject, took up his position at the conductor's desk and handled the baton with great vigour and remarkable skill. I felt safe as far as he was concerned, and all doubt as to his ability as musical director vanished on the spot. But it was a somewhat difficult task to overcome Karl's misgivings about himself, owing to the idea ingrained in his mind that he never could become a practical musician. A growing shyness and secret antipathy towards me soon manifested itself and became more noticeable in this young man, in spite of the fact that he was certainly gifted. It was impossible to keep him any longer in his position or to ask him to conduct again.

Bülow also soon encountered unexpected difficulties. The manager and his staff, who had been spoiled by my having conducted on the occasion already mentioned, were always on the look-out for some fresh excuse for requisitioning my services.

I did, in fact, conduct again a few times, partly to give the public a favourable impression of the operatic company, which was really quite a good one, and partly to show my young friends, especially Bülow, who was so eminently adapted for a conductor, the most essential points which the leader of an orchestra ought to know.

Hans was always equal to the occasion, and I could with a clear conscience say there was no need for me to take his place whenever he was called upon to conduct. However, one of the artistes, a very conceited singer, who had been somewhat spoiled by my praise, annoyed him so much by her ways that she succeeded in forcing me to take up the baton again. When a couple of months later we realised the impossibility of carrying on this state of things indefinitely, and were tired of the whole affair, the management consented to free us from our irksome duties. About this time Hans was offered the post of musical director at St. Gall without any special conditions being attached to his engagement, so I sent the two boys off to try their luck in the neighbouring town, and thus gained time for further developments.

Herr Eduard von Bülow had, after all, come to the conclusion that it would be wiser to abide by his son's decision, though he did not do so without evincing a good deal of ill-humour towards me. He had not replied to a letter I had written him to explain my conduct in the matter, but I afterwards learned that he had visited his son in Zürich by way of patching up a reconciliation.

I went several times to St. Gall to see the young men, as they remained there during the winter months. I found Karl lost in gloomy thought: he had again met with an unfavourable reception when conducting Gluck's Overture to *Iphigenia*, and was keeping aloof from everybody. Hans was busily rehearsing with a very poor company and a horrible orchestra, in a hideous theatre. Seeing all this misery, I told Hans that for the time being he had picked up enough to pass for a practical musician or even for an experienced conductor.

The question now was to find him a sphere which would give him a suitable scope for his talents. He told me that his father was going to send him to Freiherr von Poissl, the manager of the Munich Court Theatre, with a letter of introduction. But his mother soon intervened, and wanted him to go to Weimar to continue his musical training under Liszt. This was all I could desire; I felt greatly relieved and heartily recommended the young man, of whom I was very fond, to my distinguished friend.

He left St. Gall at Easter, 1851, and during the long period of his stay in Weimar I was released from the responsibility of looking after him.

Meanwhile Ritter remained in melancholy retirement, and not being able to make up his mind whether or not he should return to Zürich, where he would be disagreeably reminded of his unlucky début, he preferred for the present to stay in seclusion at St. Gall.

The sojourn of my young friends at St. Gall had been pleasantly varied during the previous winter by a visit to Zürich, when Hans made his appearance as pianist at one of the concerts of the musical society there. I also took an active part in it by conducting one of Beethoven's symphonies, and it was a great pleasure to us both to give each other mutual encouragement.

I had been asked to appear again at this society's concerts during the winter. However, I only did so occasionally, to conduct a Beethoven symphony, making it a conditon that the orchestra, and more especially the string instruments, should be reinforced by capable musicians from other towns.

As I always required three rehearsals for each symphony, and many of the musicians had to come from a great distance, our work acquired quite an imposing and solemn character. I was able to devote the time usually taken up by a rehearsal to the study of one symphony, and accordingly had leisure to work out the minutest details of the execution, particularly as the technical difficulties were not of an insuperable character. My facility in interpreting music at that time attained a degree of perfection I had not hitherto reached, and I recognised this by the unexpected effect my conducting produced.

The orchestra contained some really talented and clever musicians, among whom I may mention Fries, an oboist, who, starting from a subordinate place, had been appointed a leading player. He had to practice with me, just as a singer would do, the more important parts allotted to his instrument in Beethoven's symphonies. When we first produced the Symphony in C minor, this extraordinary man played the small passage marked *adagio* at the *fermata* of the first movement in a manner I have never heard equalled. After my retirement from the directorship of these concerts he left the orchestra and went into business as a music-seller.

The orchestra could further boast of a Herr Ott-Imhoff, a highly cultured and well-to-do man who belonged to a noble family, and had joined the orchestra as a patron and as an amateur musician. He played the clarionet with a soft and charming tone which was somewhat lacking in spirit. I must also mention the worthy Herr Bär, a cornet-player, whom I appointed leader of the brass instruments, as he exercised a great influence on that part of the orchestra. I cannot remember ever having heard the long, powerful chords of the last movement of the C minor Symphony executed with such intense power as by this player in Zürich, and can only compare the recollection of it with the impressions I had when, in my early Parisian days, the Conservatoire orchestra performed Beethoven's Ninth Symphony.

Our production of the Symphony in C minor made a great impression on the audience, especially on my intimate friend Sulzer, who had previously kept aloof from any kind of music. He became so incensed when an attack was made on me by a newspaper that he answered the gratuitous critic in a satirical poem composed with the skill of a Platen.

As I have already said, Bülow was invited in the course of the winter to give a pianoforte recital at a concert at which I promised to produce the *Sinfonia Eroica*.

With his usual audacity he chose Liszt's piano arrangement of the *Tannhäuser* Overture, a work as brilliant as it is difficult, and therefore a somewhat hazardous undertaking. However, he caused quite a sensation, and I myself was astounded at his execution. Up to this time I had not paid it the attention it deserved, and it inspired me with the greatest confidence in his future. I frequently had occasion to admire his masterly skill both as conductor and accompanist.

During that winter, apart from the occasions in my young friend's life already briefly alluded to, there were frequent opportunities of displaying his capabilities. My acquaintances used to foregather in my house, and formed quite a little club for the purposes of mutual enjoyment, which, however, would hardly have been successful without Bülow's assistance.

I sang suitable passages from my opera, which Hans accompanied with an expressiveness which delighted me very much. On an occasion like this I also read aloud extracts from my manuscripts. For instance, during a series of successive evenings I read the whole of my longer work, *Oper und Drama,* written in the course of this winter, and was favoured by a steadily growing and remarkably attentive audience.

Now that after my return I had secured a certain degree of peace and tranquillity of mind, I began to think of resuming my more serious studies. But somehow the composition of *Siegfried's Death* did not seem to appeal to me. The idea of sitting down deliberately to write a score which should never go further than the paper on which it was written, again discouraged me; whereas I felt more and more strongly impelled to lay a foundation on which it might some day be possible to present such a work, even though the end had to be gained by roundabout means. To secure this object it seemed above all necessary to approach those friends, both at home and abroad, who interested themselves in my art, in order to expound to them more clearly the problems that demanded solution, which, although definite enough to my own mind, had scarcely as yet even entered into their heads. A singularly favourable opportunity for so doing offered itself one day when Sulzer showed me an article on 'Opera' in Brockhaus's *Modern Encyclopædia.* The good man was fully convinced that in the opinions expressed in this article I should find a preliminary basis for my own theories. But a hasty glance sufficed to show me at once how entirely erroneous they were, and I tried hard to point out to Sulzer the fundamental difference between the accepted views, even of very sensible people, and my own conceptions of the heart of the matter. Finding it naturally impossible, even with all the eloquence at my command, to elucidate my ideas all at once, I set about preparing a methodical plan for detailed treatment of the subject as soon as I got home. In this way I was lead to write this book which was published under the title of *Oper und Drama*, a task which kept me fully occupied for several months, in fact until February, 1851.

But I had to pay heavily for the exhausting toil expended on the conclusion of this work. According to my calculations, only a few days of persevering industry were needed for the completion of my manuscript, when my parrot, which usually watched me on my writing-table, was taken seriously ill. As it had already completely recovered from several similar attacks, I did not feel very anxious. Although my wife begged me to fetch a veterinary surgeon who lived in a village which was rather far off, I preferred to stick to my desk, and I put off going from one day to the next. At last one evening the all-important manuscript was finished, and the next morning our poor Papo lay dead on the floor. My inconsolable grief over this melancholy loss was fully shared by Minna, and by our mutual affection for this treasured pet we were once more tenderly united in a way likely to conduce to our domestic happiness.

In addition to our pets, our older Zürich friends had also remained faithful to us, in spite of the catastrophe which had befallen my family life. Sulzer was without a doubt the worthiest and most important of these friends. The profound difference between us both in intellect and temperament seemed only to favour this relationship, for each was constantly providing surprises for the other; and as the divergencies between us were radical, they aften gave rise to most exhilarating and instructive experiences. Sulzer was extraordinarily excitable and very delicate in health. It was quite against his own original desire that he had entered the service of the state, and in doing so he had sacrificed his own wishes to a conscientious performance of duty in the extremest sense of the word, and now, through his acquaintance with me, he was drawn more deeply into the sphere of æsthetic enjoyment than he regarded as justifiable. Probably he would have indulged less freely in these excesses, had I taken my art a little less seriously. But as I insisted upon attaching an importance to the artistic destiny of mankind which far transcended the mere aims of citizenship, I sometimes completely upset him. Yet, on the other hand, it was just this intense earnestness which so strongly attracted him to me and my speculations. This

not only gave rise to pleasant conversation and calm discussion
between us, but also, owing to a fiery temper on both sides,
sometimes provoked violent explosions, so that, with trembling
lips, he would seize hat and stick and hurry away without a
word of farewell.   Such, however, was the intrinsic worth of
the man, that he was sure to turn up again the next evening
at the accustomed hour, when we both felt as though nothing
whatever had passed between us.   But when certain bodily
ailments compelled him to remain indoors for many days, it
was difficult to gain access to him, for he was apt to become
furious when any one inquired about his health.   On these
occasions there was only one way of putting him in a good
temper, and that was to say that one had called to ask a favour
of him.   Thereupon he was pleasantly surprised, and would
not only declare himself ready to oblige in any way that was
in his power, but would assume a really cheerful and benevolent
demeanour.

A remarkable contrast to him was presented by the musician
Wilhelm Baumgartner, a merry, jovial fellow, without any
aptitude for concentration, who had learned just enough about
the piano to be able, as teacher at so much an hour, to earn
what he required for a living.   He had a taste for what was
beautiful, provided it did not soar too high, and possessed a
true and loyal heart, full of a great respect for Sulzer, which
unfortunately could not cure him of a craving for the public-
house.

Besides this man, there were two others who had also from
the very first formed part of our circle.   Both of them were
friends of the pair I have already mentioned; their names were
Hagenbuch, a worthy and respectable deputy cantonal secretary; and Bernhard Spyri, a lawyer, and at that time editor
of the *Eidgenössische Zeitung*.   The latter was a singularly good-
tempered man, but not overburdened with intellect, for which
reason Sulzer always treated him with special consideration.

Alexander Müller soon disappeared from our midst, as he
became more and more engrossed by domestic calamities, bodily
infirmities, and the mechanical drudgery of giving lessons by
the hour.   As for the musician Abt, I had never felt particularly drawn towards him, in spite of his *Schwalben*, and he

too speedily left us to carve a brilliant career for himself in Brunswick.

In the meantime, however, our Zürich circle was enriched by all kinds of additions from without, mainly due to the political shipwrecks. On my return, in January, 1850, I had already found Adolph Kolatschek, a plain, though not unprepossessing-looking man, though he was a bit of a bore. He imagined himself born to be an editor, and had founded a German monthly magazine, which was to open a field for those who had been outwardly conquered in the recent movements to continue their fight in the inner realm of the spirit. I felt almost flattered at being picked out by him as an author, and being informed that 'a power like mine' ought not to be absent from a union of spiritual forces such as was to be established by his enterprise. I had previously sent him from Paris my treatise on *Kunst und Klima;* and he now gladly accepted some fairly long extracts from my still unpublished *Oper und Drama,* for which he moreover paid me a handsome fee. This man made an indelible impression on my mind as the only instance I have met of a really tactful editor. He once handed me the manuscript of a review on my *Kunstwerk der Zukunft,* written by a certain Herr Palleske, to read, saying that he would not print it without my express consent; though he did not press me to give it. It was a superficial article, without any true comprehension of the subject, and couched in most arrogant terms. I felt that if it appeared in this particular journal it would certainly demand inconvenient and wearisome rejoinders from me, in which I should have to restate my original thesis. As I was by no means inclined to enter upon such a controversy, I agreed to Kolatschek's proposal, and suggested that he had better return the manuscript to its author for publication elsewhere.

Through Kolatschek I also learned to know Reinhold Solger, a really excellent and interesting man. But it did not suit his restless and adventurous spirit to remain cooped up in the small and narrow Swiss world of Zürich, so that he soon left us and went to North America, where I heard that he went about giving lectures and denouncing the political situation in Europe. It was a pity that this talented man never succeeded

in making a name for himself by more important work. His
contributions to our monthly journal, during the brief term of
his stay in Zürich, were certainly among the best ever written
on these topics by a German.

In the new year, 1851, Georg Herwegh also joined us, and
I was delighted to meet him one day at Kolatschek's lodgings.
The vicissitudes which had brought him to Zürich came to my
knowledge afterwards in a somewhat offensive and aggressive
manner. For the present, Herwegh put on an aristocratic swag-
ger and gave himself the airs of a delicately nurtured and
luxurious son of his times, to which a fairly liberal interpolation
of French expletives at least added a certain distinction. Nevertheless, there was something about his person, with his quick,
flashing eye and kindliness of manner, which was well calculated to exert an attractive influence. I felt almost flattered
by his ready acceptance of my invitation to my informal
evening parties, which may, perhaps, have been fairly agreeable gatherings, as Bülow entertained us with music, though
to me personally they afforded no mental sustenance whatever.
My wife used to declare that, when I proceeded to read from
my manuscript, Kolatschek promptly fell asleep, while Herwegh gave all his attention to her punch. When, later on,
as I have already mentioned, I read my *Oper und Drama* for
twelve consecutive evenings to our Zürich friends, Herwegh
stayed away, because he did not wish to mix with those for
whom such things had not been written. Yet my intercourse
with him became gradually more cordial. Not only did I respect his poetical talent, which had recently gained recognition, but I also learned to realise the delicate and refined qualities of his richly cultivated intellect, and in course of time
learned that Herwegh, on his side, was beginning to covet my
society. My steady pursuit of those deeper and more serious
interests which so passionately engrossed me seemed to arouse
him to an ennobling sympathy, even for those topics which,
since his sudden leap into poetic fame, had been, greatly to his
prejudice, smothered under mere showy and trivial mannerisms,
altogether alien to his original nature. Possibly this process
was accelerated by the growing difficulties of his position, which
he had hitherto regarded as demanding a certain amount of

outward show. In short, he was the first man in whom I met with a sensitive and sympathetic comprehension of my most daring schemes and opinions, and I soon felt compelled to believe his assertion that he occupied himself solely with my ideas, into which, certainly, no other man entered so profoundly as he did.

This familiarity with Herwegh, in which an element of affection was certainly mingled, was further stimulated by news which reached me respecting a new dramatic poem which I had sketched out for the coming spring. Liszt's preparations in the late summer of the previous year for the production in Weimar of my *Lohengrin* had met with more success than, with such limited resources, had hitherto seemed possible. This result could naturally only have been obtained by the zeal of a friend endowed with such rich and varied gifts as Liszt. Though it was beyond his power to attract quickly to the Weimar stage such singers as *Lohengrin* demanded, and he had been compelled on many points to content himself with merely suggesting what was intended to be represented, yet he was now endeavouring by sundry ingenious methods to make these suggestions clearly comprehensible. First of all, he prepared a detailed account of the production of *Lohengrin*. Seldom has a written description of a work of art won for it such attentive friends, and commanded their enthusiastic appreciation from the outset, as did this treatise of Liszt's, which extended even to the most insignificant details. Karl Ritter distinguished himself by providing an excellent German translation of the French original, which was first published in the *Illustrirte Zeitung*. Shortly after this Liszt also issued *Tannhäuser* in French, accompanied by a similar preface on its origin, and these pamphlets were the chief means of awakening, now and for long after, especially in foreign countries, not only a surprisingly sympathetic interest in these works, but also an intimate understanding of them such as could not possibly have been attained by the mere study of my pianoforte arrangements. But, far from being satisfied with this, Liszt contrived to attract the attention of intellects outside Weimar to the performances of my operas, in order, with kindly compulsion, to force them upon the notice of all who had ears to hear and eyes to see. Although his good intentions did not altogether succeed with Franz Dingelstedt, who would only commit himself to a confused report on *Lohengrin* in the *Allgemeine Zeitung*, yet his enthusiastic eloquence completely and decisively captured Adolf Stahr for my work. His detailed view of *Lohengrin* in the Berlin *National-Zeitung*, in which he claimed a high importance for my opera, did not remain without permanent influence upon the German public. Even in the narrow circle of professional musicians its effects seem not to have been unimportant; for Robert Franz, whom Liszt dragged almost by force to a performance of *Lohengrin,* spoke of it with unmistakable enthusiasm. This example gave the lead to many other journals, and for some time it seemed as though the otherwise dull-witted musical press would energetically champion my cause.

I shall shortly have occasion to describe what it was that eventually gave quite a different direction to this movement. Meanwhile Liszt felt emboldened by these kindly signs to encourage me to renew my creative activity, which had now for some time been interrupted. His success with *Lohengrin* gave him confidence in his ability to execute a yet more hazardous undertaking, and he invited me to set my poem of *Siegfried's Death* to music for production at Weimar. On his recommendation, the manager of the Weimar theatre, Herr von Ziegesar, offered to make a definite contract with me in the name of the Grand Duke. I was to finish the work within a year, and during that period was to receive a payment of fifteen hundred marks (£75).

It was a curious coincidence that about this time, and also through Liszt, the Duke of Coburg invited me to arrange the instrumentation for an opera of his own composition, for which he offered me the sum of two thousand seven hundred marks (£135). In spite of my position as an outlaw, my noble patron and would-be employer offered to receive me in his castle at Coburg, where, in quiet seclusion with himself and Frau Birchpfeiffer, the writer of the libretto, I might execute the work. Liszt naturally expected nothing more from me than a decent excuse for declining this offer, and suggested my pleading ' bodily and mental depression.' My friend told me afterwards that the Duke had desired my co-operation with him in his score on account of my skilful use of trombones. When he inquired, through Liszt, what my rules for their manipulation were, I replied that before I could write anything for trombones I required first to have some ideas in my head.

On the other hand, however, I felt very much tempted to entertain the Weimar proposal. Still weary from my exhausting labour on *Oper und Drama*, and worried by many things which had a depressing effect on my spirits, I seated myself for the first time for many months at my Härtel grand-piano, which had been rescued from the Dresden catastrophe, to see whether I could settle down to composing the music for my ponderous heroic drama. In rapid outline I sketched the music for the Song of the Norns, or Daughters of the Rhine, which in this first draft was only roughly suggested. But when I attempted to turn Brunhilda's first address to Siegfried into song my courage failed me completely, for I could not help asking myself whether the singer had yet been born who was capable of vitalising this heroic female figure. The idea of my niece Johanna occurred to me, whom, as a matter of fact, I had already destined for this rôle when I was still in Dresden on account of her various personal charms. She had now entered upon the career of prima donna at Hamburg, but, judging from all the reports I had received, and especially from the attitude towards me that she openly adopted in her letters to her family, I could only conclude that my modest hopes of enlisting her talents on my behalf were doomed to disappointment. I was, moreover, confused by the fact that a second Dresden prima donna, Mme. Gentiluomo Spatzer, who had once enraptured Marschner with Donizetti's dithyrambics, kept hovering perpetually before my mind as a possible substitute for Johanna. At last, in a rage, I sprang up from the piano, and swore that I would write nothing more for these silly fastidious schoolgirls. Whenever I saw any likelihood of being again brought into closer contact with the theatre I was filled with an indescribable disgust which, for the time being, I was unable to overcome. It was some little consolation to discover that bodily ill-health might possibly be at the bottom of this mental disorder. During the spring of this year I had been suffering from a curious rash, which spread over my whole body.

For this my doctor prescribed a course of sulphur-baths, to be taken regularly every morning. Although the remedy excited my nerves so much that later on I was obliged to adopt radical measures for the restoration of my health, yet in the meantime the regular morning walk to the town and back, surrounded by the fresh green and early spring flowers of May, acted as a cheerful stimulant on my mental condition. I now conceived the idea of the poem of *Junger Siegfried*, which I proposed to issue as a heroic comedy by way of prelude and complement to the tragedy of *Siegfrieds Tod*. Carried away by my conception, I tried to persuade myself that this piece would be easier to produce than the other more serious and terrible drama. With this idea in my mind I informed Liszt of my purpose, and offered the Weimar management to compose a score for *Junger Siegfried*, which as yet was unwritten, in return for which I would definitely accept their proposal to grant me a year's salary of fifteen hundred marks. This they agreed to without delay, and I took up my quarters in the attic-room evacuated the previous year by Karl Ritter, where, with the aid of sulphur and May-blossom, and in the highest spirits, I proposed to complete the poem of *Junger Siegfried*, as already outlined in my original design.

I must now give some account of the cordial relations which, ever since my departure from Dresden, I had maintained with Theodor Uhlig, the young musician of the Dresden orchestra, which I have already described, and which by this time had developed into a genuinely productive association. His independent and indeed somewhat uncultivated disposition had been moulded into a warm, almost boundless devotion to myself, inspired both by sympathy for my fate and a thorough understanding of my works. He also had been among the number of those who had visited Weimar to hear my *Lohengrin*, and had sent me a very detailed account of the performance. As Härtel, the music-dealer in Leipzig, had willingly agreed to my request to publish *Lohengrin* on condition that I should not demand any share in the profits, I entrusted Uhlig with the preparation of the pianoforte arrangement. But it was more the theoretical questions discussed in my works that formed the chief link that bound us together by a serious correspondence. The characteristic which especially touched me about this man, whom from his training I could regard merely as an instrumentalist, was that he had grasped with clear understanding and perfect agreement those very tendencies of mine which many musicians of apparently wider culture than his own regarded with almost despairing horror, as being dangerous to the orthodox practice of their art. He forthwith acquired the literary facility necessary for the expression of his agreement with my views, and gave tangible proof of this in a lengthy treatise on 'Instrumental Music,' which appeared in Kolatschek's German monthly journal. He also sent to me another strictly theoretical work on the 'Structure of Musical Theme and Phrase.' In this he showed the originality of his ideas about Mozart's and Beethoven's methods, to an extent which was only equalled by the thoroughness with which he had mastered the question, especially where he discussed their highly characteristic differences. This clear and exhaustive treatise appeared to me admirably adapted to form the basis for a new theory of the higher art of musical phrasing, whereby Beethoven's most obscure construction might be explained, and elaborated into a comprehensible system that would allow of further application. These treatises attracted the attention of Franz Brendel, the astute publisher of the *Neue Zeitschrift für Musik,* to their brilliant young author. He was invited by Brendel to join the staff of his paper, and soon succeeded in changing his chief's previous attitude of indecision. As Brendel's aims were on the whole perfectly honourable and serious, he was quickly and definitely led to adopt those views which from this time began to make a stir in the musical world under the title of the 'New Tendency.' I thereupon felt impelled to contribute an epoch-making article to his paper on these lines. I had noticed for some time that such illsounding catch-phrases as 'Jewish ornamental flourishes' (Melismas), 'Synagogue Music,' and the like were being bandied about without any rhyme or reason beyond that of giving expression to meaningless irritation. The question thus raised regarding the significance of the modern Jew in music stimulated me to make a closer examination of Jewish influence and the characteristics peculiar to it. This I did in a lengthy treatise on 'Judaism in Music.' Although I did not wish to hide my identity, as its author, from all inquiries, yet I considered it advisable to adopt a pseudonym, lest my very seriously intended effort should be degraded to a purely personal matter, and its real importance be thereby vitiated. The stir, nay, the genuine consternation, created by this article defies comparison with any other similar publication. The unparalleled animosity with which, even up to the present day, I have been pursued by the entire press of Europe can only be understood by those who have taken an account of this article and of the dreadful commotion which it caused at the time of its publication. It must also be remembered that almost all the newspapers of Europe are in the hands of Jews. Apart from these facts, it would be impossible to understand the unqualified bitterness of this lasting persecution, which cannot be adequately explained on the mere ground of a theoretical or practical dislike for my opinions or artistic works. The first outcome of the article was a storm which broke over poor Brendel, who was entirely innocent, and, indeed, hardly conscious of his offence. This erelong developed into a savage persecution which aimed at nothing less than his ruin. Another immediate result was that the few friends whom Liszt had induced to declare themselves in my favour forthwith took refuge in a discreet silence. As it soon seemed advisable, in the interests of their own productions, to give direct evidence of their estrangement from me, most of them passed over to the ranks of my enemies. But Uhlig clung to me all the more closely on this account. He strengthened Brendel's weaker will to endurance, and kept helping him with contributions for his paper, some of them profound and others witty and very much to the point. He fixed his eye more particularly on one of my chief antagonists, a man named Bischoff, whom Hiller had discovered in Cologne, and who first invented for me and my friends the title of *Zukunftsmusiker* ('Musicians of the Future'). With him he entered into a prolonged and somewhat diverting controversy. The foundation had now been laid for the problem of the so-called *Zukunftsmusik* ('Music of the Future'), which was to become a European scandal, in spite of the fact that Liszt quickly adopted the title himself with good-humoured pride. It is true that I had to some extent suggested this name in the title of my book, *Kunstwerk der Zukunft;* but it only developed into a battle-cry when ' Judaism in Music ' unbarred the sluices of wrath upon me and my friends.

My book, *Oper und Drama,* was published in the second half of this year, and, so far as it was noticed at all by the leading musicians of the day, naturally only helped to add fuel to the wrath which blazed against me. This fury, however, assumed more the character of slander and malice, for our movement had meantime been reduced by a great connoisseur in such things, Meyerbeer, to a clearly defined system, which he maintained and practised with a sure hand until his lamented death.

Uhlig had come across my book, *Oper und Drama,* during the early stages of the furious uproar against me. I had presented him with the original manuscript, and as it was nicely bound in red, I hit upon the idea of writing in it, by way of dedication, the words, ' *Red,* my friend, is *my* theory,' in contradistinction to the Gothic saying, ' Grey, my friend, is all theory.' This gift elicited an exhilarating and most delightful correspondence with my lively and keen-sighted young friend, who, after two long years of separation, I felt sincerely desirous of seeing again. It was not an easy matter for the poor fiddler, whose pay was barely that of a chamber musician, to comply with my invitation. But he gladly tried to overcome all difficulties, and said he would come early in July. I decided to go as far as Rorschach, on the Lake of Constance, to meet him, so that we might make an excursion through the Alps as far as Zürich. I went by a pleasant detour through the Toggenburg, travelling on foot as usual. In this way, cheerful and refreshed, I reached St. Gall, where I sought out Karl Ritter, who, since Bülow's departure, had remained there alone in curious seclusion. I could guess the reason of his retirement, although he said that he had enjoyed very agreeable intercourse with a St. Gall musician named Greitel, of whom I never heard anything further. Though very tired after my long walking tour, I could not refrain from submitting the manuscript of my *Junger Siegfried,* which I had just finished, to the quick and critical judgment of this intelligent young man, who was thus the first person to hear it. I was more than gratified by its effect upon him, and, in high spirits, persuaded him to forsake his strange retreat and go with me to meet Uhlig, so that we might all three proceed over the Säntis for a long and pleasant stay in Zürich.

My first glance at my guest, as he landed at the familiar harbour of Rorschach, filled me at once with anxiety for his health, for it revealed but too plainly his tendency to consumption. In order to spare him, I wished to give up the proposed mountain climb, but he eagerly protested that exercise of this kind in the fresh air could only do him good after the drudgery of his wretched fiddling. After crossing the little canton of Appenzell, we had to face the by no means easy crossing of the Säntis. It was my first experience also of travelling over an extensive snow-field in summer. After reaching our guide's hut, which was perched on a rugged slope, where we regaled ourselves with exceedingly frugal fare, we had to climb the towering and precipitous pinnacle of rock which forms the summit of the mountain, a few hundred feet above us. Here Karl suddenly refused to allow us, and to shake him out of his effeminacy I had to send back the guide for him, who, at our request, succeeded in bringing him along, half by force. But now that we had to clamber from stone to stone along the precipitous cliff, I soon began to realise how foolish I had been in compelling Karl to share our perilous adventure. His dizziness evidently stupefied him, for he stared in front of him as though he could not see, and we had to hold him fast between our alpenstocks, every moment expecting to see him collapse, and tumble into the abyss. When we at last attained the summit, he sank senseless on the ground, and I now fully understood what a terrible responsibility I had undertaken, as the yet more dangerous descent had still to be made. In an agony of fear, which, while it made me forget my own danger altogether, filled me with a vision of my young friend lying shattered on the rocks below, we at last reached the guide's cottage in safety. As Uhlig and myself were still determined to descend the precipitous further side of the mountain, a feat which the guide informed us was not without danger, I resolved to leave young Ritter behind in the hut, as the indescribable anguish I had just endured on his behalf had been a warning to me. Here he was to await the return of our guide, and in his company take the not very dangerous path by which we had come. We accordingly parted, as he was to return in the direction of Gall, while we two roamed through the lovely Toggenburg valley, and the next day by Rappersweil to the Lake of Zürich, and so home. Not until many days later did Karl relieve our anxiety concerning him by arriving at Zürich. He remained with us a short time, and then departed, probably wishing to escape being tempted into more mountain climbing, which we had certainly planned. I heard from him afterwards when he had settled for some time in Stuttgart, where he seemed to be doing well. He soon made great friends with a young actor, and lived on terms of great intimacy with him.

I was sincerely delighted by the close intercourse I now had with the gentle young Dresden chamber musician, whose manly strength of character and extraordinary mental endowments greatly endeared him to me. My wife said that his curly golden hair and bright blue eyes made her think an angel had come to stay with us. For me his features had a peculiar and, considering his fate, pathetic interest, on account of his striking resemblance to King Friedrich August of Saxony, my former patron, who was still alive at that time, and seemed to confirm a rumour which had reached me that Uhlig was his natural son. It was entertaining to hear his news of Dresden, and all about the theatre, and the condition of musical affairs in that city. My operas, which had once been its glory, had now quite vanished from the repertoire. He gave me a choice example of my late colleagues' opinion of me by relating the following incident. When *Kunst und Revolution* and *Kunstwerk der Zukunft* appeared, and were being discussed among them, one of them remarked: ' Ha! he may worry a long time before he will be able to write conductor before his name again.' By way of illustrating the advance made in music. he related the manner in which Reissiger, having on one occasion to conduct Beethoven's Symphony in A major, which had been previously executed by me, had helped himself out of a sudden dilemma. Beethoven, as is well known, marks the great finale of the last movement with a prolonged *forte,* which he merely heightens by a *sempre più forte*. At this point Reissiger, who had conducted the Symphony before me, thinking the opportunity a favourable one, had introduced a *piano*, in order at least to secure an effective *crescendo*. This I had naturally ignored, and had instructed the orchestra to play with their full strength throughout. Now, therefore, that the conducting of this work had once more fallen into my predecessor's hands, he found it difficult to restore his unlucky *piano;* but, feeling that he must save his authority, which had been compromised, he made a rule that *mezzo forte* should be played instead of *forte*.

But the most painful news he gave me was about the state of utter neglect into which my unhappy operatic publications had fallen in the hands of the court music-dealer Meser, who, seeing that money had to be continually paid out, while nothing came in, regarded himself as a sacrificial lamb whom I had lured to the slaughter. Yet he steadily refused all inspection of his books, maintaining that he thereby protected my property, as all I possessed having been confiscated, it would otherwise be seized at once. A pleasanter topic than this was *Lohengrin*. My friend had completed the pianoforte arrangement, and was already busy correcting the engraver's proofs.

By his enthusiastic advocacy of the water cure, Uhlig gained an influence over me in another direction, and one which was of long duration. He brought me a book on the subject by a certain Rausse, which pleased me greatly, especially by its radical principles, which had something of Feuerbach about them. Its bold repudiation of the entire science of medicine, with all its quackeries, combined with its advocacy of the simplest natural processes by means of a methodical use of strengthening and refreshing water, quickly won my fervent adherence. He maintained, for instance, that every genuine medicine can only act upon our organism in so far as it is a poison, and is therefore not assimilated by our system; and proved, moreover, that men who had become weak owing to a continuous absorption of medicine, had been cured by the famous Priesnitz, who had effectually driven out the poison contained in their bodies by expelling it through the skin. I naturally thought of the disagreeable sulphur baths I had taken during the spring, and to which I attributed my chronic and severe state of irritability. In so doing I was probably not far wrong. For a long while after this I did my best to expel this and all other poisons which I might have absorbed in the course of time, and by an exclusive water regimen restore my original healthy condition. Uhlig asserted that by persevering conscientiously in a water cure, he was perfectly confident of being able to renew his own bodily health entirely, and my own faith in it also grew daily.

At the end of July we started on an excursion through the centre of Switzerland. From Brunnen, on the Lake of Lucerne, we proceeded via Beckenried to Engelberg, from which place we crossed the wild Surenen-Eck, and on this occasion learned how to glide over the snow fairly easily. But in crossing a swollen mountain torrent Uhlig had the misfortune to fall into the water. By way of quieting my uneasiness about him, he at once exclaimed that this was a very good way of carrying out the water cure. He made no fuss about the drying of his clothes, but simply spread them out in the sun, and in the meanwhile calmly promenaded about in a state of nature in the open air, protesting that this novel form of exercise would do him good. We occupied the interval in discussing the important problem of Beethoven's theme construction, until, by way of a joke, I told him that I could see Councillor Carns of Dresden coming up behind him with a party, which for a moment quite frightened him. Thus with light hearts we reached the Reuss valley near Attinghausen, and in the evening wandered on as far as Amsteg, and the next morning, in spite of our great fatigue, at once visited the Madran valley. There we climbed the Hüfi glacier, whence we enjoyd a splendid view over an impressive panorama of mountains, bounded at this point by the Tödy range. We returned the same day to Amsteg, and as we were both thoroughly tired out, I dissuaded my companion from attempting the ascent of the Klausen Pass to the Schächen valley, which we had planned for the following day, and induced him to take the easier way home via Flüelen. When, early in August, my young friend, who was always calm and very deliberate in his manner, set out on his return journey to Dresden, I could detect no signs of exhaustion about him. He was hoping on his arrival to lighten the heavy burden of life a little by undertaking the conductorship of the *entr'acte* music at the theatre, which he proposed to organise artistically, and thus set himself free from the oppressive and demoralising service of the opera. It was with sincere grief that I accompanied him to the mail-coach, and he too seemed to be seized with sudden foreboding. As a matter of fact, this was the last time we ever met.

But for the present we carried on an active correspondence, and as his communications were always pleasant and entertaining, and for a long time constituted almost my sole link with the outside world, I begged him to write me long letters as often as possible. As postage was expensive at that time, and voluminous letters touched our pockets severely, Uhlig conceived the ingenious idea of using the parcel post for our correspondence. As only packets of a certain weight might be sent in this way, a German translation of Beaumarchais' *Figaro*, of which Uhlig possessed an ancient copy, enjoyed the singular destiny of acting as ballast for our letters to and fro. Every time, therefore, that our epistles had swelled, to the requisite length, we announced them with the words: ' Figaro brings tidings to-day.'

Uhlig meanwhile found much pleasure in the *Mittheilung an meine Freunde* (' A Communication to my Friends'), which, immediately after our separation, I wrote as a preface to an edition of my three operas, the *Fliegender Holländer*, *Tannhäuser*, and *Lohengrin*. He was also amused to hear that Härtel, who had accepted the book for publication on payment of ten louis d'or, protested so vigorously against certain passages in this preface, which wounded his orthodoxy and political feelings, that I thought seriously of giving the book to another firm. However, he finally persuaded me to give way, and I pacified his tender conscience by a few trifling alterations.

With this comprehensive preface, which had occupied me during the whole of the month of August, I hoped that my excursion into the realms of literature would be ended once and for all. However, as soon as I began to think seriously about taking up the composition of *Junger Siegfried*, which I had promised for Weimar, I was seized with depressing doubts which almost amounted to a positive reluctance to attempt this work. As I could not clearly discern the reason of this dejection, I concluded that its source lay in the state of my health, so I determined one day to carry out my theories about the advantages of a water cure, which I had always propounded with great enthusiasm. I made due inquiries about a neighbouring hydropathic establishment, and informed my wife that I was going off to Albisbrunnen, which was situated about three miles from our abode. It was then about the middle of September, and I had made up my mind not to come back until I was completely restored to health.

Minna was quite frightened when I announced my intention, and looked upon it as another attempt on my part to abandon my home. I begged of her, however, to devote herself during my absence to the task of furnishing and arranging our new flat as comfortably as possible. This, although small, was conveniently situated on the ground floor of the Vordern Escher Häuser im Zeltweg. We had determined to move back to the town, on account of the great inconvenience of the situation of our present quarters, especially during winter time. Everybody, of course, was astonished at the idea of my undertaking a water cure so late in the season. Nevertheless, I soon succeeded in securing a fellow-patient. I was not fortunate enough to get Herwegh, but Fate was kind in sending me Hermann Müller, an ex-lieutenant in the Saxon Guards, and a former lover of Schröder-Devrient, who proved a most cheerful and pleasant companion. It had become impossible for him to maintain his position in the Saxon army, and although he was not exactly a political refugee, every career was closed to him in Germany, and yet he met with all the consideration of an exiled patriot when he came to Switzerland to try and make a fresh start in life. We had seen a good deal of each other in my early Dresden days, and he soon felt at home in my house, where my wife always gave him a warm welcome. I easily persuaded him to follow me shortly to Albisbrunnen to undergo a thorough treatment for an infirmity from which he was suffering. I established myself there as comfortably as I could, and I looked forward to excellent results. The cure itself was superintended in the usual superficial way by a Dr. Brunner, whom my wife, on one of her visits to this place, promptly christened the

'Water Jew,' and whom she heartily detested. Early at five o'clock in the morning I was wrapped up and kept in a state of perspiration for several hours; after that I was plunged into an icy cold bath at a temperature of only four degrees; then I was made to take a brisk walk to restore my circulation in the chilly air of late autumn. In addition I was kept on a water diet; no wine, coffee, or tea was allowed; and this régime, in the dismal company of nothing but incurables, with dull evenings only enlivened by desperate attempts at games of whist, and the prohibition of all intellectual occupation, resulted in irritability and overwrought nerves. I led this life for nine weeks, but I was determined not to give in until I felt that every kind of drug or poison I had ever absorbed into my system had been brought to the surface. As I considered that wine was most dangerous, I presumed that my system still contained many unassimilated substances which I had absorbed at various dinner-parties at Sulzer's, and which must evaporate in profuse perspiration. This life, so full of privations, which I led in rooms miserably furnished with common deal and the usual rustic appointments of a Swiss *pension*, awoke in me by way of contrast an insuperable longing for a cosy and comfortable home; indeed, as the year went on, this longing became a passionate desire. My imagination was for ever picturing to itself the manner and style in which a house or a dwelling ought to be appointed and arranged, in order to keep my mind pleasantly free for artistic creation.

At this time symptoms of a possible improvement in my position appeared. Karl Ritter, unfortunately for himself, wrote to me from Stuttgart while I was at the hydro, describing his own private attempts to secure the benefits of a water cure — not by means of baths, but by drinking quantities of water. I had found out that it was most dangerous to drink large quantities of water without undergoing the rest of the treatment, so I implored Karl to submit to the regular course, and not to have an effeminate fear of privations, and to come at once to Albisbrunnen. He took me at my word, and to my great delight arrived in a few days' time at Albisbrunnen. Theoretically he was filled with enthusiasm for hydropathy, but he soon objected to it in practice; and he denounced the use of cold milk as indigestible and against the dictates of Nature, as mother's milk was always warm. He found the cold packs and the cold baths too exciting, and preferred treating himself in a comfortable and pleasant way behind the doctor's back. He soon discovered a wretched confectioner's shop in the neighbouring village, and when he was caught buying cheap pastry on the sly, he was very angry. He soon grew perfectly miserable, and would fain have escaped, had not a certain feeling of honour prevented him from doing so. The news reached him here of the sudden death of a rich uncle, who had left a considerable fortune to every member of Karl's family. His mother, in telling him and me of the improvement in her position, declared that she was now able to assure me the income which the two families of Laussot and Ritter had offered me some time ago. Thus I stepped into an annual income of two thousand four hundred marks for as long as I required it, and into partnership with the Ritter family.

This happy and encouraging turn of events made me decide to complete my original sketch of the *Nibelungen*, and to bring it out in our theatres without paying any regard to the practicability of its various parts. In order to do this I felt that I must free myself from all obligations to the management of the Weimar theatre. I had already drawn six hundred marks salary from this source, but Karl was enchanted to place this sum at my disposal in order that I might return it. I sent the money back to Weimar with a letter expressing my most grateful acknowledgments to the management for their conduct towards me, and at the same time I wrote to Liszt, giving him the fullest particulars of my great plan, and explaining how I felt absolutely compelled to carry it out.

Liszt, in his reply, told me how delighted he was to know that I was now in a position to undertake such a remarkable work, which he considered in every respect worthy of me if only on account of its surprising originality. I began to breathe freely at last, because I had always felt that it was merely self-deception on my part to maintain that it would be possible to produce *Junger Siegfried* with the limited means at the disposal of even the best German theatre.

My water cure and the hydropathic establishment became

more and more distasteful to me; I longed for my work, and
the desire to get back to it made me quite ill. I tried obstinately to conceal from myself that the object of my cure had
entirely failed; indeed, it had really done me more harm than
good, for although the evil secretions had not returned, my
whole body seemed terribly emaciated. I considered that I
had had quite enough of the cure, and comforted myself with
the hope that I should derive benefit from it in the future.
I accordingly left the hydropathic establishment at the end of
November. Müller was to follow me in a few days, but Karl,
wishing to be consistent, was determined to remain until he
perceived a similar result in himself to the one I had experienced or pretended I had experienced. I was much pleased
with the way in which Minna had arranged our new little flat
in Zürich. She had bought a large and luxurious divan, several carpets for the floor and various dainty little luxuries, and
in the back room my writing-table of common deal was covered with a green tablecloth and draped with soft green silk
curtains, all of which my friends admired immensely. This
table, at which I worked continually, travelled with me to
Paris, and when I left that city I presented it to Blandine
Ollivier, Liszt's elder daughter, who had it conveyed to the
little country house at St. Tropèz, belonging to her husband,
where, I believe, it stands to this day. I was very glad to
receive my Zürich friends in my new home, which was so much
more conveniently situated than my former one; only I quite
spoilt all my hospitality for a long time by my fanatical agitation for a water diet and my polemics against the evils of wine
and other intoxicating drinks. I adopted what seemed almost
a new kind of religion: when I was driven into a corner by
Sulzer and Herwegh, the latter of whom prided himself on his
knowledge of chemistry and physiology, about the absurdity
of Rausse's theory of the poisonous qualities contained in wine,
I found refuge in the moral and æsthetic motive which made
me regard the enjoyment of wine as an evil and barbarous substitute for the ecstatic state of mind which love alone should
produce. I maintained that wine, even if not taken in excess,
contained qualities producing a state of intoxication which a
man sought in order to raise his spirits, but that only he who

experienced the intoxication of love could raise his spirits in the noblest sense of the word. This led to a discussion on the modern relations of the sexes, whereupon I commented on the almost brutal manner in which men kept aloof from women in Switzerland. Sulzer said he would not at all object to the intoxication resulting from intercourse with women, but in his opinion the difficulty lay in procuring this by fair means. Herwegh was inclined to agree with my paradox, but remarked that wine had nothing whatever to do with it, that it was simply an excellent and strengthening food, which, according to Anacreon, agreed very well with the ecstasy of love. As my friends studied me and my condition more closely, they felt they had reason to be very anxious about my foolish and obstinate extravagances. I looked terribly pale and thin; I hardly slept at all, and in everything I did I betrayed a strange excitement. Although eventually sleep almost entirely forsook me, I still pretended that I had never been so well or so cheerful in my life, and I continued on the coldest winter mornings to take my cold baths, and plagued my wife to death by making her show me my way out with a lantern for the prescribed early morning walk.

I was in this state when the printed copies of *Oper und Drama* reached me, and I devoured rather than read them with an eccentric joy. I think that the delightful consciousness of now being able to say to myself, and prove to the satisfaction of everybody, and even of Minna, that I had at last completely freed myself from my hateful career as conductor and opera composer, brought about this immoderate excitement. Nobody had a right to make the demands upon me which two years ago had made me so miserable. The income which the Ritters had assured me for life, and the object of which was to give me an absolutely free hand, also contributed to my present state of mind, and made me feel confidence in everything I undertook. Although my plans for the present seemed to exclude all possibility of being realised, thanks to the indifference of an inartistic public, still I could not help inwardly cherishing the idea that I should not be for ever addressing only the paper on which I wrote. I anticipated that before long a great reaction would set in with regard to the public and everything connected with our social life, and I believed that in my boldly planned work there lay just the right material to supply the changed conditions and real needs of the new public whose relation to art would be completely altered with what was required. As these bold expectations had arisen in my mind in consequence of my observations of the state of society in general, I naturally could not say much about them to my friends. I had not mistaken the significance of the general collapse of the political movements, but felt that their real weakness lay in the inadequate though sincere expression of their cause, and that the social movement, so far from losing ground by its political defeat, had, on the contrary, gained in energy and expansion. I based my opinion upon the experience I had had during my last visit to Paris, when I had attended, among other things, a political meeting of the so-called social democratic party. Their general behaviour made a great impression upon me; the meeting took place in a temporary hall called Salle de la Fraternité in the Faubourg St. Denis; six thousand men were present, and their conduct, far from being noisy and tumultuous, filled me with a sense of the concentrated energy and hope of this new party. The speeches of the principal orators of the extreme left of the Assemblée Nationale astonished me by their oratorical flights as well as by their evident confidence in the future. As this extreme party was gradually strengthening itself against everything that was being done by the reactionary party then in power, and all the old liberals had joined these social democrats publicly and had adopted their electioneering programme, it was easy to see that in Paris, at all events, they would have a decided majority at the impending elections for the year 1852, and especially in the nomination of the President of the Republic. My own opinions about this were shared by the whole of France, and it seemed that the year 1852 was destined to witness a very important reaction which was naturally dreaded by the other party, who looked forward with great apprehension to the approaching catastrophe. The condition of the other European states, who suppressed every laudable impulse with brutal stupidity, convinced me that elsewhere too this state of affairs would not continue long, and every one seemed to look forward with great expectations to the decision of the following year.

I had discussed the general situation with my friend Uhlig, as well as the efficacy of the water-cure system; he had just come home fresh from orchestral rehearsals at the Dresden theatre, and found it very difficult to agree to a drastic change in human affairs or to have any faith in it. He assured me that I could not conceive how miserable and mean people were in general, but I managed to delude him into the belief that the year 1852 would be pregnant with great and important events. Our opinions on this subject were expressed in the correspondence which was once more diligently forwarded by *Figaro*.

Whenever we had to complain of any meanness or untoward circumstance, I always reminded him of this year, so great with fate and hope, and at the same time I hinted that we had better look forward quite calmly to the time when the great 'upheaval' should take place, as only then, when no one else knew what to do, could we step in and make a start.

I can hardly express how deeply and firmly this hope had taken possession of me, and I can only attribute all my confident opinions and declarations to the increased excitement of my nerves. The news of the *coup d'état* of the 2nd of December in Paris seemed to me absolutely incredible, and I thought the world was surely coming to an end. When the news was confirmed, and events which no one believed could ever happen had apparently occurred and seemed likely to be permanent, I gave the whole thing up like a riddle which it was beneath me to unravel, and turned away in disgust from the contemplation of this puzzling world. As a playful reminiscence of our hopes of the year 1852, I suggested to Uhlig that in our correspondence during that year we should ignore its existence and should date our letters December '51, in consequence of which this said month of December seemed of eternal duration.

Soon afterwards I was overpowered by an extraordinary depression in which, somehow, the disappointment about the turn of political events and the reaction created by my exaggerated water cure, almost ruined my health. I perceived the triumphant return of all the disappointing signs of reaction which excluded every high ideal from intellectual life, and from which I had hoped the shocks and fermentations of the past few years had freed us for ever. I prophesied that the time was approaching when intellectually we should be such paupers that the appearance of a new book from the pen of Heinrich Heine would create quite a sensation. When, a short time afterwards, the *Romancero* appeared from the pen of this poet who had fallen into almost complete neglect, and was very well reviewed by the newspaper critics, I laughed aloud; as a matter of fact, I suppose I am among the very few Germans who have never even looked at this book, which, by the way, is said to possess great merit.

I was now compelled to pay a great deal of attention to my physical condition, as it gave me much cause for anxiety and necessitated a complete change in my methods. I introduced this change very gradually and with the co-operation of my friends. My circle of acquaintances had widened considerably this winter, although Karl Ritter, who had escaped from Albisbrunnen a week after my own departure and had tried to settle in our neighbourhood, ran off to Dresden, as he found Zürich much too slow for his youthful spirits. A certain family of the name of Wesendonck, who had settled in Zürich a short time before, sought my acquaintance, and took up their abode in the same quarters in the Hintern Escherhäuser where I had lived when I first came to Zürich. They had taken the flat there on the recommendation of the famous Marschall von Bieberstein, who moved in after me in consequence of the revolution in Dresden. I remember, on the evening of a party there, that I displayed uncontrolled excitement in a discussion with Professor Osenbrück. I tormented him with my persistent paradoxes all through supper to such an extent that he positively loathed me, and ever afterwards carefully avoided coming into contact with me.

The acquaintance with the Wesendoncks was the means of giving me the entrée to a delightful home, which in point of comfort was a great contrast to the usual run of houses in Zürich. Herr Otto Wesendonck, who was a few years younger than I was, had amassed a considerable fortune through a partnership in a silk business in New York, and seemed to make all his plans subservient to the wishes of the young wife whom he had married a few years before. They both came from the Lower Rhine country, and, like all the inhabitants of those parts, were fair haired. As he was obliged to take up his abode in some part of Europe which was convenient for the furtherance of his business in New York, he chose Zürich, presumably because of its German character, in preference to Lyons. During the previous winter they had both attended the performance of a symphony of Beethoven under my conductorship, and knowing what a sensation this performance had aroused in Zürich, they thought it would be desirable to include me in their circle of friends.

About this time I was persuaded to undertake the directorship of the augmented orchestra in view of the performance of some musical masterpieces at three concerts to be given early in the new year under the auspices of the Société Musicale on conditions arranged in advance.

It gave me infinite pleasure on one of these occasions to conduct an excellent performance of Beethoven's music to *Egmont*. As Herwegh was so anxious to hear some of my own music I gave the *Tannhäuser* Overture, as I told him, entirely to please him, and I prepared a descriptive programme as a guide. I also succeeded in giving an excellent rendering of the *Coriolanus* Overture, to which I had also written an explanatory programme. All this was taken up with so much sympathy and enthusiasm by my friends that I was induced to accede to the request of Löwe, who was at that time manager of the theatre, and implored me to give a performance of the *Fliegender Holländer*. For the sake of my friends I agreed to enter into negotiations with the opera company, an undertaking which, though it only lasted a very short time, was exceedingly objectionable. It is true that humane considerations animated me as well, as the performance was for the benefit of Schöneck, a young conductor, whose real talent for his art had completely won me over to him.

The efforts which this unaccustomed excursion into the regions of opera rehearsals, etc., cost me, greatly contributed to the overwrought state of my nerves, and I was obliged, in spite of all my rooted prejudices against doctors, to break faith with myself and, in accordance with the Wesendonck's special recommendation, to place myself in the hands of Dr. Rahn-

Escher, who, by his gentle manner and soothing ways, succeeded after a time in bringing me into a healthier condition.

I longed to get well enough to be able to take in hand the completion of my combined *Nibelungen* poem. Before I could summon up the courage to begin, I thought I would wait for the spring, and in the meanwhile I occupied myself with a few trifles, amongst other things a letter to Liszt on the founding of a Goethe Institution (*Goethe Stiftung*), stating my ideas on the necessity of founding a German National Theatre, as also a second letter to Franz Brendel about the line of thought which in my opinion should be taken up in founding a new musical journal.

I recollect a visit from Henri Vieuxtemps at this time, who came to Zürich with Belloni to give an evening concert, and he again delighted me and my friends with his violin playing.

With the approach of spring I was agreeably surprised by a visit from Hermann Franck, with whom I had an interesting conversation about the general course of events since I had lost sight of him.

In his quiet way he expressed his astonishment at the enthusiastic manner in which I had got mixed up in the Dresden revolution. As I quite misunderstood his remark, he explained that he thought me capable of enthusiasm in everything, but he could hardly credit me with having taken a serious part in anything so foolish as trivial matters of that kind. I now learned for the first time what the prevalent opinion was about these much-maligned occurrences in Germany, and I was in a position to defend my poor friend Röckel, who had been branded as a coward, and to put not only his conduct but also my own in a different light to that in which it had been regarded hitherto even by Hermann Franck, who afterwards expressed his sincere regret that he had so misunderstood us.

With Röckel himself, whose sentence had by royal mercy been commuted to lifelong imprisonment, I carried on at this time a correspondence, the character of which soon showed that his life was more cheerful and happy in his enforced captivity than mine with its hopelessness, in spite of the freedom I enjoyed.

At last the month of May arrived, and I felt I needed change of air in the country in order to strengthen my weakened nerves and carry out my plans in regard to poetry. We found a fairly comfortable *pied-à-terre* on the Rinderknecht estate. This was situated halfway up the Zürich Berg, and we were able to enjoy an alfresco meal on the 22nd of May — my thirty-ninth birth-day — with a lovely view of the lake and the distant Alps. Un-fortunately a period of incessant rain set in which scarcely stopped throughout the whole summer, so that I had the great-est struggle to resist its depressing influence. However, I soon got to work, and as I had begun to carry out my great plan by beginning at the end and going backwards, I continued on the same lines with the beginning as my goal. Consequently, after I had completed the *Siegfrieds Tod* and *Junger Sieg-fried,* I next attacked one of the principal subjects, the *Walküre,* which was to follow the introductory prelude of the *Rheingold.* In this way I completed the poem of the *Walküre* by the end of June. At the same time I wrote the dedication of the score of my *Lohengrin* to Liszt, as well as a rhymed snub to an un-provoked attack on my *Fliegender Holländer* in a Swiss news-paper. A very disagreeable incident in connection with Her-wegh pursued me to my retreat in the country. One day a cer-tain Herr Haug, who described himself as an ex-Roman general of Mazzini's time, introduced himself to me with a view of form-ing a sort of conspiracy against him, on behalf, as he said, of the deeply offended family of the 'unfortunate lyric poet'; however, he did not succeed in getting any assistance from me. A much pleasanter incident was a long visit from Julia, the eldest daughter of my revered friend Frau Ritter, who had married Kummer, the young Dresden chamber musician, whose health seemed so entirely undermined that they were going to consult a celebrated hydropathic doctor who practised only a few miles from Zürich. I now had a good opportunity of abusing this water cure about which my young friends were so eager, and had always believed that I was perfectly mad on it also. But we left the chamber musician to his fate, and rejoiced at the long and pleasant visit of our amiable and charming young friend.

As I was quite satisfied with the success of my work, and the weather was exceptionally cold and rainy, we made up our

minds to return to our cosy winter residence in Zürich at the
end of June. I was resolved to stay there until the appearance of some real summer weather, when I intended to take a
walking tour over the Alps, which I felt would be of great
advantage to my health. Herwegh had promised to accompany me, but as he was apparently prevented from doing so, I
started alone in the middle of July, after arranging with my
travelling companion to meet me in Valais. I began my walking tour at Alpnach, on the Lake of Lucerne, and my plan was
to wander by unfrequented paths to the principal points of
the Bernese Oberland. I worked pretty hard, paying a visit,
for instance, to the Faulhorn, which at that time was considered a very difficult mountain to climb. When I reached
the hospice on the Grimsel by the Hasli Thal, I asked the host,
a fine, stately-looking man, about the ascent of the Siedelhorn.
He recommended me one of his servants as a guide, a rough,
sinister-looking man, who, instead of taking the usual zig-zag
paths up the mountain, led me up in a bee line, and I rather
suspected he intended to tire me out. At the top of the Siedel-.
horn I was delighted to catch a glimpse, on one side, of the
centre of the Alps, whose giant backs alone were turned to us;
and on the other side, a sudden panorama of the Italian Alps,
with Mont Blanc and Monte Rosa. I had been careful to take
a small bottle of champagne with me, following the example of
Prince Pückler when he made the ascent of Snowdon; unfortunately, I could not think of anybody whose health I could
drink. We now descended vast snow-fields, over which my
guide slid with mad haste on his alpenstock; I contented myself with leaning carefully on the iron point of mine, and
coming down at a moderate pace.

I arrived at Obergestelen dead tired, and stayed there two
days, to rest and await the arrival of Herwegh. Instead of
coming himself, however, a letter arrived from him which
dragged me down from my lofty communings with the Alps
to the humdrum consideration of the unpleasant situation in
which my unhappy friend found himself as a result of the
incident I have already described. He feared that I had
allowed myself to be taken in by his adversary, and had consequently formed an unfavourable opinion of him. I told him

to make his mind easy on that score, and to meet me again, if
possible, in Italian Switzerland. So I set out for the ascent
of the Gries glacier, and the climb across the pass to the
southern side of the Alps, in the company of my sinister guide
alone. During the ascent an extremely sad sight kept meeting
my eyes; an epidemic of foot-rot had broken out among
cows in the Upper Alps, and several herds passed me in single
file on their way to the valley, where they were going to be
doctored. The cows had become so lean that they looked like
skeletons, and dragged themselves pitiably down the slopes, and
the smiling country with the fat meadow-land seemed to take
a savage delight in gazing on this sad pilgrimage. At the foot
of the glacier, which stood out sheer and steep before me, I
felt so depressed, and my nerves were so overwrought, that I
said I wished to turn back. I was thereupon met by the coarse
sarcasm of my guide, who seemed to scoff at my weakness. My
consequent anger braced up my nerves, and I prepared myself
at once to climb the steep walls of ice as quickly as possible, so
that this time it was he who found difficulty in keeping up
with me. We accomplished the walk over the back of the
glacier, which lasted nearly two hours, under difficulties which
caused even this native of Grimsel anxiety, at least on his own
account. Fresh snow had fallen, which partially concealed the
crevasses, and prevented one from recognising the dangerous
spots. The guide, of course, had to precede me here, to ex-
amine the path. We arrived at last at the opening of the upper
valley which gives on to the Formazza valley, to which a steep
cutting, covered with snow and ice, led. Here my guide again
began his dangerous game of conducting me straight over the
steepest slopes instead of going in a safe zig-zag; in this way
we reached a precipitous moraine, where I saw such unavoidable danger ahead, that I insisted upon my guide going back
with me some distance, until we struck a path that I had
noticed which was not so steep. He was obliged to give in,
much against the grain. I was deeply impressed by the first
signs of cultivation that we saw in our descent from the desolate
wilds. The first scanty meadow-land accessible to cattle was
called the Bettel-Matt, and the first person we met was a marmot hunter. The wild scenery was soon enlivened by the
marvellous swirl and headlong rush of a mountain river called

the Tosa, which at one spot breaks into a superb waterfall with
three distinct branches. After the moss and reeds had, in the
course of our continuous descent, given place to grass and
meadows, and the shrubs had been replaced by pine trees, we at
last arrived at the goal of our day's journey, the village of
Pommath, called Formazza by the Italian population, which is
situated in a charming valley. Here, for the first time in my
life, I had to eat roast marmot. After having paid my guide,
and sent him on his homeward journey, I started alone on the
following morning on my further descent of the valley, although
I had only partially recovered from my fatigue, owing to lack
of sleep. It was not until the November of this year, when the
whole of Switzerland was thrown into a state of consternation
by the news that the Grimsel inn had been set fire to by the
host himself, who hoped by this means to obtain the renewal
of the lease from the authorities, that I learned my life had
been in danger under the guidance of this man. As soon as
his crime was discovered, the host drowned himself in the little
lake, on the borders of which the inn is situated. The serving-
man, however, whom he had bribed to arrange the fire, was
caught and punished. I knew by the name that he was the same
man that the worthy innkeeper had given me as companion on
my solitary journey across the glacier pass, and I heard at the
same time that two travellers from Frankfort had perished on
the same pass a short time before my own journey. I consequently realised that I had in a really remarkable manner
escaped a fatal danger which had threatened me.

I shall never forget my impressions of my journey through
the continually descending valley. I was particularly astonished at the southern vegetation which suddenly spreads out
before one on climbing down from a steep and narrow rocky
pass by which the Tosa is confined. I arrived at Domodossola
in the afternoon in a blaze of sunshine, and I was reminded
here of a charming comedy by an author whose name I have
forgotten, which I had once seen performed with a refinement
worthy of Platen, and to which my attention had been drawn
by Eduard Devrient in Dresden. The scene of the play was
laid in Domodossola, and described exactly the impressions

I myself received on coming down from the Northern Alps into
Italy, which suddenly burst upon one's gaze. I shall also never
forget my first simple, but extremely well-served, Italian dinner.
Although I was too tired to walk any further that day, I was
very impatient to get to the borders of Lake Maggiore, and
I accordingly arranged to drive in a one-horse chaise, which
was to take me on the same evening as far as Baveno. I felt
so contented while bowling along in my little vehicle that I
reproached myself for want of consideration in having rudely
declined the offer of company which an officer passing through
the Vetturino made me by means of the driver. I admired the
daintiness of the house decorations and the pleasant faces of
the people in the pretty villages I passed through. A young
mother, strolling along and singing as she spun the flax, with
her baby in her arms, also made a never-to-be-forgotten impression on me. Soon after sunset I caught sight of the Borromean Islands rising gracefully out of Lake Maggiore, and again
I could not sleep for excitement at the thought of what I might
see on the following day. The next morning the visit to the
islands themselves delighted me so much that I could not understand how I had managed to come upon anything so charming,
and wondered what would result from it. After stopping only
one day, I left the place with the feeling that I had now to flee
from something to which I did not belong, and went round
Lake Maggiore, up past Socarno, to Bellinzona, where I was
once again on Swiss soil; from there I proceeded to Lugano,
intending, if I followed out my original plan of travel, to stay
there some time. But I soon suffered from the intense heat;
even bathing in the sun-scorched lake was not refreshing.
Apart from the dirty furniture, which included the *Denksopha*
('thinking sofa') from the *Clouds* by Aristophanes, I was
sumptuously lodged in a palatial building, which in the winter
served as the government house of the canton of Tessin, but
in the summer was used as a hotel. However, I soon fell again
into the condition that had troubled me so long, and prevented
me from taking any rest, owing to my extreme nervous strain
and excitement, whenever I felt disposed to idle pleasantly.
I had taken a good many books with me, and proposed
to entertain myself with Byron. Unfortunately it required a

great effort on my part to take any pleasure in his works, and the difficulty of doing so increased when I began to read his *Don Juan*. After a few days' time I began to wonder why I had come, and what I wanted to do here, when suddenly Herwegh wrote saying that he and several friends intended to join me at this place. A mysterious instinct made me telegraph to my wife to come also. She obeyed my call with surprising alacrity, and arrived unexpectedly in the middle of the night, after travelling by post-chaise across the St. Gotthard Pass. She was so fatigued that she at once fell into a sound sleep on the *Denksopha*, from which the fiercest storm that I ever remember failed to awaken her. On the following day my Zürich friends arrived.

Herwegh's chief companion was Dr. François Wille. I had learned to know him some time before at Herwegh's house: his chief characteristics were a face much scarred in students' duels, and a great tendency to witty and outspoken remarks. He had recently been staying near Meilen on the Lake of Zürich, and he often asked me to visit him there with Herwegh. Here we saw something of the habits and customs of a Hamburg household, which was kept up in a fairly prosperous style by his wife, the daughter of Herr Sloman, a wealthy shipowner. Although in reality he remained a student all his life, he had made himself a position and formed a large circle of acquaintances by editing a Hamburg political newspaper. He was a brilliant conversationalist, and was considered good company. He seemed to have taken up with Herwegh with the object of overcoming the latter's antipathy to Alpine climbing, and his consequent reluctance to undertake it. He himself had made preparations to walk over the Gotthard Pass with a Professor Eichelberger, and this had made Herwegh furious, as he declared that walking tours were only permissible where it was impossible to drive, and not on these broad highways. After making an excursion into the neighbourhood of Lugano, during which I got heartily sick of the childish sound of the church bells, so common in Italy, I persuaded my friends to go with me to the Borromean Islands, which I was longing to see again. During the steamer trip on Lake Maggiore, we met a delicate-looking man with a long cavalry moustache, whom in private was humourously dubbed General Haynau, and the distrust with which we affected to treat him was a source of some amusement to us.

We soon found that he was an extremely good-natured Hanoverian nobleman, who had been travelling about Italy for some time for pleasure, and who was able to give us very useful information concerning intercourse with the Italians. His advice was of great service when we were visiting the Borromean Islands, where my acquaintances parted from my wife and myself to travel back by the nearest route, whereas we intended proceeding further across the Simplon and through Le Valais to Chamounix.

From the fatigue my tour had so far occasioned me, I felt that it would be some time before I started on a similar one again. I was therefore eager to see what was best worth seeing in Switzerland as thoroughly as possible now that I had the chance. Moreover, I was just then, and indeed had been for some time, in that impressionable humour from which I might anticipate important results to myself from novel scenery, and I did not like to miss Mont Blanc. A view of it was attended with great difficulties, amongst which may be mentioned our arrival by night at Martigny, where, owing to the crowded state of the hotels, we were everywhere refused accommodation, and it was only on account of a little intrigue between a postillion and a maidservant that we found clandestine shelter for the night in a private house from which the owners were absent.

We dutifully visited the so-called Mer de Glace in the Val de Chamounix and the Flégère, from which I obtained a most impressive view of Mont Blanc. However, my imagination was less busied with the ascent of that peak than with the spectacle I beheld when crossing the Col des Géants, as the great elevation that we attained did not appeal to me so much as the unbroken and sublime wildness of the latter. For some time I cherished the intention of undertaking just one more venture of the kind. While descending the Flégère, Minna had a fall and sprained her ankle; the consequence of this was so painful as to deter us from any further adventures. We therefore saw ourselves forced to hasten on our journey home via Geneva.

But even from this more important and grander expedition, and almost the only one I had ever undertaken purely for recreation, I returned with a strangely unsatisfied feeling, and I could not resist the longing for something decisive in the distance, that would give a fresh direction to my life.

On reaching home I found announcements of a new and quite different turn in my destiny. These consisted of inquiries and commissions from various German theatres anxious to produce *Tannhäuser*. The first to apply was the Schwerin Court Theatre. Röckel's youngest sister, who afterwards married the actor Moritz (whom I had known from my earliest youth), had now come to Germany as a youthful singer from England, where she had been educated. She had given such an enthusiastic account of the impression produced upon her by *Tannhäuser* at Weimar, to an official at the theatre there named Stocks, who held the position of treasurer, that he had studied the opera most assiduously, and had now induced the management to undertake to produce it. The theatres at Breslau, Prague, and Wiesbaden soon followed; at the last of these my old friend Louis Schindelmeisser was acting as conductor. In a short time other theatres followed suit; but I was most astonished when the Berlin Court Theatre made inquiries through its new manager, Herr von Hülsen. From this last incident I felt justified in assuming that the Crown Princess of Prussia, who had always had a friendly feeling towards me, fostered by my faithful friend Alwine Frommann, had again been intensely interested by the performance of *Tannhäuser* at Weimar, and had given the impetus to these unexpected developments.

Whilst I was rejoicing over commissions from the smaller theatres, those of the largest German stage were a source of anxiety. I knew that at the former there were zealous conductors, devoted to me, who had certainly been roused by the desire of having the opera performed; in Berlin, on the other hand, matters were quite different. The only other conductor besides Taubert, whom I had known previously as a man devoid of talent, and at the same time very conceited, was Heinrich Dorn, of whom I retained most unpleasant recollections from my earliest years and from our joint stay in Riga. I felt little drawn towards either of these, nor did I perceive any possibility of undertaking the direction of my own work; and from my knowledge of their capabilities as well as of their ill-will, I had every reason to question any successful rendering of my opera under their conductorship. Being an exile, I was unable to go to Berlin in person in order to supervise my work, so I immediately begged Listz's permission to nominate him as my representative and *alter ego,* to which he willingly agreed. When I afterwards made Liszt's appointment one of my conditions, objection was raised on the part of the general manager at Berlin on the score that the nomination of a Weimar conductor would be regarded as a gross insult to the Prussian court conductors, and I must consequently desist from demanding it. Thereupon prolonged negotiations ensued with a view to compromising the matter, which resulted in the production of *Tannhäuser* at Berlin being considerably delayed.

However, while *Tannhäuser* was now rapidly spreading to the middle-class German theatres, I became a prey to great uneasiness as to the quality of these performances, and could never get a very clear idea of them. As my presence was prohibited everywhere, I had recourse to a very detailed pamphlet which was to serve as a guide to the production of my work, and convey a correct idea of my purpose. I had this somewhat voluminous work printed at my own expense and tastefully bound, and to every theatre that had given an order for the operatic score I sent a number of copies of it, with the understanding that they were to be given to the conductor, stage manager, and principal performers for perusal and guidance. But from that time I have never heard of a single person who had either read this pamphlet or taken any notice of it. In the year 1864, when all my own copies had been exhausted, owing to my painstaking distribution of them, I found to my great delight, among the theatrical archives, several copies that had been sent to the Munich Court Theatre, quite intact and uncut. I was therefore in the agreeable position of being able to procure copies of the missing pamphlet for the King of Bavaria, who wished to see it, as well as for myself and some friends.

It was a singular coincidence that the news of the diffusion of my opera through the German theatres should synchronise with my resolve to compose a work in the conception of which I had been so decidedly influenced by the necessity of being absolutely indifferent to our own theatres; yet this unexpected turn of events in no wise affected my treatment of my design. On the contrary, by keeping to my plan, I gained confidence and let things take their own course, without attempting in any way to promote the performances of my operas. I just let people do as they liked, and looked on surprised, while continual accounts reached my ears of remarkable successes; none of them, however, induced me to alter my verdict on our theatres in general or on the opera in particular. I remained unshaken in my resolve to produce my *Nibelungen* dramas just as though the present operatic stage did not exist, since the ideal theatre of my dreams must of necessity come sooner or later. I therefore composed the libretto of the *Rheingold* in the October and November of that year, and with that I brought the whole cycle of the Nibelungen myth as I had evolved it to a conclusion. At the same time I was rewriting *Junger Siegfried* and *Siegfrieds Tod*, especially the latter, in such a way as to bring them into proper relation with the whole; and by so doing, important amplifications were made in *Siegfrieds Tod* which were in harmony with the now recognised and obvious purpose of the whole work. I was accordingly obliged to find for this last piece a new title suited to the part it plays in the complete cycle. I entitled it *Götterdämmerung*, and I changed the name *Junger Siegfried* to *Siegfried*, as it no longer dealt with an isolated episode in the life of the hero, but had assumed its proper place among the other prominent figures in the framework of the whole.

The prospect of having to leave this lengthy poem for some time entirely unknown to those whom I might expect to be interested in it was a source of great grief to me. As the theatres now and then surprised me by sending me the usual royalties on *Tannhäuser*, I devoted a part of my profits to having a number of copies of my poem neatly printed for my own use. I arranged that only fifty copies of this *édition de luxe* should be struck off. But a great sorrow overtook me before I had completed this agreeable task. It is true, I met on all sides with indications of sympathetic interest in the completion of my great lyric work, although most of my acquaintances regarded the whole thing as a chimera, or possibly a bold caprice. The only one who entered into it with any heartiness or real enthusiasm was Herwegh, with whom I frequently discussed it, and to whom I generally read aloud such portions as were completed. Sulzer was much annoyed at the remodelling of *Siegfrieds Tod*, as he regarded it as a fine and original work, and thought it would be deprived of that quality if I decided to alter it to any extent. He therefore begged me to let him have the manuscript of the earlier version to keep as a remembrance; otherwise it would have been entirely lost. In order to get an idea of the effect of the whole poem when rendered in complete sequence, I decided, only a few days after the work was completed in the middle of December, to pay a short visit to the Wille family at their country seat, so as to read it aloud to the little company there. Besides Herwegh, who accompanied me, the party there consisted of Frau Wille and her sister, Frau von Bissing. I had often entertained these ladies with music in my own peculiar fashion during my pleasant visits to Mariafeld, about two hours' walk from Zürich. In them I had secured a devoted and enthusiastic audience, somewhat to Herr Wille's annoyance, as he often admitted that he had a horror of music; nevertheless, he ended in his jovial way by taking the matter good humouredly.

I arrived towards evening, and we attacked *Rheingold* at once, and as it did not seem very late, and I was supposed to be capable of any amount of exertion, I went on with the *Walküre* until midnight. The next morning after breakfast it was *Siegfried's* turn, and in the evening I finished off with *Götterdämmerung*. I thought I had every reason to be satisfied with the result, and the ladies in particular were so much moved that they ventured no comment. Unfortunately the effort left me in a state of almost painful excitement; I could not sleep, and the next morning I was so disinclined for conversation that I left my hurried departure unexplained. Herwegh, who accompanied me back alone, appeared to divine my state of mind, and shared it by maintaining a similar silence.

However, I now wished to have the pleasure of confiding the whole completed work to my friend Uhlig at Dresden.

I carried on a regular correspondence with him, and he had followed the development of my plan, and was thoroughly acquainted with every phase of it. I did not want to send him the *Walküre* before the *Rheingold* was ready, as the latter should come first, and even then I did not want him to see the whole thing until I could send him a handsomely printed copy. But at the beginning of the autumn I discerned in Uhlig's letters grounds for feeling a growing anxiety as to the state of his health. He complained of the increase in his serious paroxysms of coughing, and eventually of complete hoarseness. He thought all this was merely weakness, which he hoped to overcome by invigorating his system with the cold-water treatment and long walks. He found the violin work at the theatre very exhausting, but if he took a sharp seven hours' walk into the country he invariably felt much better. However, he could not rid himself of his chest attacks or of his hoarseness, and had a difficulty in making himself heard even when speaking to a person quite near him. Up to that time I had been unwilling to alarm the poor fellow, and always hoped that his condition would necessitate his consulting a doctor, who would naturally prescribe rational treatment. Now, however, as I was continually hearing nothing from him but assurances of his confidence in the principles of the water cure, I could contain myself no longer, and I entreated him to give up this madness and place himself in the hands of a sensible doctor, for in his condition what he most needed was, not strength, but very careful attention. The poor man was extremely alarmed at this, as he gathered from my remarks that I feared he was already in an advanced stage of consumption. 'What is to become of my poor wife and children,' he wrote, 'if that is really the case?' Unhappily, it was too late; with the last strength that was left him he tried to write to me again, and finally my old friend Fischer, the chorus-master, carried out Uhlig's instructions, and when these were no longer audible he had to bend down close to his lips. The news of his death followed with frightful rapidity. It took place on the 3rd of January, 1853. Thus, in addition to Lehrs, another of my really devoted friends was carried off by consumption. The handsome copy of the *Ring des Nibelungen* I had intended for him lay uncut before me, and I sent it to his youngest boy, whom he had christened Siegfried. I asked his widow to let me have any pamphlets of a theoretical nature he might have left behind, and I came into possession of several important ones, among them the longer essay on ' Theme-Structure.' Although the publication of these works would involve a great deal of trouble, owing to the necessity of revising them, I asked Härtel of Leipzig if he would pay the widow a fair sum for a volume of Uhlig's writings. The publisher declared he could not undertake to bring it out without payment, as works of that nature were quite unremunerative. It was obvious to me, even at that time, how thoroughly every musician who had taken a keen interest in me had made himself disliked in certain circles.

Uhlig's melancholy death gave my home-circle the whip-hand over me with regard to my theories on the subject of water cures. Herwegh impressed upon my wife that she must insist upon my taking a glass of good wine after all the exertion I underwent at the rehearsals and concerts which I was attending throughout that winter. By degrees, also, I again accustomed myself to enjoy such mild stimulants as tea and coffee, my friends meanwhile perceiving to their joy that I was once more becoming a man amongst men. Dr. Rahn-Escher now became a welcome and comforting friend and visitor, who for many years thoroughly understood the management of my health, and especially the misgivings arising from the overwrought state of my nerves. He soon verified the wisdom of his treatment, when in the middle of February I had undertaken to read my tetralogy aloud on four consecutive evenings before a larger audience. I had caught a severe cold after the first evening, and on the morning of the day for the second reading I awoke suffering from severe hoarseness. I at once informed the doctor that my failure to give the reading would be a serious matter to me, and asked him what he advised me to do to get rid of the hoarseness as speedily as possible. He recommended me to keep quiet all day, and in the evening to be taken well wrapped up to the place where the readings were to be held. When I got there I was to take two or three cups of weak tea, and I should be all right; whereas if I worried over the failure to keep my engagement I might become seriously worse. And, indeed, the reading of this stirring work went off capitally, and I was, moreover, able to continue the readings on the third and fourth evenings, and felt perfectly well. I had secured a large and handsome room for these meetings in the Hôtel Baur au lac, and had the gratifying experience of seeing it fuller and fuller each evening, in spite of having invited only a small number of acquaintances, giving them the option of bringing any friends who they thought would take a genuine interest in the subject and not come out of mere curiosity. Here, too, the verdict seemed altogether favourable, and it was from the most serious university men and government officials that I received assurances of the greatest appreciation as well as kindly remarks, showing that my poem and the artistic ideas connected with it had been fully understood. From the peculiar earnestness with which they gave vent to their opinions, which in this case were so confidently unanimous, the idea occurred to me to try how far this favourable impression might be utilized to serve the higher aims of art. In accordance with the superficial views generally prevailing on the subject, every one seemed to think I might be induced to make terms with the theatre. I tried to think out how it would be possible to convert the ill-equipped Zürich theatre into a highly developed one by adopting sound principles, and I laid my views before the public in a pamphlet entitled ' A Theatre in Zürich.' The edition, consisting of about a hundred copies, was sold, yet I never noticed the least indication of any result from the publication; the only outcome was, that at a banquet of the Musical Society my excellent friend, Herr Ott-Imhoff, expressed his entire disagreement with the statements uttered by various people, that these ideas of mine were all very grand, but unfortunately quite impracticable. Nevertheless, my propositions lacked the one thing that would have made them valuable in his eyes, namely my consent to take over the management of the theatre in person, as he would not entrust the carrying out of my ideas to anyone but myself. However, as I was obliged to declare then and there that I would not have anything to do with such a scheme, the matter dropped, and in my inmost heart I could not help thinking that the good people were quite right.

Meanwhile, the sympathetic interest in my works was increasing. As I now had to refuse firmly to yield to my friends' wishes for a performance of my principal works at the theatre, I begged to be allowed to arrange a selection of characteristic pieces, which could easily be produced at concerts, so soon as I could obtain the requisite support. A subscription list was accordingly circulated, and it had the satisfactory result of inducing several well-known art patrons to put their names down to guarantee expenses. I had to undertake to engage an orchestra to suit my requirements. Skilled musicians from far and near were summoned, and after interminable efforts I began to feel that something really satisfactory would be achieved.

I had made arrangements that the performers should stay at Zürich a whole week from Sunday to Sunday. Half of this time was allotted exclusively to rehearsals. The performance was to take place on Wednesday evening, and on Friday and Sunday evenings there were to be repetitions of it. The dates were the 18th, 20th, and 22nd of May, my fortieth birthday falling on the last-named date. I had the joy of seing all my directions accurately carried out. From Mayence, Wiesbaden, Frankfort, and Stuttgart, and on the other side, from Geneva, Lausanne, Bâle, Berne, and the chief towns in Switzerland, picked musicians arrived punctually on Sunday afternoon. They were at once directed to the theatre, where they had to arrange their exact places in the orchestral stand I had previously designed at Dresden — and which proved excellent here too — so as to begin rehearsing the first thing next morning without delay or interruption. As these people were at my disposal in the early morning and in the evening, I made them learn a selection of pieces from the *Fliegender Holländer*, *Tannhäuser*, and *Lohengrin*. I had greater trouble in trying to train them for a chorus, but this too turned out very satisfactorily. There was nothing in the way of solo-singing, except the Ballad of Senta from the *Holländer*, which was sung by the wife of the conductor Heim in a good though untrained voice, and with an amount of spirit that left nothing to be desired. As a matter of fact, the performances could hardly be called public concerts, but were rather of the nature of family entertainments. I felt

I was fulfilling a sincere desire on the part of a larger circle of acquaintances by introducing them to the true nature of my music, rendered as intelligibly as circumstances permitted. As, at the same time, it was desirable that they should have some knowledge of the poetical basis of it, I invited those who intended to be present at my concerts to come for three evenings to the Musical Society's concert-hall to hear me read aloud the libretto of the three operas, portions of which they were about to hear. This invitation met with an enthusiastic response, and I was now able to hope that my audience would come better prepared to listen to the selections from my operas than had ever been the case before. The fact that pleased me most in the performances on these three evenings was that I was able for the first time to produce something from *Lohengrin* myself, and could thus get an idea of the effect of my combination of the instrumental parts in the overture to that work.

Between the performances there was a banquet which, with the exception of a subsequent one at Pesth, was the only function of the sort ever held in my honour. I was sincerely and deeply affected by the speech of the aged President of the Musical Society, Herr Ott-Usteri. He drew the attention of all those musicians who had come together from so many places to the significance of their meeting, and its objects and results, and recommended as a trustworthy guide to them on their homeward journey the conviction they had all doubtless arrived at, that they had come into close and genuine touch with a wonderful new creation in the realm of art.

The sensation produced by these evening concerts spread through the whole of Switzerland in ever-widening circles. Invitations and requests for further repetitions of them poured in from distant towns. I was assured that I might well repeat the three performances in the following week without any fear of seeing a diminution in the audience. When this project was discussed, and I pleaded my own fatigue, and also expressed the desire to retain for these concerts their unique character by not allowing them to become commonplace, I was very glad to have the powerful and intelligent support of my friend Hagenbuch, who on this occasion was indefatigable. The

festival was concluded, and the guests were dismissed at the
appointed time.

I had hoped to be able to welcome Liszt among the visitors,
as he had celebrated a 'Wagner week' at Weimar in the
previous March by performing three operas of which I had
only given portions here. Unfortunately he was unable to
leave just then, but by way of amends he promised me a visit
at the beginning of July. Of my German friends, only the
faithful Mme. Julie Kummer and Mme. Emilie Ritter arrived
in time. As these two ladies had gone on to Interlaken at the
beginning of June, and I also began to feel in great need of a
change, I started with my wife, towards the end of the month,
for a short holiday. The visit was spoilt in the most dismal
fashion by continuous rain; and on the 1st of July, as we were
starting in desperation on our homeward journey to Zürich
with our lady friends, magnificent summer weather set in,
which lasted a considerable time. With affectionate enthusiasm we at once attributed this change to Liszt, as he arrived
in Switzerland in the best of spirits immediately after we had
returned to Zürich. Thereupon followed one of those delightful
weeks, during which every hour of the day becomes a treasured
memory. I had already taken more roomy apartments on the
second floor in the so-called Vorderen Escher Häusern, in
which I had before occupied a flat that was much too small
on the ground floor. Frau Stockar-Escher, who was part
owner of the house, was enthusiastically devoted to me. She
was full of artistic talent herself, being an excellent amateur
painter in water-colours, and had taken great pains to rearrange
the new dwelling as luxuriously as possible. The unexpected
improvement in my circumstances brought about by the continued demands for my operas, allowed me to indulge my
desire for comfortable domestic arrangements, which had been
reawakened since my stay at the hydropathic establishment,
and which, after being repressed, had become quite a passionate
longing.

I had the flat so charmingly furnished with carpets and
decorative furniture that Liszt himself was surprised into
admiration as he entered my *petite élégance,* as he called it.
Now for the first time I enjoyed the delight of getting to know

my friend better as a fellow-composer. In addition to many of his celebrated pianoforte pieces, which he had only recently written, we went through several new symphonies with great ardour, and especially his *Faust* Symphony. Later on, I had the opportunity of describing in detail the impressions I received at this time in a letter which I wrote to Marie von Wittgenstein, which was afterwards published. My delight over everything I heard by Liszt was as deep as it was sincere, and, above all, extraordinary stimulating. I even thought of beginning to compose again after the long interval that had elapsed. What could be more full of promise and more momentous to me than this long-desired meeting with the friend who had been engaged all his life in his masterly practice of music, and had also devoted himself so absolutely to my own works, and to diffusing the proper comprehension of them. Those almost bewilderingly delightful days, with the inevitable rush of friends and acquaintances, were interrupted by an excursion to the Lake of Lucerne, accompanied only by Herwegh, to whom Liszt had the charming idea of offering a ' draught of fellowship ' with himself and me from the three springs of the Grütli.

After this my friend took leave of us, after having arranged for another meeting with me in the autumn.

Although I felt quite disconsolate after Liszt's departure, the officials of Zürich took good care that I should soon have some diversion, of a kind to which I had hitherto been a stranger. It took the form of the presentation of a masterpiece of calligraphy in the shape of a ' Diploma of Honour,' awarded me by the Zürich Choral Society, which was ready at last. This was to be awarded to me with the accompaniment of an imposing torchlight procession, in which the various elements of the Zürich population, who, either as individuals or members of societies, were favourably disposed to me, were to take part. So it came to pass that one fine summer evening a large company of torchbearers approached the Zeltweg, to the accompaniment of loud music. They presented a spectacle such as I had never seen before, and made a unique impression on my mind. After the singing, the voice of the President of the Choral Society could be heard rising from the street. I was so much affected by the incident that my unconquerable optimism quickly overpowered every other sensation. In my speech of acknowledgment I indicated plainly that I saw no reason why Zürich itself should not be the chosen place to give an impetus to the fulfilment of the aspirations I cherished for my artistic ideals, and that it might do so on proper civic lines. I believe this was taken to refer to a special development of the men's choral societies, and they were quite gratified at my bold forecasts. Apart from this confusion, for which I was responsible, that evening's ceremony and its effects on me were very cheerful and beneficial.

But I still felt the peculiar disinclination and fear of taking up composing again that I had previously experienced after protracted pauses in musical production. I also felt very much exhausted by all I had done and gone through, and the ever-recurring longing to break completely with everything in the past, that had unfortunately haunted me since my departure from Dresden, as well as the desire and yearning for new and untried surroundings, fostered by that anxiety, now acquired fresh and tormenting vigour. I felt that before entering on such a gigantic task as the music to my drama of the *Nibelungen,* I must positively make one final effort to see whether I could not, in some new environment, attain an existence more in harmony with my feelings than I could possibly aspire to after so many compromises. I planned a journey to Italy, or such parts of it as were open to me as a political refugee. The means for carrying out my wish were readily placed at my disposal through the kindness of my friend Wesendonck, who has ever since that time been devoted to me. However, I knew it was inadvisable to take that journey before the autumn, and as my doctor had recommended some special treatment for strengthening my nerves — even if only to enjoy Italy — I decided first of all to go to St. Moritz Bad in the Engadine. I started in the latter half of July, accompanied by Herwegh. Strangely enough, I have often found that what other people could note in their diaries merely as an ordinary visit or a trivial expedition, assumed me the character of an adventure. This occurred on our journey to the Bad, when, owing to the coaches being crowded, we were detained at Chur in an incessant downpour of rain. We were obliged to pass the time in reading at a most uncomfortable inn. I got hold of Goethe's *West-östlichen Divan*, for the reading of which I had been prepared by Daumer's adaptation of *Hafiz*. To this day I never think of Goethe's words in elucidating these poems without recalling that wretched delay in our journey to the Engadine. We did not get on much better at St. Moritz; the present convenient Kurhaus was not then in existence, and we had to put up with the roughest accommodation; this was particularly annoying to me on Herwegh's account, as he had not gone there for health, but simply for enjoyment. However, we were soon cheered by the lovely views of the grand valleys, which were quite bare but for the Alpine pastures, that met our eyes on our way down the steep slopes into the Italian valleys. After we had secured the schoolmaster at Samaden as a guide to the Rosetch glacier, we embarked on more serious expeditions. We had confidently looked forward to exceptional enjoyment in thus penetrating beyond the precipices of the great Mont Bernina, to which we gave the palm for beauty above Mont Blanc itself. Unfortunately the effect was lost on my friend, owing to the tremendous exertions by which the ascent and crossing of the glacier were attended. Once again, but this time to an even greater degree, I felt the sublime impression of the sacredness of that desolate spot, and the almost benumbing calm which the disappearance of all vegetation produces on the pulsating life of the human organism. After we had been wandering for two hours, deep in the glacier path, we partook of a meal we had brought with us, and champagne, iced in the fissures, to strengthen us for our wearisome return. I had to cover the distance nearly twice over, as, to my astonishment, Herwegh was in such a nervous condition that I had repeatedly to go backwards and forwards, showing him the way up and down before he would decide to follow. I then realised the peculiarly exhausting nature of the air in those regions, as on our way back we stopped at the first herdsman's cottage, and were refreshed with some delicious milk. I swallowed such quantities of it that we were both perfectly amazed, but I experienced no discomfort whatever in consequence.

The waters, whether for internal or external use, are known

to be powerfully impregnated with iron, and in taking them I had the same experience as on previous occasions. With my extremely excitable nervous system, they were a source of more trouble than relief to me. The leisure hours were filled up by reading Goethe's *Wahlverwandtschaften,* which I had not read since I was quite young. This time I absolutely devoured the book from beginning to end, and it also became a source of heated discussions between Herwegh and myself. As Herwegh possessed an extensive knowledge of the characteristics of our great poetic literature, he felt it incumbent on him to defend the character of Charlotte against my attacks. My vehemence on the subject showed what a strange creature I still was at over forty, and in my heart of hearts I had to admit that Herwegh judged Gothe's poem objectively more correctly than I did, as I always felt depressed by a kind of moral bondage, to which Herwegh, if he had ever experienced it at all, submitted placidly, owing to his peculiar relations with his strong-minded wife. When the time came to an end, and I realised that I had not much to hope for from the treatment, we returned to Zürich. This was about the middle of August, and I now began to look forward impatiently to my tour in Italy. At last, in the month of September, which I had been told was quite suitable for visiting Italy, I set off on the journey via Geneva, full of indescribable ideas of what was before me, and of what I might see as the outcome of my search. Once again amid all sorts of strange adventures, I reached Turin by special mail-coach over Mont Cenis. Finding nothing to detain me there more than a couple of days, I hurried on to Genoa. There, at any rate, the longed-for marvels seemed to be within reach. The grand impression produced on me by that city overcomes, even to this day, any longing to visit the rest of Italy. For a few days I was in a dream of delight; but my extreme loneliness amidst these impressions soon made me feel that I was a stranger in that world, and that I should never be at home in it. Absolutely inexperienced as I was in searching out the treasures of art on a systematic plan, I gave myself up in this new world to a peculiar state of mind that might be described as a musical one, and my main idea was to find some turning-point that might induce me to remain there in quiet enjoyment. My only object still was to find a refuge where I might enjoy the congenial peace suited to some new artistic creation. In consequence, however, of thoughtlessly indulging in ices, I soon got an attack of dysentery, which produced the most depressing lassitude after my previous exaltation. I wanted to flee from the tremendous noise of the harbour, near which I was staying, and seek for the most absolute calm; and thinking a trip to Spezia would benefit me, I went there by steamer a week later. Even this excursion, which lasted only one night, was turned into a trying adventure, thanks to a violent head-wind. The dysentery became worse, owing to sea-sickness, and in the most utterly exhausted condition, scarcely able to drag myself another step, I made for the best hotel in Spezia, which, to my horror, was situated in a noisy, narrow street.

After a night spent in fever and sleeplessness, I forced myself to take a long tramp the next day through the hilly country, which was covered with pine woods. It all looked dreary and desolate, and I could not think what I should do there. Returning in the afternoon, I stretched myself, dead tired, on a hard couch, awaiting the long-desired hour of sleep. It did not come; but I fell into a kind of somnolent state, in which I suddenly felt as though I were sinking in swiftly flowing water. The rushing sound formed itself in my brain into a musical sound, the chord of E flat major, which continually re-echoed in broken forms; these broken chords seemed to be melodic passages of increasing motion, yet the pure triad of E flat major never changed, but seemed by its continuance to impart infinite significance to the element in which I was sinking. I awoke in sudden terror from my doze, feeling as though the waves were rushing high above my head. I at once recognised that the orchestral overture to the *Rheingold,* which must long have lain latent within me, though it had been unable to find definite form, had at last been revealed to me. I then quickly realised my own nature; the stream of life was not to flow to me from without, but from within. I decided to return to Zürich immediately, and begin the composition of my great poem. I telegraphed to my wife to let her know my decision, and to have my study in readiness.

The same evening I took my place on the coach going to Genoa
along the Riviera di Levante. I again had the opportunity
of getting exquisite impressions of the country during this
journey, which lasted over the whole of the following day.
It was, above all, the colouring of the wonders that presented
themselves to my eyes which gave me such delight — the red-
ness of the rocks, the blue of the sky and the sea, the pale green
of the pines; even the dazzling white of a herd of cattle worked
upon me so powerfully that I murmured to myself with a sigh,
'How sad it is that I cannot remain to enjoy all this, and thus
gratify my sensuous nature.'

At Genoa I again felt so agreeably stimulated that I suddenly
thought I had only yielded to some foolish weakness, and resolved to carry out my original plan. I was already making
arrangements for travelling to Nice along the celebrated Riviera
di Ponente, of which I had heard so much, but I had scarcely
decided on my former plans, when I realised that the fact which
refreshed and invigorated me was not the renewal of my delight
over Italy, but the resolve to take up my work again. And
indeed, as soon as I made up my mind to alter this plan, the
old condition set in once more, with all the symptoms of
dysentery. I thereupon understood myself, and giving up the
journey to Nice, I returned direct by the nearest route via
Alessandria and Novara.

This time I passed the Borromean Islands with supreme
indifference, and got back to Zürich over the St. Gotthard.

When I had once returned, the only thing that could have
made me happy would have been to start at once on my great
work. For the present, however, I saw that it would be
seriously interrupted by my appointment with Liszt, who was
to be in Bâle at the beginning of October. I was restless and
annoyed at being so unsettled, and spent the time in visiting
my wife, who, thinking that I would be away longer, was
taking the waters at Baden am Stein. As I was easily prevailed
upon to try any experiment of this kind if only the person who
recommended it were sufficiently sanguine, I allowed myself
to be persuaded into taking a course of hot baths, and the
process heightened my excitment considerably.

At last the time for the meeting in Bâle arrived. At the invita-

tion of the Grand Duke of Baden, Liszt had arranged and
conducted a musical festival in Karlsruhe, the aim of which
was to give the public an adequate interpretation of our
respective works. As I was not yet allowed to enter the territory of the German confederation, Liszt had chosen Bâle as
the place nearest to the Baden frontier, and had brought with
him some young men who had been his devoted admirers in
Karlsruhe, to give me a hearty welcome.

I was the first to arrive, and in the evening, while sitting
alone in the dining-room of the hotel, 'Zu den drei Königen,'
the air of the trumpet fanfare (from *Lohengrin*) announcing
the King's arrival, sung by a strong though not numerous chorus
of men's voices, reached me from the adjacent vestibule. The
door opened and Liszt entered at the head of his joyful little
band, whom he introduced to me. I also saw Bülow again, for
the first time since his adventurous winter visit to Zürich and
St. Gall, and with him Joachim, Peter Cornelius, Richard
Pohl, and Dionys Pruckner.

Liszt told me that he was expecting a visit from his friend
Caroline von Wittgenstein and her young daughter Marie the
next day. The bright and merry spirit which prevailed at
that gathering (which, like everything that Liszt promoted,
in spite of its intimate nature, was characterised by magnificent
unconventionality) grew to a pitch of almost eccentric hilarity
as the night wore on. In the midst of our wild mood I suddenly
missed Pohl. I knew him to be a champion of our cause
through having read his articles under the pseudonym of
'Hoplit.' I stole away and found him in bed suffering from a
splitting headache. My sympathy had such an effect upon
him that he declared himself suddenly cured. Jumping out of
bed, he allowed me to help him dress hurriedly, and again joining our friends we sat up till the night was far advanced and
enjoyed ourselves thoroughly. On the following day our hap-
pinesss was complete when the ladies arrived, who for the next
few days formed the centre of our little party. In those days
it was impossible for any one coming into contact with Princess
Caroline not to be fascinated by her bright manner and the
charming way in which she entered into all our little plans.

She was as much interested in the more important questions

that affected us as in the accidental details of our life in relation to society, and she had the magnetic power of extracting the very best out of those with whom she associated. Her daughter gave one quite a different impression. She was barely fifteen and had a rather dreamy look on her young face, and was at the stage 'in which womanhood and childhood meet,' thus allowing me to pay her the compliment of calling her 'the child.' During our lively discussions and outbursts of merriment, her dark pensive eyes would gaze at us so calmly that we unconsciously felt that in her innocence she unwittingly understood the cause of our gaiety. In those days I suffered from the vanity of wishing to recite my poems aloud (a proceeding which, by the bye, annoyed Herwegh very much), and consequently it was no difficult task to induce me to read out my *Nibelungen* drama. As the time of our parting was drawing near, I decided I would read *Siegfried* only.

When Liszt was obliged to leave for Paris on a visit to his children, we all accompanied him as far as Strasburg. I had decided to follow him to Paris, but the Princess intended going on from Strasburg to Weimar with her daughter.

During the few spare hours of our short stay in Strasburg I was asked to read some of my work to the ladies, but could not find a suitable opportunity. However, on the morning of our intended parting, Liszt came to my room to tell me that the ladies had, after all, decided to accompany us to Paris, and added, laughing, that Marie had induced her mother to change her plans, as she wished to hear the rest of the *Nibelungen* poems. The prolonging of our journey, with all its delightful incidents, was quite in accordance with my taste.

We were very sorry to part from our younger friends. Bülow told me that Joachim, who had been holding himself rather aloof, could not forget my tremendous article on 'Judaism,' and that he consequently felt shy and awkward in my presence. He also said that when Joachim had asked him (Bülow) to read one of his compositions, he had inquired with a certain gentle diffidence, whether I should be able to trace 'anything Jewish' in it.

This touching trait in Joachim's character induced me to say a few particularly friendly words to him at parting and to embrace him warmly. I never saw him again,[1] and heard to my astonishment that he had taken up a hostile attitude to both Liszt and myself, almost immediately after we had left. The other young men were the victims, on their return to Germany, of a very funny although unpleasant experience, that of coming into contact with the police at Baden. They had entered the town singing the same bright tune of the fanfare from *Lohengrin,* and they had a good deal of difficulty in giving a satisfactory account of themselves to the inhabitants.

Our journey to Paris and our stay there were full of important incidents, and left indelible traces of our exceptionally devoted friendship. After great difficulty we found rooms for the ladies in the Hôtel des Princes, and Liszt then suggested that we should go for a stroll on the boulevards, which at that hour were deserted. I presume that our feelings on this occasion must have differed as much as our reminiscences. When I entered the sitting-room the next morning, Liszt remarked, with his characteristic little smile, that the Princess Marie was already in a great state of excitement at the thought of further readings. Paris did not offer much attraction to me, and as Princess Caroline desired to arouse as little attention as possible, and Liszt was frequently called away on private business, we took up our reading, where we had left it off in Bâle, on the very first morning of our stay in Paris, even before we had been outside the hotel. I was not allowed to stop reading on the following days until the *Ring des Nibelungen* was quite finished. Finally Paris claimed our attention, but while the ladies were visiting the museums I was unfortunately obliged to stay in my room, tortured by continually recurring nervous headaches. Liszt, however, induced me occasionally to join them in their excursions. At the beginning of our stay he had engaged a box for a performance of *Robert le Diable,* because he wanted the ladies to see the great opera house under the most favourable conditions. I believe that my friends shared the terrible depression from which I was suffering on this occasion. Liszt, however, must have had other motives for going. He had asked me to wear evening dress, and seemed very pleased I had done so when at the interval he invited me to go for a stroll

[1] This was written in 1869.

with him through the foyer. I could see he was under the influence of certain reminiscences of delightful evenings spent in this selfsame foyer, and that the dismal performance of this night must have cast a gloom over him. We stole quietly back to our friends, hardly knowing why we had started on this monotonous expedition. One of the artistic pleasures I enjoyed most was a concert given by the Morin-Chevillard Quartette Society, at which they played Beethoven's Quartettes in E flat major and C sharp minor; the excellent rendering of this work impressed me in very much the same way as the performance of the Ninth Symphony by the Conservatoire orchestra had once done. I had again the opportunity of admiring the great artistic zeal with which the French master these treasures of music, which even to this day are so coarsely handled by the Germans.

This was the first time that I really became intimately acquainted with the C sharp minor quartette, because I had never before grasped its melody. If, therefore, I had nothing else to remind me of my stay in Paris, this would have been an unfading memory. I also carried away with me other equally significant impressions. One day Liszt invited me to spend an evening with him and his children, who were living very quietly in the care of a governess in Paris.

It was quite a novelty to me to see Liszt with these young girls, and to watch him in his intercourse with his son, then a growing lad. Liszt himself seemed to feel strange in his fatherly position, which for several years had only brought him cares, without any of the attendant pleasures.

On this occasion we again resumed our reading of the last act of *Götterdämmerung,* which brought us to the longed-for end of the tetralogy. Berlioz, who looked us up during that time, endured these readings with quite admirable patience. We had lunch with him one morning before his departure, and he had already packed his music for his concert tour through Germany. Liszt played different selections from his *Benvenuto Cellini,* while Berlioz sang to them in his peculiarly monotonous style. I also met the journalist, Jules Janin, who was quite a celebrity in Paris, although it took me a long time to realise this; the only thing that impressed me about him was his

colloquial Parisian French, which was quite unintelligible
to me.

A dinner, followed by a musical evening at the house of the
celebrated pianoforte manufacturer, Erard, also remains in my
memory. At this house, as well as at a dinner-party given by
Liszt at the Palais Royal, I again met his children. Daniel,
the youngest of them, particularly attracted me by his bright-
ness and his striking resemblance to his father, but the girls
were very shy. I must not forget to mention an evening spent
at the house of Mme. Kalergis, a woman of exceptional individuality, whom I met here for the first time since the early
performance of *Tannhäuser* in Dresden. When at dinner she
asked me a question about Louis Napoleon, I forgot myself so
far in my excitement and resentment as to put an end to all
further conversation by saying that I could not understand
how anybody could possibly expect great things from a man
whom no woman could really love. After dinner, when Liszt
sat down at the piano, young Marie Wittgenstein noticed that
I had withdrawn silently and rather sadly from the rest of the
company; this was due partly to my headache, and partly to
the feeling of isolation that came over me in these surroundings.
I was touched by her sympathy and evident wish to divert me.

After a very fatiguing week my friends left Paris. As I had
again been prevented from starting on my work, I now decided
not to leave Paris until I had restored my nerves to that state
of calm which was indispensable to the fulfilment of my great
project. I had invited my wife to meet me on our way back
to Zürich, to give her the opportunity of seeing Paris again,
where we had both suffered so much. After her arrival, Kietz
and Anders turned up regularly for dinner, and a young Pole,
the son of my old and beloved friend, Count Vincenz
Tyszkiewicz, also came to see us very often.

This young man (who had been born since the early days of
my friendship with his father) had devoted himself passionately
to music, as so many do nowadays. He had made quite a stir
in Paris after a performance of *Freischütz* at the Grand Opera,
by declaring that the many cuts and alterations which had
been made were a fraud on the initiated public, and he had sued
the management of the theatre for the return of the entrance

money, which he regretted ever having paid. He also had an idea of publishing a paper with the view of drawing attention to the slovenly conduct of musical affairs in Paris, which in his opinion was an insult to public taste.

Prince Eugen von Wittgenstein-Sayn, a young amateur painter who had belonged to Liszt's circle of intimate friends, painted a miniature of me, for which I had to give him several sittings; it was done under Kietz's guidance, and turned out pretty well.

I had an important consultation with a young doctor named Lindemann, a friend of Kietz's; he strongly advised me to give up the water cure, and tried to convert me to the toxic theory. He had attracted the attention of Parisian society by inoculating himself with various poisons in the hospital before witnesses, in order to show their effects upon the system, an experiment which he carried out in an accurate and thoroughly effective manner. With regard to my own case, he stated that it could be easily remedied if we ascertained by careful experiments what metallic substance would specifically influence my nervous system. He unhesitatingly recommended me, in case of very violent attacks, to take laudanum, and in default of that poison he seemed to consider valerian an excellent remedy.

Tired out, restless and exceedingly unstrung, I left Paris with Minna towards the end of October, without in the least understanding why I had spent so much money there. Hoping counterbalance this by pushing my operas in Germany, I calmly retired to the seclusion of my Zürich lodgings, fully decided not to leave them again until some parts, at least, of my *Nibelungen* dramas were set to music.

In the beginning of November I started on this long-postponed work. For five and a half years (since the end of March, 1848) I had held aloof from all musical composition, and as I very soon found myself in the right mood for composing, this return to my work can best be compared to a reincarnation of my soul after it had been wandering in other spheres. As far as the technique was concerned, I soon found myself in a difficulty when I started to write down the orchestral overture, conceived in Spezia in a kind of half-dream, in my usual way of sketching it out on two lines. I was compelled to resort to the complete score-formula; this tempted me to try a new way of sketching, which was a very hasty and superficial one, from which I immediately wrote out the complete score.

This process often led to difficulties, as the slightest interruption in my work made me lose the thread of my rough draft, and I had to start from the beginning before I could recall it to my memory.

I did not let this occur in regard to *Rheingold*. The whole of this composition had been finished in outline on the 16th of January, 1854, and consequently the plan for the musical structure of this work in four parts had been drawn in all its thematic proportions, as it was in this great prelude that these thematic foundations of the whole had to be laid.

I remember how much my health improved during the writing of this work; and my surroundings during that time consequently left very little impression on my mind.

During the first months of the new year I also conducted a few orchestral concerts. To please my friend Sulzer, I produced, amongst other works, the overture to Gluck's *Iphigenia in Aulis,* after having written a new finale to it. The necessity for altering the finale by Mozart induced me to write an article for the Brendel musical journal on this artistic problem. These occupations did not, however, prevent me from working at the *Rheingold* score, which I quickly dotted down in pencil on a few single sheets. On the 28th May I finished the instrumentation of the *Rheingold.* There had been very little change in my life at home; things had remained the same during the last few years, and everything went smoothly. Only my financial position was rather precarious, owing to the past year's expenses for furniture, etc., and also to the more luxurious mode of living I had adopted, on the strength of my belief that my operas, which were now better known, would bring me in a larger income.

The most important theatres, however, still held back, and to my mortification all my efforts at negotiation with Berlin and Vienna proved fruitless. In consequence of these disappointments I suffered great worries and cares during the greater part of that year. I tried to counteract these by new work, and instead of writing out the score of *Rheingold* I began the composition of the *Walküre*. Towards the end of July I had finished the first scene, but had to interrupt my work on account of a journey to the south of Switzerland.

I had received an invitation from the ' Eidgenossische Musik-gesellschaft' to conduct their musical festival at Sion that year. I had refused, but at the same time promised that if possible I would conduct Beethoven's Symphony in A major at one of the gala concerts. I intended on the way to call on Karl Ritter, who had gone to live with his young wife at Montreux on the Lake of Geneva. The week I spent with this young couple gave me ample opportunities for doubting whether their happiness would be of long duration.

Karl and I left shortly afterwards for the musical festival in Valais. On our way we were joined at Martigny by an extraordinary young man, Robert von Hornstein, who had been introduced to me on the occasion of my great musical festival the year before as an enthusiast and a musician. This quaint mortal was regarded as a very welcome addition to our party, particularly by young Ritter, and both young people looked forward with great enthusiasm to the treat in store for them; Hornstein had come all the way from Swabia to hear me conduct the festival in the canton of Valais. We arrived in the midst of the musical festivities, and I was terribly disappointed to find how very badly and inartistically the preliminary arrangements had been made. I was so taken aback, after having received the worst possible impression of the sound of the very scanty orchestra in a small church, which served as church and concert-hall combined, and was so furious at the thought of having been dragged into such an affair, that I merely wrote a few lines to Methfessel, the organising director of the festival, who had come from Berne, and took my leave, without further ceremony. I escaped by the next post-chaise that was just on the point of leaving, and I did this so expeditiously that even my young friends were unaware of my departure. I purposely kept the fact of my sudden flight from them; I had my own reasons for doing so, and as they were rather interesting from a psychological point of view, I have never forgotten them.

On coming back to dinner that day feeling miserable and depressed after the disappointing impression I had just received, my annoyance was treated with foolish and almost insulting roars of laughter by my young friends. I presumed that their merriment was the result of remarks made at my expense before I came in, as neither my admonitions nor even my anger could induce them to behave differently. I quitted the dining-room in disgust, paid my bill and left, without giving them any opportunity of noticing my departure. I spent a few days in Geneva and Lausanne, and decided to call on Frau Ritter on my way back; and there I again met the two young people. Evidently they also had given up the wretched festival, and been completely taken aback at my sudden departure, had almost immediately left for Montreux, in the hope of hearing news of me.

I made no mention of their rude conduct, and as Karl cordially invited me to stay with them a few days longer I accepted, principally because I was very much interested in a poetical work he had only just finished. This poem was a comedy called *Alkibiades,* which he had really treated with exceptional refinement and freedom of form. He had already told me at Albisbrunnen about the sketch of this work, and had shown me an elegant dagger into the blade of which the syllables *Alki* had been burnt.

He explained that his friend, a young actor whom he had left in Stuttgart, possessed a similar weapon, the blade of which bore the syllables *Biades.* It seemed that Karl, even without the symbolic help of the daggers, had again found the complement of his own ' Alkibiadesian ' individuality, this time in the young booby Hornstein, and it is very probable that the two, whilst in Sion, had imagined they were acting an ' Alkibiadesian ' scene before Socrates. His comedy showed me that his artistic talent was fortunately far better than his society manners. To this day I regret that this decidedly difficult play has never been produced.

Hornstein now behaved properly and desired to go to Lausanne via Vevey. We did part of the journey together on foot, and his quaint appearance with his knapsack on his back was most amusing.

I continued my journey alone from Berne to Lucerne, taking the shortest possible route to Selisberg on the Lake of Lucerne, where my wife was staying for a sour-milk cure.

The symptoms of heart disease, which I had already noticed some time previously, had increased, and this place had been recommended to her as specially invigorating and beneficial. With great patience I endured several weeks of life at a Swiss *pension*, but my wife, who had quite adapted herself to the ways of the house and seemed very comfortable, looked upon me as a disturbing element.

I found this a great trial, although the beautiful air and my daily excursions into the mountains did me a great deal of good. I even went so far as to choose a very wild spot, where, in imagination, I ordered a little house to be built in which I should be able to work in absolute peace.

Towards the end of July we went back to Zürich. I returned to my *Walküre* and finished the first act in the month of August. I was terribly depressed by my worries just at this time, and as it was more than ever necessary for me to have absolute quiet for my work, I at once agreed to my wife's departure, when she told me of her intended visit to her relations and friends in Dresden and Zwickau. She left me at the beginning of September, and wrote to me about her stay in Weimar, where the Princess Wittgenstein had received her with the greatest hospitality at Altenburg Castle. There she met Röckel's wife, who was being cared for in the most self-sacrificing way by her husband's brother. It showed a spirited and original trait in Minna's character that she decided to visit Röckel in his prison at Waldheim, solely that she might give his wife news of him, although she disliked the man intensely.

She told me of this visit, saying sarcastically that Röckel looked quite happy and bright, and that life in prison did not seem to suit him badly.

Meanwhile I plunged with renewed zeal into my work, and had finished a fair copy of the *Rheingold* score by the 26th of September. In the peaceful quietness of my house at this time I first came across a book which was destined to be of great importance to me. This was Arthur Schopenhauer's *Die Welt als Wille und Vorstellung*.

Herwegh recommended this work to me, and told me that strangely enough it had only been recently discovered, although it had been published over thirty years. In a pamphlet on this subject a certain Herr Frauenstädt had drawn the attention of the public to the book, to which I immediately felt attracted, and I at once began to study it. For a long time I had wanted to understand the real value of philosophy. My conversations with Lehrs in Paris in my very young days had awakened my longing for this branch of knowledge, upon which I had first launched when I attended the lectures of several Leipzig professors and in later years by reading Schelling and Hegel. I seemed to understand the reason of their failure to satisfy me from the writings of Feuerbach, which I studied at the same time. What fascinated me so enormously about Schopenhauer's work was not only its extraordinary fate, but the clearness and manly precision with which the most difficult metaphysical problems were treated from the very beginning.

I had been greatly drawn towards the work on learning the opinion of an English critic, who candidly confessed that he respected German philosophy because of its complete incomprehensibility, as instanced by Hegel's doctrines, until the study of Schopenhauer had made it clear to him that Hegel's lack of lucidity was due not so much to his own incapacity as to the intentionally bombastic style in which this philosopher had clothed his problems. Like every man who is passionately thrilled with life, I too sought first for the conclusions of Schopenhauer's system. With its æsthetic side I was perfectly content, and was especially astonished at his noble conception of music. But, on the other hand, the final summing-up regarding morals alarmed me, as, indeed, it would have startled any one in my mood; for here the annihilation of the will and complete abnegation are represented as the sole true and final deliverance from those bonds of individual limitation in estimating and facing the world, which are now clearly felt for the first time. For those who hoped to find some philosophical justification for political and social agitation on behalf of so-called ' individual freedom ' there was certainly no support to be found here, where all that was demanded was absolute renunciation of all such methods of satisfying the claims of personality. At first

I naturally found his ideas by no means palatable, and felt I could not readily abandon that so-called 'cheerful' Greek aspect of the world, with which I had looked out upon life in my *Kunstwerk der Zukunft.* As a matter of fact, it was Herwegh who at last, by a well-timed explanation, brought me to a calmer frame of mind about my own sensitive feelings. It is from this perception of the nullity of the visible world — so he said — that all tragedy is derived, and such a perception must necessarily have dwelt as an intuition in every great poet, and even in every great man. On looking afresh into my *Nibelungen* poem I recognised with surprise that the very things that now so embarrassed me theoretically had long been familiar to me in my own poetical conception. Now at last I could understand my *Wotan,* and I returned with chastened mind to the renewed study of Schopenhauer's book. I had learned to recognise that my first essential task was to understand the first part, namely, the exposition and enlarging of Kant's doctrine of the ideality of that world which has hitherto seemed to us so solidly founded in time and space, and I believed I had taken the first step towards such an understanding by recognising its enormous difficulty. For many years afterwards that book never left me, and by the summer of the following year I had already studied the whole of it for the fourth time. The effect thus gradually wrought upon me was extraordinary, and certainly exerted a decisive influence on the whole course of my life. In forming my judgment upon all those matters which I had hitherto acquired solely through the senses, I had gained pretty much the same power as I had formerly won in music — after abandoning the teaching of my old master Weinlich — by an exhaustive study of counterpoint. If, therefore, in later years I again expressed opinions in my casual writings on matters pertaining to that art which so particularly interested me, it is certain that traces of what I learned from my study of Schopenhauer's philosophy were clearly perceptible.

Just then I was prompted to send the venerated philosopher a copy of my *Nibelungen* poem. To its title I merely added by hand the words, 'With Reverence,' but without writing a single word to Schopenhauer himself.

This I did partly from a feeling of great shyness in addressing him, and partly because I felt that if the perusal of my poem did not enlighten Schopenhauer about the man with whom he was dealing, a letter from me, no matter how explicit, would not help him much. I also renounced by this means the vain wish to be honoured by an autograph letter from his hand. I learned later, however, from Karl Ritter, and also from Dr. Wille, both of whom visited Schopenhauer in Frankfort, that he spoke impressively and favourably of my poetry. In addition to these studies, I continued writing the music to the *Walküre*. I was living in great retirement at this time, my sole relaxation being to take long walks in the neighbourhood, and, as usual with me when hard at work at my music, I felt the longing to express myself in poetry. This must have been partly due to the serious mood created by Schopenhauer, which was trying to find ecstatic expression. It was some such mood that inspired the conception of a *Tristan und Isolde*.

Karl Ritter had just laid before me a sketch for the dramatic treatment of this subject (with which I was thoroughly acquainted through my Dresden studies), and had thereby drawn my attention to the material for this poem. I had already expressed my views to my young friend about the faultiness of his sketch. He had, in fact, made a point of giving prominence to the lighter phases of the romance, whereas it was its all-pervading tragedy that impressed me so deeply that I felt convinced it should stand out in bold relief, regardless of minor details. On my return from one of my walks I jotted down the incidents of the three acts in a concise form, with the intention of working them out more elaborately later on. In the last act I introduced an episode, which, however, I did not develop eventually, namely, the visit to Tristan's deathbed by Parsifal during his search for the Holy Grail. The picture of Tristan languishing, yet unable to die of his wound, identified itself in my mind with Amfortas in the Romance of the Grail.

For the moment I forced myself to leave this poem on one side, and to allow nothing to interrupt my great musical work. Meanwhile, through the help of friends, I succeeded in bringing about a satisfactory change in my financial position. My prospects with regard to the German theatres also seemed brighter. Minna had been in Berlin, and through the influence

of our old friend, Alwine Frommann, had had an interview
with Herr von Hülsen, the manager of the court theatre. After
losing two years in fruitless efforts, I at last felt more certain
of seeing *Tannhäuser* produced there without further obstacle,
as it had become so popular with all the theatres that its failure
in Berlin could not injure its reputation; it could only reflect
disadvantageously on the Berlin management.

In the beginning of November Minna returned from her
journey, and acting on the news she gave me about the production of *Tannhäuser* in Berlin, I allowed matters to take
their course, a decision which afterwards caused me great annoyance, as the rendering of my work was simply wretched. I got
some compensation, however, in the royalties, which were an
important and continuous source of income to me.

The Zürich Musical Society now again enlisted my interest
for their winter concerts. I promised to conduct, but only on
condition that they would give serious consideration to improving the orchestra. I had already twice proposed the forma-
tion of a decent orchestra, and I now sent in a third plan to the
committee, in which I described in detail how they might
achieve this object at a comparatively slight outlay by co-
operation with the theatre. I told them that this winter would
be the last time that I should interest myself in their concerts
unless they entertained this very reasonable proposition. Apart
from this work, I took in hand a quartette society, made up of
the soloists of the orchestra, who were anxious to study the right
interpretation of the various quartettes I had recommended.

It was a great pleasure to me to see how soon the public
patronised the efforts of these artists, who, by the way, thus
added a little extra to their incomes for a considerable time.
As far as their artistic achievements went, the work was rather
slow; the mere fact of their being able to play their respective
instruments well did not make them at once understand the
art of playing together, for which so much more is needed than
mere dynamic proportions and accents, attainable only by the
individual development of a higher artistic taste in the treatment of the instrument by its exponent.

I was too ambitious about them, and actually taught them
Beethoven's Quartette in C sharp minor, which meant endless

trouble and rehearsing. I wrote some analytical annotations for the better appreciation of this extraordinary work, and had them printed on the programme. Whether I made any impression on the audience, or whether they liked the performance, I was never able to find out. When I say that I completed the sketch of the whole of the music to the *Walküre* by the 30th of December of that year, it will suffice to prove my strenuous and active life at that time, as well as to show that I did not allow any outside distraction to disturb my rigorous plan of work.

In January, 1855, I began the instrumentation of the *Walküre*, but I was compelled to interrupt it, owing to a promise I made to some of my friends to give them a chance of hearing the overture to *Faust,* which I had written in Paris fifteen years before. I had another look at this composition, which had been the means of so important a change in my musical ideas. Liszt had produced the work in Weimar a little while before, and had written to me in very favourable terms about it, at the same time expressing his wish that I should rewrite more elaborately some parts that were only faintly indicated. So I immediately set to work to rewrite the overture, conscientiously adopting my dear friend's delicate suggestions, and I finished it as it was afterwards published by Härtel. I taught our orchestra this overture, and did not think the performance at all bad. My wife, however, did not like it; she said it seemed to her ' as if nothing good could be made out of it,' and she begged me not to have it produced in London when I went there that year. At this time I had an extraordinary application, such as I have never received again. In January the London Philharmonic Society wrote asking me if I would be willing to conduct their concerts for the season. I did not answer immediately, as I wanted to obtain some particulars first, and was very much surprised one day to receive a visit from a certain Mr. Anderson, a member of the committee of the celebrated society, who had come to Zürich on purpose to ensure my acceptance.

I was expected to go to London for four months to give eight concerts for the Philharmonic Society, for which I was to receive in all £200. I did not quite know what to do, as, from a business point of view, it was of no advantage to me, and, as far as the conducting went, it was not much in my line, unless I could rely on at least a few high-class artistic productions.

One thing only struck me as favourable, and that was the prospect of again handling a large and excellent orchestra, after having been denied one for so long, while the fact that I had attracted the attention of that remote world of music fascinated me exceedingly. I felt as if fate were calling me, and at last I accepted the invitation of this simple and amiable-looking Englishman, Mr. Anderson, who, fully satisfied with the result of his mission, immediately left for England wrapped in a big fur coat, whose real owner I only got to know later on. Before following him to England, I had to free myself from a calamity which I had brought upon myself through being too kind-hearted. The managing director of the Zürich theatre for that year, an obtrusive and over-zealous person, had at last made me accede to his wish to produce *Tannhäuser,* on the plea that as this work was now performed at every opera house, it would be a very bad thing for the Zürich theatre if it were the only one to be deprived of the privilege, merely because I happened to live in the town. Besides this, my wife interfered in the matter, and the singers who played Tannhäuser and Wolfram at once put themselves under her wing. She really succeeded, too, in working on my humani-tarian feelings with regard to one of her protégés, a poor tenor who had been badly bullied by the conductor till then. I took these people through their parts a few times, and in conse-quence found myself obliged to attend the stage rehearsals to superintend their performances. What it all came to in the end was that I was driven to interfere again and again, until I found myself at the conductor's desk, and eventually conducted the first performance myself. I have a particularly vivid recollection of the singer who played Elizabeth on that occasion. She had originally taken soubrette parts, and went through her rôle in white kid gloves, dangling a fan. This time I had really had enough of such concessions, and when at the close the audience called me before the curtain, I stood there and told my friends with great frankness that this was the last time they would get me to do anything of the sort.

I advised them in future to look to the state of their theatre, as they had just had a most convincing proof of its faulty construction — at which they were all much astonished. I made a similar announcement to the ' Musikgesellschaft,' where I also conducted once more — really for the last time — before my departure. Unfortunately, they put down my protests to my sense of humour, and were not in the least spurred to exert themselves, with the result that I had to be very stern and almost rude the following winter, to deter them, once and for all, from making further demands upon me. I thus left my former patrons in Zürich somewhat nonplussed when I started for London on 26th February.

I travelled through Paris and spent some days there, during which time I saw only Kietz and his friend Lindemann, whom he regarded as a quack doctor. Arriving in London on 2nd March I first went to see Ferdinand Präger. In his youth he had been a friend of the Röckel brothers, who had given me a very favourable account of him. He proved to be an unusually good-natured fellow, though of an excitability insufficiently balanced by his standard of culture. After spending the first night at his home, I installed myself the following day with his help in a house in Portland Terrace, in the neighbourhood of Regent's Park, of which I had agreeable recollections from former visits. I promised myself a pleasant stay there in the coming spring, if only on account of its close proximity to that part of the park where beautiful copper beeches overshadowed the path. But though I spent four months in London, it seemed to me that spring never came, the foggy climate so overclouded all the impressions I received. Präger was only too eager to escort me when I went to pay the customary visits, including one to Costa. I was thus introduced to the director of the Italian Opera, who was at the same time the real leader of music in London; for he was also director of the Sacred-Music Society, which gave almost regular weekly performances of Händel and Mendelssohn.

Präger also took me to see his friend Sainton, the leader of the London orchestra. After giving me a very hearty reception he told me the remarkable history of my invitation to London. Sainton, a southern Frenchman from Toulouse, of naïve and fiery temperament, was living with a full-blooded German musician from Hamburg, named Lüders, the son of a bandsman, of a brusque but friendly disposition. I was much affected when I heard, later on, of the incident which had made these two men inseparable friends. Sainton had been making a concert tour by way of St. Petersburg, and found himself stranded at Helsingfors in Finland, unable to get any further, pursued as he was by the demon of ill-luck. At this moment the curious figure of the modest Hamburg bandsman's son had accosted him on the staircase of the hotel, asking whether he would be inclined to accept his offer of friendship and take half of his available cash, as he (Lüders) had of course noticed the awkwardness of the other's position. From that moment the two became inseparable friends, made concert tours in Sweden and Denmark, found their way back in the strangest fashion to Havre, Paris, and Toulouse, by way of Hamburg, and finally settled down in London — Sainton to take an important post in the orchestra, while Lüders got along as best he could by the drudgery of giving lessons. Now I found them living together in a pretty house like a married couple, each tenderly concerned for his friend's welfare. Lüders had read my essays on art, and my *Oper und Drama* in particular moved him to exclaim, '*Donnerwetter*, there's something in that!' Sainton pricked up his ears at this, and when the conductor of the Philharmonic concerts (the great Mr. Costa himself), for some unknown reason, quarrelled with the society before the season began and refused to conduct their concerts any longer, Sainton, to whom Mr. Anderson, the treasurer, had gone for advice in this awkward predicament, recommended them, at Lüders' instigation, to engage me. I now heard that they had not acted upon this suggestion at once. Only when Sainton happened to remark casually that he had seen me conduct in Dresden did Mr. Anderson decide to make the journey to Zürich to see me (in the fur coat lent by Sainton for the purpose), as a result of which visit I was now here. I soon discovered, too, that Sainton had in this case acted with the rashness characteristic of his nation. It had never occurred to Costa that he would be taken seriously in his statement to the Philharmonic Society, and he was thoroughly disgusted at my appointment. As he was at the head of the same orchestra which was at my disposal for the Philharmonic concerts, he was able to foster an attitude of hostility to the undertakings for which I was responsible, and even my friend Sainton had to suffer from his animosity without actually realising the source of the annoyance.

As time went on I saw this more plainly, while there was abundant material for unpleasantness of every description in other quarters. In the first place Mr. Davison, the musical critic of the *Times,* adopted a most hostile attitude, and it was from this that I first realised, clearly and definitely, the effect of my essay entitled 'Judaism in Music.' Präger had further informed me that Davison's extremely powerful position on the *Times* had accustomed him to expect every one who came to England on business connected with music to propitiate him by all sorts of delicate attentions. Jenny Lind was one whose submission to these pretensions did much to ensure her popular success; whereas Sontag considered that her rank as Countess Rossi elevated her above such considerations. As I had been completely absorbed in the delight of handling a good, full orchestra, with which I hoped to give some fine performances, it was a great blow to learn that I had no control whatever over the number of rehearsals I thought necessary for the concerts. For each concert, which included two symphonies and several minor pieces as well, the society's economical arrangements allowed me only one rehearsal. Still I went on hoping that the impression produced by the performances I conducted might even here justify the demand for a special effort. It proved absolutely impossible, however, to depart in any way from the beaten track, and, realising this, I at once felt that the fulfilment of the task I had undertaken was a terrible burden. At the first concert we played Beethoven's *Eroica,* and my success as a conductor seemed so marked that the committee of the society were evidently prepared to make a special effort for the second. They demanded selections from my own compositions as well as Beethoven's Ninth Symphony, and conceded me two rehearsals as an exceptional favour. This concert went off quite passably. I had drawn up an explanatory programme for my *Lohengrin* Overture, but the words 'Holy Grail' and 'God' were struck out with great solemnity, as that sort of thing was not allowed at secular concerts. I had to content myself with the chorus from the Italian Opera for the symphony, besides putting up with a baritone whose English phlegm and Italian training drove me to despair at the rehearsal. All I understood of the English version of the text was, 'Hail thee joy' for *Freude. schöner Götterfunken.* The Philharmonic Society appeared to have staked everything on the success of this concert, which, in fact, left nothing to be desired. They were accordingly horrified when the *Times* reporter fell on this performance, too, with furious contempt and disparagement. They appealed to Präger to persuade me to offer Mr. Davison some attentions, or at least to agree to meet that gentleman and be properly introduced to him at a banquet to be arranged by Mr. Anderson. But Präger now knew me well enough to dash their hopes of obtaining any concession of that sort from me. The banquet fell through, and, as I saw later, the society began from that time forward to regret my appointment, realising that they had an entirely intractable and pig-headed person to deal with.

As the Easter holidays began after the second concert, thereby involving a long pause, I asked my friend's advice as to whether it would not be more sensible to give up the whole thing — this conductorship of the Philharmonic concerts which I had so soon discovered to be a foolish and fruitless undertaking — and go quietly back to Zürich. Präger assured me that the execution of this resolve would in no wise be regarded as a reflection on the situation, but simply as a deplorable piece of rudeness on my part, and that the principal sufferers would be my friends. This decided me, and I stayed — without, it is true, any hope of giving a fresh impetus to musical life in London. The only stimulating incident occurred on the occasion of the seventh concert, which was the evening chosen by the Queen for her annual visit to these functions. She expressed a wish through her husband, Prince Albert, to hear the *Tannhäuser* Overture. The presence of the court certainly lent a pleasing air of ceremony to the evening, and I had, too, the pleasure of a fairly animated conversation with Queen Victoria and her Consort in response to their command. The question arose of putting my operas on the stage, and Prince Albert objected that Italian singers would never be able to interpret my music. I was amused when the Queen met this objection by saying that, after all, a great many Italian singers were really Germans. All this made a good impression and, it was obvious, served as a demonstration in my favour, without, however, influencing the real situation to any appreciable extent. The leading papers still announced, as before, that every concert I conducted was a fiasco. Ferdinand Hiller actually thought himself justified in proclaiming, for the consolation of his friends, that my day in London was coming to an end, and that my banishment was practically a certainty. This was on the occasion of the Rhenish Musical Festival, which was held at that time. As a set-off against this I reaped great satisfaction from a scene which took place at the close of the eighth and last concert which I conducted — one of those strange scenes which now and again result from the long-suppressed emotion of those concerned. The members of the orchestra had at once realised, after my successes, the advisability of avoiding any expression of sympathy with me if they wished to keep in good odour with their real though unacknowledged chief, Mr. Costa, and save themselves from a possible speedy dismissal at his hands. This was the explanation given me when the signs of appreciation, which I had become accustomed to receive from the players in the course of our work together, suddenly ceased. Now, however, at the end of the series their suppressed feelings burst forth, and they crowded round me on all sides with deafening cheers, while the audience, who usually left the hall noisily before the end, likewise formed up in enthusiastic groups and surrounded me, cheering warmly and pressing my hand. Thus both players and listeners combined to make my farewell a scene of cordiality which could hardly be surpassed.

But it was the personal relations which grew out of my stay in London that provided the strangest aspect of my life there.

Immediately after my arrival, Karl Klindworth, a young pupil of Liszt, who had been recommended to me as particularly gifted, came to see me. He became a faithful and intimate friend, not only during my stay in London, but ever after. Young as he was, the short time he had spent in London had sufficed to give him an opinion of English musical life, the justice of which I was soon compelled to admit, terrible though it was. Incapable of adapting himself to the curiously organised English musical cliques, he at once lost all reasonable prospect or hope of meeting with the recognition due to his talent. He resigned himself to making his way through the dreary wastes of English musical life solely by giving lessons like a day-labourer, being too proud to pay the smallest attentions to the ruling critics, who had fallen on him immediately as a pupil of Liszt. He was really an excellent musician, and in addition a distinguished pianist. He immediately approached me with the request to be allowed to make a pianoforte arrangement of the score of *Rheingold*, for the use only of virtuosi of the first rank. Unfortunately, he was overtaken by a tedious illness, which robbed me for a long time of the desired intercourse with him.

Although Präger and his wife stood by me with great constancy, my real centre of intimacy was the original Sainton-Lüders' household. I had a standing invitation to dine with them, and I found occasion, with few exceptions, to take my meals with these friends, whose devotion surpassed that of all the others. It was here that I generally found relaxation from the unpleasantness of my business relations in London. Präger was often present, and we frequently took an evening stroll through the foggy streets. On such occasions Lüders would fortify us against the inclemency of the London climate by an excellent punch which he could prepare under any conditions. Only once did we get separated, and that was in the terrific crowd that accompanied the Emperor Napoleon from St. James's Palace to Covent Garden Theatre one evening. He had come over to London with his Consort, on a visit to Queen Victoria, during the critical stage of the Crimean War, and the Londoners gaped at him as he passed no less greedily than other nations are apt to do under similar circumstances. It so befell that I was taken for a pushing sightseer, and proportionately punished by blows in the ribs when I was crossing the road to try and get into Regent Street from the Haymarket.

This caused me much amusement, on account of the obvious misunderstanding.

The grave annoyances which arose, partly from the peculiarly momentous quarrel between Sainton and Mr. Anderson (instigated by Costa), and which deprived me of every possibility of obtaining any influence over the society, were productive, on the other hand, of some amusing experiences. Anderson had, it seemed, succeeded in elevating himself to the post of conductor of the Queen's band, through the influence of the Queen's private coachman. As he possessed absolutely no knowledge of music, the annual court concert which he had to conduct became a very feast of absurdity to the unruly Sainton, and I heard some very funny stories about it. Another thing brought to light in the course of these imbroglios was that Mrs. Anderson, whom I had christened Charlemagne on account of her great corpulency, had appropriated to herself, among other things, the office and salary of a court trumpeter. I soon arrived at the conviction, from these and other similar reports, that my lively friend would be beaten by this snug little clique in the war of disclosures, and was able subsequently to see the decision go against him at the point when either he or Anderson had to give way. This confirmed my idea that in this free country of England things were managed in much the same way as elsewhere.

The arrival of Berlioz made a very important addition to our little company. He, too, had been brought over to London, to conduct two of the New Philharmonic Society's concerts. The society had appointed as ordinary conductor, by whose recommendation I could never discover, a certain Dr. Wilde, a typical chubby-faced Englishman, remarkably good-natured, but ludicrously incompetent. He had taken some special lessons in conducting from the Stuttgart conductor, Lindpaintner, who had trained him up to the point of at least attempting to catch up the orchestra with his beat, the orchestra itself going its own way entirely. I heard a Beethoven symphony performed in this fashion, and was surprised to hear the audience break into precisely the same applause with which it greeted one of my own strictly accurate and really fiery performances. To lend distinction to these concerts, however, they had, as I said, invited Berlioz over for some of them. I thus heard him conduct some classical works, such as a Mozart symphony, and was amazed to find a conductor, who was so energetic in the interpretation of his own compositions, sink into the commonest rut of the vulgar time-beater. Certain of his own compositions, such as the more effective fragments from the *Romeo and Juliet* Symphony, again made a particular impression on me, it is true; but I was now more consciously awake to the curious weaknesses which disfigure even the finest conceptions of this extraordinary musician than on those earlier occasions, when I only had a sense of general discomfort adequate to the magnitude of the impression.

I felt much stimulated, however, on the two or three occasions when Sainton invited me to dine with Berlioz. I was now brought face to face with this strangely gifted person, tormented and even blunted in some respects as he then was. When I saw him, a man considerably my senior, coming here merely in the hope of earning a few guineas, I could deem myself perfectly happy, and almost floating on air, by contrast; for my own coming had been brought about rather by a desire for distraction, a craving for outward inspiration. His whole being expressed weariness and despair, and I was suddenly seized with deep sympathy for this man whose talent so far surpassed that of his rivals — for this was clear as daylight to me. Berlioz seemed to be pleasantly affected by the attitude of gay spontaneity I adopted with him. His usual short, almost reserved, manner thawed visibly during the friendly hours we passed together. He told me many comical things about Meyerbeer, and the impossibility of escaping from his flattery, which was dictated by his insatiable thirst for laudatory articles. The first performance of his *Prophet* had been preceded by the customary *dîner de la veille,* and when Berlioz excused himself for staying away, Meyerbeer first reproached him tenderly, then challenged him to make good the great injustice he had done him, by writing ' a real nice article ' about his opera. Berlioz declared it was impossible to get anything detrimental to Meyerbeer inserted in a Paris paper.

I found it less easy to discuss with him matters of a more profound artistic nature, as I invariably came up against the real

Frenchman then, who, fluent and glib of tongue, was so sure of himself that it never occurred to him to doubt whether he had understood his companions aright. Once, in a pleasant glow of inspiration (having suddenly mastered the French language, to my own great surprise), I tried to express to him my idea of the 'artistic conception.' I endeavoured to describe the powerful effect of vital impressions on the temperament, how they hold us captive, as it were, until we rid ourselves of them by the unique development of our inmost spiritual visions, which are not called forth by these impressions, but only roused by them from their deep slumber. The artistic structure, therefore, appears to us as in no wise a result of, but, on the contrary, a liberation from, the vital impressions. At this point Berlioz smiled in a patronising, comprehensive way, and said: '*Nous appelons cela: digérer.*' My amazement at this prompt summing-up of my laboured communications was further justified by my new friend's outward behaviour. I invited him to be present at my last concert, and also at a small farewell feast which I was giving at home to my few friends after it. He soon left the table, saying that he felt unwell, but the friends who were left made no secret to me of their belief that Berlioz had been put out of humour by the exceedingly enthusiastic farewell with which the audience had parted from me.

The total harvest, however, of acquaintances I made in London was not particularly profitable. I took pleasure in the society of Mr. Ellerton, a dignified, agreeable man, the brother-in-law of Lord Brougham — a poet, a music-lover, and, alas! a composer. He asked to be introduced to me at one of the Philharmonic concerts, and did not hesitate to tell me that he welcomed me to London because it seemed likely that I was destined to check the exaggerated Mendelssohn worship. He was also the only Englishman who honoured me by any hospitality, and by entertaining myself and my friends at the University Club, gave me an opportunity of realising the munificence of such an establishment in London. After we had spent a very agreeable time there, I had a glimpse of the weaker side of English hospitalities of this order, though the incident was friendly enough. My host had to be taken home by two men, one holding each arm, quite as a matter of course, as it was obvious that he would not have got far across the road without this help.

I made the acquaintance, too, of a curious man, an old-fashioned but very friendly composer named Potter. I had to play a symphony of his, which entertained me by its modest dimensions and its neat development of counterpoint, the more so as the composer, a friendly elderly recluse, clung to me with almost distressing humility. I had positively to force him into accepting the right *tempo* for the *Andante* in his symphony, thus proving to him that it was really pretty and interesting. He had so little faith in his work, that he considered the only way to avoid the danger of boring people with it was to rattle through it at a disgraceful speed. He really beamed with delight and gratitude when I secured him great applause by taking this very *Andante* at my own time.

I got on less well with a Mr. MacFarrinc, a pompous, melancholy Scotsman, whose compositions, I was assured, were held in high esteem by the committee of the Philharmonic Society. He seemed too proud to discuss the interpretation of any of his works with me, and I was therefore relieved when a symphony of his, which did not appeal to me, was laid aside, the substitute chosen being an overture entitled the *Steeplechase,* which I enjoyed playing, on account of its peculiarly wild, passionate character.

My acquaintance with Beneke (a merchant) and his family was attended by much awkwardness. Wesendonck had given me a letter of recommendation to them, so that I should at least have one 'house' to go to in London. I had to travel a full German mile to Camberwell in response to their invitations, only to discover that I had dropped into the very family whose house Mendelssohn had made his home when in London. The good people did not know what to do with me, apart from congratulating me on the excellence of my Mendelssohn performances, and rewarding me with descriptions of the generous character of the deceased.

Howard, the secretary of the Philharmonic Society, a worthy and agreeable old man, was another person (the only one, he believed) in the circle of my English acquaintances who took the trouble to entertain me. I had to go once or twice to the Italian Opera at Covent Garden with his daughter. There I heard *Fidelio,* given in rather grotesque fashion by unclean Germans and voiceless Italians, and with recitatives. I consequently managed to evade paying frequent visits to this theatre. When I went to say good-bye to Mr. Howard on leaving London, I was surprised to meet Meyerbeer at his house. He had just arrived in London to conduct his *Nordstern.* As I saw him come in it occurred to me immediately that Howard, whom I had only known as the secretary of the Philharmonic Society, was also the musical critic of the *Illustrated London News;* it was in the latter capacity that the great operatic composer had called upon him. Meyerbeer was absolutely paralysed when he saw me, and this put me into such a frame of mind that we found it impossible to exchange a word. Mr. Howard, who had felt sure that we were acquainted, was much surprised at this, and asked me as I was leaving whether I did not know Meyerbeer. I answered that he had better ask Meyerbeer. On meeting Howard again that evening, I was assured that Meyerbeer had spoken of me in terms of the highest praise. I then suggested his reading certain numbers of the Paris *Gazette musicale,* in which Fétis had, some time before, given a less favourable interpretation of Meyerbeer's views about me. Howard shook his head, and could not understand how two such *great composers* could meet in so strange a manner.

A visit from my old friend Hermann Franck was a pleasant surprise. He was then staying at Brighton, and had come up to London for a few days. We conversed a great deal, and I had to make a considerable effort to put him right in his ideas about me, as he had heard the most wonderful reports from German musicians during the last few years in which our intercourse had been broken off. He was astonished, in the first place, to find me in London, where he considered it impossible for me ever to find a suitable field for my musical tendencies. I did not understand what he meant by my 'tendencies,' but I told him quite simply how I came to accept the invitation of the Philharmonic Society, and that I proposed to fulfil my contract for this year's concerts, and then to go back to my work at Zürich without further ceremony. This sounded quite

different to the state of things he had imagined, for he had felt
bound to conclude that I proposed to create a stronghold in
London from which to conduct a war of extermination against
the whole race of German musicians. This was the unanimous
explanation of my intentions which he had heard in Germany.
Nothing could be more astounding, he said, than the surprising
incongruity between the fictitious form in which I appeared to
these people, and my real nature, which he had recognised at
once on seeing me again. We joked about this, and came to a
closer understanding. I was glad to see that he valued as
much as I did the works of Schopenhauer, which had become
known in the last few years. He expressed his opinion of
them with singular decision; he considered that German intellect was destined, either to complete deterioration, in conjunction
with the national political situation, or else to an equally complete regeneration, in which Schopenhauer would play his
part. He left me — soon to meet his terrible and not less
inexplicable fate. Only a few months later, after my return
home, I heard of his mysterious death. He was staying, as I
said, at Brighton, for the purpose of putting his son, a boy of
about sixteen, into the English navy. I had noticed that the
son's obstinate determination to serve in this force was repugnant to his father. On the morning of the day on which the
ship was to sail, the father's body was found shattered in the
street, as the result of a fall from the window, while the son
was found lifeless — apparently strangled — on his bed. The
mother had died some years previously, and there was no one
left to give information as to the terrible occurrence, which,
so far as I know, has never to this day been cleared up. Franck
had, out of forgetfulness, left a map of London behind on his
visit to me; this I kept, as I did not know his address, and it
is still in my possession.

I have pleasanter, though not entirely unclouded, recollections of my relations with Semper, whom I also met in London,
where he had been settled for some time with his family. He
had always seemed to me so violent and morose when in
Dresden that I was surprised and moved to admiration by the
comparatively calm and resigned spirit with which he bore
the terrible interruption to his professional career, and by his

readiness to adapt his talent (which was of an unusually productive order) to the circumstances in which he was placed. Commissions for large buildings were out of the question for him in England, but he set his hopes, to a certain extent, on the patronage accorded him by Prince Albert, as this gave him some prospects for the future. For the time being he contented himself with commissions to design decorations for interiors and luxurious furniture, for which he was well paid. He took to this work as seriously, from an artistic point of view, as if it had been a large building. We often met, and I also spent a few evenings at his house in Kensington, when we invariably dropped into the old vein of strange, serious humour that helped us to forget the seamy side of life. The report I was able to give of Semper after my return home did much to influence Sulzer in his successful attempt to get him over to Zürich to build the new Polytechnic.

On various occasions I also visited some not uninteresting theatres in London, strictly avoiding opera-houses, of course. I was most attracted by the little Adelphi Theatre in the Strand, and I frequently made Präger and Lüders go with me. They acted some dramatised fairy-tales there under the title of *Christmas*. One of the performances interested me particularly, because it consisted of a subtly connected conglomeration of the most familiar tales, played straight through, with no break at the end of the acts. It began with ' The Goose that laid the Golden Eggs,' and was transformed into ' The Three Wishes '; this passed into ' Red Riding Hood ' (with the wolf changed into a cannibal who sang a very comical little couplet), and finished as ' Cinderella,' varied with other ingredients. These pieces were in every respect excellently mounted and played, and I gained a very good notion there of the imaginative fare in which the English people can find amusement. I found the performances at the Olympic Theatre less simple and innocent. Besides witty drawing-room pieces in the French style, which were very well played there, they acted fairy-tales such as the *Yellow Dwarf,* in which Robson, an uncommonly popular actor, took the grotesque title-rôle. I saw the same actor again in a little comedy called *Garrick Fever,* in which he ends by representing a drunken man who, when people insisted on taking him for Garrick, undertook the part of Hamlet in this condition. I was greatly astonished by many audacities in his acting on this occasion.

A small out-of-the-way theatre in Marylebone was just then trying to attract the public by Shakespeare's plays. I attended a performance of the *Merry Wives* there, which really amazed me by its correctness and precision. Even a performance of *Romeo and Juliet* at the Haymarket Theatre impressed me favourably, in spite of the great inferiority of the company, on account of its accuracy and of the scenic arrangements, which were no doubt an inheritance from the Garrick tradition. But I still remember a curious illusion in connection with this: after the first act I told Lüders, who was with me, how surprised I was at their giving the part of Romeo to an old man, whose age must at least be sixty, and who seemed anxious to retrieve his long-lost youth by laboriously adopting a sickly-sweet, feminine air. Lüders looked at the programme again, and cried, '*Donnerwetter,* it's a woman!' It was the once famous American, Miss Cushman.

In spite of every effort, I found it impossible to obtain a seat for *Henry VIII.* at the Princess's Theatre. This play had been organised according to the new stage realism, and enjoyed an incredible vogue as a gorgeous spectacular piece, mounted with unusual care.

In the province of music, with which I was more concerned, I have still to mention several of the Sacred-Music Society's concerts, which I attended in the large room at Exeter Hall. The oratorios given there nearly every week have, it must be admitted, the advantage of the great confidence which arises from frequent repetition. Neither could I refuse to recognise the great precision of the chorus of seven hundred voices, which reached quite a respectable standard on a few occasions, particularly in Händel's *Messiah*. It was here that I came to understand the true spirit of English musical culture, which is bound up with the spirit of English Protestantism. This accounts for the fact that an oratorio attracts the public far more than an opera. A further advantage is secured by the feeling among the audience that an evening spent in listening to an oratorio may be regarded as a sort of service, and is almost

as good as going to church. Every one in the audience holds
a Händel piano score in the same way as one holds a prayer-
book in church. These scores are sold at the box-office in shilling
editions, and are followed most diligently — out of anxiety, it
seemed to me, not to miss certain points solemnly enjoyed by
the whole audience. For instance, at the beginning of the
' Hallelujah Chorus ' it is considered proper for every one to
rise from his seat. This movement, which probably originated
in an expression of enthusiasm, is now carried out at each performance of the *Messiah* with painful precision.

All these recollections, however, are merged in the all-
absorbing memory of almost uninterrupted ill-health, caused
primarily, no doubt, by the state of the London climate at
that season of the year, which is notorious all over the world.
I had a perpetual cold, and I therefore followed the advice of
my friends to take a heavy English diet by way of resisting the
effect of the air, but this did not improve matters in the least.
For one thing, I could not get my home sufficiently warmed
through, and the work that I had brought with me was the
first thing to suffer. The instrumentation of the *Walküre,* which
I had hoped to finish off here, only advanced a paltry hundred
pages. I was hindered in this principally by the circumstance
that the sketches from which I had to work on the instrumentation had been written down without considering the extent
to which a prolonged interruption of my working humour might
affect the coherence of the sketch. How often did I sit before
those pencilled pages as if they had been unfamiliar hiero-
glyphics which I was incapable of deciphering! In absolute
despair I plunged into Dante, making for the first time a serious
effort to read him. The *Inferno,* indeed, became a never-to-be-
forgotten reality in that London atmosphere.

But at last came the hour of deliverance from even those
evils which I had brought upon myself by my last assumption
that I might be accepted, not to say wanted, in the great world.
The sole consolation I had was in the deep emotion of my new
friends when I took leave of them. I hurried home by way of
Paris, which was clothed in its summer glory, and saw people
really promenading again, instead of pushing through the streets
on business. And so I returned to Zürich, full of cheerful im-

pressions, on the 30th of June, my net profits being exactly one thousand francs.

My wife had an idea of taking up her sour-milk cure again on the Selisberg by Lake Lucerne, and as I thought mountain air would be good for my impaired health also, we decided to move there at once. Our project suffered a brief delay through the fatal illness of my dog Peps. As the result of old age in his thirteenth year, he suddenly exhibited such weakness that we became apprehensive of taking him up the Selisberg, for he could not have borne the fatigue of the ascent. In a few days his agony became alarmingly acute. He grew stupid, and had frequent convulsions, his only conscious act being to get up often from his bed (which was in my wife's room, as he was usually under her care) and stumble as far as my writing-table, where he sank down again in exhaustion. The veterinary surgeon said he could do no more, and as the convulsions gradually became terribly acute, I was advised to shorten the poor animal's cruel agony and free him from his pain by a little prussic acid. We delayed our departure on his account until I at last convinced myself that a quick death would be charity to the poor suffering creature, who was quite past all hope. I hired a boat, and took an hour's row across the lake to visit a young doctor of my acquaintance named Obrist, who had, I knew, come into possession of a village apothecary'. stock, which included various poisons. From him I obtained a deadly dose, which I carried home across the lake in my solitary skiff on an exquisite summer evening. I was determined only to resort to this last expedient in case the poor brute were in extremity. He slept that last night as usual in his basket by my bedside, his invariable habit being to wake me with his paws in the morning. I was suddenly roused by his groans, caused by a particularly violent attack of convulsions; he then sank back without a sound; and I was so strangely moved by the significance of the moment that I immediately looked at my watch to impress on my memory the hour at which my extraordinarily devoted little friend died; it was ten minutes past one on the 10th of July. We devoted the next day to his burial, and shed bitter tears over him. Frau Stockar-Escher, our landlady, made over to us a pretty little plot in her garden, and there we buried him, with his basket and cushions. His grave was shown me many years after, but the last time I went to look at the little garden I found that everything had undergone an elegant transformation, and there were no longer any signs of Pep's grave.

At last we really started for the Selisberg, accompanied this time only by the new parrot — a substitute for good old Papo — from the Kreutzberg menagerie, which I had bought for my wife the year before. This one was a very good and intelligent bird also, but I left him entirely to Minna, treating him with invariable kindness, but never making a friend of him. Fortunately for us, our stay in the glorious air of this summer resort, of which we had grown very fond, was favoured by continuous fine weather. I devoted all my leisure, apart from my lonely walks, to making a fair copy of that part of the *Walküre* which was fully scored, and also took up my favourite reading again — the study of Schopenhauer. I had the pleasure of receiving a charming letter from Berlioz, together with *Les Soirées de l'Orchestre,* his new book, which I found inspiriting to read, although the author's taste for the grotesque was as foreign to me here as in his compositions. Here, too, I met young Robert von Hornstein again, who proved himself a pleasant and intelligent companion. I was particularly interested in his quick and evidently successful plunge into the study of Schopenhauer. He informed me that he proposed to settle for some time in Zürich, where Karl Ritter, too, had decided to take permanent winter quarters for his young wife and himself.

In the middle of August we returned to Zürich ourselves, and I was able to devote myself steadily to completing the instrumentation of the *Walküre,* while my relations with former acquaintances remained much the same. From outside I received news of the steady persistence with which my *Tannhäuser* was, little by little, being propagated in German theatres. *Lohengrin,* too, followed in its steps, though without a first meeting with an entirely favourable reception. Franz Dingelstedt, who was at the time manager of the court theatre at Munich, undertook to introduce *Tannhäuser* there, although, thanks to Lachner, the place was not prepossessed in my favour. He seemed to have managed it fairly well; its success, however, according to him, was not so great as to allow of my promised fee being punctually paid. But my income, owing to the conscientious stewardship of my friend Sulzer, was now sufficient to permit me to work without anxiety on that account. But I met with a new vexation when colder weather set in. I suffered from innumerable attacks of erysipelas during the whole winter, each fresh attack (in consequence of some tiny error of diet, or of the least cold) being attended by violent pain. It was obviously the result of the ill effects of the London climate. What pained me most was the frequent interruption of my work on this account. The most I could do was to read when the illness was taking its course. Burnouff's *Introduction à l'Histoire du Bouddhisme* interested me most among my books, and I found material in it for a dramatic poem, which has stayed in my mind ever since, though only vaguely sketched. I may still perhaps work it out. I gave it the title of *Die Sieger.* It was founded on the simple legend of a Tschantala girl, who is received into the dignified order of beggars known as *Clakyamouni,* and, through her exceedingly passionate and purified love for Ananda, the chief disciple of Buddha, herself gains merit. Besides the underlying beauty of this simple material, a curious relation between it and the subsequent development of my musical experience influenced my selection. For to the mind of Buddha the past life (in a former incarnation) of every being who appears before him stands revealed as plainly as the present; and this simple story has its significance, as showing that the past life of the suffering hero and heroine is bound up with the immediate present in this life. I saw at once that the continuous reminiscence in the music of this double existence might perfectly well be presented to the emotions, and I decided accordingly to keep in prospect the working out of this poem as a particularly congenial task.

I had thus two new subjects stamped on my imagination, *Tristan* and *Die Sieger;* with these I was constantly occupied from this time onwards, together with my great work, the *Nibelungen,* the unfinished portion of which was still of gigantic dimensions. The more these projects absorbed me, the more did I writhe with impatience at the perpetual interruptions of my work by these loathsome attacks of illness. About this time Liszt proposed to pay me a visit that had been postponed in the summer, but I had to ask him not to come, as I could not be certain, after my late experiences, of not being tied to a sick-bed during the few days he would be able to give me. Thus I spent the winter, calm and resigned in my productive moments, but moody and irritable towards the outside world, and consequently a source of some anxiety to my friends. I was glad, however, when Karl Ritter's arrival in Zürich allowed him to become more intimate with me again. By his selecting Zürich as a settled home, for the winter months, at any rate, he showed his devotion to me in a way that did me good, and wiped out more than one bad impression. Hornstein had actually managed to come too, but could not stay. He declared he was so nervous that he could not touch a note of the piano, and made no attempt to deny that the fact of his mother's having died insane made him very much afraid of going mad himself. Although this in a way made him interesting, his intellectual gifts were marred by such weakness of character, that we were soon reduced to thinking him fairly hopeless, and we were not inconsolable when he suddenly left Zürich.

My circle had gained considerably of late by the addition of a new acquaintance, Gottfried Keller, a native of Zürich, who had just returned to the welcoming arms of his affectionate fellow-townsmen from Germany, where his writings had brought him some fame. Several of his works — in particular, a longish novel, *Der Grüne Heinrich* — had been recommended to me in favourable though not exaggerated terms by Sulzer. I was therefore surprised to find him a person of extraordinarily shy and awkward demeanour. Every one felt anxious about his prospects on first becoming acquainted with him, and it was indeed this question of his future that was the difficulty. Although everything he wrote showed great original talent, it was obvious at once that they were merely efforts in the direction of artistic development, and the inevitable inquiry arose as to what was to follow and really establish his fame. I kept continually asking him what he was going to do next. In reply he would mention all sorts of fully matured schemes, which would none of them hold water on closer acquaintance. Luckily a government post was eventually found for him (from patriotic considerations, it seemed), where he no doubt did good service, although his literary activity seemed to lie fallow after his early efforts.

Herwegh, another friend of longer standing, was less fortunate. I had worried myself for a long time about him too, trying to think that his previous efforts were merely introductions to really serious artistic achievements. He admitted himself that he felt his best was still to come. It seemed to him that he had all the material — crowds of 'ideas' — in reserve for a great poetical work; there was nothing wanting but the 'frame' in which he could paint it all, and this is what he hoped, from day to day, to find. As I grew tired of waiting for it, I set about trying to find the longed-for frame for him myself. He evidently wished to evolve an epic poem on a large scale, in which to embody the views he had acquired. As he had once alluded to Dante's luck in finding a subject like the pilgrimage through hell and purgatory into paradise, it occurred to me to suggest, for the desired frame, the Brahman myth of *Metempsychosis*, which in Plato's version comes within reach of our classical education. He did not think it a bad idea, and I accordingly took some trouble to define the form such a poem would take. He was to decide upon three acts, each containing three songs, which would make nine songs in all. The first act would show his hero in the Asiatic country of his birth; the second, his reincarnation in Greece and Rome; the third, his reincarnation in the Middle Ages and in modern times. All this pleased him very much, and he thought it might come to something. Not so my cynical friend, Dr. Wille, who had an estate in the country where we often met in the bosom of his family. He was of opinion that we expected far too much of Herwegh. Viewed at close quarters he was, after all, only a young Swabian who had received a far larger share of honour and glory than his abilities warranted, through the Jewish halo thrown around him by his wife. In the end I had to shrug my shoulders in silent acquiescence with these hopelessly unkind remarks, as I could, of course, see poor

Herwegh sinking into deeper apathy every year, until in the end he seemed incapable of doing anything.

Semper's arrival in Zürich, which had at last taken place, enlivened our circle considerably. The Federal authorities had asked me to use my influence with Semper to induce him to accept a post as teacher at the Federal Polytechnic. Semper came over at once to have a look at the establishment first, and was favourably impressed with everything. He even found cause for delight, when out walking, in the unclipped trees, ' where one might light upon a caterpillar again,' he said, and decided definitely to migrate to Zürich, and thus brought himself and his family permanently into my circle of acquaintance. True, he had small prospect of commissions for large buildings, and considered himself doomed to play the schoolmaster for ever. He was, however, in the throes of writing a great work on art, which, after various mishaps and a change of publisher, he brought out later under the title, *Der Styl*. I often found him engaged with the drawings for illustrating this book; he drew them himself very neatly on stone, and grew so fond of the work that he declared the smallest detail in his drawing interested him far more than the big clumsy architectural jobs.

From this time forward, in accordance with my manifesto, I would have nothing whatever to do with the ' Musikgesellschaft,' neither did I ever conduct a public performance in Zürich again. The members of this society could not at first be brought to believe that I was in earnest, and I was obliged to bring it home to them by a categorical explanation, in which I dwelt on their slackness and their disregard of my urgent proposals for the establishment of a decent orchestra. The excuse I invariably received was, that although there was money enough among the musical public, yet every one fought shy of heading the subscription list with a definite sum, because of the tiresome notoriety they would win among the townspeople. My old friend, Herr Ott-Imhof, assured me that it would not embarrass him in the least to pay ten thousand francs a year to a cause of that sort, but that from that moment every one would demand why he was spending his income in that way. It would rouse such a commotion that he might easily be brought to account about the administration of his property. This called to my mind Goethe's exclamation at the beginning of his *Erste Schweizer Briefe*.[1] So my musical activities at Zürich ceased definitely from that time.

On the other hand, I occasionally had music at home. Neat and precious copies of Klindworth's pianoforte score of *Rheingold*, as well as of some acts of the *Walküre*, lay ready to hand, and Baumgartner was the first who was set down to see what he could make of the atrociously difficult arrangement. Later on we found that Theodor Kirchner, a musician who had settled at Winterthur and frequently visited Zürich, was better able to play certain bits of the pianoforte score. The wife of Heim, the head of the Glee Society, with whom we were both on friendly terms, was pressed into the service to sing the parts for female voices when I attempted to play some of the vocal parts. She had a really fine voice and a warm tone, and had been the only soloist at the big performances in 1853; only she was thoroughly unmusical, and I had hard work to make her keep in tune, and it was even more difficult to get the time right. Still, we achieved something, and my friends had an occasional foretaste of my *Nibelungen* music.

But I had to exercise great moderation here too, as every excitement threatened to bring on a return of erysipelas. A little party of us were at Karl Ritter's one evening, when I hit upon the idea of reading aloud Hoffmann's *Der Goldene Topf*. I did not notice that the room was getting gradually cooler, but before I had finished my reading I found myself, to every one's horror, with a swollen, red nose, and had to trail laboriously home to tend the malady, which exhausted me terribly

---

[1] This doubtless refers to the following passage: ' And the Swiss call themselves free! These smug bourgeois shut up in their little towns, these poor devils on their precipices and rocks, call themselves free! Is there any limit at all to what one can make people believe and cherish, provided that one preserves the old fable of "Freedom" in spirits of wine for them? Once upon a time they rid themselves of a tyrant and thought themselves free. Then, thanks to the glorious sun, a singular transformation occurred, and out of the corpse of their late oppressor a host of minor tyrants arose. Now they continue to relate the old fable; on all sides it is drummed into one's ears *ad nauseam* — they have thrown off the yoke of the despot and have remained free. And there they are, ensconced behind their walls and imprisoned in their customs, their laws, the opinion of their neighbours, and their Philistine suburbanism' (*Goethe's Werke, Briefe aus der Schweiz, Erste Abteilung*.) — EDITOR.

every time. During these periods of suffering I became more and more absorbed in developing the libretto of *Tristan*, whereas my intervals of convalescence were devoted to the score of the *Walküre*, at which I toiled diligently but laboriously, completing the fair copy in March of that year (1856). But my illness and the strain of work had reduced me to a state of unusual irritability, and I can remember how extremely bad-tempered I was when our friends the Wesendoncks came in that evening to pay a sort of congratulatory visit on the completion of my score. I expressed my opinion of this way of sympathising with my work with such extraordinary bitterness that the poor insulted visitors departed abruptly in great consternation, and it took many explanations, which I had great difficulty in making, to atone for the insult as the days went on. My wife came out splendidly on this occasion in her efforts to smooth things over. A special tie between her and our friends had been formed by the introduction of a very friendly little dog into our house, which had been obtained by the Wesendoncks as a successor to my good old Peps. He proved such a good and ingratiating animal that he soon gained my wife's tender affection, while I, too, always felt very kindly towards him. This time I left the choice of a name to my wife, however, and she invented, apparently as a pendant to Peps, the name Fips, which I was quite willing for him to have. But he was always more my wife's friend, as, despite my great sense of justice, which made me recognise the excellence of these animals, I never was able to become so attached to them as to Peps and Papo.

About the time of my birthday I had a visit from my old friend Tichatschek of Dresden, who remained faithful to his devotion and enthusiasm for me — as far as so uncultured a person was capable of such emotions. On the morning of my birthday I was awakened in a touching way by the strains of my beloved *Adagio* from Beethoven's E minor Quartette. My wife had invited the musicians in whom I took a special interest for this occasion, and they had, with subtle delicacy, chosen the very piece of which I had once spoken with such great emotion. At our party in the evening Tichatschek sang several things from *Lohengrin*, and really amazed us all by the brilliancy of voice he still preserved. He had also succeeded, by perseverance, in overcoming the irresolution of the Dresden management, due to their subserviency to the court, with regard to further performances of my operas. They were now being given there again, with great success and to full houses. I took a slight cold on an excursion which we made with our visitor to Brunnen on Lake Lucerne, and thus brought on my thirteenth attack of erysipelas. One of the terrible southern gales, which make it impossible to heat the rooms at Brunnen, made my sufferings this time more acute, added to the fact that I went through with the excursion, in spite of my painful condition, rather than spoil our guest's pleasure by turning back sooner. I was still in bed when Tichatschek left, and I decided at least to try a change of air in the south, because this dreadful malady seemed to me to haunt the locality of Zürich. I chose the Lake of Geneva, and decided to look out for a well-situated country resort in the neighbourhood of Geneva or thereabouts, where I could start on a cure which my Zürich doctor had prescribed. I therefore started for Geneva in the beginning of June. Fips, who was to accompany me into my rural retreat, caused me great anxiety on the journey; I nearly changed my destination, on account of an attempt to dislodge him from my carriage in the train for part of the journey. It was thanks to the energetic way in which I carried my point that I started my cure at Geneva, as I should otherwise probably have gone in a different direction.

In Geneva I put up first at the familiar old Hôtel de l'Écu de Genève, which called up various reminiscences to my mind. Here I consulted Dr. Coindet, who sent me to Mornex on Mont Salève, for the sake of its good air, and recommended me a *pension*. My first thought on arrival was to find a place where I should be undisturbed, and I persuaded the lady who kept the *pension* to make over to me an isolated pavilion in the garden which consisted of one large reception-room. Much persuasion was needed, as all the boarders — precisely the people I wished to avoid — were indignant at having the room originally intended for their social gatherings taken away. But at last I secured my object, though I had to bind myself to vacate my drawing-room on Sunday mornings, because it was then stocked with benches and arranged for a service, which seemed to mean a good deal to the Calvinists among the boarders. I fell in with this quite happily, and made my sacrifice honourably the very first Sunday by betaking myself to Geneva to read the papers. The next day, however, my hostess informed me that the boarders were very annoyed at only being able to hold the service, and not the week-day games in my drawing-room. I was given notice, and looked round for other quarters, which I found in the house of a neighbour.

This neighbour was a Dr. Vaillant, who had taken an equally fine site on which to erect a hydropathic institute. I first made inquiries about warm baths, as my Zürich doctor had advised the use of these with sulphur, but there was no prospect of obtaining any such thing. Dr. Vaillant's whole manner pleased me so much, however, that I told him my troubles. When I asked him which of two things I should drink: hot sulphur bath-water or a certain stinking mineral water, he smiled and said: '*Monsieur, vous n'êtes que nerveux.* All this will only excite you more; you merely need calming. If you will entrust yourself to me, I promise that you will have so far recovered by the end of two months as never to have erysipelas again.' And he kept his word.

I certainly formed a very different opinion of hydrotherapic methods through this excellent doctor from any I could have acquired from the 'Water Jew' of Albisbrunnen and other raw amateurs. Vaillant had been famous as a doctor in Paris itself (Lablache and Rossini had consulted him), but he had the misfortune of becoming paralysed in both legs, and after four years of helpless misery, during which he lost his whole practice and sank into utter misery, he came across the original Silesian hydrotherapeutist, Priessnitz, to whom he was conveyed, with the result that he recovered completely. There he learned the method that had proved so effective, refined it from all the brutalities of its inventor, and tried to recommend himself to the Parisians by building a hydro at Meudon. But he met with no encouragement. His former patients, whom he tried to persuade into visiting his institution, merely asked whether there was dancing there in the evening. He found it impossible to keep it up, and it is to this circumstance that I owe my meeting with him there, near Geneva, where he was once more trying to exploit his cure in a practical way. He laid claim to attention, if only by the fact that he strictly limited the number of patients he took into his house, insisting that a doctor could only be responsible for the right application and success of his treatment by being in a position to observe his patients minutely at all hours of the day. The advantage of his system, which benefited me so wonderfully, was the thoroughly calming effect of the treatment, which consisted in the most ingenious use of water at a moderate temperature.

Besides this, Vaillant took a special pleasure in satisfying my wants, particularly in procuring me rest and quiet. For instance, my presence at the common breakfast, which I found exciting and inconvenient, was excused, and I was allowed to make tea in my own room instead. This was an unaccustomed treat for me, and I indulged in it, under cover of secrecy, to excess, usually drinking tea behind closed doors for two hours, while I read Walter Scott's novels, after the fatiguing exertions of my morning cure. I had found some cheap and good French translations of these novels in Geneva, and had brought a whole pile of them to Mornex. They were admirably suited to my routine, which prohibited serious study or work; but, apart from that, I now fully endorsed Schopenhauer's high opinion of this poet's value, of which I had till then been doubtful. On my solitary strolls, it is true, I generally took a volume of Byron with me, because I possessed a miniature edition, to read on some mountain height with a view of Mont Blanc, but I soon left it at home, for I realised that I hardly ever drew it from my pocket.

The only work I permitted myself was the sketching of plans for building myself a house. These, in the end, I tried to work out correctly with all the materials of an architect's draughtsman. I had risen to this bold idea after negotiations on which I entered about that time with Härtel, the music publishers at Leipzig, for the sale of my *Nibelungen* compositions. I demanded forty thousand francs on the spot for the four works, of which half was to be paid me when the building of the house began. The publishers really seemed so far favourably inclined towards my proposals as to make my undertaking possible.

Very soon, however, their opinion of the market value of my works underwent an unhappy change. I could never make out whether this was the result of their having only just examined my poem carefully and decided that it was impracticable, or whether influence had been brought to bear on them from the same quarter to which the opposition directed against most of my undertakings could be traced, and which grew more and more evident as time wore on. Be that as it may, the hope of earning capital for my house-building forsook me; but my architectural studies took their course, and I made it my aim to obtain means to fulfil them.

As the two months I had destined to Dr. Vaillant's treatment were up on the 15th of August, I left the resort which had proved so beneficial, and went straight off on a visit to Karl Ritter, who, with his wife, had taken a lovely and very unassuming little house near Lausanne for the summer months. Both of them had visited me at Mornex, but when I tried to induce Karl to have some cold-water treatment, he declared, after one trial, that even the most soothing method excited him. On the whole, though, we found a good number of agreeable topics to discuss, and he told me he would return to Zürich in the autumn.

I returned home in a fairly good humour with Fips, on whose account I travelled by mail-coach to avoid the obnoxious railway journey. My wife, too, had returned home from her sour-milk cure on the Selisberg, and in addition I found my sister Clara installed, the only one of my relatives who had visited me in my Swiss retreat. We at once made an excursion with her to my favourite spot, Brunnen on Lake Lucerne, and spent an exquisite evening there enjoying the glorious sunset and other beautiful effects of the Alpine landscape. At nightfall, when the moon rose full over the lake, it turned out that a very pretty and effective ovation had been arranged for me (I had been a frequent visitor there) by our enthusiastic and attentive host, Colonel Auf-der-Mauer. Two boats, illuminated by coloured lanterns, came up to the beach facing our hotel, bearing the Brunnen brass band, which was formed entirely of amateurs from the countryside. With Federal staunchness, and without any attempts at punctilious unison, they proceeded to play some of my compositions in a loud and irrefutable manner. They then paid me homage in a little speech, and I replied heartily, after which there was much gripping of all sorts of horny hands on my part, as we drank a few bottles of wine on the beach. For years afterwards I never passed this beach on very frequent visits without receiving a friendly handshake or a greeting. I was generally in doubt as to what the particular boatman wanted of me, but it always turned out that I was dealing with one of the brass bandsmen whose good intentions had been manifested on that pleasant evening.

My sister Clara's lengthy stay with us at Zürich enlivened our family circle very pleasantly. She was the musical one among my brothers and sisters, and I enjoyed her society very much. It was also a relief to me when her presence acted as a damper upon the various household scenes brought on by Minna, who, as a result of the steady development of her heart trouble, grew more and more suspicious, vehement and obstinate.

In October I expected a visit from Liszt, who proposed to make a fairly long stay at Zürich, accompanied by various people of note. I could not wait so long, however, before beginning the composition of *Siegfried,* and I began to sketch the overture on the 22nd of September.

A tinker had established himself opposite our house, and stunned my ears all day long with his incessant hammering. In my disgust at never being able to find a detached house protected from every kind of noise, I was on the point of deciding to give up composing altogether until the time when this indispensable condition should be fulfilled. But it was precisely my rage over the tinker that, in a moment of agitation, gave me the theme for Siegfried's furious outburst against the bungling Mime. I played over the childishly quarrelsome Polter theme in G minor to my sister, furiously singing the words at the same time, which made us all laugh so much that I decided to make one more effort. This resulted in my writing down a good part of the first scene by the time Liszt arrived on 13th October.

Liszt came by himself, and my house at once became a

musical centre. He had finished his *Faust* and *Dante* Symphonies since I had seen him, and it was nothing short of marvellous to hear him play them to me on the piano from the score. As I felt sure that Liszt must be convinced of the great impression his compositions made on me, I felt no scruples in persuading him to alter the mistaken ending of the *Dante* Symphony. If anything had convinced me of the man's masterly and poetical powers of conception, it was the original ending of the *Faust* Symphony, in which the delicate fragrance of a last reminiscence of Gretchen overpowers everything, without arresting the attention by a violent disturbance. The ending of the *Dante* Symphony seemed to me to be quite on the same lines, for the delicately introduced Magnificat in the same way only gives a hint of a soft, shimmering Paradise. I was the more startled to hear this beautiful suggestion suddenly interrupted in an alarming way by a pompous, plagal cadence which, as I was told, was supposed to represent Domenico.

' No! ' I exclaimed loudly, ' not that! Away with it! No majestic Deity! Leave us the fine soft shimmer.'

' You are right,' said Liszt. ' I said so too; it was the Princess who persuaded me differently. But it shall be as you wish.'

All well and good — but all the greater was my distress to learn later that not only had this ending of the *Dante* Symphony been preserved, but even the delicate ending of the *Faust* Symphony, which had appealed to me so particularly, had been changed, in a manner better calculated to produce an effect, by the introduction of a chorus. And this was exactly typical of my relations to Liszt and to his friend Caroline Wittgenstein!

This woman, with her daughter Marie, was soon to arrive on a visit too, and the necessary preparations were made for her reception. But before these ladies arrived, a most painful incident occurred between Liszt and Karl Ritter at my house. Ritter's looks alone, and still more, a certain abrupt contradictoriness in his way of speaking, seemed to put Liszt into a state in which he was easily irritated. One evening Liszt was speaking in an impressive tone of the merits of the Jesuits, and

Ritter's inopportune smiles appeared to offend him. At table
the conversation turned on the Emperor of the French, Louis
Napoleon, whose merits Liszt rather summarily insisted that
we should acknowledge, whereas we were, on the whole, anything but enthusiastic about the general state of affairs in
France. When Liszt, in an attempt to make clear the important influence of France on European culture, mentioned as an
instance the French *Académie,* Karl again indulged in his fatal
smile. This exasperated Liszt beyond all bounds, and in his
reply he included some such phrase as this: 'If we are not
prepared to admit this, what do we prove ourselves to be?
Baboons!' I laughed, but again Karl only smiled — this time,
with deadly embarrassment. I discovered afterwards through
Bülow that in some youthful squabble he had had the word
'Baboon-face' hurled at him. It soon became impossible to
hide the fact that Ritter felt himself grossly insulted by 'the
doctor,' as he called him, and he left my house foaming with
rage, not to set foot in it again for years. After a few days
I received a letter in which he demanded, first, a complete
apology from Liszt, as soon as he came to see me again, and
if this were unobtainable, Liszt's exclusion from my house.
It distressed me greatly to receive, soon after this, a letter
from Ritter's mother, whom I respected very much, reproaching
me for my unjust treatment of her son in not having obtained
satisfaction for an insult offered him in my house. For a long
time my relations with this family, intimate as they had been,
were painfully strained, as I found it impossible to make them
see the incident in the right light. When Liszt, after a time,
heard of it, he regretted the disturbance too, and with praise-
worthy magnanimity made the first advance towards a reconciliation by paying Ritter a friendly visit. There was nothing
said about the incident, and Ritter's return visit was made,
not to Liszt, but to the Princess, who had arrived in the meantime. After this Liszt decided that he could do nothing
further; Ritter, therefore, withdrew from our society from
this time forward, and changed his winter quarters from
Zürich to Lausanne, where he settled permanently.

Not only my own modest residence, but the whole of Zürich
seemed full of life when Princess Caroline and her daughter

took up their abode at the Hôtel Baur for a time. The curious spell of excitement which this lady immediately threw over every one she succeeded in drawing into her circle amounted, in the case of my good sister Clara (who was still with us at the time), almost to intoxication. It was as if Zürich had suddenly become a metropolis. Carriages drove hither and thither, footmen ushered one in and out, dinners and suppers poured in upon us, and we found ourselves suddenly surrounded by an increasing number of interesting people, whose existence at Zürich we had never even suspected, though they now undoubtedly cropped up everywhere. A musician named Winterberger, who felt it incumbent on him on certain occasions to behave eccentrically, had been brought there by Liszt; Kirchner, the Schumann enthusiast from Winterthur, was practically always there, attracted by the new life, and he too did not fail to play the wag. But it was principally the professors of Zürich University whom Princess Caroline coaxed out of their hole-and-corner Zürich habits. She would have them, one at a time, for herself, and again serve them up *en masse* for us. If I looked in for a moment from my regular midday walk, the lady would be dining alone, now with Semper, now with Professor Köchly, then with Moleschott, and so on. Even my very peculiar friend Sulzer was drawn in, and, as he could not deny, in a manner intoxicated. But a really refreshing sense of freedom and spontaneity pervaded everything, and the unceremonious evenings at my house in particular were really remarkably free and easy. On these occasions the Princess, with Polish patriarchal friendliness, would help the mistress of the house in serving. Once, after we had had some music, I had to give the substance of my two newly conceived poems, *Tristan und Isolde* and *Die Sieger,* to a group which, half sitting, half lying before me, was certainly not without charm.

The crown of our festivities was, however, Liszt's birthday, on the 22nd October, which the Princess celebrated with due pomp at her own house. Every one who was some one at Zürich was there. A poem by Hoffmann von Fallersleben was telegraphed from Weimar, and at the Princess's request was solemnly read aloud by Herwegh in a strangely altered voice. I then gave a performance, with Frau Heim, of the first act, and a scene from the second, of the *Walküre,* Liszt accompanying. I was able to obtain a favourable idea of the effect of our performance by the wish expressed by Dr. Wille to hear these things badly done, so that he could form a correct judgment, as he feared he might be seduced by the excellence of our execution. Besides these, Liszt's *Symphonic Poems* were played on two grand pianos. At the feast, a dispute arose about Heinrich Heine, with respect to whom Liszt made all sorts of insidious remarks. Frau Wesendonck responded by asking if he did not think Heine's name as a poet would, nevertheless, be inscribed in the temple of immortality.

' Yes, but in mud,' answered Liszt quickly, creating, as may be conceived, a great sensation.

Unfortunately, our circle was soon to suffer a great loss by Liszt's illness — a skin eruption — which confined him to his bed for a considerable period. As soon as he was a little better, we quickly went to the piano again to try over by ourselves my two finished scores of *Rheingold* and the *Walküre.* Princess Marie listened carefully, and was even able to make intelligent suggestions in connection with a few difficult passages in the poem.

Princess Caroline, too, seemed to set extraordinary store on being quite clear as to the actual intrigue concerning the fate of the gods in my *Nibelungen.* She took me in hand one day, quite like one of the Zürich professors, *en particulier,* to clear up this point to her satisfaction. I must confess it was irrefutably brought home to me that she was anxious to understand the most delicate and mysterious features of the intrigue, though in rather too precise and matter-of-fact a spirit. In the end I felt as though I had explained a French society play to her. Her high spirits in all such things were as marked as the curious amiability of her nature in other respects; for when I one day explained to her, in illustration of the first of these two qualities, that four weeks of uninterrupted companionship with her would have been the death of me, she laughed heartily. I had reason for sadness in the changes which I realised had taken place in her daughter Marie; in the three years since I had first seen her she had faded to an

extraordinary extent. If I then called her a 'child,' I could
not now properly describe her as a 'young woman.' Some
disastrous experience seemed to have made her prematurely
old. It was only when she was excited, especially in the
evening when she was with friends, that the attractive and
radiant side of her nature asserted itself to a marked extent.
I remember one fine evening at Herwegh's, when Liszt was
moved to the same state of enthusiasm by a grand-piano
abominably out of tune, as by the disgusting cigars to which
at that time he was more passionately devoted than to the
finer brands. We were all compelled to exchange our belief
in magic for a belief in actual witchcraft as we listened to his
wonderful phantasies on this pianoforte. To my great horror,
Liszt still gave evidence on more than one occasion of an
irritability which was thoroughly bad-tempered and even
quarrelsome, such as had already manifested itself in the
unfortunate scene with young Ritter. For instance, it was
dangerous, especially in the presence of Princess Caroline, to
praise Goethe. Even Liszt and myself had nearly quarrelled
(for which he seemed to be very eager) over the character of
Egmont, which he thought it his duty to depreciate because
the man allows himself to be taken in by Alba. I had been
warned, and had the presence of mind to confine myself to
observing the peculiar physiology of my friend on this occasion,
and turning my attention to his condition, much more than to
the subject of our dispute. We never actually came to blows;
but from this time forward I retained throughout my life a
vague feeling that we might one day come to such an encounter,
in which case it would not fail to be terrific. Perhaps it was
just this feeling that acted as a check on me whenever any opportunity arose for heated argument. Goodness knows that I
myself had a bad enough reputation with my friends for my
own irritability and sudden outbursts of temper!

After I had made a stay of more than six weeks, we had a
final opportunity for coming together again before my return
from this visit that had meant so much for me. We had
agreed to spend a week at St. Gall, where we had an invitation
from Schadrowsky, a young musical director, to give our support to a society concert in that district.

We stayed together at the Hecht inn, and the Princess entertained us as if she had been in her own house. She gave me and my wife a room next her own private apartment. Unfortunately a most trying night was in store for us. Princess Caroline had one of her severe nervous attacks, and in order to preclude the approach of the painful hallucination by which she was tormented at such times, her daughter Marie was obliged to read to her all through the night in a voice deliberately raised a good deal above its natural pitch. I got fearfully excited, especially at what appeared to be an inexplicable disregard for the peace of one's neighbour implied by such conduct. At two o'clock in the morning I leaped out of bed, rang the bell continuously until the waiter awoke, and asked him to take me to a bedroom in one of the remotest parts of the inn. We moved there and then, not without attracting the attention of our neighbours, upon whom, however, the circumstance made no impression. The next morning I was much astonished to see Marie appear as usual, quite unembarrassed, and without showing the least traces of anything exceptional having occurred. I now learned that everybody connected with the Princess was thoroughly accustomed to such disturbances. Here, too, the house soon filled with all sorts of guests: Herwegh and his wife came, Dr. Wille and his wife, Kirchner, and several others, and before long our life in the Hecht yielded nothing, in point of activity, to our life in the Hôtel Baur. The excuse for all this, as I have said, was the society concert of the musical club of St. Gall. At the rehearsal, to my genuine delight, Liszt impressed two of his compositions, *Orpheus* and the *Prelude,* upon the orchestra with complete success, in spite of the limited resources at his command. The performance turned out to be a really fine one, and full of spirit. I was especially delighted with the *Orpheus* and with the finely proportioned orchestral work, to which I had always assigned a high place of honour among Liszt's compositions. On the other hand, the special favour of the public was awarded to the *Prelude,* of which the greater part was encored. I conducted the *Eroica* Symphony of Beethoven under very painful conditions, as I always caught cold on such occasions, and generally became feverish afterwards. My conception and rendering of Beethoven's work made a powerful impression upon Liszt, whose opinion was the only one which had any real weight with me. We watched each other over our work with a closeness and sympathy that was genuinely instructive. At night we had to take part in a little supper in our honour, which was the occasion for expressing the noble and deep sentiments of the worthy citizens of St. Gall concerning the significance of our visit. As I was regaled with a most complimentary panegyric by a poet, it was necessary for me to respond with equal seriousness and eloquence. In his dithyrambic enthusiasm, Liszt went so far as to suggest a general clinking of glasses, signifying approval of his suggestion that the new theatre of St. Gall should be opened with a model performance of *Lohengrin*. No one offered any objection. The next day, the 24th of November, we all met, for various festivities, in the house of an ardent lover of music, Herr Bourit, a rich merchant of St. Gall. Here we had some pianoforte music, and Liszt played to us, among other things, the great Sonata of Beethoven in B flat major, at the close of which Kirchner dryly and candidly remarked, ' Now we can truly say that we have witnessed the impossible, for I shall always regard what I have just heard as an impossibility.' On this occasion, attention was called to the twentieth anniversary of my marriage with Minna, which fell on this day, and after the wedding music of *Lohengrin* had been played, we formed a charming procession *à la Polonaise* through the various rooms.

In spite of all these pleasant experiences, I should have been well content to see the end of the business and return to the peace of my home in Zürich. The indisposition of the Princess, however, retarded the departure of my friends for Germany for several days, and we found ourselves compelled to remain together in a state of nervous tension and aimlessness for some time, until at last, on the 27th November, I escorted my visitors to Rorschach, and took my leave of them there on the steamer. Since then I have never seen the Princess or her daughter, nor I think it likely I shall ever meet them again.

It was not without some misgiving that I took leave of my friends, for the Princess was really ill, and Liszt seemed to be much exhausted. I recommended their immediate return to

Weimar, and told them to take care of themselves. Great was
my surprise, therefore, when before long I received the news
that they were making a sojourn of some duration in Munich.
This followed immediately upon their departure, and was also
attended with much noisy festivity and occasional artistic
gatherings. I was thus led to the conclusion that it was foolish
of me to recommend people with such constitutions either to
do a thing or to abstain from doing it. I, for my part, returned
home to Zürich very much exhausted, unable to sleep, and
tormented by the frosty weather at this cold season of the
year. I was afraid that I had by my recent method of life
subjected myself to a fresh attack of erysipelas. I was very
pleased when I awoke the next morning to discover no trace
of what I feared, and from that day I continued to sing the
praises of my excellent Dr. Vaillant wherever I went. By the
beginning of December I had so far recovered as to be able to
resume the composition of *Siegfried*. Thus I again entered upon
my orderly method of life, with all its insignificance as far as
outward things were concerned: work, long walks, the perusal
of books, evenings spent with some friend or other of the
domestic circle. The only thing that worried me was the regret
I still felt for my quarrel with Ritter, in consequence of the
unhappy *contre-temps* with Liszt. I now lost touch entirely
with this young friend, who in so many ways had endeared
himself to me. Before the close of the winter he left Zürich
without seeing me again.

During the months of January and February (1857) I completed the first act of *Siegfried,* writing down the composition
in full to take the place of the earlier rough pencil draft, and
immediately set to work on the orchestration; but I probably
carried out Vaillant's instructions with too much zeal. Pursued by the fear of a possible return of erysipelas, I sought to
ward it off by a repeated and regular process of sweating once
a week, wrapped up in towels, on the hydropathic system. By
this means I certainly escaped the dreaded evil, but the effort
exhausted me very much, and I longed for the return of the
warm weather, when I should be relieved from the severities
of this treatment.

It was now that the tortures inflicted upon me by noisy and

musical neighbours began to increase in intensity. Apart from
the tinker, whom I hated with a deadly hatred, and with whom
I had a terrible scene about once a week, the number of pianos
in the house where I lived was augmented. The climax came
with the arrival of a certain Herr Stockar, who played the flute
in the room under mine every Sunday, whereupon I gave up
all hope of composing any more. One day my friends the
Wesendoncks, who had returned from wintering in Paris, unfolded to me a most welcome prospect of the fulfilment of my
ardent wishes in regard to my future place of abode. Wesendonck had already had an idea of having a small house built
for me on a site I was to select for myself. My own plans,
elaborated with a deceptive skill, had been already submitted
to an architect. But the acquisition of a suitable plot of land
was and still remained a great difficulty. In my walks I had
long had my eye on a little winter residence in the district of
Enge, on the ridge of the hill that separates the Lake of Zürich
from Sihlthal. It was called Lavater Cottage, as it had belonged
to that famous phrenologist, and he had been in the habit of
staying there regularly. I had enlisted the services of my
friend Hagenbuch, the Cantonal Secretary, to use all his influence to secure me a few acres of land at this spot as cheaply as
possible. But herein lay the great difficulty. The piece of land
I required consisted of various lots attached to larger estates,
and it turned out that in order to acquire my one plot it would
have been necessary to buy out a large number of different
owners. I put the difficulties of my case before Wesendonck,
and gradually created in him a desire to purchase this wide
tract of land, and lay out a fine site containing a large villa
for his own family. The idea was that I should also have a
plot there. However, the demands made upon my friend in
regard to the preliminaries and to the building of his house,
which was to be on a scale both generous and dignified, were too
many, and he also thought the enclosure of two families within
the same confines might lead in time to inconveniences on both
sides. There happened to be an unpretentious little country
house with a garden which I had admired, and which was
only separated from his estate by a narrow carriage drive; and
this Wesendonck decided to buy for me. I rejoiced beyond

measure when I heard of his intention. The shock experienced by the over-cautious buyer was consequently all the greater when one day he discovered that the present owner, with whom he had negotiated in too timid a fashion, had just sold his piece of land to somebody else. Luckily it turned out that the buyer was a mental specialist, whose sole intention in making the purchase was to instal himself with his lunatic asylum by the side of my friend. This information awakened the most terrible anticipations in Wesendonck, and put the utmost strain upon his energy. He now gave instructions that this piece of land must be acquired at any price from the unfortunate specialist. Thus, after many vexatious vicissitudes, it came into the possession of my friend, who had to pay pretty heavily for it. He allowed me to come into possession at Easter of this year, charging me the same rent as I had paid for my lodging in the Zeltweg, that is to say, eight hundred francs a year.

Our installation in this house, which occupied me heart and soul at the beginning of the spring, was not achieved without many a disappointment. The cottage, which had only been designed for use in summer, had to be made habitable for the winter by putting in heating apparatus and various other necessaries. It is true, that most of the essentials in this respect were carried out by the proprietor; but no end of difficulties remained to be solved. There was not a single thing upon which my wife and I did not constantly differ, and my position as an ordinary middle-class man without a brass farthing of my own made matters no easier. With regard to my finances, however, events took place from time to time which were well calculated to inspire a sanguine temperament with trustful confidence in the future. In spite of the bad performances of my operas, *Tannhäuser* brought me unexpectedly good royalties from Berlin. From Vienna, too, I obtained the wherewithal to give me breathing-space in a most curious way. I was still excluded from the Royal Opera, and I had been assured that so long as there was an imperial court, I was not to dream of a performance of my seditious works in Vienna. This strange state of affairs inspired my old director, Hoffmann of Riga, now director of the Josephstadt Theatre, to venture on the production of *Tannhäuser* with a special

opera company, in a summer theatre built by himself on the
Lerchenfeld outside the boundary of Vienna. He offered me
for every performance which I would license a royalty of a
hundred francs. When Liszt, whom I informed of the matter,
thought this offer was suspicious, I wrote and told him that I
proposed to follow Mirabeau's example with regard to it.
Mirabeau, when he failed to be elected by his peers to the
assembly of Notables, addressed himself to the electors of
Marseilles in the capacity of a linendraper. This pleased Liszt;
and, indeed, I now made my way, by means of the summer
theatre on the Lerchenfeld, into the capital of the Austrian
empire. Of the performance itself the most wonderful accounts
reached me. Sulzer, who on one of his journeys had passed
through Vienna and had witnessed a performance, had complained principally of the darkness of the house, which did not
allow him to read a single word of the libretto, also of its
having rained hard right into the middle of the audience.
Another story was told me some years later by the son-in-law
of Mme. Hérold, the widow of the composer of that name. He
had been in Vienna at that period on his wedding tour, and
had heard this Lerchenfeld performance. The young man assured me that, in spite of all superficial deficiencies, the production there had given him genuine pleasure, and had been
more deeply impressive than the performance in the Berlin
Court Theatre, which he had seen afterwards, and found im-
measurably inferior. The energy of my old Riga Theatre
director in Vienna brought me in two thousand francs for
twenty performances of *Tannhäuser*. After such a curious
experience, offering clear proof of my popularity, I may perhaps be excused for having felt confident about the future,
and having relied on incalculable results from my works, even
with regard to actual gain.

While I was thus occupied in arranging the little country
house for which I had longed so much, and working on the
orchestration of the first act of *Siegfried*, I plunged anew
into the philosophy of Schopenhauer and into Scott's novels,
to which I was drawn with a particular affection. I also busied
myself with elucidating my impressions of Liszt's compositions. For this purpose I adopted the form of a letter to

Marie Wittgenstein, which was published in Brendel's musical
journal.

When we moved to what I intended to be my permanent
refuge for life, I again set myself to consider the means of
obtaining a basis for the supply of the necessities of that life.
Once again I took up the threads of my negotiations with
Härtel about the *Nibelungen,* but I was obliged to put them
down as unfruitful, and little calculated to end in any success
for this work. I complained of this to Liszt, and openly told
him how glad I should be if he would bring this to the ears of
the Grand Duke of Weimar (who, from what my friend told
me, wished himself still to be regarded as the patron of my
Nibelungen enterprise), so that he might realise the difficulties
I was encountering in the matter. I added that if one could
not expect a common bookseller to assume the responsibility of
such an extraordinary undertaking, one might well hope that
the Prince, whose idea was to make it a point of honour, should
take a share, and a serious share, in the necessary preliminaries,
among which the development of the work itself must very
properly be included. My meaning was, that the Grand Duke
should take the place of Härtel, should purchase the work
from me, and pay by instalments as the score neared completion; he would thus become the owner, and, later on, could
if he liked cover his expenses through a publisher. Liszt
understood me very well, but could not refrain from dis-
suading me from taking up such an attitude towards his Royal
Highness.

My whole attention was now directed to the young Grand
Duchess of Baden. Several years had passed since Eduard
Devrient had been transferred to Karlsruhe by the Grand
Duke to be manager of the court theatre there. Since my
departure from Dresden I had always kept in touch with
Devrient, though our meetings were rare. Moreover, he had
written the most enthusiastic letters in appreciation of my
pamphlets, *Das Kunstwerk der Zukunft* and *Oper und Drama.*
He maintained that the Karlsruhe Theatre was so poorly
equipped, that he thought he could not well entertain the idea
of a performance of my operas in that house. All these conditions were suddenly changed when the Grand Duke married,

and the Crown Princess's young daughter, who had been turned into a champion of mine by my old friend Alwine Frommann, thus secured a position of independence in Karlsruhe, and was eager in her demand for the performance of my works. My operas were now being produced there also, and Devrient in his turn had the pleasure of informing me of the great interest shown in them by the young Princess, who even frequently attended the rehearsals. This made a very agreeable impression upon me. On my own initiative I expressed my gratitude in an address which I directed to the Grand Duchess herself, enclosing ' Wotan's Abschied ' from the finale of the *Walküre* as a souvenir for her album.

The 20th April was now drawing near, the day on which I was to leave my lodging in the Zeltweg (which had already been let), although I could not occupy the cottage, where the arrangements were not yet complete. The bad weather had given us colds in the course of our frequent visits to the little house, in which masons and carpenters had made themselves at home. In the worst of tempers we spent a week in the inn, and I began to wonder whether it was worth while occupying this new piece of land at all, for I had a sudden foreboding that it would be my fate to wander further afield. Eventually we moved in at the end of April, in spite of everything. It was cold and damp, the new heating apparatus did not provide any warmth, and we were both ill, and could hardly leave our beds. Then came a good omen: the first letter that reached me was one of reconciliation and love from Frau Julie Ritter, in which she told me that the quarrel, brought about by her son's conduct, was at last ended. Beautiful spring weather now set in; on Good Friday I awoke to find the sun shining brightly for the first time in this house: the little garden was radiant with green, the birds sang, and at last I could sit on the roof and enjoy the long-yearned-for peace with its message of promise. Full of this sentiment, I suddenly remembered that the day was Good Friday, and I called to mind the significance this omen had already once assumed for me when I was reading Wolfram's *Parsifal*. Since the sojourn in Marienbad, where I had conceived the *Meistersinger* and *Lohengrin,* I had never occupied myself again with that poem;

now its noble possibilities struck me with overwhelming force, and out of my thoughts about Good Friday I rapidly conceived a whole drama, of which I made a rough sketch with a few dashes of the pen, dividing the whole into three acts.

In the midst of arranging the house, a never-ending task, at which I set to work with all my might, I felt an inner compulsion to work: I took up *Siegfried* again, and began to compose the second act. I had not made up my mind what name to give to my new place of refuge. As the introductory part of this act turned out very well, thanks to my favourable frame of mind, I burst out laughing at the thought that I ought to call my new home ' Fafner's Ruhe,' to correspond with the first piece of work done in it. It was not destined to be so, however. The property continued to be called simply ' Asyl,' and I have designated it under this title in the chart of dates to my works.

The miscarriage of my prospects of support for the *Nibelungen* from the Grand Duke of Weimar fostered in me a continued depression of spirits; for I saw before me a burden of which I knew not how to rid myself. At the same time a romantic message was conveyed to me: a man who rejoiced in the name of Ferreiro introduced himself to me as the Brazilian consul in Leipzig, and told me that the Emperor of Brazil was greatly attracted by my music. The man was an adept in meeting my doubts about this strange phenomenon in the letters which he wrote; the Emperor loved everything German, and wanted me very much to come to him in Rio Janeiro, so that I might conduct my operas in person. As only Italian was sung in that country, it would be necessary to translate my libretto, which the Emperor regarded as a very easy matter, and actually an improvement to the libretto itself. Strange to say, these proposals exercised a very agreeable influence on me. I felt I could easily produce a passionate musical poem which would turn out quite excellent in Italian, and I turned my thoughts once more, with an ever-reviving preference, towards *Tristan und Isolde.* In order in some way to test the intensity of that generous affection for my works protested by the Emperor of Brazil, I promptly sent to Señor Ferreiro the expensively bound volumes containing the pianoforte versions of my three earlier operas, and for a long time I indulged in the hope of some very handsome return from their gracious and splendid reception in Rio Janeiro. But of these pianoforte versions, and the Emperor of Brazil and his consul Ferreiro, I never heard a single syllable again as long as I lived. Semper, it is true, involved himself in an architectonic entanglement with this tropical country: a competition was invited for the building of a new opera house in Rio; Semper had announced that he would take part in it, and completed some splendid plans which afforded us great entertainment, and appeared to be of special interest, among others, to Dr. Wille, who thought that it must be a new problem for an architect to sketch an opera house for a black public. I have not learned whether the results of Semper's negotiations with Brazil were much more satisfactory than mine; at all events, I know that he did not build the theatre.

A violent cold threw me for a few days into a state of high fever; when I recovered from it, my birthday had come. As I was sitting once more in the evening on my roof, I was surprised at hearing one of the songs of the Three Rhine Maidens, from the finale of *Rheingold,* which floated to my ears from the near distance across the gardens. Frau Pollert, whose troubles with her husband had once stood in the way of a second performance in Magdeburg of my *Liebesverbot* (in itself a very difficult production), had again appeared last winter as a singer, and also as the mother of two daughters, in the theatrical firmament of Zürich. As she still had a fine voice, and was full of goodwill towards me, I allowed her to practise the last act of *Walküre* for herself, and the Rhine Maidens scenes from the *Rheingold* with her two daughters, and frequently in the course of the winter we had managed to give short performances of this music for our friends. On the evening of my birthday the song of my devoted lady friends surprised me in a very touching way, and I suddenly experienced a strange revulsion of feeling, which made me disinclined to continue the composition of the *Nibelungen,* and all the more anxious to take up *Tristan* again. I determined to yield to this desire, which I had long nourished in secret, and to set to work at once on this new task, which I had wished to regard only as a short interruption to the great one. However, in order to prove to myself that I was not being scared away from the older work by any feeling of aversion, I determined, at all events, to complete the composition of the second act of *Siegfried,* which had only just been begun. This I did with a right good will, and gradually the music of *Tristan* dawned more and more clearly on my mind.

To some extent external motives, which seemed to me both attractive and advantageous to the execution of my task, acted as incentives to make me set to work on *Tristan.* These motives became fully defined when Eduard Devrient came on a visit to me at the beginning of July and stayed with me for three days. He told me of the good reception accorded to my despatch by the Grand Duchess of Baden, and I gathered that he had been commissioned to come to an understanding with me about some enterprise or other; I informed him that I had decided to interrupt my work on the *Nibelungen* by composing an opera, which was bound by its contents and requirements to put me once more into relation with the theatres, however inferior they might be. I should do myself an injustice if I said that this external motive alone inspired the conception of *Tristan,* and made me determine to have it produced. Nevertheless, I must confess that a perceptible change had come over the frame of mind in which, several years ago, I had contemplated the completion of the greater work. At the same time I had come fresh from my writings upon art, in which I had attempted to explain the reasons for the decay of our public art, and especially of the theatre, by seeking to establish some connection between these reasons and the prevailing condition of culture. It would have been impossible for me at that time to have devoted myself to a work which compelled me to study its immediate production at one of our existing theatres. It was only an utter disregard of these theatres, as I have taken occasion to observe before, that could determine me to take up my artistic work again. With regard to the *Nibelungen* dramas, I was compelled to adhere without flinching to the one essential stipulation that it could only be produced under quite exceptional conditions, such as those I afterwards described in the preface to the printed edition of the poem. Nevertheless, the successful popularisation of my earlier operas had so far influenced my frame of mind that, as I approached the completion of more than half of my great work, I felt I could look forward with growing confidence to the possibility that this too might be produced. Up to this point Liszt had been the only person to nourish the secret hope of my heart, as he was confident that the Grand Duke of Weimar would do something for me, but to judge from my latest experience these prospects amounted to nothing, while I had grounds for hoping that a new work of similar design to *Tannhäuser* or *Lohengrin* would be taken up everywhere with considerable alacrity. The manner in which I finally executed the plan of *Tristan* shows clearly how little I was thinking of our operatic theatres and the scope of their capabilities. Nevertheless, I had still to fight a continuous battle for the necessaries of life, and I succeeded in deceiving myself so far as to persuade myself that in interrupting the composition of the *Nibelungen* and taking up *Tristan,* I was acting in the practical spirit of a man who carefully weighs the issues at stake. Devrient was much pleased to hear that I was undertaking a work that could be regarded as practical. He asked me at which theatre I contemplated producing my new work. I answered that naturally I could only have in view a theatre in which it would be possible for me to superintend the task of production in person. My idea was that this would either be in Brazil or, as I was excluded from the territory of the German Confederation, in one of the towns lying near the German frontiers, which I presumed would be able to place an operatic company at my disposal. The place I had in my mind was Strasburg, but Devrient had many practical reasons for being wholly opposed to such an undertaking; he was of opinion that a performance in Karlsruhe could be arranged more easily and would meet with greater success. My only objection to this was, that in that town I should be debarred from taking a personal share in the study and production of my work. Devrient, however, thought that, as far as this was concerned, I might feel justified in entertaining some hope, as the Grand Duke of Baden was so well disposed towards me, and took an active interest in my work. I was highly delighted to learn this. Devrient also spoke with great sympathy of the young tenor Schnorr, who, besides possessing admirable gifts, was keenly attracted by my operas. I was now in the best of tempers, and acted the host to Devrient for all I was worth. One morning I played and sang to him the whole of the *Rheingold,* which seemed to give him great pleasure. Half seriously, and half in joke, I told him that I had written the character of Mime especially for him, and that if, when the work was ready, it was not too late, he might have the pleasure of taking the part. As Devrient was with me, he had, of course, to do his share of reciting. I invited all the friends in our circle, including Semper and Herwegh, and Devrient read us the Mark Antony scenes from Shakespeare's *Julius Cæsar.* So happy was his interpretation of the part, that even Herwegh, who had approached the recitation from its outset in a spirit of ridicule, freely acknowledged the success of the practised actor's skilful manipulation. Devrient wrote a letter from my house to the Grand Duke of Baden, telling him his impressions about me and what he had found me like. Soon after his departure I received an autograph letter from the Grand Duke, couched in very amiable terms, in which he first thanked me most profusely for the souvenir I had presented to his wife for her album, and at the same time declared his intention of championing my cause, and, above all, of securing my return to Germany.

From this time forward my resolve to produce *Tristan* had to be seriously entertained, as it was written in plain letters in my book of fate. To all these circumstances I was indebted for the continuation of the favourable mood in which I now brough the second act of *Siegfried* to a close. My daily walks were directed on bright summer afternoons to the peaceful Sihlthal, in whose wooded surroundings I listened long and attentively to the song of the forest birds, and I was astonished to make the acquaintance of entirely new melodies, sung by singers whose forms I could not see and whose names I did not know. In the forest scene of *Siegfried* I put down, in artistic imitation of nature, as much as I could remember of these airs. At the beginning of August I had carefully sketched the composition of the second act. I was glad I had reserved the third act with the awakening of Brünhilda for the time when I should again be able to go on with the opera, for it seemed to me that all the problems in my work were now happily solved, and that all that remained was to get pure joy out of it.

As I firmly believed in the wisdom of husbanding my artistic power, I now prepared to write out *Tristan*. A certain strain was put upon my patience at this point by the arrival of the excellent Ferdinand Präger from London. His visit, in other respects, was a source of genuine pleasure to me, for I was bound to recognise in him a faithful and life-long friend. The only difficulty was, that he laboured under the delusion that he was exceptionally nervous, and that he was persecuted by fate. This was a source of considerable annoyance to me, as with the best will in the world, I could not muster up any sympathy for him. We helped ourselves out of the dilemma by an excursion to Schaffhausen, where I paid my first visit to the famous Rhine Falls, which did not fail to impress me duly.

About this time the Wesendoncks moved into their villa, which had now been embellished by stucco-workers and upholsterers from Paris. At this point a new phase began in my relations with this family, which was not really important, but nevertheless exercised considerable influence on the outward conduct of my life. We had become so intimate, through being such near neighbours in a country place, that it was impossible to avoid a marked increase in our intimacy if only through meeting one another daily. I had often noticed that Wesendonck, in his straightforward open manner, had shown uneasiness at the way in which I made myself at home in his house. In many things, in the matter of heating and lighting the rooms, and also in the hours appointed for meals, consideration was shown me which seemed to encroach upon his rights as master of the house. It needed a few confidential discussions on the subject to establish an agreement which was half implied and half expressed. This understanding had a tendency, as time wore on, to assume a doubtful significance in the eyes of other people, and necessitated a certain measure of precaution in an intimacy which had now become exceedingly close. These precautions were occasionally the source of great amusement to the two parties who were in the secret. Curiously enough, this closer association with my neighbour coincided with the time when I began to work out my libretto, *Tristan und Isolde.*

Robert Franz now arrived in Zürich on a visit. I was delighted by his agreeable personality, and his visit reassured me that no deep significance need be attached to the somewhat strained relations which had sprung up between us since the time when he took up the cudgels for me on the occasion of the production of *Lohengrin.* The misunderstanding had been chiefly due to the intermeddling of his brother-in-law Heinrich (who had written a pamphlet about me). We played and sang together; he accompanied me in some of his songs, and my compositions for the *Nibelungen* seemed to please him. But one day, when the Wesendoncks asked him to dinner to meet me, he begged that he might be alone with the family without any other guests, because if I were there he would not attain the importance by which he set so much store. We laughed over this, and I did so the more heartily because I was sometimes quite grateful to be saved the trouble of talking to people so curiously uncommunicative as I found Franz to be. After he left us, he never sent us a word of himself or his doings again.

When I had almost finished the first act of *Tristan,* a newly married couple arrived in Zürich, who certainly had a prominent claim on my interest. It was about the beginning of September that Hans von Bülow arrived with his young wife Cosima (a daughter of Liszt's) at the Raben Hotel. I invited them to my little house, so that they might spend the whole time of their stay in Zürich with me, as their visit was mainly on my account.

We spent the month of September together most pleasantly. In the meanwhile I completed the libretto of *Tristan und Isolde,* and at the some time Hans made me a fair copy of each act. I read it over, act by act, to my two friends, until at last I was able to get them all together for a private reading, which made a deep impression on the few intimate friends who composed the audience. As Frau Wesendonck appeared to be particularly moved by the last act, I said consolingly that one ought not to grieve over it, as, under any circumstances, in a matter so grave things generally turned out in this way, and Cosima heartily agreed. We also had a good deal of music together,

as in Bülow I had at last found the right man to play Klindworth's atrocious arrangement of my *Nibelungen* scores.   But
the two acts of *Siegfried,* which had only been written down as
rough drafts, were mastered by Hans with such consummate
skill that he could play them as if they had really been arranged
for the piano.   As usual, I took all the singing parts; sometimes we had a few listeners, amongst whom Mme. Wille was
the most promising.   Cosima listened silently with her head
bowed; if pressed for an expression of opinion, she began
to cry.

Towards the end of September my young friends left me
to travel back to their destination in Berlin, and begin their
married life like good citizens.

For the time being we had sounded a sort of funeral peal
over the *Nibelungen* by playing so much of it, and it was now
completely laid aside.   The consequence was, that when later
on we took it out of its folio for similar gatherings, it wore a
lack-lustre look, and grew ever fainter, as if to remind us of
the past.   At the beginning of October, however, I at once
began to compose *Tristan,* finishing the first act by the new
year, when I was already engaged in orchestrating the prelude.
During that time I developed a dreamy, timorous passion for
retirement.   Work, long walks in all winds and weathers,
evenings spent in reading Calderon — such was my mode of life,
and if it was disturbed, I was thrown into the deepest state
of irritation.   My connection with the world confined itself
almost entirely to my negotiations with the music-seller Härtel
about the publication of *Tristan.*   As I had told this man
that, by way of contrast to the immense undertaking of the
Nibelungen, I had in my mind a practicable work, which, in
its demands upon the producer, confined itself, to all intents
and purposes, to the engagement of a few good singers, he
showed such keenness to take up my offer that I ventured to
ask four hundred louis d'or.   Thereupon Härtel answered that
I was to read his counter offer, made, in a sealed letter which
he enclosed, only on condition that I at once agreed to waive
my own demands entirely, as he did not think the work I proposed to write was one which could be produced without difficulties.   In the sealed enclosure I found that he offered me only

one hundred louis d'or, but he undertook, after a period of five years, to give me a half-share in the proceeds, with the alternative of buying out my rights for another hundred louis d'or. With these terms I had to comply, and soon set to work to orchestrate the first act, so as to let the engraver have one batch of sheets at a time.

Besides this, I was interested at that time in the expected crisis of the American money market in the month of November, the consequences of which, during a few fatal weeks, threatened to endanger the whole of my friend Wesendonck's fortune. I remember that the impending catastrophe was borne with great dignity by those who were likely to be its victims; still the possibility of having to sell their house, their grounds, and their horses cast an unavoidable gloom over our evening meetings; and, after a while, Wesendonck went away to make arrangements with various foreign bankers.

During that time I spent the mornings in my house composing *Tristan,* and every evening we used to read Calderon, which made a deep and permanent impression upon me, for I had become fairly familiar with Spanish dramatic literature, thanks to Schack. At last the dreaded American crisis happily blew over, and it was soon apparent that Wesendonck's fortune had considerably increased. Again, during the winter evenings, I read *Tristan* aloud to a wider circle of friends. Gottfried Keller was pleased with the compact form of the whole, which really contained only three full scenes. Semper, however, was very angry about it: he objected that I took everything too seriously, and said that the charm in the artistic construction of such material consisted in the fact that the tragic element was broken up in such a way that one could extract enjoyment even from its most affecting parts. That was just what pleased him in Mozart's *Don Juan,* one met the tragic types there, as if at a masquerade, where even the domino was preferable to the plain character. I admitted that I should get on much more comfortably if I took life more seriously and art more lightly, but for the present I intended to let the opposite relations prevail.

As a matter of fact people shook their heads. After I

had sketched the first act of the composition, and had developed the character of my musical production more precisely. I thought with a peculiar smile of my first idea of writing this work as a sort of Italian opera, and I became less anxious at the absence of news from Brazil. On the other hand, my attention was particularly drawn at the end of this year to what was going on in Paris in regard to my operas. A young author from that city wrote asking me to entrust him with the translation of my *Tannhäuser,* as the manager of the Théâtre Lyrique, M. Carvalho, was taking steps to produce that opera in Paris. I was alarmed at this, as I was afraid that the copyright of my works had not been secured in France, and that they might dispose of them there at their own sweet will. To this I most strongly objected. I was well aware how this undertaking would be carried out, from an account I had read a short time before of the performance of Weber's *Euryanthe* at that very Théâtre Lyrique, and of the objectionable elaborations or rather mutilations which had been effected for the purposes of production. As Liszt's elder daughter Blandine had recently married the famous lawyer E. Ollivier, and I could consequently rely on substantial help from them, I made up my mind to go to Paris for a week, and look after the matter about which I had been approached, and, at any rate, secure my author's rights legally. In addition to this I was in a very melancholy state of mind, to which overwork and constant occupation on the kind of task that Semper had, perhaps with justice, denounced as being too serious, had contributed by reason of the strain on my mental powers.

If I remember rightly, I gave evidence of this state of mind (which curiously enough led me to despise all worldly cares) in a letter I wrote to my old friend Alwine Frommann on New Year's Eve 1857.

With the beginning of the new year 1858 the necessity for a break in my work became so manifest, that I positively dreaded beginning the instrumentation of the first act of *Tristan und Isolde,* until I had allowed myself the trip for which I longed. For at that moment, unfortunately, neither Zürich, nor my home, nor the company of my friends afforded me any relaxation.

Even the agreeable and immediate proximity of the Wesendonck family increased my discomfort, for it was really intolerable to me to devote all my evenings to conversations and entertainments in which my kind friend Otto Wesendonck felt obliged to take as much part as myself and the rest of us. His apprehension that everything in his house would very soon follow my lead instead of his, gave him that peculiar aggressiveness with which a man who believes himself neglected interpolates himself like an extinguisher into every conversation carried on in his presence.

All this soon became oppressive and irksome to me, and no one who did not realise my condition, and show signs of sympathising with it, could excite my interest, and even then it was a very languid one. So I made up my mind in the middle of the severe winter weather, and notwithstanding the fact that for the present I was quite unprovided with the necessary means, and was consequently obliged to take all sorts of tiresome precautions, to carry out my excursion to Paris. I felt a growing presentiment that I was going away never to return. I reached Strasburg on the 15th of January, too much upset to travel any further just then. From there I wrote to Eduard Devrient at Karlsruhe, asking him to request the Grand Duke to send an adjutant to meet me at Kehl on my return from Paris, to accompany me on a visit to Karlsruhe, as I particularly wanted to become acquainted with the artists who were to sing in _Tristan_. A little later I was taken to task by Eduard Devrient for my impertinence in expecting to have grand-ducal adjutants at my disposal, from which I gathered that he had attributed my request to a desire for some mark of honour, whereas my idea had been that that was the only possible way in which I, a political outlaw, could venture to visit Karlsruhe, though my object was a purely professional one. I could not help smiling at this strange misconception, but I was also startled at this proof of shallowness in my old friend, and began to wonder what he might do next.

I was trudging wearily along in the twilight through the public promenade of Strasburg, to restore my overwrought nerves, when I was suddenly taken aback by seeing on a theatre poster the word _TANNHÄUSER_.

Looking at the bill more closely, I saw that it was the Overture to *Tannhäuser* that was to be given as a prelude to a French play. The exact meaning of this I did not quite understand, but of course I took my seat in the theatre, which was very empty. The orchestra, looking all the larger from contrast with the empty house, was assembled in a huge space and was a very strong one. The rendering given of my overture under the conductor's baton was really a very good one.

As I was sitting rather near the front in the stalls, I was recognised by the man who was playing the kettledrum, as he had taken part in my Zürich performances in 1853. The news of my presence spread like wildfire through the whole orchestra until it reached the ears of the conductor, and led to great excitement. The small audience, who had evidently put in appearance simply on account of the French play, and who were not at all inclined to pay any particular attention to the overture, were very much astonished when, at the conclusion of the overture, the conductor and the whole orchestra turned round in the direction of my stall, and gave vent to enthusiastic applause, which I had to acknowledge with a bow. All eyes followed me eagerly as I left the hall after this scene, to pay my respects to the conductor. It was Herr Hasselmann, a native of Strasburg, and apparently a very good-natured, amiable fellow. He accompanied me to my hotel and, amongst other things, told me the circumstances connected with the performance of my overture. These somewhat surprised me. According to the terms of a legacy left by a wealthy citizen of Strasburg, a great lover of music, who had already contributed very largely to the building of the theatre, the orchestra, whose flourishing condition was due to his beneficence, had to give, during the usual theatrical performances, one of the greater instrumental works with a full band once a week. This time, as it happened, it was the turn for the overture to *Tannhäuser*. The feeling that was uppermost in my mind was one of envy that Strasburg should have produced a citizen whose like had never seen the light of day in any of the towns in which I had been connected with music, and more particularly Zürich.

Whilst I was discussing the state of music in Strasburg with Conductor Hasselmann, Orsini's famous attempt on the life of the Emperor took place in Paris. I heard some vague rumours of it on my journey the following morning, but it was not until the 17th, on my arrival in Paris, that I heard the full details of it from the waiter in my hotel. I looked upon this event as a malicious stroke of fate, aimed at me personally. Even at breakfast on the following morning, I feared I should see my old acquaintance, the agent of the Ministry of the Interior, walk in and demand my instant departure from Paris as a political refugee. I presumed that as a visitor at the Grand Hôtel du Louvre, then newly opened, I should be regarded by the police with greater respect, than at the little hotel at the corner of the Rue des Filles St. Thomas, where I had once stayed for the sake of economy. I had originally intended to take up my quarters at an hotel I knew in the Rue le Pelletier, but the outrage had been perpetrated just at that spot, and the principal criminals had been pursued and arrested there. It was a strange coincidence! Supposing I had arrived in Paris just two days earlier, and had gone there!!!

After thus apostrophising the demon of my fate, I hunted up M. Ollivier and his young wife. In the former I soon found a very taking and active friend, who at once resolutely took in hand the matter which was my chief object in Paris. One day we called on a notary who was a friend of his, and who seemed to be under an obligation to him. I there gave Ollivier a formal and carefully considered power of attorney, to represent my proprietary rights as author, and in spite of many official formalities in the way of stamps I was treated with perfect hospitality, so that I felt I was well sheltered under my friend's protection. In the course of my walks with my friend Ollivier in the Palais de Justice and in the Salle des pas perdus, I was introduced to the most celebrated lawyers in the world strolling about there in their berrettas and robes, and I was soon on such intimate terms with them that they formed a circle around me, and made me explain the subject of *Tannhäuser*. This pleased me greatly. I was no less delighted by my conversation with Ollivier regarding his political views and position. He still believed in the Republic which would come to stay after the inevitable overthrow of the Napoleonic rule. He and his friends did not intend to provoke a revolution, but they held themselves in readiness for the moment when it should come, as it necessarily must, and fully resolved this time not to give it up again to the plunder of base conspirators. In principle he agreed with the logical conclusions of socialism; he knew and respected Proudhon, but not as a politician; he thought nothing could be founded on a durable basis except through the initiative of political organisation. By means of simple legislation, which had already passed several enactments protecting the public good against the abuses of private privilege, even the boldest demands for a commonwealth based on equal rights for all would gradually be met.

I now noticed with great satisfaction that I had made considerable progress in the development of my character, as I could listen to and discuss these and other topics without getting into a state of excitement, as I used formally to do in similar discussions.

Blandine impressed me at the same time most favourably with her gentleness, her cheerfulness, and a certain quiet wit added to a quick mental perception. We very soon understood each other; the slightest suggestion sufficed to create a mutual understanding on any subject in which we were interested.

Sunday arrived, and with it a concert at the Conservatoire. As I had hitherto been present only at rehearsals, and had never got so far as the performances, my friends succeeded in procuring a seat for me in the box of Mme. Hérold, the widow of the composer, a woman of sympathetic disposition, who at once declared herself warmly in favour of my music. It is true her knowledge of it was slight, but she had been won over to it by the enthusiasm of her daughter and son-in-law, who, as I have previously mentioned, had heard *Tannhäuser* during their honeymoon in Vienna and Berlin. This was really a pleasant surprise. Added to this, I now heard for the first time in my life a performance of Haydn's *Seasons*, which the audience enjoyed immensely, as they thought the steady florid vocal cadences, which are so rare in modern music, but which so frequently occur at the conclusion of the musical phrases in Haydn's music, very original and charming. The rest of the day was spent very pleasantly in the bosom of the Hérold family. Towards the end of the evening a man came in whose appearance was hailed with marked attention. This was Herr Scudo, who, I found out afterwards, was the famous musical editor of the *Revue des deux Mondes*. His influence with other journals was considerable, but so far it had certainly not been in my favour. The kind hostess wished me to make his acquaintance, so that he might have a good impression of me, but I told her such an object could not be attained through the medium of a drawing-room conversation, and later on I was confirmed in my opinion that the reasons why a gentleman of this type, who possesses no knowledge of the subject, declares himself hostile to an artist, having nothing whatever to do with his convictions or even with his approval or disapproval. On a subsequent occasion these good people had to suffer for having interested themselves in me, as, in a report of my concerts by Herr Scudo, they were held up to ridicule as a family of strong democratic tendencies.

I now looked up my friend Berlioz, whose acquaintance I had recently renewed in London, and on the whole I found him kindly disposed.

I informed him that I had only just come to Paris on a short pleasure trip. He was at that time busy composing a grand opera, *Die Trojaner*. In order to get an impression of the work, I was particularly anxious to hear the libretto Berlioz had written himself, and he spent an evening reading it out to me. I was disappointed in it, not only as far as it was concerned, but also by his singularly dry and theatrical delivery. I fancied that in the latter I could see the character of the music to which he had set his words, and I sank into utter despair about it, as I could see that he regarded this as his masterpiece, and was looking forward to its production as the great object of his life.

I also received an invitation with the Olliviers from the Erard family, at whose house I again met my old friend the widow of Spontini. We spent a rather charming evening there, during which, strange to say, I had to be responsible for the musical entertainment at the piano. They declared they had thoroughly entered into the spirit of the various selections I had played from my operas in my now characteristic fashion, and that they had enjoyed them immensely. At any rate, such intimate heartfelt playing had never before been heard in that gorgeous drawing-room. Apart from this, I made one great acquisition, through the friendly courtesy of Mme. Erard and her brother-in-law Schäffer, who since the death of her husband had carried on the business, in the shape of a promise of one of the celebrated grand-pianos of their manufacture. With this the gloom of my excursion to Paris seemed to be turned into light, for I was so rejoiced at it, that I looked upon every other result as chimerical, and upon this as the only reality.

After that I left Paris on the 2nd of February in a more cheerful frame of mind, and on my homeward journey went to look up my old friend Kietz in Epernay, where M. Paul Chandon, who had known Kietz since boyhood, had interested himself in the ruined painter by taking him into his house, and giving him a number of commissions for portraits. As soon as I arrived I was irresistibly drawn into Chandon's hospitable house, and could not refuse to remain there for a couple of days. I found in Chandon a passionate admirer of my operas, particularly of *Rienzi,* the first performance of which he had witnessed during his Dresden days. I also visited the marvellous wine vaults at Champagne, which extended for miles into the heart of the rocky ground. Kietz was painting a portrait in oils, and the opinion entertained by every one that it would very soon be finished rather amused me.

After much superfluous entertainment I at last freed myself from this unexpected hospitality and returned to Zürich on the 5th of February, where I had arranged by letter for an evening party immediately after my arrival, as I thought I had much to relate which I could tell them all collectively instead of by means of long and wearisome communications to individual friends. Semper, who was one of the company, was annoyed that he had stayed in Zürich whilst I had been in Paris, and he became quite furious over my cheerful adventures and declared I was an impudent child of fortune, while he looked upon it as the greatest calamity that he should be chained to that wretched hole Zürich. How I smiled inwardly at his envy of my fortune!

My affairs were making but little progress, as my operas had been sold to almost every theatre and I had very little left out of the proceeds. I now heard nothing about all these performances except that they were yielding very little money. I resigned myself to the fact of bringing out *Rienzi,* as it was just suited to our inferior class of theatre. Before offering it for sale, it was desirable to have it performed again in Dresden; but this, it was said, was impossible on account of the impression created by the Orsini outrage. So I worked on at the instrumentation of the first act of *Tristan,* and during that time I could not help feeling that most probably other objections, besides those of political captiousness, would be raised against the spread of this work. I therefore continued my work vaguely and somewhat hopelessly.

In the month of March Frau Wesendonck informed me that she thought of having a kind of musical entertainment in her house to celebrate her husband's birthday. She had a predilection for a little serenade music, which, with the help of eight instrumentalists from Zürich, I had arranged during the winter for the occasion of her own birthday. The pride of the Wesendonck villa was a spacious hall which had been very elegantly decorated by Parisian stucco-workers, and I had once remarked that music would not sound at all badly there. We had tested it on a small scale, but now it was to be tried on a larger one. I offered to bring together a respectable orchestra to perform fragments of the Beethoven symphonies, consisting mainly of the brighter parts, for the entertainment of the company. The necessary preparations required a good deal of time, and the date of the birthday had to be overstepped. As it was, we had nearly reached Easter, and our concert took place almost at the end of March. The musical At Home was most successful. A full orchestra for the Beethoven pieces played with the greatest éclat under my conductorship, to the assembly of guests scattered about in the surrounding rooms, selections from the symphonies. Such an unprecedented home concert seemed to throw every one into a great state of excitement.

The young daughter of the house presented me at the beginning of the performance with an ivory baton, carved from a design by Semper, the first and only complimentary one I ever received. There was no lack of flowers and ornamental trees, under which I stood when conducting, and when to suit my taste for musical effect we concluded, not with a loud, but with a deeply soothing piece, like the *Adagio* from the Ninth Symphony, we felt that Zürich society had indeed witnessed something quite unique, and my friends on whom I had bestowed this mark of distinction were deeply touched by it.

This festival left on me the most melancholy impressions; I felt as though I had reached the meridian of my life, that I had in fact passed it, and that the string of the bow was overstretched. Mme. Wille told me afterwards that she had been overcome by similar feelings on that evening. On the 3rd of April I sent the manuscript of the score of the first act of *Tristan und Isolde* to Leipzig to be engraved; I had already promised to give Frau Wesendonck the pencil-sketch for the instrumentation of the prelude, and I sent this to her accompanied by a note in which I explained to her seriously and calmly the feelings that animated me at the time. My wife had for some time been anxious as to her relations with our neighbour; she complained with increasing bitterness that she was not treated by her with the attention due to the wife of a man whom Frau Wesendonck was so pleased to welcome in her house, and that when we did meet, it was rather by reason of that lady's visits to me than to her. So far she had not really expressed any jealousy. As she happened to be in the garden that morning, she met the servant carrying the packet for Frau Wesendonck, took it from him and opened the letter. As she was quite incapable of understanding the state of mind I had described in the letter, she readily gave a vulgar interpretation to my words, and accordingly felt herself justified in bursting into my room and attacking me with the most extraordinary reproaches about the terrible discovery she had made. She afterwards admitted that nothing had vexed her so much as the extreme calmness and apparent indifference with which

I treated her foolish conduct. As a matter of fact I never said a word; I hardly moved, but simply allowed her to depart. I could not help realising that this was henceforth to be the intolerable character of the conjugal relations I had resumed eight years before. I told her peremptorily to keep quiet and not be guilty of any blunder either in judgment or in act, and tried to make her realise to what a serious state of affairs this foolish occurrence had brought us. She really seemed to understand what I meant, and promised to keep quiet and not to give way to her absurd jealousy. Unfortunately the poor creature was already suffering from a serious development of heart disease, which affected her temper; she could not throw off the peculiar depression and terrible restlessness which enlargement of the heart causes, and only a few days after she felt that she must relieve her feelings, and the only possible way in which she could think of doing so was by warning our neighbour, Frau Wesendonck, with an emphasis she thought was well meant, against the consequences of any imprudent intimacy with me.

As I was returning from a walk I met Herr Wesendonck and his wife in their carriage just starting for a drive. I noticed her troubled demeanour in contrast to the peculiarly smiling and contented expression of her husband. I realised the position clearly when I afterwards met my wife looking wonderfully cheerful. She held out her hand to me with great generosity, assuring me of her renewed affection. In answer to my question, whether she had by any chance broken her promise, she said confidently that like a wise woman she had been obliged to put things into proper order. I told her she would very probably experience some very unpleasant consequences through breaking her word. In the first place, I thought it essential she should take steps to improve her health as we had previously arranged, and told her she had better go as soon as possible to the health resort she had been recommended at Brestenberg on the Hallwyler Lake. We had heard wonderful accounts of the cures of heart disease which the doctor there had effected, and Minna was quite prepared to submit to his treatment. A few days later, therefore, I took her and her parrot to the pleasantly situated and well-appointed watering-place which was about three hours distant. Meantime, I avoided asking any questions as to what had taken place in regard to our neighbours. When I left her at Brestenberg and took my leave she quite seemed to realise the painful seriousness of our position. I could say very little to comfort her, except that I would try, in the interests of our future life together, to mitigate the dreaded consequences of her having broken her word.

On my return home I experienced the unpleasant effects of my wife's conduct towards our neighbour. In Minna's utter misconstruction of my purely friendly relations with the young wife, whose only interest in me consisted in her solicitude for my peace of mind and well-being, she had gone so far as to threaten to inform the lady's husband. Frau Wesendonck felt so deeply insulted at this, as she was perfectly unconscious of having done any wrong, that she was absolutely astounded at me, and said she could not conceive how I could have led my wife into such a misunderstanding. The outcome of this disturbance was that, thanks to the discreet mediation of our mutual friend Mme. Wille, I was absolved from any responsibility for my wife's conduct; still, I was given to understand that henceforth it would be impossible for the injured lady to enter my house again, or indeed to continue to have any intercourse with my wife. They did not seem to realise, and would not admit, that this would entail the giving up of my home and my removal from Zürich. I hoped that although my relations with these good friends had been disturbed, they were not really destroyed, and that time would smooth things over. I felt that I must look forward to an improvement in my wife's health, when she would admit her folly, and thus be able to resume her intercourse with our neighbours in a reasonable manner.

Some time elapsed, during which the Wesendonck family took a pleasure trip of several weeks to Northern Italy.

The arrival of the promised Erard grand-piano made me painfully conscious of what a tin kettle my old grand-piano from Breitkopf und Härtel had been, and I forthwith banished it to the lower regions, where my wife begged she might keep it as a souvenir ' of old times.' She afterwards took it with her to Saxony, where she sold it for three hundred marks. The new piano appealed to my musical sense immensely, and whilst I was improvising I seemed to drift quite naturally into the soft nocturnal sounds of the second act of *Tristan*, the composition of which I now began to sketch out. This was at the beginning of May. My work was unexpectedly interrupted by the command of the Grand Duke of Weimar to meet him on a certain day in Lucerne, where he was staying after his return from Italy. I availed myself of this opportunity to have a lengthy interview at the hotel in Chamberlain von Beaulieu's room, with my former nominal patron whose acquaintance I had made at the time of my flight.

From this interview with Karl Alexander I gathered that my attitude towards the Grand Duke of Baden, in regard to the performance of *Tristan*, in Karlsruhe, had made an impression on the Weimar court, for while he made particular mention of that matter, I gathered from what he said that he was also anxious about my *Nibelungen* work, in which he declared he had always taken the liveliest interest, and wanted my assurance that this composition would be produced at Weimar. I had no serious objection to that. Moreover, I was vastly entertained by the personality of this free-and-easy good-natured Prince, who, though he sat chatting next to me on a narrow sofa, was evidently anxious by his singularly choice language to impress me as a man of culture. I was much struck to find that his dignified bearing was not in the least disturbed when Herr von Beaulieu, with the object of amusing us, made some rather clumsy remarks which were meant to be witty. After the Grand Duke had asked me in the most guarded way my opinion of Liszt's compositions, I was surprised to notice by his general bearing that he was not at all uncomfortable when the chamberlain expressed the most contemptuous opinions about the Grand Duke's famous friend, saying that Liszt's composing was a mere mania on his part. This gave me a strange insight into this royal friendship, and I had some difficulty in keeping serious during the interview. I had to pay the Grand Duke another visit on the following morning, but on that occasion I saw him without his chamberlain, whose absence certainly had a favourable effect on the Prince's remarks about his friend

Liszt, whose inspiring conversation and advice he loudly asserted that he could not praise enough. I was surprised to see the Grand Duchess walk in upon us, and was received by her with a most condescending bow, the formality of which I have never forgotten. I looked upon my meeting with these exalted personages as an exceedingly amusing adventure in my travels. I have never heard from them since.[1] Later on, when I called on Liszt at Weimar, just before he left there, he could not even induce the Grand Duke to receive me!

A short time after my return from that expedition Karl Tausig called with a letter of introduction from Liszt; he was then sixteen years of age, and astonished everybody by his dainty appearance and his unusual precocity of understanding and demeanour. He had already been greeted in Vienna, on his public appearance as a pianist, as a future Liszt. He gave himself all the airs of a Liszt, and already smoked the strongest cigars to such an extent that I felt a perfect horror of them. Otherwise I was very glad he had made up his mind to spend some time in the neighbourhood, all the more so as I could appreciate to the utmost his amusing, half-childish, though very intelligent and knowing personality, and, above all, his exceptionally finished piano-playing and quick musical faculty. He played the most complicated pieces at sight, and knew how to use his astonishing facility in the most extravagant tricks for my entertainment. He afterwards came to live quite near us; he was my daily guest at all meals, and accompanied me on my usual walks to the Sihlthal. He soon tried to wriggle out of these, however. He also went with me on a visit to Minna at Brestenberg. As I had to repeat these expeditions regularly every week, being anxious to watch the result of the treatment, Tausig endeavoured to escape from these also, as neither Brestenberg nor Minna's conversation seemed to appeal to him. However, he could not avoid meeting her when, feeling obliged to interrupt her cure for a few days to look after her household affairs, she returned at the end of May. I noticed by her manner that she no longer attached any importance to the recent domestic upheaval; the view she took of the matter was that there had been a little 'love affair'

[1] This was dictated in 1869.

which she had put straight. As she referred to this with a certain amount of unpleasant levity, I was obliged, though I would willingly have spared her on account of the state of her health, to explain clearly and firmly, that in consequence of her disobedience and her foolish conduct towards our neighbour, the possibility of our remaining on the estate, where we had only just settled with so much difficulty, was a matter of the most serious doubt, and I felt bound to warn her that we must be prepared for the necessity of a separation, as I was fully determined that if this dreaded event took place, I would not agree to live under similar domestic conditions elsewhere. The earnestness with which I dwelt on the character of our past life together, on that occasion, so impressed and shocked her that, fully realising it was through her fault that the home it had cost us so much pain to build up had been destroyed, she broke into a low wail of lamentation for the first time in our lives. This was the first and only occasion on which she gave me any token of loving humility, when late at night she kissed my hand as I withdrew. I was deeply touched at this, and the idea flashed across my mind that possibly a great and decided change might take place in the character of the poor woman, and this determined me to renew my hope of the possibility of continuing the life we had resumed.

Everything contributed to the maintenance of this hope: my wife returned to Brestenberg to complete the second part of her cure; the most glorious summer weather favoured my disposition to work at the second act of *Tristan*; the evenings with Tausig cheered me up, and my relations with my neighbours, who had never borne me any ill-will, seemed to me to favour the possibility of a dignified and desirable understanding in the future. It was quite probable that if my wife went on a visit to her friends in Saxony after her cure, time would eventually cover the past with oblivion, and her own future conduct as well as the changed attitude of our deeply offended neighbour, would make it possible to renew our mutual intercourse in a dignified way.

I was still further cheered by the prospect of the arrival of an agreeable visitor, as well as by some satisfactory negotiations with two of the most important German theatres.

In June the Berlin manager approached me about *Lohengrin,* and we soon came to an agreement. In Vienna, too, the forced intrusion of *Tannhäuser* had produced its effect on the attitude of the management of the court theatre. Just recently the well-known conductor, Karl Eckert, had been entrusted with the technical management of the Opera. He seized the happy opportunity afforded by the possession of a very good company of singers, and by the closing of the theatre for much needed restoration, to give the company time to study *Lohengrin,* with the object of securing the acceptance of this new and difficult work by the court authorities. He thereupon made me his offers. I wanted to insist on the author's rights on the same terms as those granted in Berlin, but he would not agree to this, because the takings of the house were very small, owing to the lack of space in the old theatre. On the other hand, Conductor Esser called on me one day; he had come from Vienna to make all arrangements, and in the name of the management he offered me about two thousand marks, cash down, for the first twenty performances of *Lohengrin,* and promised me a further sum of two thousand marks on their completion. The frank and genial manner of the worthy musician won me over, and I closed with him at once. The result was that Esser went through the score of *Lohengrin* with me there and then, with great conscientiousness and zeal, and paid special attention to all my wishes. With every confidence in a favourable result I bid him farewell, and he hurried back to Vienna to set to work at once.

I then completed the composition sketches for the second act of *Tristan* in excellent spirits, and began the more detailed execution of it, but I did not get quite through the first scene, as I was exposed to continual interruptions. Tichatschek came to pay me another visit, and took up his abode in my little spare room, to recover, as he said, from the effects of his recent exertions. He boasted that he had again introduced my operas, which had been repeatedly forbidden, into the repertoire of the Dresden theatre, and had also taken part in them himself with great success.

Lohengrin was also to be produced there. Although this was very gratifying, I did not in the least know what to do with

the good man at such close quarters. Fortunately I was able
to hand him over to Tausig, who understood my embarrassment, and kept Tichatschek to himself pretty well the whole
day, by playing cards with him. The young tenor Niemann,
of whose great talent I had heard so much, soon arrived with
his bride, the famous actress Seebach, and owing to his almost
gigantic frame, he struck me as being just the man for
Siegfried. The fact of having two famous tenors with me
at the same time gave rise to the annoyance that neither of
them would sing anything to me, as they were ill at ease in
each other's presence. I quite believed, however, that Niemann's
voice must be on a par with his imposing personality. About
that time (15th July) I fetched my wife from Brestenberg.
During my absence my servant, who was a cunning Saxon,
had thought fit to erect a kind of triumphal arch to celebrate
the return of the mistress of the house. This led to
great complications, as, much to her delight, Minna was convinced that this flower-bedecked triumphal arch would greatly
attract the attention of our neighbours, and thought this would
be sufficient to prevent them from regarding her return home
as a humiliating one. She insisted with triumphant joy upon
the decorations remaining up for several days. About the same
time the Bülows, true to their promise, paid another visit.
The unfortunate Tichatschek again put off his departure, and
consequently continued to occupy our one small spare
room, so I was obliged to let my friends stay at the
hotel several days longer. However, the visits they paid to
the Wesendoncks as well as to me soon afforded me an opportunity of hearing, much to my surprise, of the effect the
triumphal arch had produced on our neighbour's young
wife, who was still nursing her injured feelings. When I
heard of her passionate protests I realised to what a pass things
had come, and immediately gave up all hope of putting
a peaceful end to the discordant situation. Those were days
of terrible anxiety. I wished myself in the most distant desert,
and yet was in the awkward position of having to keep my
house open to a succession of visitors. At last Tichatschek
took his departure, and I could at least devote the remainder
of my stay to the pleasant duty of entertaining favourite

guests. The Bülows really seemed to me to have been providentially sent for the purpose of quelling the horrible excitement that prevailed in the house. Hans made the best of things when, on the day of his arrival, he caught me in the midst of a terrific scene with Minna, as I had just told her plainly that from what I could see of the present position of affairs, our stay here was no longer possible, and that I was only deferring my departure until after the visit of our young friends. This time, however, I had to admit that she was not altogether to blame.

We spent another whole month together in the cottage, which, by the way, I had unconsciously christened Asyl. It was an extremely trying period, and the experiences I went through every day only confirmed me in my decision to give up the house. Under the circumstances my young guests also had to suffer, as my worry communicated itself to all who were in sympathy with me. Klindworth, who was coming on a visit from London, to add to the gloom of this extraordinary ménage, soon joined us. So the house was suddenly filled, and the table surrounded by sad, mysteriously depressed guests, whose wants were ministered to by one who was shortly to leave her home for ever.

It seemed to me that there must be one human being in existence specially qualified to bring light and reconciliation, or at least tolerable order, into the gloom and trouble by which we were all surrounded. Liszt had promised me a visit, but he was so happily situated beyond the reach of these harassing conditions, he had had such experience of the world, and possessed that innate *aplomb* to such an extraordinary degree, that he did not seem to me to be very likely to approach these misunderstandings in a rational spirit. I almost felt inclined to make my final decision dependent on the effect of his expected visit. It was in vain that we begged of him to hasten his journey; he offered to meet me at the Lake of Geneva a month later! Then my courage failed. Intercourse with my friends now afforded me no satisfaction, for although they could not understand why I should be turned out of a home that suited me so well, yet it was apparent to every one that I could not remain under these

conditions. We still had music every now and then, but it
was in a half-hearted and absent-minded fashion. To make
matters worse, we had a national vocal festival inflicted upon
us, during which I was obliged to face all kinds of demands;
matters did not always pass off without unpleasantness, as
amongst others I had to decline to see Franz Lachner, who
had been specially engaged for the festival, and did not return
his call. Tausig certainly delighted us by carolling Lachner's
' Old German Battle Song' in the upper octave, which, thanks
to his boyish falsetto, was within his reach; however, even his
pranks were no longer able to cheer us. Everything, which
under other circumstances would have made this summer month
one of the most stimulating in my life, now contributed to
my discomfort, as did also the stay of the Countess d'Agoult,
who, having come on a visit to her daughter and son-in-law,
attached herself to our party for the time being. By way
of filling up the house, Karl Ritter also came after much
grumbling and sulking, and once again proved himself to be
very interesting and original.

As the time for the general leave-taking at last drew near, I
had arranged all the details connected with the breaking up of
my home. I settled the necessary business part by a personal
visit to Herr Wesendonck, and in the presence of Bülow I took
leave of Frau Wesendonck, who, in spite of her ever-recurring
misconceptions on the matter, eventually reproached herself
bitterly when she saw that these misunderstandings had ended
by breaking up my home. My friends were much distressed
at parting from me, whilst I could only meet their expressions
of sorrow with apathy. On the 16th August the Bülows also
left; Hans was bathed in tears and his wife Cosima was gloomy
and silent. I had arranged with Minna that she should remain
there for about a week to clear up and dispose of our little
belongings as she thought best. I had advised her to entrust
these unpleasant duties to some one else, as I hardly thought it
possible that she would be fitted for such a wretched task,
which, under the circumstances, would be very trying to her.
She replied reproachfully that ' it would be a fine thing if,
with all our misfortunes, we neglected our property. Order
there must be.' I afterwards learned to my disgust that she

carried out the removal and her own departure with such formality, by advertising in the daily papers that the effects would be sold cheaply owing to sudden departure, and thereby exciting much curiosity, that perplexed rumours were spread about giving the whole affair a scandalous signification, which afterwards caused much unpleasantness both to me and the Wesendonck family.

On the 17th August, the day after the departure of the Bülows (whose stay had been the only reason for detaining me), I got up at early dawn after a sleepless night, and went down into the dining-room, where Minna was already expecting me to breakfast, as I intended to start by the five o'clock train. She was calm; it was only when accompanying me in the carriage to the station that she was overpowered by her emotion under the trying circumstances. It was the most brilliant summer day with a bright, cloudless sky; I remember that I never once looked back, or shed a tear on taking leave of her, and this almost terrified me. As I travelled along in the train I could not conceal from myself an increasing feeling of comfort; it was obvious that the absolutely useless worries of the past weeks could not have been endured any longer, and that my life's ambition demanded a complete severance from them. On the evening of the same day I arrived in Geneva; here I wished to rest a little and pull myself together, so as to arrange my plan of life calmly. As I had an idea of making another attempt to settle in Italy, I proposed, after my former experience, to wait till the cooler autumn weather, so as not to expose myself again to the malignant influence of the sudden change of climate. I arranged to stay for a month at the Maison Fazy, deluding myself into the idea that a lengthy stay there would be very pleasant. I told Karl Ritter, who was at Lausanne, of my intention of going to Italy, and to my surprise he wrote saying that he also intended to give up his home and go to Italy alone, as his wife was going to Saxony for the winter on account of family affairs. He offered himself as my travelling companion. This suited me excellently, and as Ritter also assured me that he knew, from a previous visit, that the climate of Venice was quite agreeable at this season, I was induced to make a hasty departure. I had, however, to ar-

range about my passport. I expected that the embassies in
Berne would corroborate the fact that as a political refugee
I should have nothing to fear in Venice, which, although belonging to Austria, did not form part of the German Confederation. Liszt, to whom I also applied for information on
this point, advised me on no account to go to Venice; on
the other hand, the report that some of my friends in Berne
obtained from the Austrian ambassador pronounced it as quite
safe; so, after barely a week's stay in Geneva, I informed
Karl Ritter of my readiness to start, and called for him at
his villa in Lausanne, so that we might begin the journey
together.

We did not talk much on the way, but gave ourselves up
silently to our impressions. The route was over the Simplon
to Lake Maggiore, where I again visited the Borromean Islands
from Baveno. There, on the terrace garden of Isola Bella,
I spent a wonderful late summer morning in the company
of my young friend, who was never obtrusive, but, on the
contrary, inclined to be too silent. For the first time I felt
my mind entirely at rest, and filled with the hope of a new
and harmonious future. We continued our journey by coach
through Sesto Calende to Milan; and Karl was filled with such
a longing for his beloved Venice, that he could barely grant me
time to admire the famous Duomo; but I had no objection
to being hurried with this object in view. As we were looking
from the railway dike at Venice rising before us from the
mirror of water, Karl lost his hat out of the carriage owing
to an enthusiastic movement of delight; I thought that I
must follow suit, so I too threw my hat out; consequently
we arrived in Venice bareheaded, and immediately got into a
gondola to go down the Grand Canal as far as the Piazzetta
near San Marco. The weather had suddenly become gloomy,
and the aspect of the gondolas quite shocked me; for, in spite
of what I had heard about these peculiar vessels draped in
black, the sight of one was an unpleasant surprise: when I
had to go under the black awning, I could not help remembering the cholera-scare some time earlier. I certainly felt I
was taking part in a funeral procession during a pestilence.
Karl assured me that every one felt the same at first, but that

one soon got accustomed to it. Next came the long sail through the twists and turns of the Grand Canal. The impression that everything made on me here did not tend to dispel my melancholy frame of mind. Where Karl, on looking at the ruined walls, only saw the Cà d'Oro of Fanny Elser or some other famous palace, my doleful glances were completely absorbed by the crumbling ruins between these interesting buildings. At last I became silent, and allowed myself to be put down at the world-famous Piazzetta, and to be shown the palace of the Doges, though I reserved to myself the right of admiring it until I had freed myself from the extremely melancholy mood into which my arrival in Venice had thrown me.

Starting on the following morning from the Hôtel Danieli, where we had found only a gloomy lodging, I began by looking for a residence that would suit me for my prolonged stay. I heard that one of the three Giustiniani palaces, situated not far from the Palazzo Foscari, was at present very little patronised by visitors, on account of its situation, which in the winter is somewhat unfavourable. I found some very spacious and imposing apartments there, all of which they told me would remain uninhabited. I here engaged a large stately room with a spacious bedroom adjoining. I had my luggage quickly transferred there, and on the evening of 30th August I said to myself, ' At last I am living in Venice.' My leading idea was that I could work here undisturbed. I immediately wrote to Zürich asking for my Erard ' Grand ' and my bed to be sent on to me, as, with regard to the latter, I felt that I should find out what cold meant in Venice. In addition to this, the grey-washed walls of my large room soon annoyed me, as they were so little suited to the ceiling, which was covered with a fresco which I thought was rather tasteful. I decided to have the walls of the large room covered with hangings of a dark-red shade, even if they were of quite common quality. This immediately caused much trouble; but it seemed to me that it was well worth surmounting, when I gazed down from my balcony with growing satisfaction on the wonderful canal, and said to myself that here I would complete *Tristan*. I also had a little more decorating done;

I arranged to have dark-red portières, even if they were of the cheapest material, to cover the common doors which the Hungarian landlord had had put into the ruined palace in place of the original valuable ones, which had probably been sold. In addition, the host had contrived to get some showy furniture, such as a few gilded chairs, covered with common cotton plush; but the most prominent article was a finely carved gilded table-pedestal, on which was placed a vulgar pinewood top which I had to cover with a plain red cloth. Finally the Erard arrived; it was placed in the middle of the large room, and now wonderful Venice was to be attacked by music.

However, the dysentery I had previously suffered from in Genoa laid hold of me again, and rendered me incapable of any intellectual activity for weeks. I had already learned to appreciate the matchless beauty of Venice, and I was full of hope that my joy in it would give me back my power to satisfy my reviving artistic yearnings. On one of my first promenades on the Riva I was accosted by two strangers, one of whom introduced himself as Count Edmund Zichy, the other as Prince Dolgoroukow. They had both left Vienna barely a week before, where they had been present at the first performances of my *Lohengrin;* they gave me the most satisfactory reports about the result of it, and by their enthusiasm I could see that their impressions were very favourable. Count Zichy left Venice soon afterwards, but Prince Dolgoroukow decided to stay on for the winter. Although I certainly intended to avoid company, this Russian, who was about fifty years of age, soon managed to make me yield to his persuasions. He had an earnest and extremely expressive face (he prided himself on being of direct Caucasian descent), and showed remarkable culture in every respect, a wide knowledge of the world, and above all a taste for music, in the literature of which he was also so well versed that it amounted to a passion. I had at first explained to him that owing to the state of my health I was bound to renounce all society, and that I needed quiet more than anything. Apart from the difficulty of avoiding him altogether on the limited walks in Venice, the restaurant at Albergo San Marco where I joined Ritter every day for meals led to inevitable meetings with this stranger, to whom I eventually became sincerely attached. He had taken up his abode in that hotel, and I could not prevent him from taking his meals there. During my stay in Venice we met almost daily, and continued to be on very friendly terms. On the other hand I had a great surprise, on returning to my apartments one evening, to be informed that Liszt had just arrived. I rushed eagerly to the room pointed out to me as his, and there, to my horror, saw Winterberger the pianist, who had introduced himself to my host as a mutual friend of myself and of Liszt, and in the confusion of the moment the host had concluded that the new arrival was Liszt himself. As a matter of fact I had recently got to know this young man as a follower of Liszt during his comparatively long stay in Zürich; he was considered an excellent organist, and was also called into requisition as second at the piano when there were arrangements for two pianofortes. Except for some foolish behaviour on his part I had not noticed anything particular about him. I was surprised, however, that he should have selected my address as his lodging in Venice. He told me that he was merely the precursor of a certain Princess Galitzin, for whom he had to arrange winter quarters in Venice; that he knew nobody there, but having heard in Vienna that I was staying here, it was very natural he should apply first at my hotel. I argued with him that this was not an hotel, and announced that if his Russian Princess thought of taking up her abode next to me, I should move out at once. He then reassured me, by telling me that he had only wanted to make a good impression on the host by mentioning the Princess, as he thought she had already engaged rooms elsewhere. As I again asked what he thought of doing in this palace, and drew his attention to the fact that it was very expensive, and that I put up with the large outlay simply because it was most essential that I should be undisturbed, and have no neighbours, and hear no piano, he tried to pacify me by the assurance that he would certainly not be a burden to me, and that I could make my mind easy about his presence in the same house until he could arrange to move elsewhere. His next attempt was to work his way into the good graces of Karl Ritter; they both discovered a living-room in the palace at a sufficient distance from mine to be out of earshot. In this way I consented to put up with his proximity, although it was a long time before I allowed Ritter to bring him to me of an evening.

A Venetian piano-teacher, Tessarin by name, was more successful than Winterberger in winning favour with me. He was a typical handsome Venetian, with a curious impediment in his speech; he had a passion for German music, and was well acquainted with Liszt's new compositions, and also with my own operas. He admitted that having regard to his surroundings he was a 'white raven' in matters musical. He also succeeded in approaching me through Ritter, who seemed to be devoting himself in Venice to the study of human nature rather than to work. He had taken a small and extremely modest dwelling on the Riva dei Schiavoni, which, being in a sunny position, required no artificial heating. This was in reality less for himself than for his scanty luggage, as he was hardly ever at home, but was running about in the daytime after pictures and collections; in the evening, however, he studied human nature in the cafés on the Piazza San Marco. He was the only person I saw regularly every day; otherwise I rigorously avoided any other society or acquaintance. I was repeatedly asked by the Princess Galitzin's private physician to call upon that lady, who came to Venice very shortly and appeared to be living in grand style. Once, when I wanted the piano scores of *Tannhäuser* and *Lohengrin,* and had heard that the Princess was the only person in Venice who possessed them, I was bold enough to ask her for them, but I did not feel it incumbent on me to call on her for that purpose. On only one occasion did any stranger succeed in interrupting my seclusion, and then it was because his appearance had pleased me when I had met him in the Albergo San Marco; this was Rahl the painter, from Vienna. I once went so far as to arrange a sort of soirée for him, Prince Dolgoroukow, and Tessarin the pianoforte teacher, at which a few of my pieces were played. It was then that Winterberger made his début.

All my social experiences during the seven months I spent in Venice were limited to these few attempts at friendly intercourse, and apart from these my days were planned out with the utmost regularity during the whole time. I worked till two o'clock, then I got into the gondola that was always in waiting, and was taken along the solemn Grand Canal to the bright Piazzetta, the peculiar charm of which always had a cheerful effect on me. After this I made for my restaurant in the Piazza San Marco, and when I had finished my meal I walked alone or with Karl along the Riva to the Giardino Pubblico, the only pleasure-ground in Venice where there are any trees, and at nightfall I came back in the gondola down the canal, then more sombre and silent, till I reached the spot where I could see my solitary lamp shining from the night-shrouded façade of the old Palazzo Giustiniani. After I had worked a little longer Karl, heralded by the swish of the gondola, would come in regularly at eight o'clock for a few hours' chat over our tea. Very rarely did I vary this routine by a visit to one of the theatres. When I did, I preferred the performances at the Camploi Theatre, where Goldoni's pieces were very well played; but I seldom went to the opera, and when I did go it was merely out of curiosity. More frequently, when bad weather deprived us of our walk, we patronised the popular drama at the Malibran Theatre, where the performances were given in the daytime. The admission cost us six kreuzers. The audiences were excellent, the majority being in their shirt-sleeves, and the pieces given were generally of the ultra-melo-dramatic type. However, one day to my great astonishment and intense delight I saw there *Le Baruffe Chioggiote*, the grotesque comedy that had appealed so strongly to Goethe in his day, at this very theatre. So true to nature was this performance that it surpassed anything of the kind I have ever witnessed.

There was little else that attracted my attention in the oppressed and degenerate life of the Venetian people, and the only impression I derived from the exquisite ruin of this wonderful city as far as human interest is concerned was that of a watering-place kept up for the benefit of visitors. Strangely enough, it was the thoroughly German element of good military music, to which so much attention is paid in the Austrian army, that brought me into touch with public life in Venice. The conductors in the two Austrian regiments quartered there began playing overtures of mine, *Rienzi* and *Tannhäuser* for instance, and invited me to attend their practices in their barracks. There I also met the whole staff of officers, and was treated by them with great respect. These bands played on alternate evenings amid brilliant illuminations in the middle of the Piazza San Marco, whose acoustic properties for this class of production were really excellent. I was often suddenly startled towards the end of my meal by the sound of my own overtures; then, as I sat at the restaurant window giving myself up to impressions of the music, I did not know which dazzled me most, the incomparable piazza magnificently illuminated and filled with countless numbers of moving people, or the music that seemed to be borne away in rustling glory to the winds. Only one thing was wanting that might certainly have been expected from an Italian audience: the people were gathered round the band in thousands listening most intently, but no two hands ever forgot themselves so far as to applaud, as the least sign of approbation of Austrian military music would have been looked upon as treason to the Italian Fatherland. All public life in Venice also suffered by this extraordinary rift between the general public and the authorities; this was peculiarly apparent in the relations of the population to the Austrian officers, who floated about publicly in Venice like oil on water. The populace, too, behaved with no less reserve, or one might even say hostility, to the clergy, who were for the most part of Italian origin. I saw a procession of clerics in their vestments passing along the Piazza San Marco accompanied by the people with unconcealed derision.

It was very difficult for Ritter to induce me to interrupt my daily arrangements even to visit a gallery or a church, though, whenever we had to pass through the town, the exceedingly varied architectonic peculiarities and beauties always delighted me afresh. But the frequent gondola trips towards the Lido constituted my chief enjoyment during practically the whole of my stay in Venice. It was more especially on our homeward journeys at sunset that I was always overpowered by unique impressions. During the first part of our stay in the September of that year we saw on one of these occasions the marvellous apparition of the great comet, which at that time was at its highest brilliancy, and was generally said to portend an imminent catastrophe. The singing of a popular choral society, trained by an official of the Venetian arsenal, seemed like a real lagoon idyll. They generally sang only three-part naturally harmonised folk-songs. It was new to me not to hear the higher voice rise above the compass of the alto, that is to say, without touching the soprano, thereby imparting to the sound of the chorus a manly youthfulness hitherto unknown to me. On fine evenings they glided down the Grand Canal in a large illuminated gondola, stopping before a few palaces as if to serenade (when requested and paid for so doing, be it understood), and generally attracted a number of other gondolas in their wake. During one sleepless night, when I felt impelled to go out on to my balcony in the small hours, I heard for the first time the famous old folk-song of the *gondolieri*. I seemed to hear the first call, in the stillness of the night, proceeding from the Rialto about a mile away like a rough lament, and answered in the same tone from a yet further distance in another direction. This melancholy dialogue, which was repeated at longer intervals, affected me so much that I could not fix the very simple musical component parts in my memory. However, on a subsequent occasion I was told that this folk-song was of great poetic interest. As I was returning home late one night on the gloomy canal, the moon appeared suddenly and illuminated the marvellous palaces and the tall figure of my gondolier towering above the stern of the gondola, slowly moving his huge sweep. Suddenly he uttered a deep wail, not unlike the cry of an animal; the cry gradually gained in strength, and formed itself, after a long-drawn 'Oh!' into the simple musical exclamation 'Venezia!' This was followed by other sounds of which I have no distinct recollection, as I was so much moved at the time. Such were the impressions that to me appeared the most characteristic of Venice during my stay there, and they remained with me until the completion of the second act of *Tristan*, and possibly even suggested to me the long-drawn wail of the shepherd's horn at the beginning of the third act.

These sensations, however, did not manifest themselves

very easily or consecutively. Bodily sufferings and my usual
cares, that never quite left me, often considerably hindered and
disturbed my work. I had scarcely settled down comfortably
in my rooms, the northerly aspect of which exposed them to
frequent gusts of wind (from which I had practically no protection in the form of heating appliances), and had barely got over
the demoralising effect of dysentery, when I fell a victim to a
specific Venetian complaint, namely a carbuncle on my leg, as
the result of the extreme change of climate and of air. This
happened just when I was intending to resume the second act,
that had been so cruelly interrupted. The malady, which
I had first regarded as slight, soon increased and became exceedingly painful, and I was obliged to call in a doctor, who
had to treat me carefully for nearly four weeks. It was in the
late autumn, towards the end of November, that Ritter left
me to pay a visit to his relations and friends in Dresden and
Berlin; I therefore remained quite alone during this long illness, with no other society than that of the servants of the
house. Incapable of work, I amused myself by reading the
History of Venice by Count Daru, in which I became much
interested, as I was on the spot. Through it I lost some of
my popular prejudices against the tyrannical mode of government in ancient Venice. The ill-famed Council of Ten and
the State Inquisition appeared to me in a peculiar, although
certainly horrible, light; the open admission that in the
secrecy of its methods lay the guarantee of the power of the
state, seemed to me so decidedly in the interests of each and
every member of the marvellous republic, that the suppression
of all knowledge was very wisely considered a republican duty.
Actual hypocrisy was entirely foreign to this state constitution;
moreover the clerical element, however respectfully treated by
the government, never exercised an unworthy influence on the
development of the character of the citizens as in other parts
of Italy. The terrible selfish calculations of state reasons were
turned into maxims of quite an ancient heathen character,
not really evil in themselves, but reminiscent of similar
maxims among the Athenians, which, as we read in Thucydides,
were adopted by them in all simplicity, as the foundations of
human morality.

In addition to this I once more took up, by way of a restorative, as I had often done before, a volume of Schopenhauer, with whom I became on intimate terms, and I experienced a sensation of relief when I found that I was now able to explain the tormenting gaps in his system by the aids which he himself provided.

My few associations with the outer world now became calmer, but one day I was distressed by a letter from Wesendonck in which he informed me of the death of his son Guido, who was about four years old; it depressed me to think that I had refused to stand godfather to him, on the pretext that I might bring him bad luck. This event touched me deeply, and as I was longing for a thorough rest, I mapped out for myself a short journey across the Alps, with the idea that I might spend Christmas with my old friends, and offer them my condolences. I informed Mme. Wille of this idea, and in reply received, strange to say, from her husband instead of from herself, some quite unexpected particulars regarding the extremely unpleasant curiosity which my sudden departure from Zürich had caused, especially in reference to the part my wife had played in it, and at which the Wesendonck family had been so much annoyed. As I also heard how skilfully Wesendonck had treated the matter, some agreeable communications followed couched in conciliatory terms. It was much to Minna's credit that in her relations towards me she had by her letters proved herself wise and considerate, and while staying in Dresden, where she met her old friends, she lived quietly, and I always provided for her amicably. By so doing she strengthened the impression she had made on me at the time of that touching nocturnal scene, and I willingly put before her the possibility of a domestic reunion, provided that we could establish a home that promised to be a permanent one, which at that time I could only picture to myself as feasible in Germany, and if possible in Dresden. To obtain some idea as to whether it was possible to carry out such an arrangement, I lost no time in applying to Lüttichau, as I had received favourable reports from Minna about his kindly feeling and warm attachment to me. I really went so far as to write to him cordially and in detail. It was another lesson

for me when in return I received occasionally a few dry lines
in a businesslike tone, in which he pointed out that at that
moment nothing could be done with respect to my desired return to Saxony.   On the other hand, I learned through the
police authorities in Venice, that the Saxon ambassador in
Vienna ardently wished to drive me even out of Venice.   This
proved unsuccessful, however, as I was sufficiently protected
by a Swiss passport, which to my great delight the Austrian
authorities duly respected.   The only hope I had with regard
to my longed-for return to Germany was based on the friendly
efforts of the Grand Duke of Baden.   Eduard Devrient, to
whom I also applied for more definite information respecting
our project of a first performance of *Tristan*, informed me that
the Grand Duke looked upon my presence at the performance
as an understood thing; whether he was taking any steps on
his own account against the League, in case his direct efforts
to obtain the King of Saxony's permission should be fruitless,
or whether he intended to accomplish it in some other way,
he did not know.   Consequently I realised that I could not
count on the possibility of an early settlement in Germany.

A great deal of my time was taken up in correspondence with
the object of procuring the necessary means of subsistence,
which at that time, owing to the divided household, made no
small calls upon my purse.   Fortunately a few of the larger
theatres had not yet come to terms about my operas, so I
might still expect some fees from them, whereas those from
the more active theatres had already been spent.   The Stuttgart Court Theatre was the last to apply for *Tannhäuser*.   At
that time I had a particular affection for Stuttgart, owing to
the reasons I have already mentioned; this was also true of
Vienna, which had been the first place to produce *Lohengrin*,
and, in consequence of its success, thought it necessary to secure
Tannhäuser.   My negotiations with Eckert, who was director
at that time, quickly led to satisfactory results.

All this happened during the course of the winter and early
spring of 1859.   Otherwise I lived very quietly and with great
regularity, as I have described.   After recovering the use of
my leg, I was able in December to begin my regular gondola
trips to the Piazzetta again and the return journeys in the

evening, and also to give myself up for some time uninterruptedly to my musical work. I spent Christmas and New Year's Eve quite alone, but in my dreams at night I often found myself in society, which had a very disturbing effect on my rest.

At the beginning of 1859 Karl Ritter suddenly turned up again at my rooms for his usual evening visits. His anxiety about the performance of a dramatic piece he had written had taken him to the shores of the Baltic. This was a work he had completed a short time before *Armida*, much of which again showed his great talent. The tendency of the whole play is to show terrible glimpses of the poet's soul, and these prevent one from passing a favourable judgment on some parts of the piece, but other parts, notably the meeting of Rinaldo with Armida, and the violent birth of their love, are depicted by the author with real poetic fire. As is the case with all such works, which are in reality always hampered by the superficiality of the dilettante, much should have been altered and rewritten for stage effect. Karl would not hear of this; on the contrary, he thought he had discovered, in an intelligent theatrical manager in Stettin, the very man who would lay aside any such considerations as were peculiar to me. He had, however, been disappointed in this hope, and had come back to Venice intending to carry out his fond desire of living aimlessly. To wander through Rome clad in the garb of a capuchin, studying the treasures of art from hour to hour, was the kind of existence he would have preferred to any other.

He would not hear of a remodelled version of *Armida*, but declared his intention to set to work on some new dramatic material which he had taken from Machiavelli's *Florentine Histories*. He would not specify what this material was more definitely, lest I should dissuade him from using it, inasmuch as it contained only situations, and absolutely no indication of any purpose. He seemed no longer to have any desire to give himself up to musical work, although even in this respect the young man showed himself to me in a thoroughly interesting light by a fantasy for the piano which he had written soon after his arrival in Venice. Nevertheless he displayed a more highly intelligent appreciation than before of the development of the second act of *Tristan*, in which I had at last made regular progress. In the evening I frequently played to him, Winterberger and Tessarin, the portions I had completed during the day, and they were always deeply moved. During the previous interruption in my work, which had lasted rather a long time, Härtel had engraved the first act of the score, and Bülow had arranged it for the piano. Thus a portion of the opera lay before me in monumental completeness, while I was still in a fruitful state of excitement with regard to the execution of the whole. And now in the early months of the year the orchestration of this act, which I continued to send in groups of sheets to the publisher to be engraved, also neared completion. By the middle of March I was able to send off the last sheets to Leipzig.

It was now necessary to make new decisions for my plan of life. The question presented itself as to where I was going to compose the third act; for I wished to begin it only in a place where I had a prospect of finishing it undisturbed. It seemed as if this was not destined to be the case in Venice. My work would have occupied me until late into the summer, and on account of my health I did not think I dared spend the hot weather in Venice. Its climate about this time of the year did not commend itself to me. Already I had found great disadvantages and anything but favourable results from the fact that it was not possible to enjoy the invigorating recreation of rambling about in this place. Once in the winter, when I wanted a good walk, I had gone by train to Viterbo to take my fill of exercise by tramping inland for several miles towards the mountains. Inhospitable weather had opposed my progress, and this, added to other unfavourable circumstances, resulted in my bringing away from my excursion nothing more valuable than a favourable opinion of the city of lagoons, to which I fled as to a place of refuge against the dust of the streets and the spectacle of horses being cruelly used. Moreover, it now turned out that my further stay in Venice no longer depended wholly on my own will. I had been recently cited (very politely) before a commissioner of police, who informed me, without mincing the matter, that there had been an incessant agitation on the part of the Saxon embassy in Vienna against my remaining in what was a part of the Austrian Empire. When I explained that I only wished to extend my stay to the beginning of spring, I was advised to obtain permission to do so from the Archduke Maximilian, who as viceroy resided in Milan, preferring my request on the ground of ill-health as alleged by a doctor's certificate. I did this, and the Archduke issued immediate instructions by telegram to the Administrative Government of Venice, to leave me in peace.

But soon it became clear to me that the political situation, which was putting Austrian Italy into a state of ferment, might develop into an occasion for renewing active precautionary measures against strangers. The outbreak of war with Piedmont and France became more and more imminent, and the evidence of deep agitation in the Italian population grew more unmistakable every moment. One day, when I was sauntering up and down the Riva with Tessarin, we came upon a fairly large crowd of strangers, who, with a mixture of respect and curiosity, were watching the Archduke Maximilian and his wife as they were taking the air during a short visit to Venice. The situation was rapidly conveyed to me by my Venetian pianist, who nudged me violently and sought to drag me away from the spot by my arm: in order that, as he explained, I might be spared the necessity of raising my hat to the Archduke. Seeing the stately and very attractive figure of the young Prince passing along, I slipped by my friend with a laugh, and took honest pleasure in being able by my greeting to thank him for his protection, although, of course, he did not know who I was.

Soon, however, everything began to assume a more serious aspect, and to look gloomy and depressing. Day by day the Riva was so crowded with troops newly disembarked, that it became quite unavailable for a promenade. The officers of these troops, on the whole, made a very favourable impression on me, and their homely German tongue, as they chatted harmlessly with one another, reminded me pleasantly of home. In the rank and file, on the other hand, I could not possibly feel any confidence, for in them I saw chiefly the dull servile features of certain leading Slav races in the Austrian monarchy. One could not fail to recognise in them a certain brute force, but it was no less clear that they were entirely devoid of that naïve intelligence which is such an attractive characteristic of the

Italian people. I could not but grudge the former race their victory over the latter. The facial expression of these troops recurred forcibly to my memory in the autumn of this year in Paris, when I could not avoid comparing the picked French troops, the Chasseurs de Vincennes and the Zouaves, with these Austrian soldiers; and without any scientific knowledge of strategy, I understood in a flash the battles of Magenta and Solferino. For the present I learned that Milan was already in a state of seige and was almost completely barred to foreigners. As I had determined to seek my summer refuge in Switzerland on the Lake of Lucerne, this news accelerated my departure; for I did not want to have my retreat cut off by the exigencies of war. So I packed up my things, sent the Erard once more over the Gotthard, and prepared to take leave of my few acquaintances. Ritter had resolved to remain in Italy; he intended to go to Florence and Rome, whither Winterberger, with whom he had struck up a friendship, had hurried in advance. Winterberger declared that he was provided by a brother with money enough to enjoy Italy — an experience which he declared necessary for his recreation and recovery, from what disease I do not know. Ritter therefore counted upon leaving Venice within a very short time. My leave-taking with the worthy Dolgoroukow, whom I left in great suffering, was very sincere, and I embraced Karl at the station, probably for the last time, for from that moment I was left without any direct news of him, and have not seen him to this day.

On the 24th of March, after some adventures caused by the military control of strangers, I reached Milan, where I allowed myself to stay three days to see the sights. Without any official guide to help me, I contented myself with following up the simplest directions I could obtain to the Brera, the Ambrosian Library, the 'Last Supper' of Leonardo da Vinci, and the cathedral. I climbed the various roofs and towers of this cathedral at all points. Finding, as I always did, that my first impressions were the liveliest, I confined my attention in the Brera chiefly to two pictures which confronted me as soon as I entered; they were Van Dyck's 'Saint Anthony before the Infant Jesus' and Crespi's 'Martyrdom of Saint Stephen.' I realised on this occasion that I was not a good judge of pictures, because when once the subject has made a clear and sympathetic appeal to me, it settles my view, and nothing else counts. A strange light, however, was shed on the effect made by the purely artistic significance of a masterpiece, when I stood before Leonardo da Vinci's 'Last Supper' and had the same experience as every one else. This work of art, although it is almost entirely destroyed as a picture, produces such an extraordinary effect on the mind of the spectator, that even after a close examination of the copies hanging beside it representing it in a restored state, when he turns to the ruined picture the fact is suddenly revealed to the eye of his soul that the contents of the original are absolutely inimitable. In the evening I made all haste to get to the Italian comedy again. I grew very fond of it, and found it had installed itself here in the tiny *Teatro Re* for the benefit of a small audience of the lower orders. The Italians of to-day unfortunately despise it heartily. Here, too, the comedies of Goldoni were played with, as it seemed to me, considerable and ingenious skill. On the other hand, it was my fate to be present at a performance in the Scala Theatre, where, in a setting of an external magnificence that was extraordinary, it was proved true that Italian taste was degenerating sadly. Before the most brilliant and enthusiastic audience one could wish for, gathered together in that immense theatre, an incredibly worthless fake of an opera by a modern composer, whose name I have forgotten, was performed. The same evening I learned, however, that although the Italian public was passionately fond of song, it was the ballet which they regarded as the main item; for, obviously, the dreary opera at the beginning was only intended to prepare the way for a great choregraphic performance on a subject no less pretentious than that of Antony and Cleopatra. In this ballet I saw even the cold politician Octavianus, who until now had not so far lost his dignity as to appear as a character in any Italian opera, acting in pantomime and contriving fairly successfully to maintain an attitude of diplomatic reserve. The climax, however, was reached in the scene of Cleopatra's funeral. This afforded the immense staff of the ballet an opportunity for displaying the most varied picturesque effects in highly characteristic costumes.

After receiving these impressions all by myself, I travelled to Lucerne one brilliant spring day by way of Como, where everything was in full blossom, through Lugano, which I knew already, and the Gotthard, which I had to cross in small open sledges along towering walls of snow. When I reached Lucerne the weather was bitterly cold, in contrast with the genial spring I had enjoyed in Italy. The allowance of money I had made for my stay in Lucerne was based on the assumption that the big Hôtel Schweizerhof was quite empty from about this time until the summer season began, and that without further preliminaries I should be able to find a lodging there both spacious and free from noise. This hope had not been entertained in vain. The courteous manager of the hotel, Colonel Segesser, allotted to me a whole floor in the annexe on the left, to occupy at my pleasure. I could make myself quite comfortable here in the larger rooms at a moderate price. As the hotel at this time of the year had only a very small staff of servants, it was left to me to make arrangements for some one to wait upon me For this purpose I found a careful woman well suited to look after my comfort. Many years afterwards, remembering the good services she had rendered me, especially later on when the number of guests had increased, I engaged her as my housekeeper.

Soon my things arrived from Venice. The Erard had been obliged to cross the Alps again when the snow was on the ground. When it was set up in my spacious drawing-room, I said to myself that all this trouble and expense had been incurred to enable me at last to complete the third act of *Tristan und Isolde*. There were times when this seemed to me to be an extravagant ambition; for the difficulties in the way of finishing my work seemed to make it impossible. I compared myself to Leto who, in order to find a place in which to give birth to Apollo and Artemis, was hunted about the world and could find no resting-place until Poseidon, taking compassion on her, caused the island of Delos to rise from the sea.

I wished to regard Lucerne as this Delos. But the terrible influence of the weather, which was intensely cold and continuously wet, weighed upon my spirits in a most unfriendly fashion until the end of May. As such great sacrifice had been made to find this new place of refuge, I thought every day had been uselessly frittered away which had not contributed something to my work of composing. For the greater part of my third act I was occupied with a subject sad beyond words; it came to such a pass that it is only with a shudder that I can recall the first few months of this emigration to Lucerne.

A few days after my arrival I had already visited the Wesendoncks in Zürich. Our meeting was melancholy, but in no way embarrassed. I spent some days in my friends' house, where I saw my old Zürich acquaintances again, and felt as though I were passing from one dream to another. In fact, everything assumed an air of unsubstantiality for me. Several times in the course of my stay in Lucerne I repeated this visit, which was twice returned to me, once on the occasion of my birthday.

Besides the work on which I was now somewhat gloriously engaged, I was also heavy with cares about keeping myself and my wife alive. Of my own accord and out of necessary respect for the circumstances in which my friends the Ritters were placed, I had already in Venice felt myself for the future obliged to decline their voluntary support. I was beginning to exhaust the little that I could contrive to extract with difficulty from those of my operas which up to this period it had been possible to produce. It was settled that I should take up the *Nibelungen* work when Tristan was finished, and I thought it my duty to find out some way of making my future existence easier. This *Nibelungen* work spurred me to the attempt. The Grand Duke of Weimar still kept up his interest in it, to judge from the communications I had received from him during the previous year. I therefore wrote to Liszt and repeated my request that he would make a serious proposal to the Grand Duke to buy the copyright of the work and arrange for its publication, with the right of disposing of it to a publisher on his own terms. I enclosed my former negotiations with Härtel, which had been broken off, and which were now intended to serve as a fair basis for what may be called the business arrangement that Liszt was to enter into with the Grand Duke. Liszt soon gave me an embarrassed hint that his Royal Highness was not really keen on it. This was quite enough for me.

On the other hand, I was driven by circumstances to come to an agreement with Meser in Dresden about the unfortunate copyright of my three earlier operas. The actor Kriete, one of my principal creditors, was making piteous demands for the return of his capital. Schmidt, a Dresden lawyer, offered to put the matter right, and after a long and heated correspondence it was arranged that a certain H. Müller, successor to Meser, who had died a short time before, should enter into possession of the copyright of these publications. On this occasion I heard of nothing but of the costs and expenditure to which my former agent had been put; but it was impossible to get any clear account of the receipts he had taken from my works beyond the fact that the lawyer admitted to me that the late Meser must have put aside some thousands of thalers, which, however, it would not be possible to lay hands on, as he had not left his heirs any funds at all.

In order to pacify the woeful Kriete, I was eventually obliged to agree to sell my rights in the works Meser had published for nine thousand marks, which represented the exact sum I owed to Kriete and another creditor who held a smaller share. With regard to the arrears of interest still owing on the money at compound rate, I remained Kriete's personal debtor; the joint sum amounted in the year 1864 to five thousand four hundred marks, which were duly claimed of me about this time with all the pressure of the law. In the interests of Pusinelli, my chief creditor, who could only be provided under this arrangement with inadequate payment, I reserved to myself the French copyright of these three operas, in the event of this music being produced in France through my efforts at finding a publisher to purchase it in that country.

According to the contents of a letter from the lawyer Schmidt, this reservation of mine had been accepted by the present publisher in Dresden. Pusinelli in a friendly spirit forbore to take advantage of the benefits accruing to him from this arrangement, in regard to the capital he had formerly lent me. He assured me he would never claim it. Thus one possibility remained open to me for the future: that if my operas could make their way into France, although there would be no question of any profit coming to me through those works of mine, I should be reimbursed for the capital I had spent on them and for that which I had been obliged to guarantee. When, later on, my Paris publisher Flaxland and I came to make out an agreement, Meser's successor in Dresden announced himself as absolute proprietor of my operas, and actually succeeded in putting so many obstacles in Flaxland's way in the conduct of his French business, that the latter was compelled to purchase peace at the price of six thousand francs. The natural result of this was that Flaxland was placed in the position of being able to deny that it was I who owned the French copyright of my work. Upon this I made repeated appeals to Adolph Schmidt, the lawyer, to give evidence in my favour, asking nothing more of him than that he should forward to me a copy of the correspondence referring to the rights I had reserved, which had become valid in the Lucerne transaction. To all the letters addressed to him on this subject, however, he obstinately refused an answer, and I learned later on from a Viennese lawyer that I must give up hoping to get this kind of evidence, as I had no legal means in my possession to force the advocate to give it, if he were not so inclined.

While, owing to this, I had little opportunity of improving my prospects for the future, I had at least the satisfaction of seeing the score of *Tannhäuser* engraved at last. As the stock of my earlier autograph copies had come to an end, chiefly through the wasteful management of Meser, I had already persuaded Härtel when I was in Venice to have the score engraved. Meser's successor had acquired the complete rights of this work, and therefore regarded it as a point of honour not to give up the score to another publisher; consequently he took over the task of producing it at his own cost. Unluckily fate demanded that just a year later I had to revise and reconstruct the first two scenes completely. To this day it is a subject of regret to me not to have been able to introduce this fresh piece of work into the engraved score.

The Härtels, never faltering in their assumption that *Tristan* might provide good food for the theatre, set their men busily to work upon engraving the score of the second act, while I was at work on the third. The process of registering corrections, while I was in the throes of composing the third act — one long ecstasy — wielded over me a strange, almost uncanny influence; for in the first scenes of this act it was made clear to me that in this opera (which had been most unwarrantably assumed to be an easy one to produce), I had embodied the most daring and most exotic conception in all my writings. While I was at work on the great scene of *Tristan,* I found myself often asking whether I was not mad to want to give such work to a publisher to print for the theatre. And yet I could not have parted with a single accent in that tale of pain, although the whole thing tortured me to the last degree.

I tried to overcome my gastric troubles by using (among other things) Kissingen water in moderate doses. As I was fatigued and made incapable of work by the early walks I had to take during this treatment, it occurred to me to take a short ride instead. For this purpose the hotel manager lent me a horse, aged twenty-five, named Lise. On this animal I rode every morning as long as it would carry me. It never conveyed me very far, but turned back regularly at certain spots without taking the slightest notice of my directions.

Thus passed the months of April, May, and the greater part of June, without my completing even half of my composition for the third act, and all the while I was contending with a mood of the deepest melancholy. At last came the season for the visitors to arrive; the hotel with its annexes began to fill, and it was no longer possible to think of maintaining my exceptional privilege with regard to the use of such choice quarters. It was proposed to move me to the second storey of the main building, where only travellers who spent the night on their way to other places in Switzerland were put up, whereas in the annexes people were lodged who came to make a long stay, and who used their rooms day and night. As a matter of fact, this arrangement answered admirably. From this time forward I was completely undisturbed during the hours of my work in my little sitting-room with its adjoining bedchamber, as the rooms engaged for the night by strangers in this storey were perfectly empty in the daytime.

Really splendid summer weather set in eventually, lasting a good two months with a continuously cloudless sky. I enjoyed the curious charm of protecting myself against the extremes of the sun's heat by carefully keeping my room cool and dark, and going out on to my balcony only in the evening to surrender myself to the influence of the summer air. Two good horn-players gave me great pleasure by providing a performance of simple folk-songs almost regularly in a skiff on the lake. In my work, too, I had now luckily passed the critical point, and in spite of its sorrowful character, the more subdued mood of that part of my poem which I had still to master, threw me into a sincere spiritual ecstasy, during which I completed the composition of the whole work by the beginning of August, fragments only remaining to be orchestrated.

Lonely as was my life, the exciting events of the Italian war provided me plenty of interest. I followed this struggle, as unexpected as it was significant, through the thrilling course of its successes and reverses. Still I did not remain entirely without company. In July, Felix Dräsecke, whom I had not known before, came to Lucerne for a lengthy visit. After hearing a performance of the prelude to *Tristan und Isolde* conducted by Liszt, he had almost immediately determined to make himself personally acquainted with me. I was completely terrified by his arrival, and was at a loss to know what to do with him. Moreover, as his talk was in a certain facetious vein, overflowing with stories of persons and circumstances for which I was gradually losing all appreciation, he soon began to bore me, a fact which astonished him, and which he recognised so clearly that he thought he had better leave after a few days. This made me in my turn embarrassed, and I now took special care to deprive him of the bad opinion he had formed of me. I soon learned to like him, and for a considerable time, until shortly before his departure from Lucerne, he was my daily companion, from whose intercourse I derived much pleasure, as he was a highly gifted musician and by no means a prig. But Dräsecke was not my only visitor.

Wilhelm Baumgartner, my old Zürich acquaintance, came to spend a few weeks in Lucerne out of kindness to me. And lastly Alexander Séroff from St. Petersburg came to stay some time in the neighbourhood. He was a remarkable man, of great intelligence, and openly prepossessed in favour of Liszt and myself. He had heard my *Lohengrin* in Dresden and wanted to know more of me — an ambition I was obliged to satisfy by playing *Tristan* to him in the rough-and-ready fashion which was peculiar to me. I went up Mount Pilatus with Dräsecke, and again had to look after a companion who suffered from giddiness. To celebrate his departure I invited him to take an excursion to Brunnen and the Grütli. After this we took leave of each other for the time being, as his moderate resources did not permit him to remain any longer, and I too was seriously thinking of taking my departure.

The question now arose as to where I was to go. I had addressed letters, first through Eduard Devrient, and finally direct to the Grand Duke of Baden, asking the latter for a guarantee that I might settle, if not in Karlsruhe itself, at least in some small place in the neighbourhood. This would suffice to set at rest a craving, which could no longer be suppressed, for intercourse now and then with an orchestra and a company of singers, if only to hear them play. I learned later that the Grand Duke had really bestirred himself in the matter by writing to the King of Saxony. But the view still prevailed in that quarter that I could not be granted an amnesty, but could only hope to receive an act of grace; it being assumed, of course, that I would first have to report myself to a magistrate for examination. Thus the fulfilment of my wish remained impossible, and I shrank in dismay before the problem of how to secure a performance of my *Tristan* which I could superintend in person, as I had determined to do. I was assured that the Grand Duke would know what measures to resort to in order to meet the situation. But the question was, where was I to turn for a place in which to settle with some prospect of being able to remain there. I longed for a permanent home again. After due consideration I decided that Paris was the only place where I could make sure of now and then hearing a good orchestra and a first-class quartette. Without these stimulating influences Zürich at last became unbearable, and in no other city but Paris, where I could stay undisturbed, could I safely reckon on being able to obtain artistic recreation of a sufficiently high standard.

At last I had to bestir myself to come to a decision about my wife. We had now been apart from each other for a whole year. After the hard lessons she had received from me, and which, according to her letters, had left a deep impression upon her, I was justified in assuming that the renewal of our life in common might be made tolerable; especially as it would remove the grave difficulty of her maintenance. I therefore agreed with her that she should join me late in the autumn in Paris. In the meantime I was willing to look for a possible abode there, and undertook to arrange for the removal of our furniture and household goods to the French capital. In order to carry out this plan financial assistance was imperative, as the means at my disposal were quite inadequate. I then made to Wesendonck the same offer in regard to my *Nibelungen* that I had made to the Grand Duke of Weimar, that is to say, I proposed that he should buy the copyright for publishing the work. Wesendonck acceded to my wishes without demur, and was ready to buy out each of the completed portions of my work in turn for about the same sum as it was reasonable to suppose a publisher would pay for it later on. I was not able to fix my departure, which took place on the 7th of September, when I went for a three days' visit to my friends in Zürich. I spent these days at the Wesendonck's, where I was well looked after and saw my former acquaintances, Herwegh, Semper, and Gottfried Keller. One of the evenings I spent with them was marked by an animated dispute with Semper over the political events of the time. Semper professed to recognise, in the recent defeat of Austria, the defeat of the German nationality; in the Romance element represented by Louis Napoleon, he recognised a sort of Assyrian despotism which he hated both in art and politics. He expressed himself with such emphasis that Keller, who was generally so silent, was provoked into a lively debate. Semper in his turn was so aggravated at this, that at last in a fit of desperation he blamed me for luring him into the enemy's camp, by being the cause of his invitation to the Wesendonck's. We made it up before we parted that night, and met again on several occasions after this, when we took care never again to let our discussions become so passionate. From Zürich I went to Winterthur to visit Sulzer. I did not see my friend himself, but only his wife and the boy she had borne to him since my last visit; the mother and child made a very touching and friendly impression on me, particularly when I realised that I must now regard my old friend in the light of a happy father.

On the 15th of September I reached Paris. I had intended to fix my abode somewhere in the neighbourhood of the Champs Élysées, and with this object in view at once looked out for temporary lodgings in that district, which I found eventually in the Avenue de Matignon. My main object was to discover my desired peaceful place of refuge in some small house remote from the thoroughfares. I at once bestirred myself to find this, and thought it my duty to make use of every acquaintance I could call to mind. The Olliviers were not in Paris at the time; Countess d'Agoult was ill, and was also busy arranging her departure for Italy, and unable to receive me. She referred me to her daughter the Countess Charnacé, upon whom I called, but without being able to explain to her the purpose I had in view. I also looked up the Hérold family, who had received me in such a friendly way on my last visit to Paris; but I found Mme. Hérold in a strange and morbidly excitable state of mind, the result of ill-health, so that instead of discussing my views with her, my only thought was to keep her calm and avoid upsetting her by even the slightest appeal for help. In my passionate longing to find a home I decided to get no further information, but set about the matter myself. At last I discovered in the Rue Newton near the Barrière de l'Étoile, a side street off the Champs Élysées, not yet completed in accordance with a former plan of Paris, a nice little villa with a small garden. I took this on a three-years' agreement at a rent of four thousand francs a year. Here, at all events, I might look for complete quiet and total isolation from the noise of the streets. This fact alone prepossessed me very much in taking the little house, the late occupier of which had been the well-known author Octave Feuillet, who was at that time under the patronage of the imperial court. But I was puzzled that the building, in spite of my being unable to detect anything old in its structure, had been so neglected inside. The proprietor could in no way be induced to do anything to restore the place and make it habitable, even if I had consented to pay a higher rent. The reason of this I discovered some time afterwards: the estate itself was doomed in consequence of the plans for the rebuilding of Paris; but the time had not yet come to make the official announcement of the government's intentions to the proprietors, because, had this been done, their claims to compensation would have become valid at once. I consequently laboured under the pleasant delusion that whatever I was obliged to spend on interior decoration and on restoring the property would, in the course of years, prove to be money well invested. I therefore proceeded to give the necessary instructions for the work without hesitating, and ordered my furniture to be sent from Zürich, thinking that as fate had driven me to my choice, I could regard myself as a resident of Paris for the rest of my life.

While the house was being prepared, I tried to get my bearings as to what could be extracted for my future existence out of the popularity of my artistic works. The first thing I did was to look up M. de Charnal and to get information from him about the translation of the libretto of my *Rienzi* with which he had been entrusted. It turned out that M. Carvalho, the director of the Théâtre Lyrique, would hear of absolutely nothing but *Tannhäuser*. I prevailed upon Carvalho to visit me to talk the matter over. He declared that he was most certainly inclined to produce one of my operas, only it must be *Tannhäuser*, because, as he explained, this opera was identified with me among the Parisians, who would think it ridiculous to produce any other work under the name of 'Wagner.' As to my choice of a translator for the poem of this opera he seemed to entertain grave doubts: he asked whether I had not made a mistake, whereupon I tried to get more definite information about the capabilities of M. de Charnal, and discovered to my horror that this charming young man, who boasted that he had collaborated in a melodrama called *Schinderhannes*, which he thought was a German romantic subject, had not had the slightest conception of the character of the work he was handling.

As his enthusiasm moved me, I tried to shape some verses with him and make them practicable for musical purposes; but I failed utterly, and all my trouble was in vain. Bülow had once drawn my attention to Auguste de Gaspérini, a young doctor who had ceased to practise, and whose acquaintance he had made in Baden-Baden, where he discovered that he was extraordinarily fond of my music. I called upon him without loss of time, and as he was not in Paris, I wrote to him. This man sent his friend Leroy to me with a letter of recommendation. He was a well-educated Parisian music-master, who won my esteem by his attractive personality. My confidence in him was aroused, because he at once dissuaded me from associating myself with an obscure journalist on a theatrical newspaper (in which character M. de Charnal finally disclosed himself), and advised me to go to Roger, a highly gifted and experienced operatic singer, who had been a favourite with the Parisian public and was master of the German language. This lifted a load from my heart: I accepted the invitation which Leroy arranged for me through another friend, who took me down to Roger's country place one day to meet him. I have forgotten the name of this large estate which was occupied by the Paris tenor, whose fame had been so celebrated up to that time; the château had once belonged to a marquis, and was built in a very sumptuous style and surrounded by extensive hunting-grounds. It was the desire to handle a gun and make use of these grounds (which he loved) that, only a short time before, had landed this charming singer in a terrible disaster which had shattered his right arm.

I found Roger, some months after the accident, completely recovered; but the forearm had had to be amputated. The question now was whether a famous mechanician, who had promised to make him a perfect substitute for the lost limb even in the matter of free gesticulation, would be able to carry out his task. He succeeded fairly well, as I saw with my own eyes some time later, when I witnessed Roger act in a benefit performance which the Grand Opera had given him, and use his arm so ingeniously that he received great applause for this reason alone. In spite of this he had to accept the fact that he was regarded as 'disabled,' and that his career at the Grand

Opera in Paris had come to a close. For the time being he seemed to be glad to secure for himself some sort of literary occupation, and accepted with much pleasure my proposal that he should make a translation of *Tannhäuser* for practical use. He sang to me the French text of some of the main themes which he had already translated, and they seemed to me good. After I had spent a day and a night with the singer, who had once been such a popular favourite, and was now condemned to look forward to a sad decline, I felt in very good spirits and full of hope, more especially as his intelligent way of approaching my opera gave me a pleasing idea of the extent to which it was possible to cultivate the French mind. In spite of this I had soon to give up the notion of Roger's working for me, as for a long time he was entirely absorbed in trying to make secure the position into which he had fallen through his terrible accident. He was so busy with his own affairs that he could hardly give me an answer to my inquiries, and for the time being I lost sight of him altogether.

I had come to this arrangement with Roger more by chance than out of necessity, as I continued to adhere firmly to my plan simply to seek a suitable *pied-à-terre* in Paris. My serious artistic enterprises, on the other hand, were still directed to Germany, from which, from another point of view, I was an enforced exile. Soon, however, the whole aspect of affairs changed: the proposed performance of *Tristan* in Karlsruhe, on which I had continued to keep an eye, was finally announced as abandoned. I had to remain uncertain as to the precise reason why this undertaking had been given up, which at an earlier stage had apparently been pursued with so much zeal. Devrient pointed out to me that all his attempts to secure an appropriate representation of the rôle of Isolde had been shattered by my deciding against the singer Garrigues (who had already married young Schnorr), and that he felt his incapacity to offer advice on the rest of the business all the more keenly because Schnorr, the tenor, whose devotion to me was so great, had himself despaired of being able to execute the last portion of the task assigned to him. I realised at once that this was an obstacle which I should have been able to overcome, together with all its disastrous consequences, if I had been permitted, even for a brief space of time, to visit Karlsruhe. But the mere expression of this wish seemed, as soon as it was reiterated, to arouse the bitterest feelings against me. Devrient expressed his opinion on the matter with so much violence and brutality that I could not help seeing that what kept me from Karlsruhe was mainly his personal disinclination to have me there, or to be interfered with in the conduct of his theatre.

A less potent factor in the situation I found in the painful feeling now aroused in the Grand Duke at the prospect of not being able to fulfil the promise he had once held out to me, that I should visit him in Karlsruhe, where he was in residence; if the main object for the visit were to subside under pressure of other considerations, he could only regard this circumstance in the light of an almost desirable event. At the same time I received from Bülow, who had gone several times to Karlsruhe, fairly broad hints as to what Devrient was aiming at. Full light was shed on the affair at a later stage; for the present it was a matter of the utmost importance for me to face the fact that I was entirely cut off from Germany, and must think of a fresh field for the production of *Tristan*, which lay so near my heart. I rapidly sketched a plan for starting a German theatre in Paris itself, such as had existed in bygone years with the co-operation of Schröder-Devrient. I thought I could safely rely on the possibility of doing so, as the most eminent singers of the German theatre were known to me, and would gladly follow me if I were to summon them to Paris on such a mission. I received messages of ready acceptance, in the event of my succeeding in founding a German opera season in Paris on a solid basis, from Tichatschek, Mitterwurzer, Niemann the tenor, and also Luise Meyer in Vienna. My immediate and besetting care was then to discover in Paris a suitable man for the task, who would undertake the execution of my plan at his own risk. My object was to secure the Salle Ventadour for a spring season of two months after the close of the Italian opera. There would then be performances of my operas, *Tannhäuser, Lohengrin*, and finally *Tristan*, by a chosen company and chorus of German singers, for the benefit of the Parisian public in general and myself in particular.

With this purpose in mind, my anxieties and endeavours now

took a totally different direction from that towards which they had tended when I first settled again in Paris; to cultivate acquaintances, especially among those who had influence, was now of the utmost importance to me. For this reason I was glad to hear that Gaspérini had arrived in Paris for good. Although I had only known him very slightly before, I now immediately communicated my plans to him, and was introduced in the friendliest way to a rich man who was well disposed towards him, a M. Lucy, who, so I was told, was not without influence, and was at that time Receiver-General in Marseilles. Our deliberations convinced us that the most necessary, and indeed indispensable, thing was to find some one to come forward and finance our enterprise. My friend Gaspérini could not but agree that, on the strength of the opinions he had himself advanced, it was natural I should look upon M. Lucy as the very man we wanted; but he thought it advisable to put our wishes before his friend with some caution, for though Lucy had much *chaleur de cœur*, he was principally a man of business and understood but little of music. Above all, it was necessary that my compositions should become well known in Paris, so that further enterprises might be founded on the results thus obtained. With this object in view I decided to arrange a few important concerts. To effect this I had to welcome my old friend Belloni, Liszt's former secretary, into the circle of my closer acquaintances. He immediately enlisted a companion of his in our cause, a highly intelligent man called Giacomelli, whom I never knew to be anything but good-natured. He was the editor of a theatrical journal and was cordially recommended to me by Belloni, as much for his excellent French as for his exceptional capabilities in other respects. My new protector's strange editorial office became from this time one of my most important places of rendezvous, which I frequented almost daily, and where I met all the curious creatures with whom, for the purpose of theatrical and similar matters, one is obliged to mix in Paris. The next thing to be considered was how to obtain the most suitable hall for my intended concerts. It was evident that I should appear to greatest advantage before the Parisian public if I could secure the theatre and orchestra of the Grand Opera.

For this I had to address myself to the Emperor Napoleon, which I did in a concise letter composed for me by Gaspérini. The hostility of Fould, who was at that time the Minister of the Household to Napoleon, would probably have to be reckoned with, on account of his friendly relations to Meyerbeer. The injurious and dreaded influence of this personage we hoped to counteract by that of M. Mocquard, Napoleon's secretary, who, as Ollivier declared, composed all the imperial speeches. In an *élan* of fiery generosity Lucy decided to appeal to the friend of his youth, for as such he regarded Mocquard, in a letter of recommendation to him on my behalf. As even this communication received no answer from the Tuileries, I and my more practical friends, Belloni and Giacomelli, with whom I held consultations, grew more doubtful every day of our own power as opposed to that of the Minister of the Household, and we therefore entered into negotiations with Calzado, the director of the Italian Opera, instead. We met with a direct refusal in this quarter, whereupon I finally decided to seek a personal interview with the man. By a power of persuasion which astonished even myself, and, above all, by holding out the prospect of my *Tristan* at the Italian Opera possibly proving a huge success, I actually succeeded in at last obtaining his consent to let the Salle Ventadour for three evenings with a week's interval between each. But even my passionate eloquence, which Giacomelli extolled on our way home, could not persuade him to lower the rent, which he fixed at four thousand francs an evening, merely for the hire and lighting of the hall.

After this the most important point was to get a first-class orchestra for my concerts, and my two agents had, for the time being, more than enough to do in this respect. In consequence of their endeavours on my behalf I now began to notice the first signs of a hostile, and hitherto unsuspected, attitude towards me and my undertaking on the part of my old friend Berlioz. Full of the favourable impression he had made upon me when we met in London in 1855, which was strengthened by a friendly correspondence he had kept up for a time, I had called at his house as soon as I arrived in Paris. As he was not in I turned back into the street, where I met him on his way home, and noticed that the sight of me occasioned a convulsive movement of fright, which showed itself in his whole physiognomy and bearing in a way which was almost gruesome. I saw at a glance how matters stood between us, but concealed my own uneasiness under an appearance of natural concern about his state of health, which he immediately assured me was one of torture, and that he could only bear up against the most violent attacks of neuralgia with the help of electric treatment, from which he was just returning. In order to allay his suffering I offered to leave him immediately, but this made him so far ashamed of his attitude that he pressed me to return with him to his house. Here I succeeded in making him feel somewhat more friendly towards me by disclosing my real intentions in Paris: even the concerts I proposed giving were merely to serve the purpose of so far attracting public attention as to make it possible to establish German opera here, so that when I wished to do so I could superintend the representation of such of my own works I had not yet heard; while, on the other hand, I completely renounced the idea of a French production of *Tannhäuser*, such as the manager Carvalho had seemed to contemplate. In consequence of these explanations I was apparently for a time on quite a friendly footing with Berlioz. I consequently thought that, with regard to the engagement of musicians for the proposed concerts, I could not on this occasion do better than refer my agents to this experienced friend, whose advice would certainly prove invaluable. They afterwards informed me that Berlioz had at first shown himself sympathetically inclined, but his manner had suddenly changed one day when Mme. Berlioz entered the room where they were discussing matters, and exclaimed in a tone of angry surprise, ' *Comment, je crois que vous donnez des conseils pour les concerts de M. Wagner?* ' Belloni then discovered that this lady had just accepted a valuable bracelet sent her by Meyerbeer. Being a man of the world he said to me, ' Do not count upon Berlioz,' and there the whole matter ended.

From this time forward Belloni's bright face was clouded over with an expression of the deepest anxiety. He thought he had discovered that the whole Parisian press was exceedingly

hostile towards me, which he had not the slightest doubt was due
to the tremendous agitation Meyerbeer had set on foot from
Berlin. He discovered that an urgent correspondence had been
carried on from there with the editors of the principal Paris
journals, and that amongst others the famous *Fiorentino* had
already taken advantage of Meyerbeer's alarm at my Parisian
enterprise, to threaten him with praise of my music, thus
naturally exciting Meyerbeer to further bribery. This increased
Belloni's anxiety, and he advised me, above all, to try and find
financial support for my plans, or if I had no prospect of this,
to rely on the imperial power alone. He pointed out that it
was absolutely impossible for me to carry out the concerts
entirely on my own responsibility without financial support,
and his arguments had the effect of making me decide to be
careful; for what with my journey to Paris and my installation
there, my funds were thoroughly exhausted. So I was again
forced to enter into negotiations with the Tuileries about the
letting of the Opera House and its orchestra free of charge.
Ollivier now came forward with judicious advice and introductions, which brought me into touch with all kinds of people,
and, amongst others, with Camille Doucet (a leading member of
Fould's ministry and also a dramatic author). By this means I
hoped to penetrate into the presence of Meyerbeer's admirer,
the unapproachable and terrible Minister of State. One result
of these introductions, however, was that I formed a lasting
friendship with Jules Ferry, though our acquaintance proved
quite useless to the immediate purpose in hand. The Emperor
and his secretary remained obstinately silent, and this even
after I had obtained the Grand Duke of Baden's consent to
the intercession of his ambassador in Paris on my behalf, and
also that of the Swiss ambassador, Dr. Kern, whose combined
forces were to try and enlighten me, and possibly also the
Emperor, about Fould's manœuvres. But it was useless — all
remained silent as before.

Under these circumstances I regarded it as a freak of fate
that Minna should announce her readiness to join me in Paris,
and that I should have to expect her arrival shortly. In the
selection as well as in the arrangement of the little house in
the Rue Newton I had had particular regard to our future

existence together. My living-room was separated from hers by a staircase, and I had taken care that the part of the house to be occupied by her should not be wanting in comfort. But, above all, the affection which had been revived by our last reunion in Zürich had prompted me to furnish and decorate the rooms with special care, so that they might have a friendly appearance and make life in common with this woman, who was becoming quite a stranger to me, more possible to bear. On account of this I was afterwards reproached with a love of luxury. There was also a possibility of arranging a drawing-room in our house, and though I had not intended to be extravagant, I finally discovered that, in addition to the trouble of negotiations with unreliable Parisian workmen, I was drawn into expenses I had not counted upon. But I comforted myself with the reflection that, as it could not be helped now, Minna would at least be pleased when she entered the house she was henceforth to manage. I also thought it necessary to get a maid for her, and a particularly suitable person was recommended me by Mme. Hérold. I had also engaged a man-servant as soon as I arrived, and although he was rather a thick-headed Swiss from Valais, who had at one time belonged to the Pope's bodyguard, he soon became quite devoted to me. In addition to these two servants there was my wife's former cook, whom she had taken with her from Zürich, and by whom she was accompanied when at last I was able to go and meet her at the station on the 17th of November. Here Minna immediately handed me the parrot and her dog Fips, which involuntarily reminded me of her arrival in the harbour of Rorschach ten years ago. Just as she had done on that occasion also, she now immediately gave me to understand that she did not come to me out of need, and that if I treated her badly she knew quite well where to go. Moreover, there was no denying that since then a not unimportant change had taken place in her; she owned that she was filled with a similar anxiety and fear like a person feels who is about to enter a new situation, and did not know whether she would be able to stand it. Here I sought to divert her thoughts by acquainting her with my public position, which as my wife she would naturally share. Unfortunately she could not understand this at all, and it failed to make any appeal to her, while her attention was immediately absorbed by the interior arrangement of our house. The fact of my having taken a man-servant merely filled her with scorn; but that, under the title of lady's maid, I should have provided her with what I had really considered a very necessary attendant, made her furious. This person, whom Mme. Hérold had recommended to me with the assurance that she had shown angelic patience in the care of her sick and aged mother, speedily became so demoralised by Minna's treatment of her that, at the end of a very short time, I of my own accord hurriedly dismissed her, and in doing so was violently reproached by my wife for giving the woman a small tip. To an even greater extent did she succeed in spoiling my man-servant, who finally refused to obey her orders, and when I found fault with him became so impertinent towards me also that I had to send him away at the shortest notice. He left a very good complete set of livery behind, which I had just bought at great expense, and which remained on my hands, as I felt no inclination ever to have a man-servant again. On the other hand, I cannot but bear the highest testimony in favour of the Swabian Therese, who from this time forward performed the entire service of the household alone during the whole of my sojourn in Paris. This woman, who was gifted with unusual penetration, at once grasped my painful position towards her mistress, and understanding my wife's faults, succeeded by her indefatigable activity in turning matters to the best advantage for me as well as for the household, and thus neutralising their bad effect.

So in this last reunion with Minna I once more entered upon a state of existence which I had repeatedly lived through before, and which it seemed was now to start afresh. This time it was almost a blessing that there could be no question of quiet retirement, but that, on the contrary, it was necessary to enter upon an endless succession of worldly relations and activities, to which I was again driven by fate entirely against my choice and inclination.

With the opening of the year 1860 a very unexpected turn of affairs made it seem possible that I should succeed in carrying out my plans. The musical director Esser in Vienna informed me that Schott, the music publisher of Mayence, wished to obtain a new opera by me for publication. I had nothing to offer at present but the *Rheingold;* the peculiar composition of this work, meant only as a prelude to the *Nibelungen* trilogy I meant to write, made it difficult for me to offer it as an opera without adding any further explanation. However, Schott's eagerness, at all costs, to have a work of mine to add to his catalogue of publications was so great that I no longer hesitated, and, without concealing from him the fact that he would have great difficulty in propagating this work, I offered to place it at his disposal for the sum of ten thousand francs, promising him at the same time the option of purchasing the three main operas which were to follow at the same price for each. In the event of Schott accepting my offer, I immediately formed a plan of spending the sum thus unexpectedly acquired for the furthering of my Paris undertaking.

Tired out with the obstinate silence maintained by the imperial cabinet, I now commissioned my agents to close with Signor Calzado for three concerts to be given at the Italian Opera, as well as to obtain the necessary orchestra and singers. When the arrangements for this had been set in motion, I was again made anxious by Schott's tardy offers of lower terms; in order not to alienate him, however, I wrote to the musical director Schmidt in Frankfort commissioning him to continue the negotiations with Schott on considerably reduced terms, to which I gave my consent. I had scarcely sent off this letter when an answer from Schott reached me, in which he at last expressed his willingness to pay me the sum of ten thousand francs for which I had asked. I thereupon sent a telegram to Schmidt promptly cancelling the commission with which I had just charged him.

With renewed courage I and my agents now followed up our plans, and the necessary preparations for the concerts engaged my whole attention. I had to look out for a choir, and for this I thought it necessary to reinforce the expensively paid company of the Italian Opera by a German society of singers who had been recommended to me and who were under the direction of a certain Herr Ehmant. In order to ingratiate myself with its members, I had one evening to visit their meeting-place in the

Rue du Temple, and cheerfully accommodate myself to the smell of beer and the fumes of tobacco with which the atmosphere was laden, and in the midst of which sturdy German artists were to reveal their capabilities to me. I was also brought into contact with a M. Chevé, the teacher and director of a French national choral society, whose rehearsals took place in the École de Médecine. I there met an odd enthusiast, who, by his method of teaching people to sing without notes, hoped to bring about the regeneration of the French people's genius. But the worst trouble was occasioned by the necessity of my having the different orchestral parts of the selections I was going to have played copied out for me. For this task I hired several poor German musicians, who remained at my house from morning till night, in order to make the necessary arrangements, which were often rather difficult, under my direction.

In the midst of these absorbing occupations Hans von Bülow looked me up. He had come to Paris for some length of time, as it turned out, more to assist me in my undertaking than to follow his own pursuit as a concert virtuoso. He was staying with Liszt's mother, but spent the greater part of the day with me, in order to give help wherever it was needed, as, for instance, with the immediate preparation of the copies. His activity in all directions was extraordinary, but he seemed, above all, to have set himself the task of making certain social connections, that he and his wife had formed during their visit to Paris the year before, useful to my undertaking. The result of this was felt in due course, but for the present he helped me to arrange the concerts, the rehearsals for which had begun.

The first of these took place in the Herz Hall, and led to such an agitation on the part of the musicians against me that it was almost as bad as a riot. I had continually to remonstrate with them about habits on their part, which I on my side felt unable to overlook, and tried to prove, on common-sense grounds, how impossible it was to give way to them. My $\frac{6}{8}$ time, which I took as $\frac{4}{4}$ time, particularly incensed them, and with tumultuous protestations they declared it should be taken *alla-breva*. In consequence of a sharp call to order and an allusion on my part to the discipline of a well-drilled orchestra, they declared they were not 'Prussian soldiers,' but free men.

At last I saw that one of the chief mistakes had lain in the faulty setting up of the orchestra, and I now formed my plan for the next rehearsal. After a consultation with my friends I went to the concert-room on the next occasion the first thing in the morning and superintended the arranging of the desks myself, and ordered a plentiful lunch for the musicians to which, at the beginning of the rehearsal, I invited them in the following manner. I told them that on the result of our meeting of that day depended the possibility of my giving my concerts; that we must not leave the concert-room till we were quite clear about it. I therefore requested the members to rehearse for two hours, then to partake of a frugal lunch prepared for them in the adjoining salon, whereupon we would immediately hold a second rehearsal for which I would pay them. The effect of this proposal was miraculous: the advantageous arrangement of the orchestra contributed to the maintenance of the general good-humour, and the favourable impression made upon every one by the prelude to *Lohengrin,* which was then played, rose to enthusiasm, so that at the conclusion of the first rehearsal both players and audience, amongst whom was Gaspérini, were delighted with me. This friendly disposition was most agreeably displayed at the principal rehearsal, which took place on the stage of the Italian Opera House. I had now gained sufficient control to allow me to dismiss a careless cornet-player from the orchestra with a severe reproof, without incurring any difficulties owing to their *esprit de corps.*

At last the first concert took place on the 25th of January (1860); all the pieces which I had chosen from my various operas, including *Tristan und Isolde,* met with an entirely favourable, nay enthusiastic, reception from the public, and I even had the experience of one of my pieces, the march from *Tannhäuser,* being interrupted by storms of applause. The pleasure thus expressed was aroused, it seems, because the audience was surprised to find that my music, of which there had been so many contradictory reports, contained such long phrases of connected melody. Well satisfied as I was, both with the way in which the concert had been carried out and its enthusiastic reception, I had on the following days to overcome contrary impressions caused by the papers giving vent to their

feelings against me. It was now clear that Belloni had been
quite right in supposing that they were hostile to me, and his
foresight, which had led us to omit inviting the press, had
merely roused our opponents to greater fury. As the whole
undertaking had been arranged more for the stimulation of
friends than to excite praise, I was not so much disturbed by
the blustering of these gentlemen as by the absence of any sign
from the former. What caused me most anxiety was that the
apparently well-filled house should not have brought us better
returns than was found to be the case. We had made from
five to six thousand francs, but the expenses amounted to eleven
thousand francs. This might be partially covered if, in the
case of the two less expensive concerts still to come, we could
rely on considerably higher returns. Belloni and Giacomelli
shook their heads, however; they thought it better not to close
their eyes to the fact that concerts were not suited to the taste
of the French people, who demanded the dramatic element
as well, that is to say, costumes, scenery, the ballet, etc., in
order to feel satisfied. The small number of tickets sold for
the second concert, which was given on the 1st of February,
actually put my agents to the necessity of filling the room
artificially, so as at least to save appearances. I had to allow
them to do as they thought best in this matter, and was afterwards astonished to learn how they had managed to fill the
first places in this aristocratic theatre in such a way as to deceive
even our enemies. The real receipts amounted to little over
two thousand francs, and it now required all my determination
and my contempt for the miseries that might result not to
cancel the third concert to be given on the 8th of February.
My fees from Schott, a part of which, it is true, I had to devote
to the household expenses of my troubled domestic existence,
were all spent, and I had to look round for futher subsidies.
These I obtained with great difficulty, through Gaspérini's mediation, from the very man to win whose assistance in a much
wider sense had been the whole object of the concerts. In
short, we had to have recourse to M. Lucy, the Receiver-General
of Marseilles, who was to come to Paris at the time my concerts
were being given, and upon whom my friend Gaspérini had
assumed that an important Parisian success would have the

effect of making him declare his readiness to finance my project of establishing German opera in Paris. M. Lucy, on the contrary, did not appear at the first concert at all, and was only present at a part of the second, during which he fell asleep. The fact that he was now called upon to advance several thousands of francs for the third concert naturally seemed to him to protect him against any further demands on our part, and he felt a certain satisfaction at being exempt from all further participation in my plans, at the price of this loan. Although, as a matter of fact, this concert now seemed useless, it nevertheless gave me great pleasure, as much through the spirited performance itself as on account of its favourable reception by the audience, which, it is true, my agents had again to supplement in order to give the appearance of a full hall, but which, nevertheless, showed a marked increase in the number of tickets paid for.

The realisation of the deep impression I had made on certain people had more effect upon me at this time than the dejection I felt at having to all outward appearances failed in this enterprise. It was undeniable that the sensation I had produced had directly, as the comments of the press had indirectly, aroused extraordinary interest in me. My omission to invite any journalists seemed to be regarded on all sides as a wonderful piece of audacity on my part. I had foreseen the attitude likely to be adopted by the majority of reporters, but I was sorry that even such men as M. Franc-Marie, the critic of the *Patrie,* who at the end of the concert had come forward to thank me with deep emotion, should have found themselves forced to follow the lead of the others, without compromising, and even to go so far as to deny their true opinion of me. Berlioz aroused a universal feeling of anger amongst my adherents, by an article which began in a roundabout way, but ended with an open attack on me which he published in the *Journal des Débats.* As he had once been an old friend, I was determined not to overlook this treatment, and answered his onslaught in a letter which, with the greatest difficulty, I managed to get translated into good French, and succeeded, not without trouble, in having it inserted in the *Journal des Débats.* It so happened that this very letter had the effect of drawing those on whom my concerts had already made an impression more enthusiastically towards me. Amongst others a M. Perrin introduced himself to me; he had formerly been director of the Opéra Comique, and was now a well-to-do *bel esprit* and painter, and later became director of the Grand Opera. He had heard *Lohengrin* and *Tannhäuser* performed in Germany, and expressed himself in such a way as led me to suppose that he would make it a point of honour to bring these operas to France should he at any time be in a position to do so. A certain Count Foucher de Careil had also become acquainted with my operas in the same way, through seeing them performed in Germany, and he too became one of my distinguished and lasting friends. He had made a name by various publications on German philosophy, and more especially through a book on Leibnitz, and it could not but prove interesting to me to be brought through him into touch with a form of the French genius as yet unknown to me.

It is impossible to record all the passing acquaintances with whom I was brought in contact at this time, amongst whom a Russian Count Tolstoi was conspicuously kind; but I must here mention the excellent impression made upon me by the novelist Champfleury's amiable pamphlet, of which I and my concerts formed the subject. In a series of light and airy aphorisms he displayed such a comprehension of my music, and even of my personality, that I had never again met with such a suggestive and masterly appreciation, and had only come across its equal once before in Liszt's lucubrations on *Lohengrin* and *Tannhäuser*. My personal acquaintance with Champfleury, which followed, brought me face to face with a very simple and in a certain sense easy-tempered individual, such as one seldom meets, and belonging to a type of Frenchman fast becoming extinct.

The advances made me by the poet Baudelaire were in their way still more significant. My acquaintance with him began with a letter in which he told me his impressions of my music and the effect it had produced upon him, in spite of his having thought till then that he possessed an artistic sense for colouring, but none for sound. His opinions on the matter, which he expressed in the most fantastic terms and with audacious self-assurance, proved him, to say the least, a man of extra-

ordinary understanding, who with impetuous energy followed
the impressions he received from my music to their ultimate
consequences. He explained that he did not put his address
to his letter in order that I might not be led to think that he
wanted something from me. Needless to say, I knew how to
find him, and had soon included him among the acquaintances
to whom I announced my intention of being at home every
Wednesday evening.

I had been told by my older Parisian friends, amongst whom
I continued to count the faithful Gaspérini, that this was the
right thing to do in Paris; and so it came about that, in accordance with the fashion, I used to hold a *salon* in my small house
in the Rue Newton, which made Minna feel that she occupied
a very dignified position, though she only knew a few scraps of
French, with which she could barely help herself out. This
salon, which the Olliviers also attended in a friendly way, was
crowded for a time by an ever-growing circle. Here an old
acquaintance of mine, Malwida von Meysenburg, again came
across me, and from that time forth became a close friend for
life. I had only met her once before; this was during my
visit to London in 1855, when she had made herself known to
me by a letter in which she enthusiastically expressed her agreement with the opinions contained in my book *Das Kunstwerk
der Zukunft*. The occasion on which we had met in London
had been at an evening party at the house of a family called
Althaus, when I found her full of the desires and projects
for the future perfection of the human race to which I had
given expression in my book, but from which, under the influence of Schopenhauer and a profound realisation of the
intense tragedy of life and the emptiness of its phenomena, I
had turned away with almost a feeling of irritation. I found
it very painful in discussing the question, not to be understood
by this enthusiastic friend and to have to appear to her in the
light of a renegade from a noble cause. We parted in London
on very bad terms with one another. It was almost a shock to
me to meet Malwida again in Paris. Very soon, however, all
unpleasant recollections of our discussion in London were
wiped out, as she at once explained to me, that our dispute had
had the effect of making her decide to read Schopenhauer at

once. When, by earnest study, she had made herself acquainted
with his philosophy, she came to the conclusion that the opinions
she had at that time expressed and eagerly maintained concerning the happiness of the world must have vexed me on account
of their shallowness. She then declared herself to be one of my
most zealous followers in the sense that she, from now, became
a true friend who was ever anxious for my welfare. When the
laws of propriety compelled me to introduce her as a friend of
mine to my wife, she could not help noticing at the first glance
the misery of our merely nominal life in common, and realising the discomfort resulting from it, made it her business to
interpose with affectionate solicitude. She also quickly saw
the difficult position in which I was placed in Paris with my
almost purposeless enterprises and the absence of all material
security. The tremendous expenses I had incurred in giving
the three concerts had not remained a secret from any of those
concerned about me. Malwida also soon guessed the difficulties
in which I found myself, since no prospect was opened on any
side which could be looked upon as a practical result of my
enterprise and a compensation for the sacrifices I had made.
Entirely of her own accord she felt it her duty to try and
obtain help for me, which she endeavoured to get from a certain
Mme. Schwabe, the widow of a rich English tradesman, in
whose house she had found shelter as governess to the eldest
daughter, and whom she now proposed to introduce to me. She
did not conceal from herself or from me what a disagreeable
task the cultivation of this acquaintance might be to me;
nevertheless she relied on the kindness she thought this somewhat grotesque woman possessed, as well as on her vanity,
which would prompt her to repay me for the distinction she
obtained by frequenting my *salon*. As a matter of fact I was
entirely at the end of my resources, and I only found courage
to deny my poverty-stricken condition in public on account of
the horror I felt when I learned that a collection was being
made for me amongst the Germans in Paris to indemnify me
for the expense I had incurred in giving the three concerts.
When the news of this reached me I immediately interfered
with the declaration that the idea that I was in distress in
consequence of the losses I had sustained was founded on a

false report, and that I should be obliged to refuse all efforts made on my behalf. On this supposition Mme. Schwabe, who regularly attended my soirées and as regularly fell asleep while any music was going on, was however induced, through the solicitations of Malwida, to offer me her personal assistance. She gave me about three thousand francs, of which at this moment I was certainly in the greatest need; as I did not wish to accept this money as a gift, I gave the lady, who in no way exacted it, a written agreement of my own accord, by which I undertook to return this sum at the end of a year. She good-naturedly accepted this, not as a security but merely in order to satisfy my feelings. When, at the end of this time, I found it impossible to meet my obligation, I turned to Malwida, who was still in Paris, and asked her to tell Mme. Schwabe, who had left, how matters stood, and to obtain her consent to the renewal of the agreement for another year. Malwida earnestly assured me I need not take the trouble to ask for a renewal, as Mme. Schwabe had never looked upon the sum given me as anything but a contribution towards my undertaking, in which she flattered herself that she took great interest. We shall see later on how the case really stood.

During this stirring time I was deeply moved and surprised to receive a present from an admirer in Dresden called Richard Weiland; it was an artistic silver ornament representing a sheet of music surrounded by a crown of laurels; upon the sheet were engraved the first bars from the principal themes of my various operas up to *Rheingold* and *Tristan*. The modest fellow once paid me a visit afterwards and told me that he had gone regularly to different places in order to see the productions of my operas, which had given him the opportunity of comparing the representation of *Tannhäuser* in Prague, in which the overture had lasted twenty minutes, with the one in Dresden, which, under my direction, had only taken twelve minutes.

My acquaintance with Rossini also proved agreeably stimulating to me in another way; a comic writer had attributed an anecdote to him according to which, when his friend Caraffa declared himself an admirer of my music, he had served him his fish without sauce at dinner, and explained in so doing that his friend liked music without melody. Rossini openly protested against this in an article in which he designated the story as a *mauvaise blague* and at the same time declared that he would never allow himself such a jest at the expense of a man who was trying to extend his influence in the artistic world. When I heard of this, I did not for a moment hesitate to pay Rossini a visit, and was received by him in the friendliest manner, which I afterwards described in a memorandum devoted to reminiscences of him. I was also glad to hear that my old acquaintance Halévy, during the controversy occasioned by my music, had taken my part in a kindly way, and I have already described my visit to him and our conversation on that occasion.

In spite of all these pleasant and stimulating events, nothing occurred to make my position less uncertain. I was still kept in doubt as to whether I should receive an answer from the Emperor Napoleon to my request for the use of the Opera House for the repetition of my concerts. Only by obtaining this, and having no preliminary expenses in consequence, could I gain the benefit which was becoming more and more necessary to me. It remained an understood thing that the Minister Fould was assiduously using his influence to turn the Emperor against me. As, on the other hand, I had made the surprising discovery that Marshal Magnan had been present at all three of my concerts, I hoped to enlist this gentleman's sympathy, which might be turned to good account, as the Emperor was particularly indebted to him since the events of the 2nd of December. I was anxious to circumvent Fould's intrigues, as the man had become most obnoxious to me, and I consequently introduced myself to the Marshal, and was one day surprised to see a hussar ride up to my door, who got down from his horse, rang the bell, and handed my astonished man-servant a letter from Magnan, in which he summoned me to his presence.

I was therefore duly received at the Commandant's residence by this military man, whose bearing struck me as stately, almost to the point of rudeness. He chatted very intelligently with me, frankly confessing his delight in my music, and listening very attentively to the report of my flagrantly futile addresses to the Emperor, as well as to my expressions of suspicion regarding Fould. I was told later that he spoke very plainly to Fould that very evening at the Tuileries on my behalf.

This much at least is certain, that from that moment I noticed that my affairs took a more favourable turn in that quarter. Yet the deciding factor was found at last in a movement on my behalf from a source I had hitherto entirely disregarded. Bülow, arrested by his interest in the outcome of these matters, continued to prolong his stay in Paris. He had come with letters of introduction from the Princess-Regent of Prussia to the Ambassador, Count Pourtalès. His hope that the latter might eventually express a desire to have me presented to him had so far remained unfulfilled. In order, therefore, to compel him to make my acquaintance, he finally adopted the plan of inviting the Prussian Ambassador and his attaché, Count Paul Hatzfeld, to lunch at Vachette's, a first-class restaurant, where I was to accompany him. The result of this meeting was certainly everything that could be desired. Not only did Count Pourtalès charm me with the simplicity and undisguised warmth of his conversation and attitude towards me, but from this time forward Count Hatzfeld used to visit me and also frequented my Wednesday evening At Homes, and at last brought me the news that there was a distinct movement in my favour at the Tuileries. Finally, one day he requested me to go with him to call on the Emperor's military chamberlain, Count Bacciochi, and from this official I received the first hints of a reply to my earlier application to his Imperial Majesty, who now expressed a wish to know why I wanted to give a concert in the Grand Opera House. No one, he said, took any serious interest in such enterprises, and it could do me no good. He thought it might perhaps be better if he were to persuade M. Alphonse Royer, the director of this imperial institution, to come to some understanding with me respecting the composition of an opera written on purpose for Paris. As I would not agree to his suggestion, this and other subsequent interviews remained for the time being without result. On one of these occasions Bülow accompanied me, and we were both struck by a ridiculous habit peculiar to this singular old man, whom Belloni said he had known in his youth as a box-office clerk at the Scala Theatre in Milan. He suffered from involuntary spasmodic movements of the hands, the result of certain not very creditable physical infirmities, and probably to conceal these he continually toyed with a small stick, which he tossed to and fro with seeming affectation. But even after I had at last succeeded in gaining access to the imperial officials, it seemed as though next to nothing would be done on my behalf, when suddenly one morning Count Hatzfeld overwhelmed me with news that on the preceding evening the Emperor had given orders for a performance of my *Tannhäuser*. The decisive word had been spoken by Princess Metternich. As I happened to be the subject of conversation near the Emperor, she had joined the circle, and on being asked for her opinion, she said she had heard *Tannhäuser* in Dresden, and spoke in such enthusiastic terms in favour of it that the Emperor at once promised to give orders for its production. It is true that Fould, on receiving the imperial command the same evening, broke out into a furious rage, but the Emperor told him he could not go back upon his promise, as he had pledged his word to Princess Metternich. I was now once more taken to Bacciochi, who this time received me very seriously, but first of all made the singular inquiry as to what was the subject of my opera. This I had to outline for him, and when I had finished, he exclaimed with satisfaction, ' *Ah! le Pape ne vient pas en scène? C'est bon! On nous avait dit que vous aviez fait paraître le Saint Père, et ceci, vous comprenez, n'aurait pas pu passer. Du reste, monsieur, on sait à présent que vous avez énormément de génie; l'Empereur a donné l'ordre de représenter votre opéra.*' He moreover assured me that every facility should be placed at my disposal for the fulfilment of my wishes, and that henceforth I must make my arrangements direct with the manager Royer.

This new turn of affairs put me into a state of vague agitation, for at first my inner conviction could only make me feel that singular misunderstandings would be sure to arise. For one thing, all hope of being able to carry out my original plan of producing my work in Paris with a picked German company was now at an end, and I could not conceal from myself that I had been launched upon an adventure which might turn out well or badly. A few interviews with the manager Royer sufficed to enlighten me as to the character of the enterprise entrusted to me. His chief anxiety was to convince me of the necessity of rearranging my second act, because according to him it was absolutely necessary for a grand ballet to be introduced at this point. To this and similar suggestions I hardly deigned to reply, and as I went home asked myself what I should do next, in case I decided to refuse to produce my *Tannhäuser* at the Grand Opera.

Meanwhile other cares, more immediately connected with my personal affairs, pressed heavily upon me, and compelled me to devote every effort to their removal. With this object in view I decided at once to carry out an undertaking suggested to me by Giacomelli, namely, a repetition of my concerts in Brussels. A contract had been made with the Théâtre de la Monnaie there for three concerts, half the proceeds of which, after the deduction of all expenses, was to be mine. Accompanied by my agent, I started on 19th March for the Belgian capital, to see whether I could not manage to recoup the money lost on my Paris concerts. Under the guidance of my mentor I found myself compelled to call upon all sorts of newspaper editors and, among other Belgian worthies, a certain M. Fétis *père*. All I knew about him was that, years before, he had allowed himself to be bribed by Meyerbeer to write articles against me, and I now found it amusing to enter into conversation with this man, who, although he assumed great airs of authority, yet in the end declared himself entirely of my opinion.

Here also I made the acquaintance of a very remarkable man, the Councillor of State Klindworth, whose daughter, or, as some said, his wife, had been recommended to me by Liszt when I was in London. But I had not seen her on that occasion, and I now had the pleasant surprise of being invited to call upon her in Brussels. While she, on her part, showed the greatest cordiality towards me, M. Klindworth provided me with inexhaustible entertainment by the narrative of his wonderful career as a diplomatist in numerous transactions of which I had hitherto known nothing. I dined with them several times, and met Count and Countess Condenhoven, the latter being a daughter of my old friend Mme. Kalergis. M. Klindworth showed a keen and lasting interest in me, which even prompted him to give me a letter of recommendation to Prince Metternich, with whose father he said he had been on very familiar terms.

He had a strange habit of interlarding his otherwise frivolous conversation with continual references to an omnipotent Providence, and when, during one of our later interviews, I once hazarded a risky retort, he quite lost his temper, and I fancied he was going to break off our connection. Fortunately this fear was not realised, either at that time or afterwards.

But except for these interesting acquaintances, I gained nothing in Brussels but anxiety and fruitless exertion. The first concert, for which season-tickets were suspended, drew a large audience. But, owing to my misconception of a clause in our agreement, the cost of musical accompaniment, which was put down to me alone, was reckoned at so high a figure by the managers, that next to nothing was left over by way of profit. This deficiency was to be recouped from the second concert, to which, however, season-ticket holders were admitted free. But beyond these persons, who, I was told, almost filled the house, there were few single-ticket holders, so that there was not enough left to pay my travelling and hotel expenses, which had been increased by the inclusion of my agent and servant. I consequently gave up the idea of having a third concert, and set off once more for Paris in a not very cheerful frame of mind, but with the gift of a vase of Bohemian glass from Mme. Street, Klindworth's daughter whom I have already mentioned. Nevertheless, my stay in Brussels, including a short trip from there to Antwerp, had served to distract my thoughts a little. As I did not at that moment feel at all inclined to devote my precious time to looking at works of art, I contented myself in Antwerp with a cursory glance at its outward aspect, which I found less rich in antiquities than I had anticipated. The situation of its famous citadel proved peculiarly disappointing. In view of the first act of my *Lohengrin* I had presumed that this citadel, which I imagined as the ancient keep of Antwerp, would from the opposite side of the Scheldt be a prominent object to the eye. Instead of which, nothing whatever was to be seen but a monotonous plain, with fortifications sunk into the earth. After this, whenever I saw *Lohengrin* again, I could not restrain a smile at the scene-painter's castle, perched aloft in the background on its stately mountain.

On returning to Paris at the end of March my sole anxiety was how to repair my impecunious and therefore hopeless position. The pressure of these monetary cares seemed all the more incongruous from the fact that the notoriety of my position had made my house, where, of course, I allowed no signs of poverty to appear, exceedingly popular. My Wednesday receptions became more brilliant than ever. Interesting strangers sought me out, in the hope that they, too, might attain to equal fortune through knowing me. Fräulein Ingeborg Stark, who afterwards married young Hans von Bronsart, put in an appearance among us, a vision of bewitching elegance, and played the piano, in which she was modestly assisted by Fräulein Aline Hund of Weimar. A highly gifted young French musician, Camille Saint-Saëns, also played a very agreeable part in our musical entertainments; a noteworthy addition to my other French acquaintances was made in the person of M. Frédéric Villot. He was Conservateur des Tableaux du Louvre, an exceedingly polished and cultured man, whom I met for the first time in Flaxland's music-shop, where I did a good deal of business. To my surprise I happened to overhear him asking about the score of *Tristan*, which he had ordered. On being introduced to him I learned, in reply to my inquiry, that he already possessed the scores of my earlier operas; and when I then asked whether he thought it possible for me to make my dramatic compositions pay, as I could not understand how he, without any knowledge of the German language, could rightly appreciate the music, which was so closely allied to the sense of the poetry, he answered wittily that it was precisely my music which afforded him the best guidance to a comprehension of the poem itself. This reply strongly attracted me to the man, and from that time I found great pleasure in keeping up an active correspondence with him. For this reason, when I brought out a translation of my operatic poems, I felt that its very detailed preface could not be dedicated to any worthier man. As he was not able to play the scores of my operas himself, he had them performed for him by Saint-Saëns, whom he apparently patronised. I thus learned to appreciate the skill and talent of this young musician, which was simply amazing. With an unparalleled sureness and rapidity of glance with regard to even the most complicated orchestral score, this young man combined a not less marvellous memory. He was not only able to play my scores, including *Tristan*, by heart, but could also reproduce their several parts, whether they were leading or minor themes. And this he did with such precision that one might easily have thought that he had the actual music before his eyes. I afterwards learned that this stupendous receptivity for all the technical material of a work was not accompanied by any corresponding intensity of productive power; so that when he tried to set up as a composer I quite lost sight of him in the course of time.

I now had to enter into closer communication with the manager of the Opera House, M. Royer, with regard to the production of *Tannhäuser*, which he had been commissioned to prepare. Two months passed before I was able to make up my mind whether to say yes or no to the business. At no single interview did this man fail to press for the introduction of a ballet into the second act. I might bewilder him, but with all the eloquence at my command I could never convince him on the point. At last, however, I could no longer refuse to consider the advisability of preparing a suitable translation of the poem.

Arrangements for this work had so far progressed very slowly. As I have already said, I had found M. de Charnal altogether incompetent, Roger had permanently disappeared from my sight, and Gaspérini showed no real desire for the work. At last a certain Herr Lindau came to see me, who protested that with the aid of young Edmond Roche he could produce a faithful translation of *Tannhäuser*. This man Lindau was a native of Magdeburg, who had fled to escape the Prussian military service. He had first been introduced to me by Giacomelli on an occasion when the French singer engaged by him to sing 'L'Étoile du Soir' at one of my concerts had disappointed us, and he had recommended Lindau as a very efficient substitute. This man promptly declared his readiness to undertake this song, with which he was quite familiar, without any rehearsal, an offer which led me to regard him as a genius sent down from heaven on purpose for me. Nothing could, therefore, equal my amazement at the unbounded impudence of the man; for on the evening of the concert he executed his task with the most amateurish timidity; he did not enunciate a single note of the song clearly, and nothing but astonishment at so unprecedented a performance appeared to restrain the audience from breaking out into marked disapproval. Yet, in spite of this, Lindau, who had all sorts of explanations and excuses to offer for his short-comings, contrived to insinuate himself into my house, if not as a successful singer, at least as a sympathetic friend. There, thanks to Minna's partiality, he soon became an almost daily guest. In spite of a certain inward repugnance towards him, I treated him with tolerant good-nature, not so much because of the 'enormous connection' he said he could influence, but because he really showed himself to be a most obliging fellow on all sorts of occasions.

But the fact that finally induced me to grant him a share in the translation of *Tannhäuser* was his suggestion that young Roche should also participate in the work.

I had become acquainted with Roche immediately after my arrival in Paris (in the September of the previous year), and this in a somewhat remarkable and flattering way. In order to receive my furniture on its arrival from Zürich I had to go to the Custom House, where I was referred to a pale, seedy-looking young man, who appeared full of life, however, with whom I had to settle my business. When I wished to give him my name, he enthusiastically interrupted me with the exclamation, '*O, je connais bien Monsieur Richard Wagner, puisque j'ai son portrait suspendu au-dessus de mon piano.*' Much astonished, I asked what he knew about me, and learned that by careful study of my pianoforte arrangements he had become one of my most fervent admirers. After he had helped me with self-sacrificing attentions to complete my tiresome business with the Custom House, I made him promise to pay me a visit. This he did, and I was able to obtain a clearer insight into the necessitous position of the poor fellow, who, so far as I was able to judge, showed signs of possessing great poetic talent. He further informed me that he had tried to eke out a precarious living as a violinist in the orchestras of the smaller vaudeville theatres, but that being a married man he would, for the sake of his family, much prefer a situation in some office with a fixed salary and prospects of promotion. I soon found that he thoroughly understood my music, which, he assured me, gave him the only pleasure he had in his hard life. As regards his power of poetical composition, I could only gather from Gaspérini and other competent judges that he could, at any rate, turn out very good verse. I had already thought of him as a translator for *Tannhäuser*, and now that the only obstacle to his doing the work, his ignorance of the German language, was removed by Lindau's proffered collaboration, the possibility of such an arrangement at once decided me to accept the latter's offer.

The first thing on which we agreed was that a fair prose translation of the whole subject should be taken in hand, and this task I naturally entrusted to Lindau alone. A serious delay, however, intervened before this was delivered to me, which was subsequently explained by the fact that Lindau was quite unable to provide even this dry version, and had pressed the work on another man, a Frenchman who knew German, and whom he induced to undertake it by holding out hopes of a fee, to be squeezed out of me later on. At the same time Roche turned a few of the leading stanzas of my poem into verse, with which I was well contented. As I was thus satisfied about the ability of my two helpers, I visited Royer in order to make my position secure by obtaining his authority for a contract with the two men. He did not seem to like my placing the work in the hands of two perfectly unknown people; but I insisted that they should at least have a fair trial. As I was obstinately resolved not to withdraw the work from Roche, but soon realised Lindau's complete inefficiency, I joined in the task myself at a cost of much exertion. We frequently spent four hours together in my room in translating a few verses, during which time I often felt tempted to kick Lindau out, for although he did not even understand the German text, he was always ready with the most impudent suggestions. It was only because I could not think of any other way of keeping poor Roche in the business that I endured such an absurd association.

This irritating and laborious work lasted for several months, during which I had to enter into fuller negotiations with Royer respecting his preparations for the production of *Tannhäuser*, and particularly with regard to the cast and distribution of the parts. It struck me as odd that hardly any of the leading singers of the Opera were suggested by him. As a matter of fact none of them aroused my sympathy, with the sole exception of Mme. Gueymard, whom I would gladly have secured for Venus, but who, for reasons I never clearly understood, was refused me. In order to form an honest opinion of the company at my disposal, I now had to attend several performances of such operas as *La Favorita, Il Trovatore,* and *Semiramis,* on which occasions my inner conviction told me so clearly that I was being hopelessly led astray, that each time I reached home I felt I must renounce the whole enterprise. On the other hand, I found continual encouragement in the generous way in which M. Royer, in obedience to authority, now offered to secure me any singer I might choose to designate. The most important item was a tenor for the title-rôle. I could think of no one but Niemann of Hanover, whose fame reached me from every quarter. Even Frenchmen such as Foucher de Careil and Perrin, who had heard him in my operas, confirmed the report of his great talent. The manager also regarded such an acquisition as highly desirable for his theatre, and Niemann was accordingly invited to come to Paris with a view of being engaged. Besides him, M. Royer wished me to agree to his securing a certain Mme. Tedesco, a tragedienne, who, on account of her beauty, would be a very valuable addition to the repertoire of his theatre, protesting that he could think of no woman better fitted for the part of Venus. Without knowing the lady I gave my consent to this excellent proposal, and moreover agreed to the engagement of a Mlle. Sax, a still unspoiled young singer with a very beautiful voice, as well as of an Italian baritone, Morelli, whose sonorous tones, as contrasted with the sickly French singers of this class, had greatly pleased me during my visits to the Opera. When these arrangements were concluded, I thought I had done all that was really necessary, though I did not cherish any very firm conviction on the matter.

Amid these labours I passed my forty-seventh birthday in a far from happy frame of mind, to which, however, on the evening of this day, the peculiarly bright glow of Jupiter gave

me an omen of better things to come. The beautiful weather,
suitable to the time of year, which in Paris is never favourable
to the conduct of business, had only tended to increase the
stringency of my needs. I was and still continued to be without any prospect of meeting my household expenses, which
had now become very heavy. As I was ever anxious, amid
all my other discomforts, to find some relief from this burden,
I had made an agreement with the music-dealer Flaxland
for the sale of all my French rights in the *Fliegender Holländer,*
Tannhäuser, and *Lohengrin* for whatever they would fetch.
Our contract stipulated that for each of these three operas
he was to pay me a sum of one thousand francs down, and
further payments on their being performed in a Paris theatre,
namely, one thousand francs after the first ten performances,
and the same amount for the following performances up to
the twentieth. I at once notified my friend Pusinelli of
this contract, having made this condition in his favour when
selling my operas to Meser's successors. This I did by way
of guaranteeing him the repayment of the capital advanced
for their publication. I begged him, however, to allow me
to retain Flaxland's first instalment on account, as otherwise
I should be stranded in Paris without the means of bringing
my operas to the point of being profitable. My friend agreed
to all my suggestions. The Dresden publisher, on the contrary, was just as disagreeable, and complained at once that
I was infringing his rights in France, and so worried Flaxland
that the latter felt justified in raising all sorts of difficulties
against me.

I had almost become involved in fresh complications in consequence, when one day Count Paul Hatzfeld appeared at my
house with a request that I would visit Mme. Kalergis, who had
just arrived in Paris, to receive certain communications from
her. I now saw the lady again for the first time since my stay
in Paris with Liszt in 1853. She greeted me by declaring how
much she regretted not having been present at my concerts
in the preceding winter, as she had thereby missed the chance
of helping me in a time of great stress. She had heard that I
had suffered great losses, the account of which she had been
told ran to ten thousand francs, and she now begged me to

accept that sum from her hand. Although I had thought it right to deny these losses to Count Hatzfeld, when an application was made to the Prussian embassy on behalf of the odious subscription-list, yet I had now no reason whatever for hiding the truth from this noble-hearted woman. I felt as though something were now being fulfilled which I had always been entitled to expect, and my only impulse was an immediate desire to show my gratitude to this rare lady by at least doing something for her. All the friction which disturbed our later intercourse sprang solely from my inability to fulfil this desire, in which I felt ever more and more confirmed by her singular character and restless, unsettled life. For the present I endeavoured to do something for her which should prove the reality of my feeling of obligation. I improvised a special performance of the second act of my *Tristan*, in which Mme. Viardot was to share the singing parts with myself, and on which occasion my friendship for the latter received a considerable impetus; while for the pianoforte accompaniment I summoned Klindworth at my own expense from London. This exceedingly select performence took place in Mme. Viardot's house. Besides Mme. Kalergis, in whose honour alone it was given, Berlioz was the only person present. Mme. Viardot had specially charged herself with securing his presence, apparently with the avowed object of easing the strained relations between Berlioz and myself. I was never clear as to the effect produced upon both performers and listeners by the presentation under such circumstances of this extraordinary selection. Mme. Kalergis remained dumb. Berlioz merely expressed himself warmly on the *chaleur* of my delivery, which may very well have afforded a strong contrast to that of my partner in the work, who rendered most of her part in low tones. Klindworth seemed particularly stirred to anger at the result. His own share was admirably executed; but he declared that he had been consumed with indignation at observing Viardot's lukewarm execution of her part, in which she was probably determined by the presence of Berlioz. By way of set-off to this, we were very pleased by the performance, on another evening, of the first act of the *Walküre*, at which, in addition to Mme. Kalergis, the singer Niemann was present.

This man had now arrived in Paris, at the request of the manager Royer, to arrange a contract. I confess I was astounded at the pose he assumed, and the airs with which he presented himself at my door with the question, 'Well, do you want me or do you not?' Nevertheless, when we went to the manager's office he pulled himself together, so as to make a good effect. In this he succeeded admirably, for every one was amazed to meet a tenor of such extraordinary physical endowments. Nevertheless, he had to submit to a nominal trial performance, for which he chose the description of the pilgrimage in *Tannhäuser*, acting and singing it upon the stage of the Grand Opera House. Mme. Kalergis and Princess Metternich, who were secretly present at this performance, were both enthusiastically prepossessed in Niemann's favour, as were also all the members of the management. He was engaged for eight months at a monthly salary of ten thousand francs. His contract referred solely to *Tannhäuser*, as I felt obliged to protest against the singer appearing before this in other operas.

The conclusion of this agreement, and the remarkable circumstances under which it had been brought about, filled me with a hitherto unknown consciousness of the power thus suddenly placed in my hands. I had also been drawn into closer contact with Princess Metternich, who was undoubtedly the good fairy of the whole enterprise, and I was now also received with flattering cordiality by her husband and by the whole diplomatic circle to which they belonged. To the Princess, in particular, people attributed an almost omnipotent influence at the French Imperial Court, where Fould, the otherwise influential Minister of State, could effect nothing against her in matters pertaining to myself. She instructed me to apply only to her for the fulfilment of all my wishes, and said she would know how to find ways and means of attaining the success of the project, on which she had now evidently set her heart, all the more firmly because she saw that I still had no real faith in the enterprise.

Under these more hopeful auspices I spent the months from summer to autumn, when rehearsals were to begin. It was a great boon to me that I was just then able to make provision for Minna's health, as the doctors had urgently prescribed her a visit to the baths of Soden, near Frankfort. She accordingly set off at the beginning of July, when I promised myself the pleasure of fetching her on the completion of her cure, as it happened that I myself had occasion to visit the Rhine at that time.

It was just at this moment that an improvement took place in my relations with the King of Saxony, who had hitherto obstinately opposed to grant me an amnesty. I owed this to the growing interest now taken in me by the other German embassies, especially those of Austria and Prussia. Herr von Seebach, the Saxon Ambassador, who was married to a cousin of my magnanimous friend, Mme. Kalergis, had shown great kindness to me, and at last he seemed to grow tired of being continually taunted by his colleagues about my objectionable position as a 'political refugee,' and consequently felt it his duty to make representations to his court on my behalf. In this action he appears to have been generously assisted by the Princess-Regent of Prussia — once more through the intervention of Count Pourtalès. I heard that on the occasion of a meeting between the German princes and the Emperor Napoleon in Baden she used her influence on my behalf with the King of Saxony. The result was that, after settling several ridiculous objections, all of which Herr von Seebach had to repeat to me, the latter was able to report that, although King John would not pardon me, nor permit my return to the kingdom of Saxony, yet he would raise no obstacle to my staying in any other state in the German Confederation which I might have to visit in pursuit of my artistic aims, provided such a state made no objection to my presence. Herr von Seebach added the further hint, that it would be advisable for me to present myself to the Princess-Regent on the occasion of my next visit to the Rhineland, in order to express my thanks for her kindly intercession, a courtesy which he gave me to understand the King of Saxony himself appeared to desire.

But before this project could be realised I had still to endure the most harassing torments with my translators of *Tannhäuser*. Amid these anxieties, and indeed throughout all my previous worries, I was again suffering from my old malady, which now seemed to have settled in my abdomen. As a remedy I was advised to take horse exercise. The painter Czermak, a friendly young man, whom Fräulein Meysenburg had introduced to me, offered his help for the necessary riding lessons. In return for a subscription for a fixed period, a man from a livery stables brought round his quietest horses, for which we had specially bargained, for the use of myself and comrade, upon which we ventured forth with the utmost caution for a ride in the Bois de Boulogne. We chose the morning hours for this exercise, so as not to meet the elegant cavaliers of the fashionable world. As I placed implicit reliance on Czermak's experience, I was naturally astonished to find that I far excelled him, if not in horsemanship, at least in courage, for I was able to endure the exceedingly disagreeable trot of my horse, whereas he loudly protested against every repetition of the experience. As I grew bolder I resolved one day to ride out alone. The groom who brought me the horse prudently kept an eye on me as far as the Barrière de l'Étoile, as he was doubtful of my ability to take my horse beyond this point. And, in fact, as I drew near to the Avenue de l'Impératrice my steed obstinately refused to go any further: he curveted sideways and backwards and frequently stood stock-still. In this he persisted until at last I decided to return, in which the prudent foresight of the groom luckily came to my rescue. He helped me down from my beast in the open street and led it home smiling. With this experience my last effort to become a horseman came to an inglorious end, and I lost ten rides, the vouchers for which remained unused in my desk.

By way of compensation I found abundant refreshment and regular exercise in solitary walks in the Bois de Boulogne, gaily accompanied by my little dog Fips, during which I learned once more to appreciate the sylvan beauty of this artificial pleasure-ground. Life also had become quieter, as is usually the case at this season in Paris. Bülow, after hearing that his déjeûner at Vachette's had produced the extraordinary result of an imperial command for the production of *Tannhäuser*, had long since gone back to Germany; and in August I also set out on my carefully planned excursion to the German Rhine districts. There I first turned my steps, via Cologne, to Coblenz, where I expected to find Princess Augusta of Prussia. Learning, however, that she was in Baden, I made my way towards Soden, whence I fetched Minna for a further tour, accompanied by her recently acquired friend, Mathilde Schiffner. We touched at Frankfort, where I met my brother Albert for the first time since leaving Dresden, as he also happened to be passing through this city.

When I was there it occurred to me that this was the residence of Schopenhauer, but a singular timidity restrained me from calling upon him. My temper just then seemed too distraught and too far removed from all that which might have formed a subject for conversation with Schopenhauer, even if I had felt strongly attracted towards him, and which alone could have furnished a reason for intruding myself upon him, in spite of such disinclination. As with so many other things in my life, I again deferred one of its most precious opportunities until that fervently expected 'more favourable season,' which I presumed was sure to come some day. When, a year after this flying visit, I again stayed some time in Frankfort to superintend the production of my *Meistersinger*, I imagined that at last this more favourable opportunity for seeing Schopenhauer had come. But, alas! he died that very year, a fact which led me to many bitter reflections on the uncertainty of fate.

During this earlier visit another fondly cherished hope also came to nothing. I had reckoned on being able to induce Liszt to meet me in Frankfort, but instead found only a letter declaring it impossible to grant the fulfilment of my wish.

From this town we went straight to Baden-Baden. Here I abandoned Minna and her friend to the seductions of the roulette-table, while I availed myself of a letter of introduction from Count Pourtalès to Countess Hacke, a lady-in-waiting on her Royal Highness, through whom I hoped to be presented to her exalted patroness. After a little delay I duly received an invitation to meet her in the Trinkhalle at five o'clock in the afternoon. It was a wet, cold day, and at that hour the whole surroundings of the place seemed absolutely devoid of life as I approached my momentous rendezvous. I found Augusta pacing to and fro with Countess Hacke, and as I approached she graciously stopped. Her conversation consisted almost entirely of assurances that she was completely powerless in every respect, in reponse to which I imprudently cited the hint received from the King of Saxony that I should offer her my personal thanks for previous intervention on my behalf. This she seemed evidently to resent, and dismissed me with an air of indifference meant to show that she took very little interest in my concerns. My old friend Alwine Frommann told me later that she did not know what there was about me that displeased the Princess, but thought it might possibly be my Saxon accent.

This time I left the much-praised paradise of Baden without carrying away any very friendly impression, and at Mannheim boarded a steamer, accompanied only by Minna, on which for the first time I was borne along the famous Rhine. It struck me as very strange that I should so often have crossed the Rhine without having once made the acquaintance of this most characteristic historical thoroughfare of mediæval Germany. A hasty return to Cologne concluded this excursion, which had lasted only a week, and from which I returned to face once more the solution of the problems of my Parisian enterprise, now opening out painfully before me.

One factor which seemed likely greatly to relieve the difficulties confronting me was to be found in the friendly relationship into which the young banker, Emil Erlanger, was pleased to enter towards me. This I owed, in the first place, to an extraordinary man named Albert Beckmann, a former Hanoverian revolutionary, and afterwards private librarian to Louis Napoleon, who was at this time a press agent for several interests, respecting which I was never quite clear. This man succeeded in making my acquaintance as an open admirer, in which capacity he showed himself remarkably obliging. He now informed me that M. Erlanger, by whom he was also employed in connection with the press, would be pleased to know me. I was on the point of bluntly declining the honour, saying that I wanted to know nothing about any banker except with regard to his money, when he answered my jest by telling me in all seriousness that it was precisely in this way that M. Erlanger desired to serve me. As a result of this invitation I made the acquaintance of a genuinely agreeable man, who, having often heard my music in Germany, had become inspired by a sympathetic interest in my person. He frankly expressed a desire that I should commit the management of my financial business entirely to his hands, which meant, in fact, nothing less than that he would permanently hold himself responsible for any needful subsidies, in return for which I was to assign to him all the eventual proceeds of my Paris undertakings. This offer was distinctly novel, and moreover exactly fell in with the needs of my peculiar situation. And, in fact, so far as my subsequent financial security was concerned, I had no further difficulties to encounter until my position in Paris was fully decided. And although my later intercourse with M. Erlanger was accompanied by many circumstances which no man's kindly courtesy could have relieved, yet I ever found in him a truly devoted friend, who earnestly studied both my own personal welfare and the success of my enterprises.

This eminently satisfactory turn of events was calculated to inspire me with high courage had the circumstances been somewhat different. As it was, it had no power to excite in me even the slightest enthusiasm for an undertaking of which the hollowness and unsuitability for me personally were clearly revealed every time I approached it. It was with a feeling of ill-humour that I met every demand made by this venture, and yet it represented the foundation of the confidence reposed in me. My mind was subjected, however, to a certain refreshing uncertainty as to the character of my scheme by a new acquaintance who was introduced to me in connection with it. M. Royer informed me that he could not ' pass ' the translation which I had taken infinite pains to conjure into existence through the two men who had volunteered to help me. He most earnestly recommended a thorough revision by M. Charles Truinet, whose pseudonym was Nuitter. This man was still young and extraordinarily attractive, with something friendly and open in his manner. He had called on me a few months ago to offer his co-operation in the translation of my operas, on the introduction of Ollivier, his colleague at the Paris bar. Proud of my connection with Lindau, however, I had refused his help; but the time had now come when, in consequence of M. Royer's strictures, Truinet's renewed offer of his services had to be taken into consideration. He understood no German, but maintained that as far as this was concerned he could place sufficient reliance upon his old father, who had travelled for a long time in Germany and had acquired the essentials of our language. As a matter of fact, there was no need for special knowledge in this respect, as the sole problem seemed to be to make the French verses less stiff and stilted which poor Roche had constructed under the shameful control of Lindau, who used to make out that he knew everything better than any one else. The inexhaustible patience with which Truinet proceeded from one change to another in order to satisfy my requirements, even with regard to the musical fitness of the version, won my sympathy for this last collaborator. From this time forward we had to keep Lindau away from the slightest interference in this new modelling of the 'book.' He had been recognised as quite incompetent. Roche, on the other hand, was retained, in so far as his work served as a basis for the new versification. As it was difficult for him to leave his custom office, he was excused from troubling about the remaining part of the work, as Truinet was quite free and could keep in daily touch with me. I now saw that Truinet's law degree was merely ornamental, and that he never had any thought of conducting a case. His chief interests lay in the administration of the Grand Opera, to which he was attached as keeper of the archives. First with one collaborator and then with another he had also worked at little plays for the vaudeville and theatres of a lower order, and even for the Bouffes Parisiens; but he was ashamed of these productions and always knew how to evade talking about this sphere of activity. I was greatly obliged to him for the final arrangement of a text to my *Tannhäuser* which could be sung and which was regarded on all sides as 'acceptable.' But I cannot remember ever having been attracted by anything poetic or even æsthetic in his nature. His value, however, as an experienced, warm-hearted, staunchly devoted friend at all times, especially in periods of the greatest distress, made itself more and more clearly felt. I can hardly remember ever meeting a man of such sound judgment on the most difficult points, or one so actively ready when occasion arose to uphold the view I advocated.

We had first of all to join forces in promoting an entirely new piece of work. In obedience to a need I had always felt, I had seized the occasion of this carefully prepared production of *Tannhäuser* to expand and considerably fill out the first Venus scene. For this purpose I wrote the text in loosely constructed German verses, so as to leave the translator quite free to work them out in a suitable French form: people told me that Truinet's verses were not at all bad; and with these as a basis I composed the extra music for the scene, and only fitted a German text to it afterwards. My annoying discussions with the management on the subject of a big ballet had determined me to make extensive additions to the scene of the ' Venusberg.' I thought that this would give the staff of the ballet a chorographic task of so magnificent a character that there would no longer be any occasion to grumble at me for my obstinacy in this matter. The musical composition of the two scenes occupied most of my time during the month of September, and at the same time I began the pianoforte rehearsals of *Tannhäuser* in the foyer of the Grand Opera.

The company, part of which had been freshly engaged for this purpose, were now assembled, and I was interested in learning the way in which a new work is studied at the French Opera.

The characteristic features of the system in Paris may be described simply as extreme frigidity and extraordinary accuracy. M. Vauthrot, the chorus-master, excelled in both these qualities. He was a man whom I could not help regarding as hostile to me, because I had never been able to win from him a single expression of enthusiasm. On the other hand, he proved to me by the most punctilious solicitude how conscientious he really was about his work. He insisted on considerable alterations in the text, so as to obtain a favourable medium for singing. My knowledge of the scores of Auber and Boieldieu had misled me into assuming that the French people were entirely indifferent as to whether the mute syllables in poetry and singing were to be sounded or not. Vauthrot maintained that this was only the case with composers, but not with good singers. He was always feeling misgivings about the length of my work, which I met with the observation that I could not understand how he could be afraid of boring the public with any opera after they had been accustomed to find pleasure in

Rossini's *Semiramis*, which was often produced. Upon this he
paused to reflect, and agreed with me so far as the monotony
of action and of music in that work was concerned. He told
me not to forget, however, that the public neither cared for
action nor music, but that their whole attention was directed to
the brilliancy of the singers. *Tannhäuser* gave little scope for
brilliancy, and, as a matter of fact, I had none of that quality at
my disposal. The only singer in my company who had any
claim to such a distinction was Mme. Tedesco, a rather grotesque
but voluptuous type of Jewess who had returned from Portugal
and Spain after having had great triumphs in Italian operas.
She did not conceal her satisfaction at having secured an
engagement at the Paris Opera through my unwilling choice
of her for the part of Venus. She gave herself no end of trouble
to solve the problem to the best of her ability — a problem which
was entirely beyond her and which was suited only to a genuine
tragedy actress. For a certain time her efforts appeared to
be crowned with success, and several special rehearsals with
Niemann led to a lively affinity between Tannhäuser and Venus.
As Niemann mastered the French pronunciation with considerable skill, these rehearsals, in which Fräulein Sax also
proved delightful, made genuine and encouraging progress.
Up to this point these rehearsals were undisturbed, as my
acquaintance with M. Dietzsch was as yet very slight. According to the rules of the Opera House, Dietzsch had
hitherto only been present at the pianoforte rehearsals as *chef
d'orchestre* and future conductor of the opera, so as to make
himself accurately acquainted with the intentions of the
singers. Still less was I disturbed by M. Cormon, the stage
manager, who was also present at the rehearsals, and with a
lively skill, characteristic of the French people, conducted the
numerous so-called 'property' rehearsals, at which the way
each scene was to be played was determined. Even when
M. Cormon or others did not understand me, they were always
ready to subordinate themselves to my decisions; for I continued
to be regarded as all-powerful, and everybody thought that
I could enforce what I wanted through Princess Metternich,
a belief which, indeed, was not without foundation. For instance, I had learned that Prince Poniatowsky was threatening

to place a serious obstacle in the way of continuing our rehearsals by reviving one of his own operas, the production of which had fallen through. The undaunted Princess met my complaints on this subject by obtaining an immediate order that the Prince's opera should be laid aside. Naturally this did not tend to ingratiate me with the Prince, and he did not fail to make me feel his displeasure when I called upon him. In the midst of all this work I was afforded some recreation by a visit from my sister Louise with part of her family. To entertain her in my own home presented the greatest difficulties owing to the strange fact that it was now becoming absolutely dangerous to approach my house. When I first took it, the proprietor gave me a fairly long lease, but would not undertake any repairs. I now discovered the reason of this was that it had just been decided by the Paris Committee of Reconstruction to clear the Rue Newton with all its side streets to facilitate the opening up of a broad boulevard from one of the bridges to the Barrière de l'Étoile. But up to the last moment this plan was officially denied, so as to avoid for as long as possible the liability of paying compensation for the land that was to be expropriated. To my astonishment I noticed that excavations were being made close to my front door; these increased in width, so that at first no carriages could pass my door, and finally my house was unapproachable even on foot. Under these circumstances the proprietor had no objection to make to my leaving the house. His sole stipulation was that I should sue him for damages, as that was the only way by which he in his turn could sue the government. About this time my friend Ollivier was debarred for three months on account of a parliamentary misdemeanour; he therefore recommended me for the conduct of my case to his friend Picard, who, as I saw later on from the legal proceedings, acquitted himself of his task with much humour. Nevertheless, there was no chance of damages for me (whether the proprietor obtained any, I cannot say); but, at all events, I had to content myself with being released from my agreement. I also obtained leave to look about for another house, and instituted my search in a neighbourhood less remote from the Opera. I found a poor cheerless spot in the Rue d'Aumale. Late in the autumn in stormy

weather we completed the arduous task of moving, in which
Louisa's daughter, my niece Ottilie, proved a capable and willing
child. Unfortunately I caught a violent cold in the course of
moving and took few precautions to check it. I again exposed
myself to the growing excitement of the rehearsals, and eventually I was struck down by typhoid fever.

We had reached the month of November. My relations had
to go home, leaving me behind in a state of unconsciousness,
in which I was consigned to the care of my friend Gaspérini.
In my fits of fever I insisted on their calling in all imaginable
medical aid, and, as a matter of fact, Count Hatzfeld did
bring in the doctor attached to the Prussian embassy. The
injustice thus done to my friend, who took the greatest care of
me, was due to no mistrust of him, but to feverish hallucinations
which filled my brain with the most outrageous and luxuriant
fancies. In this condition, not only did I imagine that Princess Metternich and Mme. Kalergis were arranging a complete
court for me, to which I invited the Emperor Napoleon, but
I actually requested that Emil Erlanger should place a villa
near Paris at my disposal, and that I should be removed to
it, as it was impossible for me to recover in the dark hole
where I was. At last I insisted on being taken to Naples,
where I promised myself a speedy recovery in free intercourse
with Garibaldi. Gaspérini held bravely out against all this
madness, and he and Minna had to use force in order to apply
the necessary mustard-plasters to the soles of my feet. During
bad nights later on in life similar vain and extravagant fancies
used to return to me, and on waking I have realised with horror
that they were the offspring of that period of fever. After five
days we mastered the fever; but I seemed to be threatened
with blindness, and my weakness was extreme. At last the
injury to my sight passed away, and after a few weeks I again
trusted myself to steal along the few streets between my house
and the Opera, to satisfy my anxiety for the continuation of the
rehearsals.

People here had indulged in the oddest ideas, and seemed to
have assumed that I was as good as dead. I learned that
the rehearsals had been needlessly suspended, and moreover
gathered from one indication after another that the affair had

practically collapsed, although in my intense desire for recovery I tried my utmost to conceal this from myself. But I was much elated and pleased to see that the translation of the four operatic librettos which had so far appeared had been published. I had written a very exhaustive preface to them addressed to M. Frédéric Villot. The translation of all this had been arranged for me by M. Challemel Lacour, a man with whom I had become acquainted at Herwegh's house in days gone by when he was a political refugee. He was a highly intelligent translator, and had now done me such admirable service that every one recognised the value of his work. I had given J. J. Weber, the bookseller in Leipzig, the German original of the preface to publish under the title of *Zukunftsmusik*. This pamphlet also reached me now, and pleased me, as it probably represented the only result of my whole Paris undertaking, which looked so brilliant on the surface.

At the same time I was now in a position to complete the new composition for *Tannhäuser*, of which the great dance scene in the Venusberg was still incomplete. I finished it at three o'clock one morning after staying up all night, just as Minna returned home from a great ball at the Hôtel de Ville to which she had been with a friend. I had given her some handsome presents for Christmas, but as far as I myself was concerned I continued, on the advice of my doctor, to assist the slow process of recovery by a beefsteak in the morning and a glass of Bavarian beer before going to bed. We did not watch the old year out; on the contrary, I retired to bed and slept calmly into 1861.

1861. — The slackness with which the rehearsals of *Tannhäuser* were being conducted when I fell ill changed at the beginning of the new year into a more decided handling of all the details connected with the intended performance. But I could not fail to notice at the same time that the attitude of all those who took part was substantially altered. The rehearsals, which were more numerous than might be expected, gave me the impression that the management was adhering to the strict execution of a command, but were not fired by any hope of successful results. Certainly I now obtained a clearer insight into the actual state of affairs. From the press, which was entirely in the hands of Meyerbeer, I knew long ago what I had

to expect. The management of the Opera, probably after repeated efforts to make the chief leaders in the press tractable,
were now likewise convinced that my *Tannhäuser* venture
would only meet with a hostile reception from that quarter.
This view was shared even in the highest circles, and it seemed
as if an attempt was being made to discover some means
whereby to win over to my side that part of the operatic public
which could turn the scales. Prince Metternich sent me an invitation one day to meet the new cabinet minister, Count Walewsky. An air of ceremony pervaded the introduction, and made it
particularly significant when the Count in a persuasive speech
endeavoured to convince me that they entertained every wish
for my good fortune and desired to help me to a brilliant success.
He added in conclusion that the power to effect this was in my
own hands, if I would only consent to introduce a ballet into
the second act of my opera; the most celebrated ballet-dancers
from St. Petersburg and London had been proposed to me,
and I had only to make my selection; their engagement would
be concluded as soon as I had entrusted the success of my
work to their co-operation. In declining these proposals I
think I was no less eloquent than he in making them. My
complete failure, however, was due to the fact that I did not
appear to understand the worthy minister when he informed
me that the ballet in the first act counted for nothing, because
those devotees of the theatre who only cared for the ballet
on an opera night were accustomed, according to the new
fashion, not to dine until eight o'clock, and so did not reach the
theatre until ten o'clock, when about half the performance was
over. I replied that I could not undertake myself to oblige these
gentlemen, but might well hope duly to impress another part
of the public. But with his imperturbable air of ceremony he
met me with the objection that these gentlemen's support could
alone be counted upon to produce a successful result, inasmuch
as they were powerful enough even to defy the hostile attitude
of the press. This precaution awakened no response in me, and
I offered to withdraw my work altogether, whereupon I was
assured with the greatest earnestness that, according to the
Emperor's command, which had to be universally respected,
I was master of the situation, and my wishes would be followed

in everything. The Count had only thought it his duty to give me a friendly piece of advice.

The consequences of this conversation soon became evident in many ways. I threw myself enthusiastically into the work of carrying out the great dance scenes of the first act, and tried to win Petitpas, the ballet-master, to my side. I asked for unheard-of combinations quite different from those generally employed in the ballet. I drew attention to the dances of the Mænads and Bacchantes, and astounded Petitpas with the mere proposition that he would be able to accomplish something of the kind with his graceful pupils, as it was well within his powers. He explained to me that by placing my ballet at the beginning of the first act I had myself renounced all claim to the step-dancers attached to the Opera, and all he could do was to offer to engage three Hungarian dancers, who had formerly danced in the fairy scenes at the Porte St. Martin, to fill the parts of the three graces. As I was quite content to dispense with the distinguished dancers belonging to the Opera, I insisted all the more that the rank and file of the ballet should be actively coached. I wanted to know that the male staff was present in full force, but I learned that it was impossible to bring it up to my requirements, unless some tailors were engaged who, for a monthly salary of fifty francs, figured in a vague way in the wings during the performances of the solo dancers. Finally I tried to produce my effects by means of the costumes, and asked for considerable funds for that purpose, only to learn, after I had been wearied by one subterfuge after another, that the management was determined not to expend a halfpenny on my ballet, which they regarded as completely wasted. Such was the substance of what my trusty friend Truinet conveyed to me. This was the first sign out of many which soon revealed to me the fact, that even in the circles of the operatic administration itself *Tannhäuser* was already regarded as labour lost and sheer waste of trouble.

The atmosphere created by this conviction now weighed with increasing pressure upon everything which was undertaken for the preparation of a performance which was postponed time after time. With the beginning of the year the rehearsals had reached the stage at which the scenes were arranged and the orchestral practices begun. Everything was conducted with a care which impressed me very agreeably at the beginning, until finally I was bored by it, because I saw that the powers of the performers were being relaxed by eternal repetition, and it was now evident that I must trust to my own ability to pull the matter quickly through as I thought best. But it was not the fatigue due to this system that finally made Niemann, the main prop in my work, recoil from the task which at the start he had undertaken with an energy full of promise. He had been informed that there was a conspiracy to ruin my work. From this time forward he was a victim to a despondency to which, in his relations with me, he sought to lend a sort of diabolical character. He maintained that so far he could only see the matter in a black light, and he brought forward some arguments that sounded very sensible; he criticised the whole Opera as an institution and the public attached to it, and also our staff of singers, of whom he maintained that not a single one understood his part as I intended it; and he exposed all the disadvantages of the undertaking, which I myself could not fail to see as soon as I came to deal with the *chef du chant,* the *régisseur,* the ballet-master, the conductor of the chorus, but, particularly, with the *chef d'orchestre.* Above all, Niemann (who at the beginning, with a full knowledge of what it involved, had imposed upon himself the task of playing his part without curtailments of any sort) insisted upon cutting down the score. He met my expression of astonishment with the remark, that I must not suppose that the sacrifice of this or that passage mattered, but that we were in the throes of an undertaking which could not be got through too quickly.

Under circumstances from which so little encouragement could be derived, the study of *Tannhäuser* dragged itself along to the brink of the so-called ' dress ' rehearsals. From all sides the friends of my past life gathered together in Paris to be present at the apotheosis of the first performance. Among these were Otto Wesendonck, Ferdinand Präger, the unfortunate Kietz, for whom I had to pay the costs of his journey and of his stay in Paris; luckily M. Chandon from Epernay came, too, with a hamper of ' Fleur du Jardin,' the finest of all his champagne brands. This was to be drunk to the success of *Tann-*

häuser. Bülow also came, depressed and saddened by the burdens of his own life, and hoping to be able to gather courage and renewed vitality from the success of my undertaking. I did not dare to tell him in so many words of the miserable state of affairs; on the contrary, seeing him so depressed, I made the best of a bad matter. At the first rehearsal, however, at which Bülow was present, he did not fail to grasp how matters stood. I no longer concealed anything from him; and we continued to indulge in sorrowful intercourse till the night of the performance, which was again and again postponed, and it was only his untiring efforts to be of use to me that gave some life to our companionship. From whatever side we regarded our grotesque undertaking, we encountered unsuitability and incompetence. For instance, it was impossible in the whole of Paris to find the twelve French horns which in Dresden had so bravely sounded the hunting call in the first act. In connection with this matter I had to deal with the terrible man Sax, the celebrated instrument-maker. He had to help me out with all kinds of substitutes in the shape of saxophones and saxhorns; moreover, he was officially appointed to conduct the music behind the scenes. It was an impossibility ever to get this music properly played.

The main grievance, however, lay in the incompetence of M. Dietzsch, the conductor, which had now reached a pitch hitherto unsuspected. In the numerous orchestral rehearsals which had been held hitherto, I had accustomed myself to use this man like a machine. From my habitual position on the stage near his desk I had conducted both conductor and orchestra. In this way I had maintained my *tempi* in such a way that I felt no doubt that on my removal all my points would remain firmly established. I found, on the contrary, that no sooner was Dietzsch left to his own resources than everything began to waver; not one *tempo*, not one *nuance* was conscientiously and strictly preserved. I then realised the extreme danger in which we were placed. Granted that no one singer was suited to his task, or qualified to achieve it so as to produce a genuine effect; granted that the ballet, and even the sumptuous mounting and vitality of the Parisian performances of the day, could contribute nothing on this occasion,

or at most but little; granted that the whole spirit of the
libretto, and that indefinable *something* which even in the worst
performances of *Tannhäuser* in Germany roused a feeling of
home, was likely here to strike an alien or at best an unfamiliar note; yet in spite of all this the character of the
orchestral music, which if rendered with emphasis was full of
suggestive expression, led one to hope that it would make an
impression even upon a Parisian audience. But it was precisely
in this particular that I saw everything submerged in a colourless
chaos, with every line of the drawing obliterated; moreover, the
singers became more and more uncertain in their work; even
the poor ballet-girls were no longer able to keep time in their
trivial steps; so that at last I thought myself obliged to interpose
with the declaration that the opera required a different conductor, and that in case of necessity I myself was ready to take
his place. This declaration brought to a climax the confusion
that had grown up around me. Even the members of the
orchestra, who had long recognised and openly ridiculed their
conductor's incompetence, took sides against me now that the
matter concerned their notorious chief. The press lashed itself
into fury over my ' arrogance,' and in the face of all the agitation caused by the affair, Napoleon III. could send me no
better advice than to forgo my requests, as in adhering to
them I should only be exposing the chances of my work to the
greatest risks. On the other hand, I was allowed to start fresh
rehearsals and have them repeated until I was satisfied.

This way out of the difficulty could lead to nothing but an
increase of fatigue for me and for the whole staff actively engaged in the undertaking, and the fact still remained that M.
Dietzsch could not be depended upon for the *tempo*. Finally, by
sheer force of will rather than of conviction, I tried to imagine
I was doing a service by holding out for the correct interpretation of a performance which, after all, had to be got through;
whereupon for the first time the impetuous musicians broke out
into rebellion against the excessive rehearsals. At this stage
I noticed that the guarantee of my practical control given by
the general management was not altogether made in good faith,
and in the face of the growing complaint on all sides against
being overfatigued I decided ' to demand the return of my

score,' as they called it; that is to say, to dispense with the production of the opera. I addressed an express request to this effect to the cabinet minister Walewsky, but received the answer that it was impossible to comply with my wishes, more particularly on account of the heavy expenses which had already been incurred in its preparation. I refused to abide by his decision, and called a conference of those friends of mine who were more closely interested in me, among whom were Count Hatzfeld and Emil Erlanger. I took counsel with them as to the means at my disposal for forbidding *Tannhäuser* to be performed at the Opera House. It happened that Otto Wesendonck was present at this conference; he was still waiting in Paris hoping to have the pleasure of attending the first performance, but he was now thoroughly convinced that the situation was hopeless, and promptly fled back to Zürich. Präger had already done likewise. Kietz alone held out faithfully, and he busied himself in trying to make some money in Paris to provide for his future, in which attempt he was hampered by many difficulties that stood in the way of his desire. This conference resulted in fresh representations being made to the Emperor Napoleon, which, however, met with the same gracious reply as before, and I was authorised to institute a fresh course of rehearsals. At last, weary to the depths of my soul, completely disillusioned, and absolutely decided in my pessimistic view of the matter, I determined to abandon it to its fate.

Having at last, in this frame of mind, given my consent to fix the date of the first performance of my opera, I was now plagued in another direction in the most astonishing way. Every one of my friends and partisans demanded a good seat for the first night; but the management pointed out that the occupation of the house on such occasions was entirely in the hands of the court and those dependent on it, and I was soon to realise clearly enough to whom these seats were to be allotted. At present I had to suffer the annoyance of being unable to serve many of my friends as I should have liked. Some of them were very quick to resent what they supposed to be my neglect of them. Champfleury in a letter complained of this flagrant breach of friendship; Gaspérini started an open quarrel because

I had not reserved one of the best boxes for his patron and my creditor Lucy, the Receiver-General of Marseilles. Even Blandine, who had been filled with the most generous enthusiasm for my work at the rehearsals she had attended, could not suppress a suspicion that I was guilty of neglecting my best friends when I was unable to offer her and her husband Ollivier anything better than a couple of stalls. It needed all Emil's *sang-froid* to obtain from this deeply offended friend a just appreciation of the honest assurance that I was in an impossible position, in which I was exposed to betrayal on all sides. Poor Bülow alone understood everything; he suffered with me, and shirked no trouble to be of use to me in all these difficulties. The first performance on the 13th of March put an end to all these complications; my friends now understood that it was to no celebration of my triumphs, as they supposed, to which they should have been invited.

I have already said enough elsewhere of the way in which this evening passed off. I was justified in flattering myself that in the end a favourable view of my opera prevailed, inasmuch as the intention of my opponents had been to break up this performance completely, and this they had found it impossible to do. But I was grieved the next day to receive nothing but reproaches from my friends, with Gaspérini at the head of them, because I had allowed the occupation of the house at the first performance to be completely wrested out of my hands. Meyerbeer, they urged, knew how to work such things differently; had he not, ever since he first appeared in Paris, refused to allow the production of a single one of his operas to take place without a guarantee that he himself should fill the auditorium, to the remotest corner? As I had not looked after my best friends, such as M. Lucy, was not the ill-success of that evening to be ascribed to my own conduct? Confronted with these and similar arguments, I had to spend the whole day in writing letters and in devoting myself to the most urgent efforts at propitiation. Above all, I was besieged with advice as to how I might recover the lost ground at the subsequent performances. As the management placed a very small number of free seats at my disposal, money had to be found for the purchase of tickets. In the pursuit of this object, which my friends were so warmly advocating and which involved much that was disagreeable, I shrank from approaching Emil Erlanger or anybody else. Giacomelli, however, had found out that Aufmordt, the merchant, a business friend of Wesendonck, had offered to help to the extent of five hundred francs. I now allowed these champions of my welfare to act according to their own ideas, and was curious to see what assistance I should derive from these resources which I had previously neglected and now utilised.

The second performance took place on the 18th of March, and, indeed, the first act promised well. The overture was loudly applauded without a note of opposition. Mme. Tedesco, who had eventually been completely won over to her part of Venus by a wig powdered with gold dust, called out triumphantly to me in the manager's box, when the 'septuor' of the finale of the first act was again vigorously applauded, that everything was now all right and that we had won the victory. But when shrill whistling was suddenly heard in the second act, Royer the manager turned to me with an air of complete resignation and said, '*Ce sont les Jockeys; nous sommes perdus.*' Apparently at the bidding of the Emperor, extensive negotiations had been entered into with these members of the Jockey Club as to the fate of my opera. They had been requested to allow three performances to take place, after which they had been promised that it should be so curtailed as to admit of its presentation only as a curtain-raiser to introduce a ballet which was to follow. But these gentlemen had not agreed to the terms. In the first place, my attitude during the first performance (which had been such a bone of contention) had been observed to be utterly unlike that of a man who would consent to the proposed line of conduct; this being so, it was to be feared that if two more performances were allowed to take place without interruption, we might hope to win so many adherents that the friends of the ballet would be treated to repetitions of this work thirty times running. To guard against this they determined to protest in time. The fact that these gentlemen meant business was now realised by the excellent M. Royer; and from that time he gave up all attempt to resist them, in spite of the support granted to our party by the Emperor and his Consort, who stoically kept their seats through the uproars of their own courtiers.

The impression made by this scene had a disastrous effect upon my friends. After the performance Bülow broke out into sobs as he embraced Minna, who had not been spared the insults of those next to her when they recognised her as the wife of the composer. Our trusty servant Therese, a Swabian girl, had been sneered at by a crazy hooligan, but when she realised that he understood German, she succeeded in quieting him for a time by calling him *Schweinhund* at the top of her voice. Poor Kietz was struck dumb with disappointment, and Chandon's ' Fleur du Jardin ' was growing sour in the storeroom.

Hearing that in spite of everything a third performance was fixed, I was confronted with only two possible solutions of the difficulty. One was, to try once more to withdraw my score; the other, to demand that my opera should be given on a Sunday, that is to say, on a non-subscriber's day. I assumed that such a performance could not be regarded by the usual ticket-holders as a provocation, for they were quite accustomed on such days to surrender their boxes to any of the general public who chanced to come and buy them. My strategical proposal seemed to please the management and the Tuileries, and was accepted. Only they refused to conform to my wish to announce this as the third and *last* performance. Both Minna and I stayed away from this, as it was just as embarrassing for me to know that my wife was insulted as to see the singers on the stage subjected to such behaviour. I was really sorry for Morelli and Mlle. Sax, who had proved their genuine devotion to me. As soon as the first performance was over, I met Mlle. Sax in the corridor on her way home, and chaffed her about being whistled off the stage. With proud dignity she replied, ' *Je le supporterai cent fois comme aujourd' hui. Ah, les misérables!* ' Morelli found himself strangely perplexed when he had to weather the onslaught of the hooligans. I had explained to him in the minutest detail how to act his part from the time when Elizabeth disappears in the third act, until the beginning of his song to the evening star. He was not to move an inch from his rocky ledge, and from this position, half turning to the audience, he was to address his farewell to the departing lady. It had been a difficult task for him to obey my instructions, as he maintained that it was against all operatic custom for the singer not to address such an important passage straight to the public from the footlights. When in the course of the performance he seized his harp to begin the song, there was a cry from the audience, ' *Ah! il prend encore sa harpe*,' upon which there was a universal outburst of laughter followed by fresh whistling, so prolonged, that at last Morelli decided boldly to lay aside his harp and step forward to the proscenium in the usual way. Here he resolutely sang his evening carol entirely unaccompanied, as Dietzsch only found his place at the tenth bar. Peace was then restored, and at last the public listened breathlessly to the song, and at its close covered the singer with applause.

As the vocalists showed a courageous determination to encounter fresh onslaughts, I could not protest. At the same time I could not endure to be in the position of a passive spectator suffering at the infliction of such unworthy methods, and as the third performance was also likely to be attended with doubtful consequences, I stayed at home. After the various acts messages reached us informing us that after the first act Truinet at once came round to my opinion that the score should be withdrawn; it was found that the 'Jockeys' had not stayed away, as was their custom, from this Sunday performance; on the contrary, they had purposely taken their seats from the beginning, so as not to allow a single scene to pass without a row. I was assured that in the first act the performance had been twice suspended by fights lasting a quarter of an hour each. By far the greater part of the public obstinately took my part against the childish conduct of the rowdies, without intending by their action to express any opinion of my work. But in opposing their assailants they were at a great disadvantage. When everybody on my side was utterly wearied out with clapping and shouting applause and calling ' Order,' and it looked as if peace were about to reign once more, the ' Jockeys ' returned afresh to their task and began cheerfully whistling their hunting-tunes and playing their flageolets, so that they were always bound to have the last word. In an interval between the acts one of these gentlemen entered the box of a certain great lady, who in the excess of her anger introduced him to one of her friends with the words, ' *C'est un de ces misérables, mon cousin.*' The young man, completely unabashed, answered, ' *Que voulez-vous?* I am beginning to like the music myself. But, you see, a man must keep his word. If you will excuse me, I will return to my work again.' He thereupon took his leave. The next day I met Herr von Seebach, the friendly Saxon Ambassador, who was as hoarse as he could be, as he and all his friends had completely lost their voices through the uproar of the previous night. Princess Metternich had remained at home, as she had already had to endure the coarse insults and ridicule of our opponents at the first two performances.

She indicated the height to which this fury had risen by mentioning some of her best friends, with whom she had engaged in so virulent a controversy that she had ended by saying: ' Away with your free France! In Vienna, where at least there is a genuine aristocracy, it would be unthinkable for a Prince Liechtenstein or Schwarzenberg to scream from his box for a ballet in *Fidelio*. I believe she also spoke to the Emperor in the same strain, so that he seriously debated whether by police intervention some check could not be put upon the unmannerly conduct of these gentlemen, most of whom, unfortunately, belonged to the Imperial Household. Some rumour of this got abroad, so that my friends believed they had really gained the day when, at the third performance, they found the corridors of the theatre occupied by a strong body of police. But it turned out later on that these precautions had only been taken to ensure the safety of the ' Jockeys,' as it was feared they might be attacked from the pit as a punishment for their insolence. It seems that the performance, which was again carried through to the end, was accompanied from start to finish by an endless tumult. After the second act the wife of von Szemere, the Hungarian revolutionary minister, joined us in a state of complete collapse, declaring that the row in the theatre was more than she could bear. No one seemed able to tell me exactly how the third act had been got through. As far as I could make out, it resembled the turmoil of a battle thick with the smoke of gunpowder.

I invited my friend Truinet to visit me the next morning, so that with his help I might compose a letter to the management withdrawing my work and, as author, forbidding any further performance of the same, as I did not wish to see my singers abused instead of myself by a section of the public from whom the Imperial administration seemed unable to protect them. The astonishing thing about the whole matter was that in thus interfering I was guilty of no bravado, for a fourth and fifth performance of the opera had been already arranged, and the management protested that they were under obligations to the public, who still continued to crowd to this opera. But through Truinet I contrived to have my letter published the next day in the *Journal des Débats*, so that at last, though with great reluctance, the management gave their consent to my withdrawal of the piece.

Thereupon the legal action taken on my behalf by Ollivier against Lindau also came to an end. The latter had put in a claim on my author's rights in the libretto, in which he said he was entitled to a share as one of the three collaborators. His counsel, Maître Marie, based his plea on a principle which I was said to have established myself, namely that the point of chief importance was not the melody, but the correct declamation of the words of the libretto, which obviously neither Roche nor Truinet could have ensured, seeing that neither of them understood German. Ollivier's argument for the defence was so energetic that he was almost on the point of proving the purely musical essence of my melody by singing the ' Abendstern.' Completely carried away by this, the judges rejected the plaintiff's claim, but requested me to pay him a small sum by way of compensation, as he seemed really to have taken some part in the work at the beginning. In any case, however, I could not have paid this out of the proceeds of the Paris performances of *Tannhäuser*, as I had decided with Truinet, on withdrawing the opera, to hand over the whole of the proceeds from my author's rights, both for libretto and music, to poor Roche, to whom the failure of my work meant the ruin of all his hopes for the amelioration of his position.

Various other connections were also dissolved by this outcome of affairs. During the past few months I had busied myself with an artistic club which had been founded, chiefly through the influence of the German embassies, among an aristocratic connection for the production of good music apart from the theatres, and to stimulate interest in this branch of art among the upper classes. Unfortunately, in the circular it had published it had illustrated its endeavours to produce good music by comparing them to those of the Jockey Club to improve the breed of horses. Their object was to enrol all who had won a name in the musical world, and I was obliged to become a member at a yearly subscription of two hundred francs. Together with M. Gounod and other Parisian celebrities, I was nominated one of an artistic committee, of which Auber was elected president. The society often held its meetings at the house of a certain Count Osmond, a lively young man, who had lost an arm in a duel, and posed as a musical dilettante. In this way I also learned to know a young Prince Polignac, who interested me particularly on account of his brother, to whom we were indebted for a complete translation of *Faust*. I went to lunch with him one morning, when he revealed to me the fact that he composed musical fantasies. He was very anxious to convince me of the correctness of his interpretation of Beethoven's Symphony in A major, in the last movement of which he declared he could clearly demonstrate all the phases of a shipwreck. Our earlier general meetings were chiefly occupied with arrangements and preparations for a great classical concert, for which I also was to compose something. These meetings were enlivened solely by Gounod's pedantic zeal, who with unflagging and nauseating garrulity executed his duties as secretary, while Auber continually interrupted, rather than assisted the proceedings, with trifling and not always very delicate anecdotes and puns, all evidently intended to urge us to end the discussions. Even after the decisive failure of *Tannhäuser* I received summonses to the meetings of this committee, but never attended it any more, and sent in my resignation to the president of the society, stating that I should probably soon be returning to Germany.

With Gounod alone did I still continue on friendly terms, and I heard that he energetically championed my cause in society. He is said on one occasion to have exclaimed: ' *Que*

Dieu me donne une pareille chute!' As an acknowledgment of this advocacy I presented him with the score of *Tristan und Isolde,* being all the more gratified by his behaviour because no feeling of friendship had ever been able to induce me to hear his *Faust.*

I now came into touch with energetic protagonists of my cause at every turn. I was particularly honoured in the columns of those smaller journals of which Meyerbeer had as yet taken no account, and several good criticisms now appeared. In one of these I read that my *Tannhäuser* was *la symphonie chantée.* Baudelaire distinguished himself by an exceedingly witty and aptly turned pamphlet on this topic; and finally Jules Janin himself astonished me by an article in the *Journal des Débats,* in which, with burning indignation, he gave a somewhat exaggerated report, in his own peculiar style, of the whole episode. Even parodies of *Tannhäuser* were given in the theatres for the delectation of the public; and Musard could find no better means of attracting audiences to his concerts than the daily announcement, in enormous letters, of the Overture to *Tannhäuser.* Pasdeloup also frequently produced some of my pieces by way of showing his sentiments. And lastly, Countess Löwenthal, the wife of the Austrian military plenipotentiary, gave a great matinée, at which Mme. Viardot sang various items from *Tannhäuser,* for which she received five hundred francs.

By some singular coincidence people managed to confound my fate with that of a certain M. de la Vaquerie, who had also made a dismal failure with a drama, *Les Funérailles de l'Honneur.* His friends gave a banquet, to which I was invited, and we were both enthusiastically acclaimed. Fiery speeches were made about the *encanaillement* of the public, containing references to politics, which were easily explained by the fact that my partner in the festivity was related to Victor Hugo. Unfortunately particular supporters had provided a small piano, on which I was literally compelled to play favourite passages from *Tannhäuser.* Whereupon the evening became a festival in my honour alone.

But a much more important result than these was that people began to recognise the reality of my popularity, and began to plan yet greater undertakings. The manager of the Théâtre Lyrique sought everywhere for a tenor suitable for *Tannhäuser,* and only his inability to find one compelled him to renounce his intention of producing my opera at once. M. de Beaumont, the manager of the Opéra Comique, who was on the verge of bankruptcy, hoped to save himself with *Tannhäuser,* with which intention he approached me with the most urgent proposals. True, he hoped at the same time to enlist Princess Metternich's intervention on his behalf with the Emperor, who was to help him out of his embarrassments. He reproached me with coldness when I failed to fall in with his glowing dreams, in which I could find no pleasure. But I was interested to learn that Roger, who now had a post at the Opéra Comique, had included part of the last act of *Tannhäuser* in the programme of a performance given for his own benefit, whereby he drew down upon his head the fury of the more influential press, but won a good reception from the public. Schemes now began to multiply. A. M. Chabrol, whose journalistic name was Lorbach, visited me on behalf of a company, whose director was an enormously wealthy man, with a plan for founding a Théâtre Wagner, of which I refused to hear anything until it could secure an experienced man of first-class reputation as manager. Eventually M. Perrin was selected for the post. This man had lived for years in the firm conviction that he would be some day appointed manager of the Grand Opera, and thought, therefore, that he ought not to compromise himself. It is true, he ascribed the failure of *Tannhäuser* entirely to Royer's incapacity, who ought to have made it his business to win over the press to his side. Nevertheless he was strongly tempted to share in the attempt because of the opportunity it afforded him of proving that, if he took the matter in hand, everything would at once wear a different aspect, and *Tannhäuser* become a great success. But as he was an exceedingly cold and cautious man, he thought he had discovered serious flaws in M. Lorbach's proposals, and when the latter began to stipulate for certain commissions, Perrin immediately fancied that he detected a not quite blameless savour of speculation in the whole business, and declared that if he wanted to found a Wagner Theatre, he would manage to procure the necessary funds in his own way. As a matter of fact, he did actually entertain the notion of securing a large café, the 'Alcazar,' and after that the 'Bazar de la Bonne Nouvelle,' for the purposes of such a theatre. It also seemed possible that the requisite capitalists would be found for his enterprise. M. Erlanger believed he could succeed in getting ten bankers to guarantee fifty thousand francs, thus placing a sum of five hundred thousand francs at M. Perrin's disposal. But the latter soon lost courage when he found that the gentlemen thus approached were willing to risk their money on a theatre for their own amusement, but not for the serious purpose of acclimatising my music in Paris.

With this disappointing experience M. Erlanger now withdrew from all further participation in my fate. From a business point of view he regarded the arrangement made with me as a sort of deal, in which he had not succeeded. The settlement of my financial position seemed likely now to be undertaken by other friends, and with this object in view the German embassies approached me with great delicacy, commissioning Count Hatzfeld to inquire into my necessities. My own view of the situation was simply that, in obedience to the Emperor's command for the production of my opera, I had wasted my time over an enterprise the failure of which had not been my fault. With perfect justice my friends pointed out how careless I had been not to secure from the first certain stipulations about compensations, a demand which the Frenchman's practical mind would at once have recognised as reasonable and obvious. As matters stood, I had demanded no return for my time and labour beyond certain author's rights in case of success. Feeling how impossible it was for me to approach either the management or the Emperor to retrieve this omission, I was content to leave Princess Metternich to intercede on my behalf. Count Pourtalès had stayed on in Berlin to try and persuade the Prince Regent to order a performance of *Tannhäuser* for my benefit. Unfortunately, the latter had been unable to secure the execution of his order owing to the opposition of his manager, Herr von Hülsen, who was hostile to me. As I had no other prospect for a long time to come but one of complete helplessness, I had no option but to leave the representation of my claim for compensation to the kindly care of my royal patroness. All these events had taken place within the short space of a month after the production of *Tannhäuser*, and now, on the 15th April, I went for a short trip to Germany, to try and find some solid ground for my future in that country.

The only person who really understood my deepest needs had already set out on the same road, away from the chaos of Parisian theatrical life. Bülow had just sent me news from Karlsruhe that the grand-ducal family were favourably disposed towards me, and I promptly formed the plan of immediately setting to work seriously on the production there of my *Tristan*, which had been so fatally deferred. Accordingly I went to Karlsruhe, and if anything could have decided me to execute my hastily formed plan, it would certainly have been the exceptionally cordial welcome I now received at the hands of the Grand Duke of Baden. This exalted personage seemed really desirous of awakening my sincerest confidence in himself. During an exceedingly intimate interview, at which his young wife was also present, the Grand Duke took pains to convince me that his profound sympathy for me was less as a composer of operas, whose excellence he neither wished nor was able to appreciate, than as the man who had suffered so much for his patriotic and independent opinions. As I naturally could not attach much value to the political importance of my past career, he imagined this arose from suspicious reticence, and encouraged me by the assurance that, although great mistakes and even offences might have been committed in this respect, these only affected those who, while they had remained in Germany, had not been made happy, and had thereby certainly atoned for their misdeeds by inward suffering. On the other hand, it was now the duty of all these guilty ones to repair the wrongs they had done to those who had been driven into exile. He gladly placed his theatre at my disposal, and gave the necessary orders to the manager. This was my old 'friend' Eduard Devrient, and the painful embarrassment he betrayed on my arrival fully justified all that Bülow had said about the complete worthlessness of those sentiments of sincere sympathy for me which he had hitherto affected. But in the happy atmosphere created by the Grand Duke's gracious reception I was soon able to bring Devrient — in appearance at least — to do as I wished, and he was compelled to assent to the proposed production of *Tristan*. As he was unable to deny that, especially since Schnorr's departure for Dresden, he did not possess the requisite singers for my work, he referred me to Vienna, expressing at the same time his astonishment that I did not try to have my operas produced there, where everything required was ready to hand. It cost me some trouble to make him understand why I preferred a few exceptionally fine performances of my works in Karlsruhe to the mere chance of having them inscribed on the repertoire of the Vienna Opera House. I obtained permission to secure Schnorr, who of course would be engaged only for the special performances at Karlsruhe, and was also allowed to choose in Vienna the other singers for our intended 'model performance.'

I was thus left to rely on Vienna, and had meanwhile to return to Paris, so as to settle my affairs there in such a way as to suit the execution of my latest project. I arrived there, after an absence of only six days, and my sole occupation was to provide money for the needs of the moment. Under these circumstances I could only feel indifferent to the many sympathetic advances and assurances which reached me with ever-growing cordiality, although at the same time they filled me with apprehension. In the meantime, the operations undertaken on a larger scale by Princess Metternich to secure me some compensation dragged along with mysterious slowness, and it was to a merchant named Stürmer, whom I had previously known in Zürich, that I owed my deliverance from my present troubles. He had constantly interested himself in my welfare while in Paris, and now by his help I was enabled, first to set my household affairs in order, and then to set off for Vienna.

Liszt had announced that he was coming to Paris some time before, and during the recent disastrous time I had longed for his presence, as I thought that, with his recognised position in the higher circles of Parisian society, he would have been able to exert a very helpful influence upon my hopelessly involved situation. A mysterious epistolary 'shrug of the shoulders' had been the only answer I had received to my various inquiries as to the cause of his delay. It seemed like irony on the part of Fate that, just as I had arranged everything for my journey to Vienna, news should come that Liszt would reach Paris in a few days. But I could only yield to the pressure of my necessities which sternly demanded that I should pick up new threads for my plan of life, and I quitted Paris about the middle of May, without awaiting my old friend's arrival.

I stopped first of all at Karlsruhe for another interview with the Grand Duke, who received me as kindly as ever, and granted me permission to engage in Vienna any singers I liked for a really fine performance of *Tristan* in his theatre. Armed with this command I went on to Vienna, where I stayed at the 'Erzherzog Karl,' and there waited for Conductor Esser to fulfil the promises he had made by letter to allow me to see a few performances of my operas. It was here that for the first time I saw my own *Lohengrin*. Although the opera had already been played very frequently, the entire company was present at the full rehearsal, as I desired. The orchestra played the prelude with such delightful warmth, the voices of the singers and many of their good qualities were so conspicuously and surprisingly pleasing, that I was too much overcome by the sensation created by them to have any desire to criticise the general performance. My profound emotion seemed to attract attention, and Dr. Hanslick probably thought this was a suitable moment for being introduced to me in a friendly way as I sat listening on the stage. I greeted him shortly, like a perfectly unknown person; whereupon the tenor, Ander, presented him a second time with the remark that Dr. Hanslick was an old acquaintance. I answered briefly that I remembered Dr. Hanslick very well, and once more turned my attention to the stage. It seems that exactly the same now happened with my Vienna friends as once before in the case of my London acquaintances, when the latter found me disinclined to respond to their efforts to make me conciliate the dreaded critics. This man, who as a budding young student had been present at the earliest performances of *Tannhäuser* in Dresden, and had written glowing reports on my work, had since become one of my most vicious antagonists, as was proved on the production of my operas in Vienna. The members of the opera company, who were all well disposed towards me, seemed to have devoted their whole attention to reconciling me, as best they could, with this critic. As they failed to do so, those who ascribe, to the enmity thus aroused, the subsequent failure of every attempt to launch my enterprise in Vienna, may be right in their opinion.

But for the present it seemed as though the flood of enthusiasm would bear down all opposition. The performance of *Lohengrin*, which I attended, was made the occasion of a frantic ovation, such as I have only experienced from the Viennese public. I was urged to have both my other operas presented also, but felt a sort of shyness at the thought of a repetition of that evening's occurrences. As I had now fully realised the serious weaknesses in the performance of *Tannhäuser*, I only agreed to a revival of the *Fliegender Holländer*, for the reason that I wished to hear the singer Beck, who excelled in that opera. On this occasion also the public indulged in similar manifestations of delight, so that, backed up by universal favour, I could begin to consider the main business on which I had come. The students of the University offered me the honour of a torchlight procession, which I declined, thereby winning the hearty approval of Esser, who, together with the chief officials of the Opera, asked me how these triumphs could be turned to account. I then presented myself to Count Lanckoronski, the Controller of the Emperor's household, who had been described to me as a peculiar person, totally ignorant of art and all its requirements. When I unfolded to him my request that he would graciously grant leave of obsence for a fairly long period to the chief singers of his Opera, namely, Frau Dustmann (*née* Luise Meyer), Herr Beck, and probably also Herr Ander, for the proposed performance of *Tristan* in Karlsruhe, the old gentleman dryly answered that it was quite impossible. He thought it much more reasonable, seeing I was satisfied with his company, that I should produce my new work in Vienna, and the courage necessary to refuse this proposition melted completely away.

As I descended the steps of the Hofburg, lost in meditation over this new turn of affairs, a stately gentleman of unusually sympathetic mien came to meet me at the door, and offered to accompany me in the carriage to my hotel. This was Joseph

Standhartner, a famous physician, who was exceedingly popular in high circles, an earnest devotee of music, thenceforth destined to be a faithful friend to me all my life.

Karl Tausig had also sought me out, and was now devoting his energies to Vienna, with the express determination of conquering this field for Liszt's compositions, and had opened his campaign there during the previous winter with a series of orchestral concerts, started and conducted by himself. He introduced me to Peter Cornelius, who had also been drawn to Vienna, and whom I only knew from our meeting in Bâle in 1853. They both raved about the recently published pianoforte arrangement of *Tristan*, which Bülow had prepared. In my room at the hotel, whither Tausig had transported a Bösendorff grand-piano, a musical orgy was soon in full swing. They would have liked me to have started rehearsing *Tristan* at once; and, in any case, I was now so bent on securing the acceptance of the proposal that my work should first be performed here, that I finally quitted Vienna with a promise to return in a few months, in order to start the preliminary study at once.

I felt no little embarrassment at the prospect of communicating my change of plan to the Grand Duke, and therefore readily yielded to the impulse of only visiting Karlsruhe after a long detour. As my birthday fell just at the time of this return journey, I resolved to celebrate it at Zürich. I reached Winterthur, via Munich, without delay, and hoped to meet my friend Sulzer there. Unfortunately he was away, and I only saw his wife, who had a pathetic interest for me, and also their little son, a lively and attractive boy. Sulzer himself, I learned, was expected back the next day, the 22nd of the month, and I accordingly spent most of the day in a small room at the inn. I had brought Goethe's *Wilhelm Meister's Wanderjahre* with me, and now for the first time was enraptured by fuller comprehension of this wonderful production. The spirit of the poet attracted me most profoundly to his work by the impression left on my mind by his lively description of the breaking-up of the players' company, in which the action almost becomes a furious lyric. Next morning at early dawn I returned to Zürich. The wonderfully clear air decided me to try the long and circuitous path through the familiar haunts of the Sihlthal to Wesendonck's estate. Here I arrived quite unannounced; and when I inquired what the habits of the household were, I learned that about this time Wesendonck usually came down to his dining-room to breakfast alone. There I accordingly seated myself in a corner, where I awaited the tall, good-tempered man, who, on entering quietly for his morning coffee, broke out into joyous astonishment on beholding me. The day passed most sociably; Sulzer, Semper, Herwegh, and Gottfried Keller were all sent for, and I thoroughly enjoyed the satisfaction of a well-contrived surprise, under such strange circumstances, as my recent fate had only just been forming the daily topic of animated discussion among these friends.

The next day I hurried back to Karlsruhe, where my announcement was received by the Grand Duke with kindly acquiescence. I could truly state that my request for leave of absence for the singers had been refused, and the projected performance in Karlsruhe thereby rendered impossible. Without any grief, but, on the contrary, with undisguised satisfaction, Eduard Devrient yielded to this fresh turn of affairs, and prophesied a splendid future for me in Vienna. Here Tausig overtook me, having already decided in Vienna to pay a visit to Paris, where he wished to see Liszt; and we accordingly continued our journey from Karlsruhe together by way of Strasburg.

When I reached Paris, I found my household on the point of breaking up. My only anxiety with regard to this was to procure means for getting away from the city, and for the prompt settlement of a future which seemed hopeless. Meanwhile Minna found an opportunity for exhibiting her talents as a housewife. Liszt had already fallen back into his old current of life, and even his own daughter, Blandine, could only manage to get a word with him in his carriage, as he drove from one visit to another. Nevertheless, impelled by his goodness of heart, he found time once to accept an invitation to 'beef-steaks' at my house. He even managed to spare me a whole evening, for which he kindly placed himself at my disposal for the settlement of my small obligations. In the presence of a few friends, who had remained true after the recent days of trouble, he played the piano to us on this occasion, during which a curious coincidence occurred. The day before poor Tausig had filled up a spare hour by playing Liszt's 'Fantaisie' on the name of Bach,[1] and now when Liszt chanced to play us the same piece, he literally collapsed with amazement before this wonderful prodigy of a man.

Another day we met for lunch at Gounod's, when we had a very dull time, which was only enlivened by poor Baudelaire, who indulged in the most outrageous witticisms. This man, *criblé de dettes,* as he told me, and daily compelled to adopt the most extravagant methods for a bare subsistence, had repeatedly approached me with adventurous schemes for the exploitation of my notorious fiasco. I could not on any account consent to adopt any of these, and was glad to find this really capable man safe under the eagle-wing of Liszt's 'ascendency.' Liszt took him everywhere where there was a possibility of a fortune being found. Whether this helped him into anything or not, I never knew. I only heard that he died a short time afterwards, certainly not from an excess of good fortune.

In addition to this festive morning, I met Liszt again at a dinner at the Austrian embassy, on which occasion he once more showed his kindly sympathy by playing several passages from my *Lohengrin* on the piano to Princess Metternich. He was also summoned to a dinner at the Tuileries, to which, however, it was not thought necessary to invite me to accompany him. With regard to this he related a conversation, which was very much to the point, with the Emperor Napoleon about the episode of my *Tannhäuser* performances in Paris, the upshot of which appears to have been that I was not in my right place at the Grand Opera House. Whether Liszt ever discussed these matters with Lamartine I do not know, I only heard that my old friend several times addressed him, to try and arrange a meeting with him, for which I was very anxious. Tausig, who at first had taken refuge chiefly with me, fell back later into his natural dependence upon his master, so that in the end he quite vanished from my sight, when he went with Liszt to visit Mme. Street in Brussels.

[1] The notes B, A, C, H, are equivalent to our English B flat, A, C, B. — EDITOR.

I was now longing to leave Paris. I had fortunately managed to get rid of my house in the Rue d'Aumale by sub-letting it, a transaction in which I was helped by a present of a hundred francs to the concierge, and was now merely waiting for news from my protectors. As I did not wish to press them, my situation became most painfully prolonged, though it was not altogether devoid of pleasant but tantalising incidents. For instance, I had won the special favour of Mlle. Eberty, Meyerbeer's elderly niece. She had been an almost rabid partisan of my cause during the painful episode of the *Tannhäuser* performances, and now seemed earnestly desirous of doing something to brighten my cheerless situation. With this object she arranged a really charming dinner in a first-class restaurant in the Bois de Boulogne, to which we and Kietz, of whom we were not yet rid, were invited, and which took place in lovely spring weather. The Flaxland family also, with whom I had had some differences over the publication of *Tannhäuser*, now exerted themselves in every possible way to show me kindness, but I could only wish that they had had no reason for doing so.

It was now settled that we must at all costs leave Paris soon. It was proposed that Minna should resume her treatment at the Soden baths and also revisit her old friends in Dresden, while I was to wait until it was time for me to return to Vienna for the preliminary study of my *Tristan*. We decided to deposit all our household belongings, well packed, with a forwarding-agent in Paris. While thus occupied with thoughts of our painfully delayed departure, we also discussed the difficulty of transporting our little dog Fips by rail. One day, the 22nd of June, my wife returned from a walk, bringing the animal back with her, in some mysterious way dangerously ill. According to Minna's account, we could only think that the dog had swallowed some virulent poison spread in the street. His condition was pitiable. Though he showed no marks of outward injury, yet his breathing was so convulsive that we thought his lungs must be seriously damaged. In his first frantic pangs he had bitten Minna violently in the mouth, so that I had sent for a doctor immediately, who, however, soon relieved our fears that she had been bitten by a mad dog.

But we could get no relief for the poor animal. He lay quietly curled up, and his breathing grew steadily shorter and more violent. Towards eleven o'clock at night he seemed to have fallen asleep under Minna's bed, but when I drew him out he was dead. The effect of this melancholy event upon Minna and myself was never expressed in words. In our childless life together the influence of domestic pets had been very important. The sudden death of this lively and lovable animal acted as the final rift in a union which had long become impossible. For the moment I had no more urgent care than to rescue the body from the usual fate of dead dogs in Paris, that of being flung out into the street for the scavengers to carry off in the morning. My friend Stürmer had a small garden behind his house in the Rue de la Tour des Dames, where I wished to bury Fips the next day. But it cost me a rare expenditure of persuasion to induce the absent owner's housekeeper to give me permission to do so. At last, however, with the help of the concierge of our house, I dug a small grave, as deep as possible, among the bushes of the garden, for the reception of our poor little pet. When the sad ceremony was completed, I covered up the grave with the utmost care and tried to make the spot as indistinguishable as possible, as I had a suspicion that Herr Stürmer might object to harbouring the dog's body, and have it removed, a misfortune which I strove to prevent.

At last Count Hatzfeld announced in the kindliest possible manner that some friends of my art, who wished to remain unknown, sympathising with my unmerited condition, had united to offer me the means of relieving my burdensome position. I considered it fitting to express my thanks for this happy consummation only to my patroness, Princess Metternich, and now set about making arrangements for the final dissolution of my Paris establishment. My first care, after concluding all these necessary labours, was to see that Minna set out at once for Germany to begin her treatment; while, as for myself, I had no better object there for the present than to pay a visit to Liszt in Weimar, where in August a German-music festival was to be celebrated with farewell performances of Liszt's compositions. Moreover Flaxland, who had now taken courage to issue my other operas in French, wished to retain me in Paris until, in collaboration with Truinet, I had completed the translation of the *Fliegender Holländer*. For this work I needed several weeks, which it was impossible for me to spend in our apartments, now entirely stripped of furniture. Count Pourtalès, hearing of this, invited me to take up my abode for this period in the Prussian embassy, a remarkable and indeed in its way unprecedented act of kindness which I accepted with a gratitude full of foreboding. On the 12th of July I saw Minna off to Soden, and the same day went to reside at the embassy, where they assigned me a pleasant little room looking out upon the garden, with a view of the Tuileries in the distance. In a pool in the garden there were two black swans, to which, in a dreamy sort of way, I felt strangely attracted. When young Hatzfeld looked me up in my room, to make inquiries about my needs in the name of my well-wishers, a strong emotion overwhelmed me for the first time in many years, and I felt a profound sense of well-being in the midst of a condition of complete impecuniosity and detachment from everything usually considered as necessary for permanent existence.

I asked permission to have my Erard brought to my room for the period of my stay, as it had not been packed away with the rest of my furniture, whereupon a handsome room was given up to me on the first floor. Here I worked every morning at the translation of my *Fliegender Holländer,* and also composed two musical album pieces, one of which, intended for Princess Metternich, contained a pretty theme which had long floated in my mind, and was afterwards published, while a similar one, for Frau Pourtalès, got somehow mislaid.

My intercourse with the family of my friend and host had not only a soothing influence upon my spirit, but also filled me with calm content. We dined together daily, and the midday meal often developed into the well-known ' diplomatic dinner.' I here made acquaintance with the former Prussian minister, Bethmann-Hollweg, the father of Countess Pourtalès, with whom I discussed in detail my ideas respecting the relations between art and the state. When at last I had succeeded in making them clear to the minister, our conversation closed with the fatal assertion that such an understanding with the supreme head of the state would always remain an impossibility, seeing that in his eyes art belonged merely to the realm of amusement.

In addition to Count Hatzfeld, the two other attachés, Prince Reuss and Count Dönhoff, often shared these domestic gatherings. The former seemed to be the politician of the company, and was particularly commended to me on account of the great and able efforts he had made on my behalf at the Imperial Court, while the latter simply appealed to me by his looks and by his attractive and open-hearted friendliness. Here, too, I was again frequently brought into social contact with Prince and Princess Metternich, but I could not help noticing that a certain embarrassment marked our demeanour. Owing to her energetic complicity in the fate of *Tannhäuser,* Princess Pauline had not only been subjected to the coarsest handling by the press, but had also suffered the most ungallant and ill-natured treatment at the hands of so-called higher society. Her husband seems to have borne all this very well, though doubtless he experienced many a bitter moment. It was difficult for me now to understand what compensation the Princess could have found in a genuine sympathy for my art for all she had been obliged to endure.

Thus I frequently spent the evenings in familiar intercourse with my amiable hosts, and was even seduced into trying to instruct them about Schopenhauer. On one occasion a larger evening assembly led to almost intoxicating excitement. Selections from several of my works were vivaciously played in a circle of friends all very much prepossessed in my favour. Saint-Saëns took the piano, and I had the unusual experience of hearing the final scene of *Isolde* rendered by the Neapolitan Princess Campo-Reale, who, to that excellent musician's accompaniment, sang it with a beautiful German accent and an astounding faithfulness of intonation.

I thus passed three weeks in peace and quiet. Meanwhile, Count Pourtalès had procured me a superior Prussian ministerial passport for my projected visit to Germany, his attempt to get me a Saxon passport having failed, owing to the nervousness of Herr von Seebach.

This time, before taking leave of Paris — for ever, as I supposed — I felt impelled to bid an intimate farewell to the few French friends who had stood by me loyally in the difficulties I had overcome. We met at a café in Rue Lafitte — Gaspérini, Champfleury, Truinet and I — and talked until late in the night. When I was about to start on my homeward way to the Faubourg St. Germain, Champfleury, who lived on the heights of Montmartre, declared that he must take me home, because we did not know whether we should ever see each other again. I enjoyed the exquisite effect of the bright moonlight on the deserted Paris streets ; only the huge business firms, whose premises extend to the uppermost floors, seemed to have turned night into day in a picturesque fashion, particularly those houses which have been pressed into the service of trade in the Rue Richelieu. Champfleury smoked his short pipe and discussed with me the prospects of French politics. His father was, he told me, an old Bonapartist of the first water, but had been moved to exclaim, a short time before, after reading the papers day after day, ' *Pourtant, avant de mourir je voudrais voir autre chose.*' We parted very affectionately at the door of the embassy.

I took leave in equally friendly fashion of a young Parisian friend, who has not yet been mentioned — Gustave Doré — who had been sent to me by Ollivier at the very outset of my Paris venture. He had proposed to make a fantastic drawing of me in the act of conducting, without, it is true, ever realising his intention. I do not know why, except, perhaps, that I did not show any particular inclination for it. Doré remained loyal to me, however, and was one of those who made a point of demonstrating their friendship just now in their extreme indignation at the outrage inflicted on me. This extraordinarily prolific artist proposed to include the *Nibelungen* among his many subjects for illustration, and I wished first to make him acquainted with my interpretation of this cycle of legends. This was undoubtedly difficult, but as he assured me he had a friend well versed in the German language and German literature, I gave myself the pleasure of presenting him with the recently published pianoforte score of *Rheingold,* the text of which would give him the clearest idea of the plan on which I had moulded the material. I thus returned the compliment of his having sent me a copy of his illustrations to Dante, which had just appeared.

Full of pleasant and agreeable impressions, which formed the only actual gain of real worth that I reaped from my Paris enterprise, I left the generous asylum offered by my Prussian friends the first week in August to go, first, to Soden by way of Cologne. Here I found Minna in the society of Mathilde Schiffner, who seemed to have become indispensable to her as an easy victim for her tyranny. I spent two extremely painful days there in trying to make the poor woman understand that she was to establish herself at Dresden (where I was not at present allowed to stay), while I looked about me in Germany — in Vienna first — for a new centre of operations. She glanced at her friend with peculiar satisfaction on hearing my proposal and my promise to remember, under any circumstances, to provide her with three thousand marks a year. This bargain set the standard of my relation to her for the rest of her life. She went with me as far as Frankfort, where I parted from her to go, for the time being, to Weimar — the town where Schopenhauer had died a short time before.

PART IV

1861-1864

AND so I again crossed Thuringia, passing the Wartburg which, whether I visited it or merely saw it in the distance, seemed so strangely bound up with my departures from Germany or my return thither. I reached Weimar at two in the morning, and was conducted later in the day to the rooms which Liszt had arranged for my use at the Altenburg. They were, as he took good care to inform me, Princess Marie's rooms. This time, however, there were no women to entertain us. Princess Caroline was already in Rome, and her daughter had married Prince Constantin Hohenlohe and gone to Vienna. There was only Miss Anderson, Princess Marie's governess, left to help Liszt entertain his guests. Indeed, I found the Altenburg was about to be closed, and that Liszt's youthful uncle Eduard had come from Vienna for this purpose, and also to make an inventory of all its contents. But at the same time there reigned an unusual stir of conviviality in connection with the Society of Musical Artists, as Liszt was putting up a considerable number of musicians himself, first and foremost among his guests being Bülow and Cornelius. Every one, including Liszt himself, was wearing a travelling cap, and this strange choice of head-dress seemed to me typical of the lack of ceremony attending this rural festival at Weimar. On the top floor of the house Franz Brendel and his wife were installed with some splendour, and a swarm of musicians soon filled the place, among them my old acquaintance Dräsecke and a certain young man called Weisheimer, whom Liszt had once sent to see me at Zürich. Tausig put in an appearance too, but excluded himself from most of our free and easy gatherings to carry on a love-affair with a young lady. Liszt gave me Emilie Genast as a companion on one or two short excursions, an arrangement with which I found no fault, as she was witty and very intelli-

gent. I made the acquaintance of Damrosch too, a violinist and
a musician. It was a great pleasure to see my old friend Alwine Frommann, who had come in spite of her somewhat
strained relations with Liszt; and when Blandine and Ollivier
arrived from Paris and became my neighbours on the Altenburg,
the days which were lively before to begin with, now became
boisterously merry. Bülow, who had been chosen to conduct
Liszt's *Faust* Symphony, seemed to me the wildest of all. His
activity was extraordinary. He had learned the entire score
by heart, and gave us an unusually precise, intelligent, and
spirited performance with an orchestra composed of anything
but the pick of German players. After this symphony the
Prometheus music had the greatest success, while I was particularly affected by Emilie Genast's singing of a song-cycle,
composed by Bülow, called *Die Entsagende*. There was little
else that was enjoyable at the festival concert with the exception of a cantata, *Das Grab im Busento* by Weisheimer, and a
regular scandal arose in connection with Dräsecke's ' German
March.' For some obscure reason Liszt adopted a challenging
and protecting attitude towards this strange composition,
written apparently in mockery by a man of great talent in other
directions. Liszt insisted on Bülow's conducting the march,
and ultimately Hans made a success of it, even doing it by
heart; but the whole thing ended in the following incredible
scene. The jubilant reception of Liszt's own works had not
once induced him to show himself to the audience, but when
Dräsecke's march, which concluded the programme, was at
last rejected by the audience in an irresistible wave of ill-
humour, Liszt came into the stage-box and, stretching out his
hands, clapped vigorously and shouted ' Bravos.' A real
battle set in between Liszt, whose face was red with anger,
and the audience. Blandine, who was sitting next to me, was,
like me, beside herself at this outrageously provocative behaviour on the part of her father, and it was a long time before
we could compose ourselves after the incident. There was
little in the way of explanation to be got out of Liszt. We only
heard him refer a few times, in terms of furious contempt, to
the audience, ' for whom the march was far and away too good.'
I heard from another quarter that this was a form of revenge

on the regular Weimar public, but it was a strange way of wreaking it, as they were not represented on this occasion. Liszt thought it was a good opportunity to avenge Cornelius, whose opera *The Barber of Bagdad* had been hissed by the Weimar public when Liszt had conducted it in person some time previously. Besides this, I could of course see that Liszt had much to bear in other directions. He admitted to me that he had been trying to induce the Grand Duke of Weimar to show me some particular mark of distinction. He first wanted him to invite me, with himself, to dine at court, but as the Duke had qualms about entertaining a person who was still exiled from the kingdom of Saxony as a political refugee, Liszt thought he could at least get me the Order of the White Falcon. This too was refused him, and as his exertions at court had been so fruitless, he was bent on making the townsmen of the Residency do their part in celebrating my presence. A torchlight procession was accordingly arranged, but when I heard of it I took all possible pains to thwart the plan — and succeeded. But I was not to get off without any ovation at all. One afternoon *Justizrath* Gille of Jena and six students grouped themselves under my window, and sang a nice little choral society song, for which attention I thanked them most warmly. A contrast to this was presented by the great banquet attended by all the musical artists. I sat between Blandine and Ollivier, and the feast developed into a really hearty ovation for the composer of *Tannhäuser* and *Lohengrin*, whom they now ' welcomed back to Germany after he had won their love and esteem during his banishment.' Liszt's speech was short but vigorous, and I had to respond in greater detail to another speaker. Very pleasant were the select gatherings which on several occasions met round Liszt's own dinner-table, and I thought of the absent hostess of Altenburg at one of them. Once we had our meal in the garden, and I had the pleasure of seeing my good friend Alwine Frommann there conversing intelligently with Ollivier, as a reconciliation with Liszt had taken place.

The day for parting was drawing near for us all, after a week of very varied and exciting experiences. A happy chance enabled me to make the greater part of my prearranged journey to Vienna in the company of Blandine and Ollivier, who had decided to visit Cosima at Reichenhall, where she was staying for a 'cure.' As we were all saying good-bye to Liszt on the railway platform, we thought of Bülow, who had distinguished himself so remarkably in the past few days. He had started a day in advance, and we exhausted ourselves in singing his praises, though I added with jesting familiarity, 'There was no necessity for him to marry Cosima.' And Liszt added, bowing slightly, 'That was a luxury.'

We travellers — Blandine and I, that is — soon fell into a frivolous mood which was much intensified by Ollivier's query, repeated after each burst of laughter, '*Qu'est-ce qu'il dit?*' He had to submit good-humouredly to our continuous joking in German, though we always responded in French to his frequent demands for *tonique* or *jambon cru,* which seemed to form the staple of his diet. It was long after midnight when we reached Nuremberg, where we were obliged to halt for the night. We got ourselves conveyed to an inn by dint of much effort, and were kept waiting there some time before the door opened. A fat and elderly innkeeper acceded to our entreaties to give us rooms, late as it was, but to accomplish this he found it necessary — after much anxious reflection — to leave us in the hall for a good long time while he vanished down a back passage. There he stood outside a bedroom door, and we heard him calling 'Margarethe' in bashful and friendly tones. He repeated the name several times with the information that visitors had arrived, and a woman answered him with oaths. After much pressing entreaty on the innkeeper's part Margarethe at last appeared, in *négligé,* and showed us, after various mysterious confabulations with the host, the rooms selected for us. The odd part of the incident was that the immoderate laughter in which we all three indulged seemed to be noticed neither by the innkeeper nor by his chambermaid. The next day we went to see some of the sights of the town, last of all the Germanisches Museum, which was in such a wretched condition at that time as to earn the contempt of my French companion particularly. The large collection of instruments of torture, which included a box studded with nails, filled Blandine with sympathetic horror.

We reached Munich that evening, and inspected it the next day (after *tonique* and ham had again been obtained) with great satisfaction, particularly on the part of Ollivier, who thought that the 'antique' style in which King Ludwig I. had had the museums built contrasted most favourably with the buildings with which, much to his indignation, it had pleased Louis Napoleon to fill Paris. I here ran across an old acquaintance, young Hornstein, whom I introduced to my friends as 'the baron.' His comical figure and clumsy behaviour gave them food for mirth, which degenerated into a positive orgy of merriment when 'the baron' thought it necessary, before we started on our night journey to Reichenhall, to take us to a *Bier-Brauerei* some distance away, so that we should see that side of Munich life. It was pitch dark and there was no light provided, except a stump of a candle to light 'the baron,' who had to go down himself to fetch the beer from the cellar. The beer certainly tasted particularly good, and Hornstein repeated his descent into the cellar several times. When, being obliged to hurry, we set off on our perilous journey across fields and ditches to the station, we found that the unwonted refreshment had somewhat dazed us. Blandine fell fast asleep as soon as she got into the carriage, only waking at daybreak when we arrived at Reichenhall. Here Cosima met us, and took us to the rooms that had been prepared for us.

We were first of all rejoiced to find Cosima's state of health much less alarming than we — I in particular — had known it to be before. She had been ordered a sour-milk cure, and we went to look on the next morning when she took her walk to the institution. Cosima appeared to lay less stress on the actual milk-drinking, however, than on the walks and the sojourn in the splendid, bracing, mountain air. Ollivier and I were generally excluded from the merriment which here too immediately set in, as the two sisters, to secure more privacy for their talks — they laughed so incessantly that they could be heard a long way off — usually shut themselves away from us in their bedrooms, and almost my only resource was to converse in French with my political friend. I succeeded in gaining admission to the sisters once or twice, to announce to them amongst other things my intention of adopting them, as their father took no more notice of them — a proposition received with more mirth than confidence. I once deplored Cosima's wild ways to Blandine, who seemed unable to understand me, until she had persuaded herself that I meant *timidité d'un sauvage* by my expression. After a few days I had really to think of continuing my journey, which had been so pleasantly interrupted. I said good-bye in the hall, and caught a glimpse of almost timid inquiry from Cosima.

I first drove down the valley to Salzburg in a one-horse carriage. On the Austrian frontier I had an adventure with the custom-house. Liszt had given me at Weimar a box of the most costly cigars — a present to him from Baron Sina. As I knew from my visit to Venice what incredible formalities make it exceedingly difficult to introduce these articles into Austria, I hit upon the plan of hiding the cigars singly among my dirty linen and in the pockets of my clothes. The officer, who was an old soldier, seemed to be prepared for precautionary measures of this sort, and drew forth the *corpora delicta* skilfully from all the folds of my little trunk. I tried to bribe him with a tip, which he actually accepted, and I was all the more indignant when, in spite of this, he denounced me to the authorities. I was made to pay a heavy fine, but received permission to buy back the cigars. This I furiously declined to do. With the receipt of the fine I had paid, however, I was also given back the Prussian thaler which the old soldier had quietly tucked away before, and when I got into my carriage to continue the journey I saw the same officer sitting placidly before his beer and bread and cheese. He bowed very politely, and I offered to give him his thaler back, but this time he refused it. I have often been angry with myself since for not asking the man's name, as I clung to the notion that he must be a particularly faithful servant, in which capacity I should like to have engaged him myself later on.

I touched at Salzburg, arriving soaked through by floods of rain, and spent the night there, and on the following day at last reached my place of destination — Vienna. I proposed to accept the hospitality of Kolatschek, with whom I had been friendly in Switzerland. He had long since been granted an amnesty by Austria, and had, on my last visit to Vienna,

called on me and offered me the use of his house, to avoid the
unpleasantness of an inn, in the event of my returning for a
longer stay. For reasons of economy alone — and these at
the time were very urgent — I had willingly accepted this offer,
and now drove direct with my hand luggage to the house described. To my surprise I at once discovered that I was in
an exceedingly remote suburb, practically cut off from Vienna
itself. The house was quite deserted, Kolatschek and his family
having gone to a summer resort at Hütteldorf. With some
difficulty I unearthed an old servant, who seemed to think
she had been warned of my arrival by her master. She showed
me a small room in which I could sleep if I liked, but was
apparently unable to provide either linen or service of any
kind. Greatly discomfited by this disappointment, I first drove
back into town to wait for Kolatschek at a certain café in
Stephan's Platz, which, according to the servant, he was likely
to visit at a particular time. I had been sitting there a good
while, making repeated inquiries for the man I expected to
see, when suddenly I saw Standhartner come in. His extreme
surprise at finding me there was intensified, as he told me, by
the fact that he had never in his life entered this café. It had
been quite a special coincidence that had brought him there on
that day and at that time. On being made aware of my situation he at once became furious at the idea of my living in
the most deserted part of Vienna when I had such pressing
business in the city, and promptly offered me his own house for
temporary quarters, as he and all his family would be away
for six weeks. A pretty niece, who, with her mother and sister,
lived in the same house, was to see to all my wants, including
breakfast, etc., and I should be able to make use of the whole
place with the greatest freedom. He took me triumphantly
home with him at once to a deserted dwelling, as the family
had already gone to their summer resort at Salzburg. I let
Kolatschek know, had my luggage brought in, and for a few
days had the pleasure of Standhartner's society and easy hospitality. I realised, however, from information given me by
my friend, that my path was beset with new difficulties. The
rehearsals for *Tristan und Isolde*, which had been planned in
the spring to take place about this time (I had arrived in Vienna

on 14th August), had been postponed indefinitely as Ander, the tenor, had sent word that he had injured his voice. On hearing this I at once concluded that my stay in Vienna would be useless; but I knew that no one would be able to suggest any other place where I could employ myself profitably.

My situation was, as I now saw plainly, quite hopeless, for every one seemed to have deserted me. A few years back I might, in a similar case, have flattered myself that Liszt would be pleased to have me at Weimar during the period of waiting, but if I returned to Germany just now I should only have to look on at the dismantling of the house — to which I have already alluded. My chief concern, then, was to find a friendly shelter somewhere. It was with this sole end in view that I turned to the Grand Duke of Baden, who had shortly before greeted me with such kindness and sympathy. I wrote him a beseeching letter, urging him to consider my necessitous condition. I pointed out that what I wanted, above all, was an asylum, however modest, and implored him to provide me with one in or near Karlsruhe, by securing me a pension of two thousand four hundred marks. Judge of my surprise on receiving a reply, not in the Grand Duke's own hand, but only signed by him, to the effect that if my request were granted, it would probably mean that I would interfere with the management of the theatre, and, as a very natural result, discussions would ensue with the director (my old friend E. Devrient, who was now doing splendidly). As the Grand Duke would in any such case feel obliged to act in the interests of justice, 'possibly to my disadvantage,' as he put it, he must, after mature consideration, regretfully decline to accede to my request.

Princess Metternich, who had suspected my embarrassment on that score also when I left Paris, had given me a warm recommendation to Count Nako and his family in Vienna, referring me with particular emphasis to his wife. Now I had made the acquaintance through Standhartner, during the short time before he left me, of young Prince Rudolph Liechtenstein — known to his friends as Rudi. His doctor, with whom he was very intimate, had spoken of him to me in the most flattering way as being a passionate admirer of my music. I often met him at meal times at the 'Erzherzog Karl,' after Standhartner had joined his family, and we planned a visit to Count Nako on his estate at Schwarzau, some distance away. The journey was made in the most comfortable fashion, partly by rail, in the company of the Prince's young wife. They introduced me to the Nakos at Schwarzau. The Count proved to be a particularly handsome man, while his wife was more of a cultured gipsy, whose talent for painting was evidenced in striking fashion by the gigantic copies of Van Dyck resplendent on the walls. It was more painful to hear her amuse herself at the piano, where she gave faithful renderings of gipsy music, which, she said, Liszt failed to do. The music to *Lohengrin* seemed to have prepossessed them all very much in my favour, and this appreciation was confirmed by other magnates who were visiting there, among them being Count Edmund Zichy, whom I had known in Venice. I was thus able to observe the character of unconstrained Hungarian hospitality, without being much edified by the subjects of conversation, and I had soon, alas! to face the question as to what I was to get from these people. I was given a decent room for the night, and on the following day took an early opportunity of looking round the beautifully kept precincts of the majestic castle, wondering in which part of the building there might be found room for me in case of a longer visit. But my remarks in praise of the size of the building were met at breakfast with the assurance that it really was hardly big enough for the family, as the young Countess in particular lived in great style with her suite. It was a cold morning in September, and we spent it out of doors. My friend Rudi seemed to be out of humour. I felt cold, and very soon took leave of the great man's board with the consciousness of having rarely found myself in the company of such nice people without discovering the smallest subject in common. This consciousness grew into a positive feeling of disgust when I was driving with several of the *cavalieri* to the station at Mödling, for I was reduced to absolute silence during the hour's drive, as they had literally only the one topic of conversation, by that time so terribly familiar to me! — namely horses.

I got out at Mödling to call on Ander the tenor, having

invited myself for that day with the intention of going through
Tristan. It was still very early on a bright morning, and the
day was gradually growing warmer. I decided to take a walk
in the lovely Brühl before looking up Ander. There I ordered
a lunch in the garden of the beautifully situated inn, and enjoyed an extremely refreshing hour of complete solitude. The
wild birds had already ceased singing, but I shared my meal
with an army of sparrows, which assumed alarming proportions.
As I fed them with bread-crumbs, they finally became so tame
that they settled in swarms on the table in front of me to seize
their booty. I was reminded of the morning in the tavern
with the landlord Homo in Montmorency. Here again, after
shedding many a tear, I laughed aloud, and set off to Ander's
summer residence. Unfortunately his condition confirmed the
statement that the injury to his voice was not merely an excuse;
but in any case I soon saw that this helpless person could
never under any circumstances be equal to the task of playing
Tristan, demi-god as he was, in Vienna. All the same I
did my best, as I was there, to show him the whole of *Tristan*
in my own interpretation of the part (which always excited
me very much), after which he declared that it might have
been written for him. I had arranged for Tausig and Cornelius,
whom I had again met in Vienna, to come out to Ander's house
that day, and I returned with them in the evening.

I spent a good deal of time with these two, who were sincerely
concerned about me and did their best to cheer me. Tausig, it
is true, was rather more reserved, as he had aspirations in high
quarters at that time. But he, too, accepted Frau Dustmann's
invitations to the three of us. She was then at Hietzing for
the summer, and there dinners were given more than once, and
also a few vocal rehearsals for Isolde, for which part her voice
seemed to possess some of the spiritual susceptibility required.
There, too, I read through the poem of *Tristan* again, still
thinking the prospect of its performance possible with the
exercise of patience and enthusiasm. For the present patience
was the quality most needed; certainly nothing was to be
obtained by enthusiasm. Ander's voice still failed him and
did not improve, and no doctor was prepared to fix a limit to
his malady.

I got through the time as best I could, and hit upon the idea of translating back into German the new scene to *Tannhäuser*, written to a French text for the performance in Paris. Cornelius had first to copy it from the original score for me, as this was in a very defective condition. I accepted his copy without inquiring further about the original left in his hands, and we shall see the result of this later on.

A musician named Winterberger also joined our party. He was an old acquaintance, and I found him in a position I much envied. Countess Banfy, an old friend of Liszt's, had taken him into her very pleasant house at Hietzing, and he was thus in excellent quarters, living at ease, and with nothing to trouble about, as the kind lady thought it her duty to keep this fellow — in other respects so undeserving — supplied with everything. Through him I again had news of Karl Ritter, and was told that he was now at Naples, where he lived in the house of a piano-maker, whose children he had to teach in return for board and lodging. It seems that Winterberger, after running through everything, had on the strength of some of Liszt's introductions started off to seek his fortune in Hungary. But things did not fall out to his satisfaction, and he was now enjoying compensation in the house of the worthy Countess. I met an excellent harpist there — also one of the family — Fräulein Mössner. By the Countess's orders she was made to betake herself and her harp to the garden, where, either at or with her harp, she had a most pert air and looked quite delightful, so that I gained an impression which lingered pleasantly in my mind. Unfortunately I became involved in a quarrel with the young lady because I would not compose a solo for her instrument. From the time when I definitely refused to humour her ambitions she took no more notice of me.

The poet Hebbel must be mentioned among the special acquaintances I made in Vienna during this difficult epoch. As it seemed not unlikely that I should have to make Vienna the scene of my labours for some time, I thought it desirable to become better acquainted with the literary celebrities living there. I prepared myself for meeting Hebbel by taking considerable trouble to read his dramatic pieces beforehand, doing my best to think that they were good and that a closer acquaintance with the author was desirable. I was not to be deterred from my purpose by my consciousness of the great weakness of his poems, although I realised the unnaturalness of his conceptions and the invariably affected and frequently vulgar form of expression. I only visited him once, and did not have a particularly long talk with him even then. I did not find any expression in the poet's personality of the eccentric force which threatens to explode in the figures of his dramas. When I heard, some years later, that Hebbel had died of softening of the bones, I understood why he had affected me so unpleasantly. He talked about the theatrical world in Vienna with the air of an amateur who feels himself neglected but continues to work in a businesslike fashion. I felt no particular desire to repeat my visit, especially after his return call in my absence, when he left a card announcing himself as ' *Hebbel, chevalier de plusieurs ordres!* '

My old friend Heinrich Laube had now long been established as director of the Royal and Imperial Court Theatre. He had felt it his duty on my previous visit to Vienna to introduce me to the literary celebrities, among whom, being of a practical turn, he counted chiefly journalists and critics. He invited Dr. Hanslick to a big dinner-party, thinking I should be particularly interested in meeting him, and was surprised that I had not a word to say to him. The conclusions Laube drew from this led him to prophesy that I should find it hard to get on in Vienna if I really hoped to make it the sphere of my artistic labours. On my return this time he welcomed me simply as an old friend, and begged me to dine with him as often as I cared to come. He was a passionate sportsman, and was able to provide the luxury of fresh game for his table. I did not avail myself very often of this invitation, however, as the conversation, which was inspired solely by the dull business routine of the stage, did not attract me. After dinner a few actors and literary men would come in for coffee and cigars, sitting at a large table where Laube's wife generally held her court, while Laube himself enjoyed his rest and his cigar in silence. Frau Laube had consented to become *Theatre Directrice* solely to please her husband, and now thought herself obliged to make long and careful speeches about things of which she had no understanding whatever. The only pleasure I had was in renewed glimpses of the good-nature which I had admired in her of old; for instance, when none of the company dared to oppose her, and I intervened with some frank criticism, she usually accepted it with unreserved merriment. To her and her husband I probably seemed a good-natured sort of fool and nothing more, for my conversation was generally in a joking strain, as I was utterly indifferent to their earnestness. In fact, when I gave my concerts in Vienna later on, Frau Laube remarked with the most friendly air of surprise that I was quite a good conductor, contrary to what she had expected after reading some newspaper report or other.

For one thing, Laube's practical knowledge was not without importance, as he could tell me all about the character of the chief inspectors of the Royal and Imperial Court Theatre. It now transpired that the Imperial Councillor, von Raymond, was a most important personage, and the aged Count Lanckoronski, the Lord High Marshall, who in other respects was extremely tenacious of his authority, could not trust himself to come to any decision in matters of finance without consulting this exceedingly competent man.

Raymond himself, whom I soon got to know and regard as a model of ignorance, took fright and felt bound to withhold his consent to my performance of *Tristan,* mainly on account of the Vienna papers, which always ran me down and scoffed at my proposal. Officially I was referred to the actual manager of the Opera, Herr Salvi, who had formerly been the singing-master of a lady-in-waiting to the Grand Duchess Sophia. He was an absolutely incapable and ignorant man, who was obliged to pretend in front of me that, according to the command of the supreme authorities, nothing lay so near his heart as the furtherance of the performance of *Tristan.* Accordingly he tried by perpetual expressions of zeal and goodwill to conceal the increasing spirit of doubt and hesitation with which even the staff was imbued.

I found out the state of affairs one day when a company of our singers was invited with me to the country house of a certain Herr Dumba, who was introduced to me as a most enthusiastic well-wisher. Herr Ander had taken the score of

Tristan with him, as if to show that he could not part with it for a single day. Frau Dustmann grew very angry about it, and accused Ander of trying to impose upon me by playing the hypocrite; for he knew as well as any one else that he would never sing that part, and that the management was only awaiting a chance of preventing the performance of *Tristan* in some way or other, and then laying the blame on her shoulders. Salvi tried most zealously to interfere in these extremely awkward revelations. He recommended me to choose the tenor Walter, and as I objected on the ground of my antipathy to the man, he next referred me to certain foreign singers whom he was quite ready to approach.

As a matter of fact, we tried a few outside players of whom the most promising was a certain Signor Morini, and I really felt so depressed and so desirous of furthering my work at any price that I attended a performance of *Luzia* by Donizetti with my friend Cornelius to see if I could extract from him a favourable judgment of the singer. Cornelius, who was apparently absorbed in listening whilst I attentively watched him, suddenly started up in a passion and exclaimed, 'Horrible! horrible!' which made us both laugh so heartily that we soon left the theatre in quite a cheerful frame of mind.

At last I carried on my negotiations with the conductor Heinrich Esser alone, as he was apparently the only honest man in the management. Although he found *Tristan* very difficult, yet he worked at it with great earnestness, and never really gave up the hope of making a performance possible, if only I would accept Walter as the tenor; but, in spite of my persistent refusal to make use of such help, we always remained good friends. As he, like myself, was a keen walker, we often explored the neighbourhood of Vienna, and our conversations during these expeditions were enthusiastic on my part and thoroughly honest and serious on his.

Whilst these *Tristan* matters were running their weary course like a chronic disease, whose outcome it is impossible to foresee, Standhartner returned at the end of September with his family. Consequently the next thing I had to do was to look out for a residence, which I chose in the Hôtel Kaiserin Elizabeth.

Through my cordial intercourse with the family of this friend I became quite intimate not only with his wife, but also with her three sons and a daughter by her first marriage, and a younger daughter by the second marriage with Standhartner. On looking back upon my former residence in my friend's house, I greatly missed the presence and kindly care bestowed upon me by his niece Seraphine, whom I have already mentioned, as well as her untiring thoughtfulness and pleasant, amusing companionship. On account of her natty figure and hair carefully curled *à l'enfant*, I had given her the name of ' The Doll.' Now I had to look after myself in the dull room of the hotel, and the expense of my living increased considerably. I remember at that time that I had only received twenty-five or thirty louis d'or for *Tannhäuser* from Brunswick. On the other hand, Minna sent me from Dresden a few leaves of the silver-spangled wreath presented by some of her friends as a souvenir of her silver wedding-day, which she had celebrated on the 24th of November. I could hardly wonder that there was no lack of bitter reproach on her part when sending me this gift; however, I tried to inspire her with the hope of having a golden wedding. For the present, seeing that I was staying without any object in an expensive Viennese hotel, I did my utmost to secure a chance of performing *Tristan*. First I turned to Tichatschek in Dresden, but obtained no promise from him. I then had recourse to Schnorr, with a similar result, and I was at last obliged to acknowledge that my affairs were in a bad way. Of this I made no secret in my occasional communications to the Wesendoncks, who, apparently to cheer me up, invited me to meet them in Venice, where they were just going for a pleasure trip. Heaven knows what my intention was as I started off in a casual sort of way by train, first to Trieste and then by steamer (which did not agree with me at all) to Venice, where I again put up in my little room at the Hôtel Danieli.

My friends, whom I found in very flourishing circumstances, seemed to be revelling in the pictures, and fully expected that a participation in their enjoyment would drive away my ' blues.' They seemed to have no desire to realise my position in Vienna. Indeed, after the ill-success of my Paris undertaking, entered upon with such glorious anticipations, I had learned to recognise among most of my friends a tacitly submissive abandonment of all hope for my future success.

Wesendonck, who always went about armed with huge fieldglasses, and was ever ready for sight-seeing, only once took me with him to see the Academy of Arts, a building which on my former visit to Venice I had only known from the outside. In spite of all my indifference, I must confess that the ' Assumption of the Virgin ' by Titian exercised a most sublime influence over me, so that, as soon as I realised its conception, my old powers revived within me, as though by a sudden flash of inspiration.

I determined at once on the composition of the *Meistersinger*.

After a frugal dinner with my old acquaintances Tessarin and the Wesendoncks, whom I invited to the Albergo San Marco, and once more exchanging friendly greetings with Luigia, my former attendant at the Palazzo Giustiniani, to the astonishment of my friends I suddenly left Venice. I had spent four dreary days there, and now started by train on my dull journey to Vienna, following the roundabout overland route. It was during this journey that the music of the *Meistersinger* first dawned on my mind, in which I still retained the libretto as I had originally conceived it. With the utmost distinctness I at once composed the principal part of the Overture in C major.

Under the influence of these last impressions I arrived in Vienna in a very cheerful frame of mind. I at once announced my return to Cornelius by sending him a small Venetian gondola, which I had bought for him in Venice, and to which I added a canzona written with nonsensical Italian words. The communication of my plan for the immediate composition of the *Meistersinger* made him almost frantic with delight, and until my departure from Vienna he remained in a state of delirious excitement.

I urged my friend to procure me material for mastering the subject of the *Meistersinger*. My first idea was to make a thorough study of Grimm's controversy on the *Song of the Meistersinger;* and the next question was how to get hold of old Wagenseil's *Nuremberg Chronicle*. Cornelius accompanied me to the Imperial Library, but in order to obtain a loan of this book, which we were fortunate enough to find, my friend was obliged to visit Baron Münch-Bellinghausen (Halm), a visit which he described to me as very disagreeable. I remained at my hotel, eagerly making extracts of portions of the *Chronicle,* which to the astonishment of the ignorant I appropriated for my libretto.

But my most urgent task was to secure some means of livelihood during the composition of my work. I applied first to the music publisher Schott at Mayence, to whom I offered the *Meistersinger* if he would make me the necessary advance. Being animated by the desire to provide myself with money for as long a time as possible, I offered him not only the literary rights, but also the rights of performance for my work, for the sum of twenty thousand francs. A telegram from Schott containing an absolute refusal at once destroyed all hope. As I was now obliged to think of other means, I decided to turn to Berlin. Bülow, who was always kindly exerting himself on my behalf, had hinted at the possibility of being able to raise a considerable sum of money there by means of a concert, which I should conduct; and as I was at the same time longing to find a home amongst friends, Berlin seemed to beckon me as a last refuge. At noon, just before the evening of my intended departure, a letter came from Schott, following on his telegram of refusal, which certainly held out some more consoling prospect. He offered to undertake the publication of the pianoforte edition of the *Walküre* at once and to advance me three thousand marks to be deducted from a future account. The joy of Cornelius at what he called the salvation of the *Meistersinger* knew no bounds. From Berlin Bülow, in great indignation and evident low spirits, wrote to me of his dreadful experiences in attempting to organise my concert. Herr von Hülsen declared that he would not countenance my visit to Berlin, while as to giving a concert at the great Kroll Restaurant, Bülow found after much deliberation that it would be quite impracticable.

Whilst I was busily engaged on a detailed scenic sketch of the *Meistersinger,* the arrival of Prince and Princess Metternich in Vienna seemed to create a favourable diversion on my behalf.

The concern expressed by my Paris patrons about me and my
position was undoubtedly real; therefore, in order to show
myself gratefully disposed towards them, I induced the management of the Opera to allow me to invite their splendid
orchestra for a few hours one morning to play some selections
from *Tristan* in the theatre by way of rehearsal. Both the
orchestra and Frau Dustmann were quite ready to grant my request in the most friendly manner, and Princess Metternich,
with some of her acquaintances, was invited to this rehearsal.
With the orchestra we played through two of the principal selections, namely, the prelude to the first act, and the beginning of
the second act, as far as the middle, while the singing part was
sustained by Frau Dustmann, the whole being so brilliantly
executed that I felt fully justified in believing I had created a
most excellent impression Herr Ander, too, had appeared
on the scene, but without knowing a single note of the music
or attempting to sing it. Both my princely friends, as well as
Fräulein Couqui, the *première danseuse,* who singularly enough
had attended the rehearsal on the sly, overwhelmed me with
enthusiastic marks of admiration. Hearing of my ardent desire
for retirement in order to go on with the composition of a
new work, the Metternichs one day suggested that they were
in a position to offer me just such a quiet retreat in Paris. The
Prince, who had now completely arranged his spacious embassy,
could place at my disposal a pleasant suite of rooms looking on
to a quiet garden, just like the one I had found in the Prussian
embassy. My Erard was still in Paris, and if I could arrange
to go there at the end of the year, I should find everything ready
for me to begin my work. With unconcealed joy I most gratefully accepted this kind invitation, and my only care now was
so to arrange my affairs that I could take my departure from
Vienna and effect my removal to Paris in a proper manner.
The arrangement that had been made through Standhartner's
mediation, that the management should pay me a part of the
stipulated fee for *Tristan,* would be a great help in this. But
as I was only to get one thousand marks, and even this was to
be subject to so many clauses and conditions as to suggest a
desire to renounce the whole transaction, I at once rejected
the offer. This fact, however, did not prevent the press, which

was always in touch with the theatrical management, from publishing that I had accepted an indemnity for the non-performance of *Tristan*. Fortunately I was able to protest against this calumny by producing proof of what I had actually done in the matter. Meanwhile, the negotiations with Schott dragged out to some length, because I would not agree at present to his suggestions about the *Walküre*. I adhered to my first offer of a new opera, the *Meistersinger*, and at last received three thousand marks as an instalment on this work. As soon as I had received the cheque, I packed up my things, when a telegram from Princess Metternich reached me, in which she begged of me to put off my departure until the 1st of January. I decided not give up my plan, being anxious to get away from Vienna, so I determined to go straight to Mayence to pursue further negotiations with Schott. My leavetaking at the station was made particularly gay by Cornelius, who whispered to me with mysterious enthusiasm a stanza of 'Sachs' which I had communicated to him. This was the verse:

> *'Der Vogel der heut' sang,*
> *Dem war der Schnabel hold gewachsen;*
> *Ward auch den Meistern dabei bang,*
> *Gar wohl gefiel er doch Hans Sachsen.'* [1]

In Mayence I got to know the Schott family, with whom I had only had a casual acquaintance in Paris, more intimately. The young musician Weisheimer, who was just then beginning his career as musical director at the local theatre, was a daily visitor at their house. At one of our dinners another young man, Städl, a lawyer, proposed a remarkable toast in my honour in a most eloquent and astonishing speech. Notwithstanding all this I had to recognise that in Franz Schott I was dealing with a very singular man, and our negotiations proceeded with extraordinary difficulty. I insisted emphatically on carrying out my first proposal, namely, that he should provide

---

'The bird who sang this morn
From Nature's self had learned his singing;
Masters that song may scorn,
For aye Hans Sachs will hear it singing.'
(Translation of the *Meistersinger*, by Frederick Jameson.) — EDITOR.

me for two successive years with funds necessary for the undisturbed execution of my work. He excused his unwillingness to do this by pretending it was painful to his feelings to drive a bargain with a man like myself by purchasing my work for a certain sum of money, including also the profits of my author's rights in the theatrical performances; that, in a word, he was a music publisher, and did not want to be anything else. I represented to him that he need only advance me the necessary amount in proper form, and that I would guarantee him the repayment of that proportion of it which might be considered due payment for the literary property, out of my future theatrical takings, which would thus be his security.

After a long time he agreed to make advances on 'musical compositions still to be delivered,' and to this suggestion I gladly acceded, insisting, however, that I must be able to depend on a total gradual payment of twenty thousand francs. As, after settling my Vienna hotel bill, I was in immediate want of money, Schott gave me a draft on Paris. From that city I now received a letter from Princess Metternich, which mystified me, inasmuch as it merely announced the sudden death of her mother, Countess Sandor, and the consequent change in her family circumstances. Once more I deliberated whether it would not be better, after all, to take at random a modest lodging in or near Karlsruhe, which in time might develop into a peaceful and permanent dwelling. Owing to my difficulty in providing Minna's allowance, which according to our agreement was three thousand marks a year, it struck me as more reasonable and certainly more economical to ask my wife to share my home. But a letter which just then reached me from her, and the main contents of which were nothing less than an attempt to incite me against my own friends, scared me away from any thought of reunion with her, and determined me to adhere to my Paris plans and keep as far away from her as possible.

So towards the middle of December I started for Paris, where I alighted at the dingy-looking Hôtel Voltaire, situated on the quay of the same name, and took a very modest room with a pleasant outlook. Here I wished to remain unrecognised (preparing myself meanwhile for my work) until I could present myself to Princess Metternich at the beginning of the new year, according to her wish. In order not to embarrass the Metternich's friends, Pourtalès and Hatzfeld, I pretended that I was not in Paris, and looked up only those of my old acquaintances who did not know these gentlemen, such as Truinet, Gaspérini, Flaxland, and the painter Czermak. I met Truinet and his father regularly at supper time in the Taverne Anglaise, to which I used to make my way unobserved through the streets at dusk. One day, on opening one of the papers there I read the news of the death of Count Pourtalès. My grief was great, and I felt particularly sorry that, out of my singular regard for the Metternichs, I had neglected to visit this man who had been a real friend to me. I at once called on Count Hatzfeld, who confirmed the sad news and told me the circumstances of the sudden death, which was the result of heart disease, the existence of which the doctor had not discovered till the very last moment. At the same time I learned the true significance of the events which had taken place at the Hôtel Metternich. The death of Countess Sandor, of which Princess Pauline had informed me, had produced the following developments: the Count, who was the famous Hungarian madman, had up to that time, in the general interest of the family, been strictly guarded by his wife as an invalid. At her death the family lived in fear of the most terrible disturbances from her husband, now no longer under control, and the Metternichs therefore thought it necessary to take him at once to Paris, and keep him there under proper supervision. For that purpose the Princess found that the only suitable suite of apartments at her command was the one previously offered to me. I at once saw it was useless to think any more of taking up my residence at the Austrian embassy, and I was left to reflect on the strange freak of fortune that had again cast me adrift in this ill-omened Paris.

At first the only course open to me was to stay in my inexpensive lodging in the Hôtel Voltaire until I had finished the libretto of the *Meistersinger,* and meanwhile set to work to find the refuge so earnestly sought for the completion of my new work. It was not an easy matter; my name and person, which everybody involuntarily regarded in the doubtful light of my Paris failure, seemed surrounded by a cloud of mist, which made me unrecognisable even to my old friends. The Olliviers also appeared to receive me with an air of distrust; at any rate, they thought it very strange to see me again so soon in Paris. I was obliged to explain the extraordinary circumstances that had brought me back, and told them that I did not contemplate a long stay. Apart from this probably deceptive impression, I soon noticed the great change that had taken place in the home life of the family. The grandmother was laid up with a broken leg, which at her age was incurable. Ollivier had taken her into his very small flat for more efficient nursing and care, and we all met for dinner at her bedside in the tiny room. Blandine had greatly changed since the previous summer, and wore a sad and serious expression, and I fancied that she was *enceinte*. Émile, although dry and superficial, was the only one who gave me any sound advice. When the fellow Lindau sent me a letter through his lawyer demanding the compensation awarded him by the law for his imaginary co-operation in the translation of *Tannhäuser,* all that Émile said on reading the letter was, ' *Ne répondez pas,*' and his advice proved as useful as it was easy to follow, for I never heard anything more of the matter. I sorrowfully made up my mind not to trouble Ollivier any more, and it was with an inexpressibly sad look that Blandine and I parted.

With Czermak, on the other hand, I entered into almost daily intercourse. I used to join him and the Truinet family of an evening at the Taverne Anglaise, or some other equally cheap restaurants which we hunted out. Afterwards we generally went to one of the smaller theatres, which, owing to pressure of work, I had not troubled about on my former visits. The best of them all was the Gymnase, where all the pieces were good and played by an excellent company. Of these pieces a particularly tender and touching one-act play called *Je dîne chez ma Mère* remains in my memory. In the Théâtre du Palais Royal, where things were not now so refined as formerly, and also in the Théâtre Déjazet, I recognised the prototypes of all the jokes with which, in spite of poor elaboration and unsuitable localisation, the German public is being entertained all the year round. Besides this I occasionally dined with the Flaxland family, who still refused to despair of my eventual success with the Parisians. For the present my Paris publisher continued to issue the *Fliegender Holländer* as well as *Rienzi*, for which he paid me fifteen hundred francs as a small fee, which I had not bargained for on the first edition.

The cause of the almost cheerful complacency with which I managed to regard my adverse situation in Paris, and which enabled me afterwards to look back on it as a pleasant memory, was that my libretto of the *Meistersinger* daily increased its swelling volume of rhyme. How could I help being filled with facetious thoughts, when on raising my eyes from the paper, after meditating upon the quaint verses and sayings of my Nuremberg Meistersinger, I gazed from the third-floor window of my hotel on the tremendous crowds passing along the quays and over the numerous bridges, and enjoyed a prospect embracing the Tuileries, the Louvre, and even the Hôtel de Ville!

I had already got far on into the first act when the momentous New Year's Day of 1862 arrived, and I paid my long-delayed visit to Princess Metternich. I found her very naturally embarrassed, but I quite cheerfully accepted her assurances of regret at being obliged to withdraw her invitation owing to circumstances with which I was already acquainted, and I did my utmost to reassure her. I also begged Count Hatzfeld to inform me when Countess Pourtalès would feel equal to receiving me.

Thus through the whole month of January I continued working on the *Meistersinger* libretto, and completed it in exactly thirty days. The melody for the fragment of Sachs's poem on the Reformation, with which I make my characters in the last act greet their beloved master, occurred to me on the way to the Taverne Anglaise, whilst strolling through the galleries of the Palais Royal. There I found Truinet already waiting for me, and asked him to give me a scrap of paper and a pencil to jot down my melody, which I quietly hummed over to him at the time. I usually accompanied him and his father along the boulevards to his flat in the Faubourg St. Honoré, and on that evening he could do nothing but exclaim, ' *Mais, quelle gaîté d'esprit, cher maître!* '

The nearer my work approached its termination, the more earnestly had I to think about a place of abode. I still imagined

that something similar to what I had lost by Liszt's abandonment of the Altenburg was in store for me. I now remembered
that in the previous year I had received a most pressing invitation from Mme. Street, to pay her and her father a long visit in
Brussels; on the strength of which I wrote to the lady and asked
if she could put me up for a time without any ceremony. She
was *en désolation* at being obliged to deny my wish. I next
turned to Cosima, who was in Berlin, with a similar request,
at which she seemed to be quite alarmed, but I quite understood
the reason of this when, on visiting Berlin later on, I saw the
style of Bülow's quarters. It struck me as very strange, on
the other hand, that my brother-in-law Avenarius, who, I heard,
was very comfortably settled in Berlin, begged me most earnestly
to go to him, and judge for myself whether I could not pay him
a long visit. My sister Cecilia, however, forbade me to take
Minna there, although she thought she could find her a lodging
in the immediate neighbourhood if she wanted to visit Berlin.
Unfortunately for herself, poor Minna could find nothing better
to do than to write me a furious letter about my sister's cruel
behaviour to her, so the possibility of a renewal of our old
squabbles deterred me at once from accepting my brother-in-
law's proposal. At last I bethought me of looking out for a
quiet retreat in the neighbourhood of Mayence, under the
financial protection of Schott. He had spoken to me about a
pretty estate there belonging to the young Baron von Hornstein.
I thought I was conferring an honour upon the latter when I
wrote to him at Munich asking permission to take up my abode
for a time at his place in the Rhine district, and was therefore
greatly perplexed when I received an answer expressing terror
at my suggestion. I now determined to go at once to Mayence,
and ordered all our furniture and household goods, which had
been stored in Paris for nearly a year, to be sent there. Before
leaving Paris, after coming to this decision, I had the consolation
of receiving a sublime exhortation to face everything with
resignation. I had previously informed Frau Wesendonck of
my situation and the chief source of my trouble, though of
course only as one writes to a sympathetic friend; she answered
by sending me a small letter-weight of cast-iron which she had
bought for me in Venice. It represented the lion of San Marco

with his paw on the book, and was intended to admonish me to imitate this lion in all things. On the other hand, Countess Pourtalès granted me the privilege of another visit to her house. In spite of her mourning, this lady did not wish to leave her sincere interest in me unexpressed on account of her sad bereavement; and when I told her what I was then doing, she asked to see my libretto. On my assuring her that in her present frame of mind she could not enter into the lively character of my *Meistersinger,* she kindly expressed a great wish to hear me read it, and invited me to spend an evening with her. She was the first person to whom I had the opportunity of reading my now completed work, and it made such a lively impression upon us both, that we were many times compelled to burst out into fits of hearty laughter.

On the evening of my departure on the first of February, I invited my friends Gaspérini, Czermak, and the Truinets to a farewell meal in my hotel. All were in capital spirits, and my good-humour enhanced the general cheerfulness, although no one quite understood what connection it could have with the subject on which I had just completed a libretto, and from the performance of which I anticipated so much.

In my anxiety to choose a suitable residence, which was now so necessary to me, I directed my steps once more to Karlsruhe. I was again received in the kindest manner by the Grand Duke and Duchess, who inquired about my future plans. It turned out, however, that the residence I so earnestly desired could not be provided for me in Karlsruhe. I was much struck by the sympathetic concern of the Grand Duke as to how I could meet the cost of my arduous life, or even my travelling expenses. I cheerfully endeavoured to set his mind at rest by telling him of the contract I had made with Schott, who had bound himself to provide me with the necessary funds in the form of advances on my *Meistersinger.* This seemed to reassure him. Later on I heard from Alwine Frommann that the Grand Duke had once said that I had been somewhat cold towards him, considering that he had been kind enough to place his purse at my disposal. But I was certainly not conscious of his having done so. The only point raised in our discussion had been whether I should go to Karlsruhe again to rehearse one of my operas there, possibly *Lohengrin,* and conduct it in person.

At any rate I started for Mayence, which I reached on the 4th February, and found the whole place flooded. Owing to the early breaking up of the ice, the Rhine had overflowed its banks to an unusual extent, and I only reached Schott's house at some considerable risk. Nevertheless, I had already arranged to read the *Meistersinger* on the evening of the 5th of that month, and had even made Cornelius promise to come from Vienna, and had sent him a hundred francs from Paris for that purpose. I had not received any answer from him, and as I now learned that the floods had spread to all the river districts of Germany, and impeded the railway traffic, I had already ceased to count upon him. I waited until the last moment and — in fact, just as the clock struck seven — Cornelius appeared. He had met with all sorts of adventures, had even lost his overcoat on the way, and reached his sister's house in a half-frozen condition only a few hours before. The reading of my libretto put us all into excellent humour, but I was very sorry I could not shake Cornelius's determination to start on his return journey the next day. He wished me to understand that his sole object in coming to Mayence was for this one reading of the *Meistersinger,* and as a matter of fact, in spite of floods and floating ice, he left for Vienna on the following day.

As we had already arranged, I began in company with Schott to search for a residence on the opposite bank of the Rhine. We had had Biebrich in our mind's eye; but as nothing suitable seemed to present itself there, we thought of Wiesbaden. At last I decided to stay at the ' Europäischer Hof ' at Biebrich, and continue my search from there. As I had always been most particular to keep aloof as far as possible from the noise of music, I decided to rent a small but very suitable flat in a large summer residence newly built by the architect Frickhöfer, and situated close to the Rhine. I was obliged to await the arrival of my furniture and household effects from Paris before I could get it in order. At last they came, and at endless trouble and expense were duly unloaded at the Biebrich custom-house, where I took possession only of those things which I required most.

I kept only what was absolutely necessary in Biebrich, intending to send the greater part to my wife in Dresden. I had already informed Minna of this, whereupon she immediately assumed that with my clumsy unpacking I should lose half the things or ruin them all. About a week after I had fairly settled down with my newly arrived Erard grand, Minna suddenly appeared in Biebrich. At first I felt nothing but sincere pleasure at her healthy appearance and untiring energy in the practical management of affairs, and even thought the best thing I could do was to let her remain with me. Unfortunately my good resolutions did not last long, as the old scenes were soon renewed. When we went to the custom-house, intending to separate her things from mine, she could not contain her anger that I had not waited for her arrival before removing on my own account the articles I required for myself. Nevertheless, she thought it only proper that I should be provided with certain household effects, and gave me four sets of knives, forks and spoons, a few cups and saucers, with plates to match. She then superintended the packing of the remainder, which was not inconsiderable, and, after arranging everything to her satisfaction, took her departure to Dresden a week later.

She now flattered herself that her establishment there would be sufficiently furnished to receive me, as she hoped, very shortly. With this idea she had taken the necessary steps with regard to the superior government officials, and these latter had been successful in obtaining a declaration from the minister that I might now send in a formal petition to the King to grant me an amnesty, and that nothing would then stand in the way of my return to Dresden.

I deliberated with considerable hesitation as to what I should do in this matter. Minna's presence had greatly increased the mental discord arising from my recent anxieties. Rough weather, defective stoves, my badly managed household, and my unexpectedly heavy expenses, particularly for Minna's establishment, all combined to mar the pleasure I had taken in pursuing the work I had started at the Hôtel Voltaire. Presumably to distract my thoughts, the Schott family invited me to witness a performance of *Rienzi* at Darmstadt, with

Niemann in the title-rôle. The ex-minister, Herr von Dalwigk, fearing that a demonstration at the theatre in my favour in the presence of the Grand Duke, might wound the latter's susceptibilities, introduced himself to me at the station and accompanied me to his own box, where he cleverly thought he could play the part of presenting me to the public on behalf of the Grand Duke. Thus everything went off pleasantly. The performance itself, in which Niemann played one of his best parts, interested me greatly; I also noticed that they cut out as much of the opera as they could, presumably in deference to the tastes of the Grand Duke, so as to extend the ballet as much as possible by repeating the lighter parts of it.

From this excursion I had again to return home through the floating ice on the Rhine. As I was still in very low spirits, I tried to introduce a few comforts into my home, and for this purpose engaged a maid-servant to prepare my breakfast; my other meals I took at the 'Europäischer Hof.'

When I found, however, that I could not recover my working mood, and feeling somewhat restless, I offered to redeem my promise and pay another visit to the Grand Duke of Baden, suggesting that I should give him a reading of the *Meistersinger*. The Grand Duke replied by a very kind telegram signed by himself, in response to which I went to Karlsruhe on the 7th March and read my manuscript to him and his wife. A drawing-room had been specially selected for this reading, in which hung a great historical picture by my old friend Pecht, portraying Goethe as a young man reading the first fragments of his *Faust* before the Grand Duke's ancestors. My work received very kind attention, and at the conclusion of the reading I was exceedingly pleased to hear the Grand Duchess recommend me particularly to find a suitable musical setting for the excellent part of Pogner, which was a friendly admission of regret that a citizen should be more zealous in the interests of art than many a prince. A performance of *Lohengrin*, under my conductorship, was once more discussed, and I was advised to make fresh terms with Eduard Devrient. Unfortunately the latter made a terrible impression on me by his production of *Tannhäuser* at the theatre. I was obliged to witness this performance seated by his side, and was astonished to realise that this 'Dramaturge,' whom I had hitherto so highly recommended, had now sunk to the most vulgar practices of the theatrical profession. To my amazement at the monstrous mistakes made in the performance, he replied, with great surprise and a certain haughty indignation, that he could not understand why I made so much fuss about such trifles, as I must know very well that in theatres it was impossible to do otherwise. Nevertheless, a model performance of *Lohengrin* was arranged for the following summer, with the co-operation of Herr Schnorr and his wife.

A much pleasanter impression was made upon me by a play I saw at the Frankfort theatre, where, in passing through that town, I saw a pretty comedy, in which the delicate and tender acting of Friederike Meyer, the sister of my Vienna singer, Mme. Dustmann, impressed me more than any German acting had ever done. I now began to calculate on the possibility of making suitable friends in the neighbourhood of Biebrich, so as not to be entirely dependent on the Schott family or on my hotel-keeper for society. I had already looked up the Raff family in Wiesbaden, where Frau Raff had an engagement at the court theatre. She was a sister of Emilie Genast, with whom I had been on friendly terms during my stay in Weimar. One excellent piece of information I heard about her was that by extraordinary thrift and good management she had succeeded in raising her husband's position of careless wastefulness to a flourishing and prosperous one. Raff himself, who by his own accounts of his dissipated life under Liszt's patronage, had led me to regard him as an eccentric genius, at once disabused me of this idea when, on a closer acquaintance, I found him an uncommonly uninteresting and insipid man, full of self-conceit, but without any power of taking a wide outlook on the world.

Taking advantage of the prosperous condition to which he had attained, thanks to his wife, he considered he was entitled to patronise me by giving me some friendly advice in regard to my position at the time. He thought it advisable to tell me that I ought in my dramatic compositions to pay more attention to the reality of things, and to illustrate his meaning he pointed to my score of *Tristan* as an abortion of idealistic extravagances.

In the course of my rambles on foot to Wiesbaden I sometimes liked to call on Raff's wife, a rather insignificant woman, but Raff himself was a person to whom I soon became perfectly indifferent. Still, when he came to know me a little better, he lowered the tone of his sagelike maxims, and even appeared to be rather afraid of my chaffing humour, against the shafts of which he knew he was defenceless.

Wendelin Weisheimer, whom I had known slightly before, often called on me in Biebrich. He was the son of a rich peasant of Osthofen, and to the astonishment of his father refused to give up the musical profession. He was particularly anxious to introduce me to his parent, that I might influence the old man's mind in favour of his son's choice of an artistic career. This involved me in excursions into their district, and I had an opportunity of witnessing young Weisheimer's talent as an orchestral conductor at a performance of Offenbach's *Orpheus* in the theatre at Mayence, where he had hitherto occupied a subordinate position. I was horrified that my sympathy for this young man should make me descend so low as to be present at such an abomination, and for a long time I could not refrain from letting Weisheimer see the annoyance I felt.

In my search for a more dignified entertainment I wrote to Friedericke Meyer in Frankfort and asked her to let me know when the performance of Calderon's comedy, *Das öffentliche Geheimniss,* would be repeated, as the last time I had seen an announcement of it, I had been too late. She was much pleased at my sympathetic inquiry, and informed me that the comedy was not likely to be revived in the immediate future, but that there was a prospect of Calderon's *Don Gutierre* being produced. I again paid a visit to Frankfort to see this play, and made the personal acquaintance of this interesting actress for the first time. I had every reason to be highly satisfied with the performance of Calderon's tragedy, although the talented actress who played the leading part was thoroughly successful only in the tenderer passages, her resources being insufficient to depict the more passionate scenes. She told me she very often visited some friends of hers in Mayence, and I followed up this communication by expressing a wish that when doing so she would look me up at Biebrich, to which she replied that

I might hope on some future occasion for the fulfilment of my wish.

A grand soirée given by the Schotts to their Mayence acquaintances was the occasion of my making friends with Mathilde Maier, whom Frau Schott, at least so she informed me, had specially selected for her 'cleverness' to be my companion at the supper table; her highly intelligent, sincere manner and her peculiar Mayence dialect distinguished her favourably from the rest of the company; nor was this distinction accompanied by anything *outré*. I promised to visit her, and thus became acquainted with an idyllic home such as I had never met before. This Mathilde, who was the daughter of a lawyer who had died leaving only a small fortune behind, lived with her mother, two aunts and a sister in a neat little house, while her brother, who was learning business in Paris, was a continual source of trouble to her. Mathilde, with her practical common-sense, attended to the affairs of the whole family, apparently to every one's complete satisfaction. I was received among them with remarkable warmth whenever, in the pursuit of my business, I chanced to come to Mayence. This happened about once a week, and on each occasion I was made to accept their hospitality. But as Mathilde had a large circle of acquaintances, among others an old gentleman in Mayence who had been Schopenhauer's only friend, I frequently met her in other people's houses, as for instance at the Raffs in Wiesbaden. From there she and her old friend Luise Wagner would often accompany me on my way home, and I would sometimes go with them further on the way to Mayence.

These meetings were full of agreeable impressions, to which frequent walks in the beautiful park of Biebrich Castle contributed. The fair season of the year was now approaching, and I was once more seized with a desire for work. As from the balcony of my flat, in a sunset of great splendour, I gazed upon the magnificent spectacle of 'Golden' Mayence, with the majestic Rhine pouring along its outskirts in a glory of light, the prelude to my *Meistersinger* again suddenly made its presence closely and distinctly felt in my soul. Once before had I seen it rise before me out of a lake of sorrow, like some distant mirage. I proceeded to write down the prelude exactly as it appears to-day in the score, that is, containing the clear outlines of the leading themes of the whole drama. I proceeded at once to continue the composition, intending to allow the remaining scenes to follow in due succession. As I was feeling in a good temper I thought I would like to pay a visit to the Duke of Nassau. He was my neighbour, and I had so often met him on my lonely walks in the park, that I considered it polite to call on him. Unfortunately there was not much to be got out of the interview which took place. He was a very narrow-minded but amiable man, who excused himself for continuing to smoke his cigar in my presence because he could not get on without it, and he thereupon proceeded to describe to me his preference for Italian opera, which I was quite content he should retain. But I had an ulterior motive in trying to prepossess him in my favour. At the back of his park stood a tiny castle of ancient appearance on the borders of a lake. It had grown into a sort of picturesque ruin, and at the time served as a studio for a sculptor. I was filled with a bold desire to acquire this small, half-tumbledown building for the rest of my life; for I had already become a prey to alarming anxiety as to whether I should be able to hold out in the quarters I had so far tenanted, as the greater part of the storey, on which I occupied only two small rooms, had been let to a family for the approaching summer, and I heard that they would enter into possession, armed with a piano. I was soon dissuaded, however, from further attempts to induce the Duke of Nassau to favour my views, for he told me that this little castle, on account of its damp situation, would be thoroughly unhealthy.

Nevertheless, I did not allow myself to be deterred from setting to work to find some lonely little house with a garden, for which I still longed. In the excursions I repeatedly undertook for this purpose I was frequently accompanied not only by Weisheimer but also by Dr. Städl, the young lawyer who at Schott's house had proposed the charming toast which I have already mentioned. He was an extraordinary man, and I could only explain his very excitable nature by the fact that he was a passionate gambler at the roulette tables in Wiesbaden. He it was who had introduced me to another friend, a practised musician, Dr. Schüler from Wiesbaden. With both these gentlemen I now weighed all the possibilities of acquiring, or at least of discovering, my little castle for the future.   On one occasion we visited Bingen with this object, and ascended the celebrated old tower there in which the Emperor Henry IV. was imprisoned long ago.   After going for some distance up the rock on which the tower was built, we reached a room on the fourth storey occupying the entire square of the building, with a single projecting window looking out upon the Rhine.

I recognised this room as the ideal of everything I had imagined in the way of a residence for myself.   I thought I could arrange for the necessary smaller apartments in the flat by means of curtains, and thus prepare for myself a splendid place of refuge for ever.   Städl and Schüler thought it possible they might help me in the fulfilment of my wishes, as they were both acquainted with the proprietor of this ruin.   Shortly afterwards, in fact, they informed me that the owner had no objection to letting me this large room at a low rent, but at the same time they pointed out the utter impracticability of carrying out my plan; nobody, they said, would be either able or willing to act as my servant there, for, amongst other things, there was no well, and the only water obtainable was from a cistern lying at a frightful depth down in the keep, and even this was not good.   Under such circumstances it did not require more than one such obstacle to deter me from the pursuit of such an extravagant scheme.   I had a similar experience with a property in Rheingau belonging to Count Schönborn. My attention had been drawn to it, because it was unoccupied by the proprietor.   Here I certainly found a number of empty rooms, out of which I should have been able to arrange something suitable for my purpose.   After obtaining further details from the land agent, who wrote on my behalf to Count Schönborn, I had to content myself with a refusal.

A strange incident that occurred about this time seriously threatened to interrupt me to some extent in the work I had begun.   Friederike Meyer kept her promise and called on me one afternoon on her return from her usual excursion to Mayence.   She was accompanied by a lady friend.   Shortly after her arrival she was suddenly overwhelmed with fear, and to the terror of all present declared she was afraid she had caught scarlet fever. Her condition soon became alarming, and she had to find accommodation immediately in the 'Europäischer Hof' hotel and send for a doctor. The certainty with which she had immediately recognised the symptoms of a disease, which in most cases can only be caught from children, could not fail to impress me strangely. But my amazement was increased when on the following morning, at a very early hour, Herr von Guaita, the manager of the Frankfort theatre, who had heard of her illness, paid a visit to the patient and expressed for her an anxiety, the intensity of which it was impossible to ascribe entirely to his interest as a theatrical manager. He took Friederike at once under his protection, and treated her with the greatest care, thus relieving me from the pangs of anxiety aroused by this strange case. I spent some time with Herr von Guaita, talking with him about the possibility of producing one of my operas in Frankfort. On the second day I was present when the sick lady was conveyed to the railway station by Guaita, who evinced towards her what appeared to me the most tender paternal solicitude. Soon after this, Herr Bürde (the husband of Madame Ney, a famous singer), who was at that time an actor at the Frankfort theatre, paid me a call. This gentleman, with whom amongst other things I discussed Friederike Meyer's talents, informed me that she was supposed to be the mistress of Herr von Guaita, a man who was held in great respect in the town on account of his noble rank, and that he had presented her with a house in which she was now living. As Herr von Guaita had not made an agreeable impression upon me, but on the contrary had struck me as a strange creature, this news filled me with a certain uneasiness. My other acquaintances who lived near my place of refuge in Biebrich were kind and friendly when, on the evening of my birthday on the 22nd of May, I entertained this little company in my flat. Mathilde Maier with her sister and her lady friend were very clever in utilising my small stock of crockery, and in a certain sense she did the honours as mistress of the house.

But my peace of mind was soon disturbed by an interchange of letters with Minna, which grew more and more unsatisfactory. I had settled her in Dresden, but wanted to spare her the humiliation of a permanent separation from me. In pursuance of this idea I had at last found myself compelled to adopt the plan she had initiated, by communicating with the Saxon Minister of Justice; and I finally petitioned for a complete amnesty from the government, and received permission to settle in Dresden. Minna now thought herself authorised to take a large flat, in which it would be easy to arrange the furniture allotted to her, assuming that after a little while I would share the abode with her, at least periodically. I had to try to meet cheerfully her demands for the wherewithal to carry out her wishes, and especially to procure the two thousand seven hundred marks she required for the purpose. The more calmly I acted in this matter, the more deeply she seemed to be offended by the quiet frigidity of my letters. Reproaches for supposed injuries in the past and recriminations of every kind now poured in from her faster than ever. At last I turned to my old friend Pusinelli. Out of affection for me he had always been a loyal helper of my intractable spouse. Through his mediation I now prescribed the strong medicine which my sister Clara a short while ago had recommended as the best remedy for the patient, and asked him to impress upon Minna the necessity for a legal separation. It seemed to be no easy task for my poor friend to carry out this proposal in earnest, but he had been asked to do it, and obeyed. He informed me that she was very much alarmed, but that she definitely refused to discuss an amicable separation, and, as my sister had foreseen, Minna's conduct now changed in a very striking manner; she ceased to annoy me and seemed to realise her position and abide by it. To relieve her heart trouble, Pusinelli had prescribed for her a cure at Reichenhall. I obtained the money for this, and apparently she spent the summer in tolerable spirits in the very place in which a year ago I had met Cosima undergoing a cure.

Once more I turned to my work, to which I always had recourse as the best means of raising my spirits so soon as interruptions were removed. One night I was disturbed by a strange event. The evening had been pleasant, and I had sketched out the pretty theme for Pogner's *Anrede,* ' Das schöne Fest Johannistag,' etc., when, while I was dozing off and still

had this tune floating in my mind, I was suddenly awakened
to full consciousness by an unrestrained outburst of a woman's
laughter above my room. This laughter, growing madder and
madder, at last turned into a horrible whimpering and frightful
howling. I sprang out of bed in a terrified condition, to
discover that the sound proceeded from my servant Lieschen,
who had been attacked with hysterical convulsions as she lay
in bed in the room overhead. My host's maid went to help
her, and a doctor was summoned. While I was horrified at
the thought that the girl would soon die, I could not help wondering at the curious tranquillity of the others who were present.
I was told that such fits were of common occurrence in young
girls, especially after dances. Without heeding this, I was
riveted to the spot for a long time by the spectacle, with the
horrible symptoms it presented. Several times I saw what
resembled a childish fit of merriment pass, like the ebb and
flow of the tide, through all the different stages, up to the most
impudent laughter, and then to what seemed like the screams
of the damned in torture. When the disturbance had somewhat subsided, I went to bed again, and once more Pogner's
'Johannistag' rose to my memory, and gradually banished the
fearful impressions that I had undergone.

One day, when I was watching young Städl at the gambling-
table in Wiesbaden, I thought he was rather like the poor
servant-girl. I had taken coffee with him and Weisheimer in
the Kur garden, and we had enjoyed one another's company,
when Städl disappeared for a time. Weisheimer led me to the
gambling-table to find him. Seldom have I witnessed a more
horrible change of expression than that now stamped on the
man who was a prey to the gambling mania. As a demon had
possessed poor Lieschen, so now a demon possessed this man.
As folk say, the devils 'pursued their evil lusts in him.' No
appeal, no humiliating admonitions could prevail upon the man
tortured by his losses in the game to summon up his moral
powers. As I remembered my own experiences of the gambling
passion, to which I had succumbed for a time when I was a
youth, I spoke to young Weisheimer on the subject, and offered
to show him how I was not afraid to make a stake on pure
chance, but that I had no belief in my luck. When a new

round of roulette began, I said to him in a voice of quiet certainty, 'Number 11 will win'; and it did. I added fuel to the fire of his astonishment at this stroke of good luck by predicting Number 27 for the next round. Certainly I remember being overcome by a spell as I spoke, and my number was in fact again victorious. My young friend was now in a state of such astonishment, that he vehemently urged me to stake something on the numbers which I foretold. Again I cannot but call to mind the curious, quiet feeling of being spellbound which possessed me as I said, 'As soon as I introduce my own personal interests into the game, my gift of prophecy will disappear at once.' I then drew him away from the gambling-table, and we took our way back to Biebrich in a fine sunset.

I now came into very painful relations with poor Friederike Meyer. She wrote and told me of her recovery and requested me to visit her, because she felt it her duty to apologise to me for the trouble in which she had involved me. As the short drive to Frankfort often helped to entertain me and distract my thoughts, I gladly fulfilled her wishes, and found her in a state of convalescence but still weak, and obviously preoccupied with the effort to fortify my mind against all disagreeable surmises about herself. She said that Herr von Guaita was like an anxious, almost hypersensitive father to her. She told me that she was very young when she left her family, and that with her sister Luise in particular she had severed all connection. She had thus come quite friendless to Frankfort, where the chance protection of Herr von Guaita, a man of mature age, had been very welcome to her. Unfortunately she had to suffer much that was painful under this arrangement, for she was most bitterly persecuted, chiefly on the score of her reputation, by her patron's family, who feared he might want to marry her. As she told me this, I could not refrain from drawing her attention to some of the consequences of the antagonism I had noticed, and I went so far as to speak of the house which people said had been given her as a present. This seemed to produce an extraordinary effect upon Friederike, who was still an invalid. She expressed the greatest annoyance at these rumours, although, as she admitted, she had long been obliged to suspect that slander of this kind would be disseminated about her; more than once she had considered the advisability of giving up the Frankfort stage, and now she was more determined than ever to do so. I saw nothing in her demeanour to shake my confidence in the truth of her story; moreover, as Herr von Guaita became more and more unintelligible to me both as a man and in the light of his incredible conduct on the occasion of Friederike's illness, my attitude towards this highly gifted girl was henceforth unconditionally on the side of her interests, which were being prejudiced by an obvious injustice. To facilitate her recovery I advised her, without delay, to take a long holiday for a tour on the Rhine.

In accordance with the instructions conveyed to him by the Grand Duke, Eduard Devrient now addressed me in reference to the appointed performance of *Lohengrin* in Karlsruhe under my superintendence. The angry and arrogant disgust expressed in his letter at my desire to see that *Lohengrin* was produced without 'cuts,' served admirably to expose to me the profound antipathy of this man whom I had once so blindly overestimated. He wrote that one of the first things he had done was to have a copy of the score made for the orchestra with the 'cuts' introduced by Conductor Rietz for the Leipzig performance, and that it would consequently be a tiresome business to put back all the passages which I wished to have restored. He regarded my request in this particular as merely malicious. I now remembered that the only performance of *Lohengrin,* which had been taken off almost immediately on account of its complete failure, was the one in Leipzig produced by Conductor Rietz. Devrient, regarding Rietz as Mendelssohn's successor and the most solid musician of 'modern times,' had concluded that this mutilation of my work was a suitable one for production in Karlsruhe. But I shuddered at the misguided light in which I had so long persisted in regarding this man. I informed him briefly of my indignation and of my decision to have nothing to do with *Lohengrin* in Karlsruhe. I also expressed my intention to make my excuses to the Grand Duke at a suitable time. Soon after this I heard that *Lohengrin* was, after all, to be produced in Karlsruhe in the usual way, and that the newly wedded Schnorrs had been specially

engaged for it. A great longing at last filled me to make the
acquaintance of Schnorr and his achievements. Without announcing my intentions, I travelled to Karlsruhe, obtained a
ticket through Kaliwoda, and heedless of all else went to the
performance. In my published *Memoirs* I have described more
accurately the impressions I received on this occasion, more particularly of Schnorr. I fell in love with him at once, and after
the performance I sent him a message to come and see me in
my room at the hotel and have a little chat. I had heard so
much of his delicate state of health that I was genuinely
delighted to see him enter the room with a lively step and a
look of joy in his eyes. Although it was late at night, and he
had undergone a considerable strain, he met my anxiety to
avoid all dissipation out of regard to his welfare, by willingly
accepting my offer to celebrate our new acquaintance with a
bottle of champagne. We spent the greater part of the night
in the best of spirits, and among our discussions those on
Devrient's character were especially instructive to me. I undertook to stay another day, so as to avail myself of an invitation
to lunch with Schnorr and his wife. As by this lengthy stay
in Karlsruhe I knew my presence would become known to
the Grand Duke, I took advantage on the following day to inform him of my arrival, and he made an appointment to meet
me in the afternoon. After talking at lunch to Frau Schnorr,
in whom I had recognised a great and well-developed theatrical
talent, and after making the most astonishing discoveries about
Devrient's behaviour in the *Tristan* affair, I had my interview
at the ducal palace. It was marked by uneasiness on both
sides. I openly stated my reasons for withdrawing my promise
with regard to the *Lohengrin* performance, and also my unalter-
able conviction that a conspiracy to interfere with the production of *Tristan* originally proposed had been the work of
Devrient. As Devrient, by his ingenious attitude, had led the
Grand Duke to believe in his profound and genuinely solicitous
friendship for me, my communications obviously pained the
Grand Duke a great deal. Still, he seemed eager to assume
that the matter turned on artistic differences of opinion between
me and his theatrical manager, and in bidding me good-bye he
expressed the hope of seeing these apparent misunderstandings

give way to a satisfactory explanation. I replied with indifference that I did not think it likely I should ever come to an
agreement with Devrient. The Grand Duke now gave vent to
genuine indignation; he had not thought, he said, that I could
so easily treat an old friend with such ingratitude. To meet
the keenness of this reproach I could at first only tender my
apologies for not having expressed my decision with the
emphasis he had a right to expect, but as the Grand Duke had
taken this matter so seriously and had thereby seemed to
justify me in expressing my real opinion of this supposed friend
with equal seriousness, I was bound, with all the earnestness at
my command, to assure him that I did not wish to have anything more to do with Devrient. At this the Grand Duke
told me, with renewed gentleness, that he declined to regard my
assurance as irrevocable, for it lay in his power to propitiate
me by other means. I took my departure with an expression
of serious regret that I could not help regarding as fruitless
any effort made in the direction contemplated by my patron.
Later on I ascertained that Devrient, who, of course, was
informed by the Grand Duke of what had taken place, looked
upon my behaviour as an attempt on my part to ruin and
supplant him. The Grand Duke had not abandoned his desire
to arrange for the performance of a concert consisting of
selections from my most recent works. Devrient had afterwards to write to me again in his official capacity on this
subject. In his letter he took occasion to make it clear that he
regarded himself as victorious over the intrigues I had practised
against him, assuring me at the same time that his distinguished
patron nevertheless wished to carry out the concert in question, as from his lofty point of view he knew very well how to
distinguish 'the art from the artist.' My answer was a simple
refusal.

I had many a conversation with the Schnorrs over the
episode, and I made an arrangement with them to visit me
soon in Biebrich. I returned there now, to be in time for
Bülow's visit, of which I had already been informed. He
arrived at the beginning of July to look for lodgings for himself
and Cosima, who followed two days later. We were immensely
pleased to meet again, and utilised the occasion to make

excursions of all sorts for the benefit of our health in the pleasant Rheingau country. We took our meals together regularly in the public dining-room of the ' Europäischer Hof ' (where the Schnorrs also came to stay), and we were generally as merry as possible. In the evening we had music in my rooms. Alwine Frommann, on her way through Biebrich, also came to the reading of the *Meistersinger*. All present seemed to be struck with surprise on hearing my latest libretto, and especially by the vernacular gaiety of the style, of which until now I had not availed myself. Frau Dustmann also, who had a special engagement for a performance at Wiesbaden, paid me a visit. Unfortunately I noticed in her a lively antipathy to her sister Friederike, a fact which, among others, strengthened my conviction that it was high time for Friederike to dissociate herself from all ties in Frankfort. After I had been enabled, with Bülow's support, to play my friends the completed parts of the composition of the *Meistersinger,* I went through most of *Tristan,* and in this process the Schnorrs had an opportunity of showing the extent to which they had already made themselves acquainted with their task. I found that both were a good deal lacking in clearness of enunciation.

The summer now brought more visitors into our neighbourhood, and amongst them several of my acquaintances. David, the Leipzig concert director, called on me with his young pupil, August Wilhelmj, the son of a Wiesbaden lawyer. We now had music in the true sense of the word, and Conductor Alois Schmitt from Schwerin contributed an odd share by performing what he called a worthless old composition of his. One evening we had a crowded party, the Schotts joining the rest of my friends, and both the Schnorrs delighted us keenly with a performance of the so-called love-scene in the third act of *Lohengrin.* We were all deeply moved by the sudden apparition of Röckel in our common dining-room at the hotel. He had been released from Waldheimer prison after thirteen years. I was astounded to find absolutely no radical change in the appearance of my old acquaintance, except for the faded colour of his hair. He himself explained this to me by observing that he had stepped out of something like a shell in which he had been ensconced for his own preservation. As we were deliberating about the field of activity on which he ought now to enter, I advised him to seek some useful employment in the service of a benevolent and liberal-minded man like the Grand Duke of Baden. He did not think he would succeed in any ministerial capacity, owing to his want of legal knowledge; on the other hand, he was eminently qualified to undertake the supervision of a house of correction, as he had obtained not only the most accurate information on this subject, but at the same time had noted what reforms were necessary. He went off to the German shooting competition taking place at Frankfort. There, in recognition of his martyrdom and his unwavering conduct, he was accorded a flattering ovation, and he stayed in Frankfort and its neighbourhool for some time.

Cäsar Willig, a painter who had received a commission from Otto Wesendonck to paint my portrait at his expense, worried me and my intimate friends at this time. Unfortunately the painter was utterly unsuccessful in his attempt to make a good likeness of me. Although Cosima was present at nearly all the sittings, and tried her utmost to put the artist on the right track, the end of it was that I had to sit for a sharp profile, to enable him to produce anything that could be in the least recognisable as a likeness. After he had performed this task to his satisfaction, he painted another copy for me out of gratitude. I sent this at once to Minna in Dresden, through whom it ultimately went to my sister Louisa. It was a horrible picture, and I was confronted with it once afterwards when it was exhibited by the artist in Frankfort.

I made a pleasant excursion with the Bülows and the Schnorrs to Bingen one evening, and availed myself of the opportunity to cross over to Rüdesheim to bring back Friederike Meyer, who had been enjoying her holiday there. I introduced her to my friends, and Cosima especially took a friendly interest in this uncommonly gifted woman. Our gaiety as we sat over a glass of wine in the open air was heightened by our being unexpectedly accosted by a traveller who approached us respectfully from a distant table; he held his glass filled, and at once greeted me politely and with the utmost warmth. He was a native of Berlin and a great enthusiast of my work. He spoke not only for himself, but also on behalf of two of his friends, who joined us at our table; and our good-humour led us ultimately to champagne. A splendid evening with a wonderful moon-rise shed its influence over the gladness of our spirits as we returned home late in the evening after this delightful excursion. When we visited Schlangenbad (where Alwine Frommann was staying) in equally high spirits, our reckless humour beguiled us into making an even longer excursion to Rolandseck. We made our first halt at Remagen, where we visited the handsome church, in which a young monk was preaching to an immense crowd, and we afterwards lunched in a garden on the bank of the Rhine. We remained that night in Rolandseck, and next morning we went up the Drachenfels. In connection with this ascent, an adventure happened which had a merry sequel. On the return journey, after getting out of the train at the railway station and crossing the Rhine, I missed my letter-case containing a note for two hundred marks; it had slipped out of my overcoat pocket. Two gentlemen who had joined us on the way from the Drachenfels immediately offered to retrace their steps, a somewhat arduous undertaking, to hunt for the lost object. After a few hours they returned, and handed me the letter-case with its contents intact. Two stone-cutters at work on the summit of the mountain had found it. They restored it at once, and the honest fellows were presented with a handsome reward. The happy issue to this adventure had, of course, to be celebrated by a good dinner with the best wine. The story was not completed for me until a long time afterwards. In 1873, on my entering a restaurant in Cologne, the host introduced himself to me as the man who, eleven years previously, had catered for us at the inn on the Rhine, and had changed that very two-hundred-mark note for me. He then told me what had happened to that note. An Englishman, to whom he had related the adventure of the note on the same day, offered to buy it from him for double its value. The host declined any such transaction, but allowed the Englishman to have the note on the promise of the latter to stand champagne to all those present at the time. The promise was fulfilled to the letter.

An invitation to Osthofen from the Weisheimer family was the origin of a less satisfactory excursion than the one described above. We put up there for one night after being compelled on the previous day to take part at all hours in the frolics of a peasant wedding-feast which was simply interminable. Cosima was the only one who managed to keep in a good temper throughout the proceedings. I supported her to the best of my abilities. But Bülow's depression, which had increased during the preceding days, grew deeper and deeper, was aggravated by every possible incident, until at last it developed into an outbreak of fury. We tried to console ourselves with the reflection that a similar infliction could never again fall to our lot. The following day, while I was preparing for my departure, and brooding over other sources of dissatisfaction at my position, Cosima induced Hans to continue the journey as far as Worms in the hope of finding something refreshing and cheering in a visit to the ancient cathedral there, and from that place they followed me later to Biebrich.

One little adventure we had at the gaming-table at Wiesbaden still lingers in my memory. Within the last few days I had received a royalty of twenty louis d'or from the theatre for an opera. Not knowing what to do with so small a sum (as my situation, on the whole, was growing worse and worse), I ventured to ask Cosima to risk half the sum at roulette in our joint interest. I observed with astonishment how, without even the smallest knowledge of the game, she staked one gold piece after another on the table, throwing it down so that it never definitely covered any particular number or colour. In this way it gradually disappeared behind the croupier's rake. I grew alarmed, and hurriedly went to another table in the hope of counteracting the effect of Cosima's unguided and misguided efforts. In this very economical pursuit luck befriended me so substantially, that I at once recovered the ten louis d'or which my fair friend had lost at the other table. This soon put us into a very merry mood. Less cheering than this adventure was our visit to a performance of *Lohengrin* in Wiesbaden. After we had been pretty well satisfied and put into a fairly good humour by the first act, the representation turned, as it proceeded, into a current of maddening misrepresentation such as I should never have believed possible. In a fury I left the theatre before the end, while Hans, urged by Cosima's reminder of the proprieties (though they were both as much infuriated as I was), endured the martyrdom of witnessing the performance to a close.

On another occasion I heard that the Metternichs had arrived at their Castle Johannisberg. Still preoccupied with my main anxiety to obtain a peaceful domicile in which to conclude the *Meistersinger,* I kept an eye on this castle, which was generally unoccupied, and announced my intention of calling on the Prince. An invitation soon followed, and the Bülows accompanied me to the railway station. I could not fail to be satisfied with the friendly reception accorded to me by my patrons. They, too, had been considering the question of finding a temporary resting-place for me in the Johannisberg Castle, and found they could give me a small flat in the house of the keeper of the castle for my sole use, only they drew my attention to the difficulty of obtaining my board. The Prince, however, had busied himself more actively with another matter, that of creating a permanent position for me in Vienna. He said that on his next stay in Vienna he would have a discussion about my affairs with Schmerling the minister, whom he thought it was most suitable to consult on such a matter. He was a man who would understand me, and perhaps be able to discover a proper position for me in the higher sense of the word, and arouse the Emperor's interest in me. If I went to Vienna again, I was simply to call on Schmerling, and he would receive me as a matter of course on account of the Prince's introduction. As the result of an invitation to the ducal court, the Metternichs had repaired without loss of time to Wiesbaden, to which city I accompanied them, and again fell in with the Bülows.

Schnorr had left us after a fortnight's stay, and now the time had also come for the Bülows to depart. I accompanied them as far as Frankfort, where we spent two more days together to see a performance of Goethe's *Tasso.* Liszt's symphonic poem *Tasso* was to precede the play. It was with odd feelings that we witnessed this performance. Friederike Meyer as the Princess and Herr Schneider as Tasso appealed to us greatly, but Hans could not get over the shameful execution of Liszt's work by the conductor, Ignaz Lachner. Before going to the theatre Friedrike gave us a luncheon at the restaurant in the Botanical Gardens. In the end the mysterious Herr von Guaita also joined us there. We now noticed with astonishment that all further conversation was carried on between them as a duologue which was quite unintelligible to us. All that we could make out was the furious jealousy of Herr von Guaita and Friederike's witty, scornful defence. But the excited man became more composed when he suggested I should arrange for a performance of *Lohengrin* in Frankfort under my own direction. I was favourably disposed to the suggestion, as I saw in it an opportunity for another meeting with the Bülows and the Schnorrs. The Bülows promised to come, and I invited the Schnorrs to be in the cast. This time we could take leave of one another cheerfully, although the increasing and often excessive ill-humour of poor Hans had drawn many an involuntary sigh from me. He seemed to be in perpetual torment. On the other hand, Cosima appeared to have lost the shyness she had evinced towards me when I visited Reichenhall in the previous year, and a very friendly manner had taken its place. While I was singing ' Wotan's Abschied ' to my friends I noticed the same expression on Cosima's face as I had seen on it, to my astonishment, in Zürich on a similar occasion, only the ecstasy of it was transfigured into something higher. Everything connected with this was shrouded in silence and mystery, but the belief that she belonged to me grew to such certainty in my mind, that when I was under the influence of more than ordinary excitement my conduct betrayed the most reckless gaiety. As I was accompanying Cosima to the hotel across a public square, I suddenly suggested she should sit in an empty wheelbarrow which stood in the street, so that I might wheel her to the hotel. She assented in an instant. My astonishment was so great that I felt all my courage desert me, and was unable to carry out my mad project.

On returning to Biebrich I was at once confronted with grave difficulties, for Schott, after keeping me some time in suspense, now definitely refused to pay me any further subsidies. The advances I had already received from my publisher had, it is true, until quite recently, served to defray all my expenses since leaving Vienna, including my wife's removal to Dresden

and my own migration to Biebrich by way of Paris, where I
had to satisfy more than one lurking creditor. But in spite
of these initial difficulties, which, I suppose, took about half
the money I was to have for the *Meistersinger* by agreement,
I had counted upon finishing my work in peace with the
remainder of the sum stipulated. But since then Schott had
put me off with vain promises about a fixed date for balancing
accounts with the bookseller. I had already been put to
great straits, and now everything seemed to depend on my
being able to hand over a complete act of the *Meistersinger* to
Schott quickly. I had got as far as the scene where Pogner is
about to introduce Walther von Stolzing to the meistersingers,
when — about the middle of August, while Bülow was still there
— an accident occurred which, though slight in itself, made me
incapable of writing for two whole months.

My surly host kept a bulldog named Leo chained up, and
neglected him so cruelly that it excited my constant sympathy.
I therefore tried one day to have him freed from vermin, and
held his head myself, so that the servant who was doing it should
not be frightened. Although the dog had learned to trust me
thoroughly, he snapped at me once involuntarily and bit me —
apparently very slightly — in the upper joint of my right-hand
thumb. There was no wound visible, but it was soon evident
that the periosteum had become inflamed from the contusion.
As the pain increased more and more with the use of the
thumb, I was ordered to do no writing until my hand was quite
healed. If my plight was not quite so terrible as the news-
papers — which announced that I had been bitten by a mad dog
— made out, it was still conducive to serious reflection on human
frailty. To complete my task, therefore, I needed, not only a
sound mind and good ideas, irrespective of any required skill,
but also a healthy thumb to write with, as my work was not a
libretto I could dictate, but music which no one but myself could
write down.

On the advice of Raff, who considered a volume of my songs
to be worth one thousand francs, I decided to offer my publisher,
by way of temporary compensation, five poems by my friend
Frau Wesendonck which I had set to music (consisting chiefly
of studies for *Tristan* with which I was occupied at the time),

so that he should at least have something on the market. The songs were accepted and published, but they seemed to have produced no softening effect on Schott's mood. I was obliged to conclude that he was acting on some one else's instigation, and I betook myself to Kissingen (where he was staying for his ' cure ') in order to get to the bottom of it and shape my next moves accordingly. An interview with him was obstinately denied me, and Frau Schott, who was posted outside his door in the rôle of guardian angel, informed me that a bad liver attack prevented him from seeing me. I now realised my position with regard to him. For the moment I drew on young Weisheimer for some money, which he gave me most willingly, supported as he was by a wealthy father, and then set to work to consider what I could do next. I could no longer count on Schott, and had in consequence lost all prospect of an unopposed performance of the *Meistersinger*.

At this juncture I was much surprised to receive a renewed official invitation to Vienna for the performance of *Tristan* at the Opera, where I was informed all obstacles had been removed, as Ander had completely recovered his voice. I was genuinely astonished to hear this, and on further inquiry arrived at the following elucidation of the transactions that had been taking place on my behalf in Vienna during the interval. Before I left there the last time Frau Luise Dustmann, who seemed to take a real pleasure in the part of Isolde, had tried to clear away the real impediment to my undertaking by persuading me to go to an evening party, where she intended to introduce me again to Dr. Hanslick. She knew that unless this gentleman could be brought round to my side nothing could be accomplished in Vienna. As I was in a good temper that evening I found it easy to treat Hanslick as a superficial acquaintance, until he drew me aside for an intimate talk, and with sobs and tears assured me he could not bear to be misunderstood by me any longer. The blame for anything that might have been extraordinary in his judgment of me was to be laid, not on any malicious intention, but solely on the narrowmindedness of an individual who desired nothing more ardently than to learn from me how to widen the boundaries of his knowledge. All this was said in such a burst of emotion that I could do nothing but soothe his grief and promise him my unreserved sympathy with his work in future. Just before leaving Vienna I actually heard that Hanslick had launched forth into unmeasured praise of myself and my amiability. This change had so affected both the singers at the Opera and also Councillor Raymond (the Lord High Steward's adviser) that at last, working from high circles downwards, it came to be regarded as a point of honour with the Viennese to have *Tristan* performed in their city. Hence my summons!

I heard at the same time from young Weisheimer, who had betaken himself to Leipzig, that he was sure he could arrange a good concert there if I could assist him by conducting my new prelude to the *Meistersinger* as well as the *Tannhäuser* Overture. He believed it would make so great a sensation that the probable sale of all the tickets would enable him to place a not inconsiderable sum at my disposal after the bare expenses had been deducted. In addition to this, I could hardly go back on my promise to Herr von Guaita with respect to a performance of *Lohengrin* at Frankfort, although the Schnorrs had been obliged to decline to take part in it. After weighing all these offers I decided to put the *Meistersinger* aside, and try to earn enough by enterprises abroad to enable me in the following spring to take up and finish my interrupted work on the spot, unaffected by Schott's humours. I therefore decided at all costs to keep on the house at Biebrich, which I really liked. Minna, on the other hand, had been pressing me to send some of the furniture which I had kept, to complete her own establishment at Dresden, namely, my bed and a few other things to which I was accustomed, ' so that when I went to see her,' she said, ' I should find everything in proper order.' I did not want to act contrary to the established fiction which was to make the parting from me easier for her ; I therefore sent her what she wanted, and bought new furniture for my home on the Rhine with the assistance of a Wiesbaden manufacturer, who allowed me fairly long credit.

At the end of September I went to Frankfort for a week to take over the rehearsals of *Lohengrin*. Here again I went through the same experience as I had so often done before. I no sooner came into contact with the members of the opera

company than I felt a desire to throw up the undertaking on
the spot; then the general consternation and the entreaties
that I would persevere caused a reaction, under the influence
of which I held out until I at last became interested in certain things for their own sake, and quite apart from any consideration of the wretched singers. The things that pleased
me were the effect of an uncurtailed performance, and the
employment of correct *tempi* and correct staging. Yet I
suppose Friederike Meyer was the only one who completely
realised these effects. The usual ' animation ' of the audience
was not lacking, but I was told later on that the subsequent
performances fell off, so that the opera had to be curtailed in
the old way to keep it going. (They were conducted by Herr
Ignaz Lachner of Frankfort, a smart, sleek man, but a wretched-
ly bad, muddle-headed conductor.)

I was the more prostrated by the effect of all this because
even the Bülows had failed to pay me their expected visit.
Cosima, as I was now informed, had passed me by in haste
on her way to Paris to offer her support for a short time to
her grandmother, who was suffering from a tedious illness, and
had now received a most painful blow by the news of the
death of Blandine after her confinement, which had taken place
at St. Tropèz.

I now shut myself up for some time in my house at Biebrich,
the weather having suddenly turned cold, and prevailed on
my thumb to prove itself capable of writing down the instrumentation of some extracts for immediate concert purposes
from the *Meistersinger,* which was now complete. I sent the
prelude to Weisheimer at once to be copied at Leipzig, and
also set the *Versammlung der Meistersinger* and Pogner's
Anrede for orchestra.

By the end of October I was at last ready to start on my
journey to Leipzig, in the course of which I was induced in
a strange way to enter the Wartburg once more. I had alighted
for a few minutes at Eisenach, and the train had just begun
to move as I was hurriedly trying to catch it. I ran after the
vanishing train involuntarily with a sharp cry to the guard,
but naturally without being able to stop it. A considerable
crowd, which had gathered on the station to watch the de ·

parture of a prince, thereupon broke into loud outbursts of laughter, and when I said to them, ' I suppose you are glad that this happened to me ? ' they replied, ' Yes, it was very funny.' On this incident I based my axiom that you can please the German public by your misfortunes if by nothing else. As there was no other train to Leipzig for five hours I telegraphed to my brother-in-law, Hermann Brockhaus (whom I had asked to put me up), telling him of my delay, and allowed a man who introduced himself as a guide to persuade me to visit the Wartburg. There I saw the partial restoration made by the Grand Duke, and also the hall containing Schwind's pictures, to all of which I was quite indifferent. I then turned into the restaurant of this show-place of Eisenach, and found several women there engaged in knitting stockings. The Grand Duke of Weimar assured me some time afterwards that *Tannhäuser* enjoyed great popularity throughout the whole of Thuringia down to the lowest peasant boy, but neither the host nor my guide seemed to know anything about it. However, I signed the visitors' book with my full name, and described in it the pleasant greeting I had received at the station, though I have never heard that any one noticed it.

Hermann Brockhaus, who had aged rather and grown stout, gave me a most cheerful reception when I arrived, late at night, at Leipzig. He took me to his house, where I found Ottilie and her family, and was installed in comfort. We had much to talk about, and my brother-in-law's remarkably good-natured way of entering into our conversation often kept us up fascinated until all hours of the morning. My connection with Weisheimer, a young and quite unknown composer, aroused some misgivings. His concert programme was in fact filled with a great number of his own compositions, including a symphonic poem, just completed, entitled *Der Ritter Toggenburg*. I should probably have raised a protest against carrying out this programme in its entirety had I attended the rehearsals in an undisturbed frame of mind, but it so happened that the hours I spent in the concert-room proved to be among the most intimate and pleasant recollections of my life, for there I met the Bülows again. Hans seemed to have felt it his duty to join me in celebrating Weisheimer's début, his contribution being a new pianoforte concerto by Liszt. To enter the old familiar hall of the Gewandhaus at Leipzig was enough in itself to cause me an uneasy feeling of depression, which was increased by my reception by the members of the orchestra — of whose estrangement I was keenly conscious — and to whom I had to introduce myself as an entire stranger. But I felt myself suddenly transported when I discovered Cosima sitting in a corner of the hall, in deep mourning and very pale, but smiling cheerfully at me. She had returned shortly before from Paris — where her grandmother now lay hopelessly bedridden — filled with grief at the inexplicably sudden death of her sister, and she now seemed, even to my eyes, to be leaving another world to approach me. Our emotions were so genuinely deep and sincere that only an unconditional surrender to the enjoyment of meeting again could bridge the chasm. All the incidents of the rehearsal affected us like a magic-lantern show of peculiarly enlivening character, at which we looked on like merry children. Hans, who was in an equally happy mood — for we all seemed to each other to be embarked on some Quixotic adventure — called my attention to Brendel, who was sitting not far from us, and seemed to be expecting me to recognise him. I found it entertaining to prolong this suspense thus occasioned, by pretending not to know him, whereat, as it appears, the poor man was much offended. Recalling my unjust behaviour on this occasion, I therefore made a point of alluding specially to Brendel's services when speaking in public some time afterwards on *Judaism in Music,* by way of atonement, as it were, to this man, who had died in the meantime. The arrival of Alexander Ritter with my niece Franziska helped to enliven us. My niece, indeed, found constant entertainment and excitement in the enormity of Weisheimer's compositions, while Ritter, who was acquainted with the text of my *Meistersinger,* described a highly unintelligible melody given to the basses in *Ritter Toggenburg* as 'the lonely gormandiser mode.'[1] Our goodhumour might have failed us in the end, however, had we not been refreshed and uplifted by the happy effect which the prelude to the *Meistersinger* (which had at last been success-

[1] *Meistersinger* (English version), Act 1, scene ii.

fully rehearsed) and Bülow's glorious rendering of Liszt's new work produced. The actual concert itself gave a final ghostly touch to an adventure to which we had looked forward so contentedly till then. To Weisheimer's horror the Leipzig public stayed away *en masse,* in response apparently to a sign from the leaders of the regular subscription concerts. I have never seen any place so empty on an occasion of this sort; besides the members of my family — among whom my sister Ottilie was conspicuous in a very eccentric cap — there was no one to be seen but a few visitors, who had come into town for the occasion, occupying one or two benches. I noticed in particular my Weimar friends, Conductor Lassen, Councillor Franz Müller, the never-failing Richard Pohl, and *Justizrath* Gille, who had all nobly put in an appearance. I also recognised with a shock of surprise old Councillor Küstner, the former manager of the Court Theatre in Berlin, and I had to respond amiably to his greeting and his astonishment at the incomprehensible emptiness of the hall. The people of Leipzig were represented solely by special friends of my family, who never went to a concert in the ordinary way, among them being my devoted friend, Dr. Lothar Müller, the son of Dr. Moritz Müller, an allopath whom I had known very well in my earliest youth. In the middle of the hall there were only the concert-giver's *fiancée* and her mother. At a little distance away, and facing this lady, I took a seat next to Cosima while the concert was in progress. My family, observing us from a distance, were offended by the almost incessant laughter which possessed us, as they themselves were in the depths of depression.

As regards the prelude to the *Meistersinger,* its successful performance affected the few friends who formed the audience so favourably that we had to repeat it there and then — to the satisfaction even of the orchestra. Indeed, their artificially nurtured distrust of me, which had been like a coating of ice, now seemed to have melted, for when I brought the concert to a close with the *Tannhäuser* Overture the orchestra celebrated my recall with a tremendous flourish of instruments. This delighted my sister Ottilie beyond measure, as she maintained that such an honour had never

been accorded before except to Jenny Lind. My friend
Weisheimer, who had really tired every one's patience in the
most inconsiderate way, afterwards developed a feeling of
dissatisfaction towards me which dated from this period. He
felt bound to confess to himself that he would have done much
better without my brilliant orchestral pieces, in which case he
might have offered the public a concert at a cheaper rate,
consisting exclusively of his own works. As it was, he had to
bear the costs — to his father's great disappointment — and also
to overcome the unnecessary humiliation of being unable to
give me any profits.

My brother-in-law was not to be deterred by these painful
impressions from carrying out the household festivities, which
had been arranged beforehand in celebration of my expected
triumphs. The Bülows were also invited to one of the banquets,
and there was an evening party at which I read the *Meistersinger*
to an imposing array of professors, and met with much appreciation. I renewed my acquaintance with Professor Weiss, too,
who interested me very much, for I remembered him from my
young days as a friend of my uncle's. He expressed himself as
particularly surprised by my skill in reading aloud.

The Bülows had now unfortunately returned to Berlin.
We had met once more on a very cold day in the street (under
unpleasant conditions, for they were paying duty calls), but
the general depression which had settled on us seemed more
noticeable, during our short leave-taking, than the fleeting
good-humour of the last few days. My friends were well aware
of the terrible and utterly forlorn condition in which I found
myself. I had been idiotic enough to count on the proceeds
from the Leipzig concert to provide at least the needs of the
moment, and I was, in the first place, put into the awkward
position of being unable to pay my landlord punctually (the
house rent at Biebrich being now due). But I was ready to
stake everything on keeping this asylum for another year, and
I had to deal with an obstinate, bad-tempered creature whom
I thought it necessary to pay in advance for the sake of securing
the place. As I had just then to supply Minna with her
quarterly allowance also, the money which *Regierungsrath*
Müller forwarded to me from the Grand Duke seemed, indeed,

a heaven-sent windfall. For after giving up Schott entirely I had, in my distress, turned to this old acquaintance and begged him to explain my situation to the Grand Duke and induce him to send me some help — to be regarded possibly as payment in advance for my new operas. In response to this I received the startling and unexpected sum of fifteen hundred marks through Müller's instrumentality. It was not until some time after that I accounted for this generosity by the supposition that the Grand Duke's amiable behaviour towards me had been a deliberate attempt to make an impression upon his friend Liszt, whom he wished to entice back to Weimar at all costs. He was certainly not mistaken in counting on the excellent effect his binding generosity to me would have on our common friend.

I was therefore in a position to go to Dresden for a few days at once, to renew my provision for Minna, and at the same time to honour her with one of the visits deemed necessary to support her in her difficult situation. Minna conducted me from the station to the flat which she had taken and furnished in Walpurgisstrasse, a street which had not been built at the time I left Dresden. She had as usual arranged her home very tastefully, and with the aim evidently of making me comfortable. I was greeted on the threshold by a little mat embroidered with the word *Salve,* and I recognised our Paris drawing-room at once in the red silk curtains and the furniture. I was to have a majestic bedroom, an exceedingly comfortable study on the other side, as well as the drawing-room at my entire disposal, while she installed herself in one little room with recesses looking on to the yard. The study was adorned by the magnificent mahogany bureau which had originally been made for my house when I was conductor at Dresden. It had been bought in by the Ritter family, after my flight from that city, and presented to Kummer, the son-in-law, from whom Minna had hired it temporarily, leaving me the option of buying it back for one hundred and eighty marks. As I showed no desire to do so her mood became gloomier. Oppressed by the fearful embarrassment which she experienced on being alone with me, she had invited my sister Clara to come on a visit from Chemnitz, and was now sharing the small room at her disposal with her. Clara proved herself extraordinarily wise and sympathetic on this as on former occasions. She pitied Minna of course, and was anxious to help her at this difficult period, though always with a view to strengthening her in the conviction that our parting was unavoidable. An exact knowledge of my extremely awkward position now seemed called for. My financial difficulties were so crushing that the only excuse for telling Minna was to silence her uneasy suspicions about me. I did, however, succeed in avoiding all explanations with her — the more easily as my meetings with Fritz Brockhaus and his family (including the married daughter Clara Kessinger), the Pusinellis, old Heine, and lastly the two Schnorrs, provided a pretext for our spending most of the time in the society of others.

I filled the mornings by making calls, and it was when I set out to pay my respects and thanks to Minister Bär for my amnesty that I trod the familiar streets of Dresden again. My first impression was one of extraordinary boredom and emptiness, for I had last seen them filled with barricades, in which fantastic condition they had looked so unusually interesting. I did not see a single familiar face on the way. Even the glover, whom I had always patronised and whose shop I now had occasion to revisit, did not seem to know me, until an oldish man rushed across the street to me and greeted me with great excitement and tears in his eyes. It turned out to be Karl Kummer of the court orchestra (looking much older), the most inspired oboist I ever met. I had taken him almost tenderly to my heart on account of his playing, and we embraced joyfully. I asked whether he still played his instrument as beautifully as before, whereupon he assured me that since I had left his oboe had failed to give real satisfaction, and it was now a long time since he had had himself pensioned off. He told me in response to my inquiries that all my old military bandsmen — including Dietz, the tall double-bass player — were either dead or pensioned off. Our manager Lüttichau and Conductor Reissiger were among those who had died, Lipinsky had returned to Poland long before, Schubert, the leader, was unfit for work, and everything seemed to me sad and strange. Minister Bär expressed to me the grave qualms he still felt

about the amnesty granted me.   True, he had ventured to sign
it himself, but was still troubled to think that my great popularity as a composer of opera would make it easy for me to
raise annoying demonstrations.   I comforted him at once by
promising only to remain a few days and to refrain from visiting
the theatre, upon which he dismissed me with a deep sigh and
an exceedingly grave face.

Very different was my reception from Herr von Beust, who
with smiling elegance of manner implied by his conversation
that I was perhaps not so innocent after all as I now seemed
to think myself.   He drew my attention to a letter of mine
which had been found in Röckel's pocket at the time.   This
was new to me, and I willingly gave him to understand that
I felt myself bound to look on the amnesty accorded me as
a pardon for my incautious behaviour in the past, and we
parted with the liveliest manifestations of friendship.

We invited some friends one evening in Minna's drawing-
room, where I read out the *Meistersinger* once more to the
people who did not know it.   After Minna had been provided
with enough money to last some time, she accompanied me
back to the station on the fourth day; but she was filled with
such fearful presentiments of never seeing me again that her
farewell was made in positive anguish.

At Leipzig I put up at an inn for one day.   There I met
Alexander Ritter, and we spent a pleasant evening together over
our punch.   The reason that had induced me to make this
short stay was the assurance given me that if I gave a concert
of my own it would not be one of the regular series.   I had
weighed this information with reference to the much-needed
money it might bring in, but I now realised that the undertaking rested on no security.   I returned in haste to Biebrich,
where I had to get my household affairs into order.   To my
great annoyance I found my landlord in a more impossible
temper than ever.   He seemed unable to forget my having
blamed him for his treatment of the dog, and also of my servant, whom I had been obliged to protect against him when
she had had a love-affair with a tailor.   In spite of receiving
payment and promises he remained peevish, and insisted that
he would have to move into my part of the house on account

of his health in the coming spring. So while I forced him,
by paying advance, to leave my household goods untouched
until Easter at least, I went about trying to find a suitable
house for the following year, visiting various places in the
Rheingau under the guidance of Dr. Schüler and Mathilde
Maier. I had no success, however, the time being so short,
but my friends promised to search untiringly for what I wanted.

At Mayence I met Friederike Meyer again. Her situation
in Frankfort seemed to have grown more and more difficult.
When she heard that I had turned away Herr von Guaita's
manager, who had been sent to Biebrich with instructions to
pay me fifteen louis d'or for conducting *Lohengrin,* she upheld
my action strongly. As for herself, she had broken with that
gentleman entirely, insisting on being released from her contract, and was now about to enter upon a special engagement
at the Burgtheater. She won my sympathy once more by
her conduct and determination, which I had to consider as
a powerful refutation of the calumnies brought up against
her. As I too was in the act of starting for Vienna, she was
glad to be able to make part of the journey in my company.
She proposed to stop a day at Nuremberg, where I could pick
her up for the next stage of the journey. This we did and
arrived in Vienna together, where my friend went to Hôtel
Munsch, while I chose the Kaiserin Elizabeth, where I now
felt at home. This was on the 15th of November. I went to
see Conductor Esser at once, and heard from him that *Tristan*
was really being studied vigorously. With Frau Dustmann,
on the other hand, I became immediately involved in very
unpleasant disagreements through my relation to her sister
Friederike, which it was easy to misunderstand. It was impossible to make her see how things really stood. In her eyes
her sister was involved in a *liaison,* and had been cast off by
her family, so that her arrival in Vienna was compromising to
them. In addition to this Friederike's own condition soon
caused me the greatest anxiety. She had made an engagement
to appear three times at the Burgtheater without considering
that just then she was not likely to make a good appearance
on the stage, particularly before the Viennese public. Her
serious illness, the recovery from which had been attended by

the most exciting circumstances, had disfigured her and made her very thin. She had also gone almost entirely bald, but nevertheless persisted in her great objection to wearing a wig. Her sister's hostility had estranged her colleagues at the theatre, and as a result of all this, and also on account of her unfortunate choice of a rôle, her appearance was a failure. There could be no question of her being taken on at that theatre. Although her weakness increased, and she suffered from constant insomnia, she still tried, in her magnanimity and her shame, to hide from me the awkwardness of her situation. She went to a cheaper inn, the 'Stadt Frankfurt,' where she intended to wait and see the result of sparing her nerves as far as possible. She seemed to be in no embarrassment as far as money was concerned, but at my request consulted Standhartner, who did not seem to know how to help her much. As open-air exercise had been strongly recommended, and as the weather was at present bitterly cold (from the end of November to the beginning of December), I hit on the idea of advising her to go to Venice for a prolonged stay. Once again there seemed no lack of means, and she followed my advice. One icy morning I accompanied her to the station, and there for the present I left her, as I hoped, to a kinder fate. She had a faithful maid with her, and I soon had the satisfaction of receiving reassuring accounts — of her health especially — from Venice.

While my relations with her had brought me troublesome complications, I still kept up my old Viennese acquaintances. A curious incident occurred at the very beginning of my visit. I had to read the *Meistersinger* aloud to the Standhartner family, as I had done everywhere else. As Dr. Hanslick was now supposed to be well disposed towards me, it was considered the right thing to invite him too. We noticed that as the reading proceeded the dangerous critic became more and more pale and depressed, and it was remarked by everyone that it was impossible to persuade him to stay on at the close, but that he took his leave there and then in an unmistakably vexed manner. My friends all agreed in thinking that Hanslick looked on the whole libretto as a lampoon aimed at himself, and had felt an invitation to the reading to be an insult. And undoubtedly the critic's attitude towards me underwent a very

remarkable change from that evening. He became uncompro-
misingly hostile, with results that were obvious to us at once.

Cornelius and Tausig had again been to see me, but I had to
work off my resentment against them both for the fit of real
ill-humour their behaviour had caused me in the previous summer. This had happened when I expected the Bülows and
the Schnorrs to stay with me together at Biebrich, and my
warm interest in these two young friends, Cornelius and Tausig,
led me to invite them too. I received Cornelius's acceptance
immediately, and was the more surprised to get a letter from
Geneva, whither Tausig (who appeared to have funds at his
disposal all of a sudden) had carried him off on a summer
excursion — no doubt of a more important and pleasanter nature. Without the least mention of any regret at not being able
to meet me that summer, they simply announced to me that ' a
glorious cigar had just been smoked to my health.' And now,
when I met them again in Vienna, I found it impossible to
refrain from pointing out to them the insulting nature of their
behaviour; but they seemed unable to understand how I could
object to their preferring the beautiful tour into French Switzerland to paying me a visit at Biebrich. I was obviously a
tyrant to them. Besides this, I thought Tausig's curious conduct at my hotel suspicious. I was told that he took his
meals in the downstairs restaurant, after which he climbed up
past my floor to the fourth storey, to pay long visits to Countess
Krockow. When I asked him about it, and learned that the
lady in question was also a friend of Cosima's, I expressed my
surprise at his not introducing me. He continued to evade
this suggestion with singularly vague phrases, and when I
ventured to tease him by the supposition of a love-affair, he
said there could be no question of such a thing, as the lady was
old. So I let him alone, but the amazement which his peculiar
behaviour then caused me was intensified some years later when
I at last learned to know Countess Krockow very well, and
was assured of her deep interest in me. It seemed that she
had desired nothing more than to make my acquaintance also
at that time, but that Tausig had always refused to find an
opportunity, and had made the excuse that I did not care about
women's society.

But we eventually resumed our lively and sociable habits when I began seriously to carry out my project of giving concerts in Vienna. Although the piano rehearsals for the principal solo parts of *Tristan* had been put in hand diligently — I had left them to Conductor Esser, who took them zealously in hand — my mistrust as to the real success of these studies was unshaken, and the point which I doubted most was not so much the capabilities of the singers as their goodwill. Moreover, Frau Dustmann's absurd behaviour disgusted me on my frequent attendance at the rehearsals. On the other hand, I now set my hopes on making a good impression, on the score of novelty alone, by performing selections from my own works still unknown to the Viennese public. In this way I could show my secret enemies that there were other means open to me of bringing my more recent compositions before the public than by the medium of the stage, where they could so easily stop me. For all the practical details of the performance Tausig now proved himself particularly useful. We agreed to hire the Theatre on the Wien for three evenings, the idea being to give one concert at the end of December and to repeat the experiment twice after a week's interval. The first thing was to copy out the orchestral parts from the sections which I cut out from my scores for the concert. There were two selections from *Rheingold* and two from the *Walküre* and the *Meistersinger*, but I kept back the prelude to *Tristan* for the present, so as not to clash with the performance of the whole work at the Opera which was still being advertised. Cornelius and Tausig, with some assistant copyists, now started on the work, which could only be carried out by experienced score-readers if it was to be done correctly. They were joined by Weisheimer, who had arrived in Vienna, having in the end decided to come to the concert. Tausig also mentioned Brahms to me, recommending him as a 'very good fellow,' who, although he was so famous himself, would willingly take over a part of their work, and a selection from the *Meistersinger* was accordingly allotted to him. And, indeed, Brahms's behaviour proved unassuming and good-natured, but he showed little vivacity and was often hardly noticed at our gatherings. I also came across Friedrich Uhl again, an old acquaintance who was now editing a political paper called *Der Botschafter* with Julius Fröbel under Schmerling's auspices. He placed his journal at my disposal, and made me give him the first act of the libretto of *Meistersinger* for his *feuilleton*. Whereupon my friends chose to think that Hanslick grew more and more venomous.

While I and my companions were overwhelmed by the preparations for the concert, there came in one day a certain Herr Moritz, whom Bülow had introduced to me in Paris as a ridiculous person. His clumsy and importunate behaviour and the idiotic messages — evidently of his own invention — which he brought me from Bülow drove me in the end to show him the door with great emphasis, for I too was carried away by Tausig's lively annoyance at this very officious intruder. He reported on this to Cosima in a manner so insulting to Bülow that she in return found it necessary to express to me in writing her intense indignation at my inconsiderate behaviour towards my best friends. I was really so surprised and dumbfounded by this strange and inexplicable event that I handed Cosima's letter to Tausig without comment, merely asking him what could be done in the face of such nonsense. He at once undertook to show Cosima the incident in a correct light and clear up the misunderstanding, and I soon had the pleasure of hearing that he had met with success.

We had now come to the point of rehearsing for the concert. The Royal Opera had supplied me with the singers needed for the selections from *Rheingold*, the *Walküre*, and *Siegfried* ('Schmiede-Lieder'), and also for *Pogner's Anrede* from the *Meistersinger*. I had only to fall back on amateurs for the three Rhine maidens. The concert director Hellmesberger was a great help to me in this matter as in every other way, and his fine playing and enthusiastic demonstrations when leading the orchestra never failed in any circumstances. After the deafening preliminary rehearsals in a small music-room in the opera house, which had perplexed Cornelius by the great noise they made, we arrived at the stage itself. In addition to the expense of hiring the place, I had to bear the cost of the requisite extension of the orchestra. The room, which was lined all round with theatrical scenery, was still extraordinarily unfavourable for sound. I hardly felt like running the risk of providing an acoustic wall and ceiling on my own account, however. Although the first performance on 26th December drew a large audience, it brought me in nothing but outrageously heavy expenses and great distress at the dismal effect of the orchestra owing to the bad acoustics. In spite of the dark outlook I decided to bear the cost of building a sound-screen, in order to enhance the effect of the two following concerts, when I flattered myself I might count on the success of the efforts that were being made to arouse interest in the highest circles.

My friend Prince Liechtenstein thought this was by no means impossible, and believed he might manage to interest the Imperial Court through Countess Zamoïska, one of the ladies-in-waiting, and he one day accompanied me through the interminable corridors of the Imperial Castle on a visit to this lady. I afterwards learned that Mme. Kalergis had also been at work here on my behalf, but she had apparently only succeeded in winning over the young Empress, for she alone was present at the performance, and without any retinue. But at the second concert I had to endure all kinds of disillusionment. In spite of all warnings to the contrary, I had fixed it for the New Year's Day of 1863. The hall was exceedingly badly filled, and my sole satisfaction was to know that by improving the acoustic properties of the place the orchestra sounded extremely well. In consequence of this the reception of the various pieces was so favourable that at the third concert, on 8th January, I was able to perform before an overflowing house, and thus obtained very gratifying testimony to the fine musical taste of the Viennese public. The by no means startling prelude to Pogner's *Anrede* from the *Meistersinger* was enthusiastically encored, in spite of the fact that the singer had already risen to his feet for the next part. At this moment I chanced to see in one of the boxes a most comforting omen for my present position; for I recognised Mme. Kalergis, who had just arrived for a prolonged stay in Vienna, to which I fondly imagined she was prompted by some idea of helping me here also. As she too was on friendly terms with Standhartner, she at once entered into consultation with him as to how I could be helped out of the critical situation in which I was once more placed by the expenses of my concerts. She confessed to our mutual friend that she had no means at her disposal, and would only be able to meet our extraordinary expenditure by contracting fresh debts. It was therefore necessary to secure wealthier patrons, among whom she mentioned Baroness von Stockhausen, the wife of the Hanoverian ambassador. This lady, who was a great friend of Standhartner's, was most kind to me, and won me the sympathy of Lady Bloomfield and her husband, the English ambassador. A soirée was given in the house of the latter, and at Frau von Stockhausen's there were also several evening assemblies. One day Standhartner brought me a thousand marks as an instalment towards my expenses, saying that they came from an anonymous donor. Meanwhile Mme. Kalergis had managed to procure two thousand marks, which were also placed at my disposal, through Standhartner, for further needs. But all her efforts to interest the court on my behalf remained entirely fruitless, in spite of her intimacy with Countess Zamoïska; for unfortunately a member of that Könneritz family from Saxony, which was everywhere turning up for my discomfiture, had now appeared as ambassador here also. He succeeded in suppressing any inclination the all-powerful Archduchess Sophie might have had towards me, by pretending that during his time I had burnt down the King of Saxony's castle.

But my patroness, undaunted still, endeavoured to help me in every conceivable way demanded by my necessities. In order to gratify my most earnest longing for a peaceful home where I could stay for a while, she managed to secure the house of the English attaché, a son of the famous Bulwer Lytton, who had been called away, but was keeping up his establishment for some time longer. Thus through her I was introduced to this exceedingly amiable young man. I dined with him one evening, together with Cornelius and Mme. Kalergis, and after dinner began to read them my *Götterdämmerung*. I did not seem to have secured a very attentive audience, however, and when I noticed this I stopped and withdrew with Cornelius. We found it very cold as we went home, and Bulwer's rooms seem also to have been insufficiently heated, so that we took refuge in a restaurant to drink a glass of hot punch. The incident has remained fixed in my memory because here for the first time I saw Cornelius in an ungovernably eccentric humour. While we thus took our pleasure, Mme. Kalergis used her influence—so I was afterwards informed —as an exceedingly powerful and irresistible female advocate to inspire Bulwer with a definite interest in my fate. In this she so far succeeded, that he unconditionally placed his house at my disposal for nine months. On considering the matter more deeply, however, I did not see what advantage this would be to me, seeing that I had no further prospect of earning any income in Vienna for my sustenance.

On the other hand, my plans were decided for me by an offer which reached me from St. Petersburg to conduct two concerts there in the month of March for the Philharmonic Society for a fee of two thousand silver roubles. For this also I had to thank Mme. Kalergis, who urgently counselled me to accept the invitation, holding out at the same time a prospect of further increasing my receipts by giving an additional concert on my own account, from which very important material results might be expected. The only thing which could have induced me to decline this invitation would have been an assurance that my *Tristan* would be staged in Vienna during the next few months; but a fresh indisposition on the part of the tenor Ander had once more brought our preparations to a standstill, and moreover I had completely lost all faith in those promises which had lured me again to Vienna. To this the effect of my visit to the minister Schmerling immediately on my return to Vienna had certainly contributed. This man had been much astonished at my referring to a recommendation by Prince Metternich, for the latter, so the minister declared, had never spoken a word to him about me. Nevertheless, he very politely assured me that it needed no such recommendation to interest him in a man of my merit. When, therefore, I mentioned the idea suggested by Prince Metternich's kindness that the Emperor might assign me some special position in Vienna, he hastened at once to inform me that he was completely powerless to influence any of the Emperor's decisions. This admission on the part of Herr von Schmerling certainly helped to explain Prince Metternich's behaviour, and I concluded that the latter had preferred an attempt to win the

Chief Chamberlain for a serious revival of *Tristan* to a fruitless effort with the minister.

As these prospects were therefore thrust into the uncertain future, I now agreed to the St. Petersburg proposal, but first of all sought about for means to provide the necessary funds. For these I relied on a concert which Heinrich Porges had already arranged for me in Prague. Consequently early in February I set out for that city, and had every reason to be satisfied with my reception there. Young Porges, an out-and-out partisan of Liszt and myself, pleased me greatly, not only personally, but by his obvious enthusiasm. The concert took place at the hall on the Sophia Island, and was crowned with great success. Besides one of Beethoven's symphonies, several selections from my newer works were given, and when next day Porges paid me about two thousand marks, with the reservation of a few smaller supplementary payments, I laughingly assured him that this was the first money I had ever earned by my own exertions. He also gave me some very pleasant introductions to several exceedingly devoted and intelligent young people, belonging both to the German and Czech parties, and among them to a teacher of mathematics called Lieblein, and an author whose name was Musiol. It was with a certain pathetic interest that, after so many years, I here discovered a friend of my earliest youth, named Marie Löwe, who had given up singing and taken to the harp instead, and was now engaged to play this instrument in the orchestra, in which capacity she assisted at my concert. On the occasion of the first performance of *Tannhäuser* in Prague, she had sent me a most enthusiastic report about it. Her admiration was now intensified, and for many years afterwards she remained tenderly attached to me. Well satisfied then, and filled with newly awakened hope, I hurried back to Vienna again in order to put the arrangement for *Tristan* on as firm a basis as possible. It was found feasible to arrange another pianoforte rehearsal in my presence of the two first acts, and I was astonished at the really passable performance of the tenor, while from Frau Dustmann I could not withhold my sincerest congratulations on her admirable execution of her difficult part. It was therefore decided that my work should be produced a little after Easter, which would fit in very well with the expected date of my return from Russia.

The hope of being now able to count on earning a large income decided me to revive my former idea of settling for good in the peace and quiet of Biebrich. As there was still time before I had to start for Russia, I returned to the Rhine to arrange matters there as rapidly as possible. Once more I lodged in Frickhöfer's house, and in the company of Mathilde Maier and her friend Luise Wagner once more hunted through the Rheingau in search of a suitable house. Not finding what I wanted, I finally entered into treaty with Frickhöfer for the erection of a small cottage on a plot of land I proposed to buy near his villa. Dr. Schüler, the man who had been introduced to me by young Städl, was to take the matter in hand, as he had both legal and business experience. Estimates were prepared, and it now depended entirely on the amount of my Russian receipts as to whether the undertaking could be begun in the following spring or not. As in any case I had to give up my rooms in Frickhöfer's house at Easter, I removed all my furniture and sent it packed to the furniture-dealer in Wiesbaden, to whom I was still indebted for the greater part of it.

Thus in the best of spirits I went first to Berlin, where I called at once on Bülow. Cosima, who was expecting an early confinement, seemed delighted to see me again, and insisted on accompanying me at once to the music-school, where we should find Hans. I entered a long room, at one end of which Bülow was giving a music-lesson. As I stood for some time in silence in the doorway, he gave an exclamation of anger at being disturbed, only to burst out into joyful laughter on recognising who it was. Our midday meal together was lively, and in excellent humour I set out with Cosima alone for a drive in a fine carriage (belonging to the Hôtel de Russie), whose grey satin lining and cushions provided us with endless fun. Bülow seemed troubled that I should see his wife in a condition of advanced pregnancy, as I had once expressed my aversion from such a sight when speaking of another woman of our acquaintance. It put us into a good-humour to be able to set his mind at rest in this case, for nothing could possibly put me out of sympathy with Cosima. So, sharing my hopes and heartily rejoicing in the turn of my fortune, these two friends accompanied me to the Königsburg railway station and saw me off on my long night journey.

In Königsburg I had to wait half a day and a night. As I had no desire to revisit my haunts in a place which had once been so fatal to me, I spent the time quietly in the room of an hotel, the position of which I did not even try to fix, and early in the morning continued my journey towards the Russian frontier. With certain uneasy memories of my former illegal passage of this frontier, I carefully scanned the faces of my fellow-passengers during the long hours of travel. Among these I was especially struck by one, a Livland nobleman of German descent, who, in the haughtiest German Tory tone, proclaimed his disgust at the Tsar's emancipation of the serfs. He wished me clearly to understand that any efforts on the part of the Russians to obtain their freedom would receive but scant support from the German nobles settled in their midst. But as we approached St. Petersburg I was genuinely frightened to find our train suddenly stopped and examined by the police. They were apparently searching for various persons suspected of complicity in the latest Polish insurrection, which had just broken out. Not far from the capital itself the empty seats in our carriage were filled by several people, whose high Russian fur caps aroused my suspicions, which were not allayed by the attention which their wearers bestowed upon me in particular. But suddenly the face of one of them brightened up, and he impulsively turned towards me and saluted me as the man whom he and several other musicians of the Imperial orchestra had come out on purpose to meet. They were all Germans, and on our arrival at the St. Petersburg railway station they joyfully introduced me to a further large contingent from the orchestra, headed by the committee of the Philharmonic Society. I had been recommended to a German boarding-house on the Newsky Prospect as a suitable residence. There I was very graciously and flatteringly received by Frau Kunst, the wife of a German merchant, in a drawing-room whose windows commanded a view of the wide and busy street, and where I was very well served. I dined in common with the other boarders and visitors, and often invited Alexander Séroff, whom I had formerly known in Lucerne, to be my guest at table. He had called on me immediately on my arrival, and I learned that he held a very poor appointment as censor of German news-papers. His person bore signs of much neglect and ill-health, and proved that he had had a hard struggle for existence; but he speedily won my respect by the great independence and truthfulness of his opinions, whereby, combined with an excellent understanding, I soon learned that he had won himself a reputation as a most influential and much-dreaded critic. I appreciated this better later on when advances were made to me from high quarters to use my influence with Séroff to assuage the bitterness of his persecution of Anton Rubinstein, who just at that time was being somewhat offensively patron-ised. On my mentioning the matter to him, he explained his reasons for believing Rubinstein's influence in Russia to be pernicious, whereupon I begged him, for my sake at least, to hold his hand a little, as I did not wish, during my brief stay in St. Petersburg, to pose as Rubinstein's rival. To this he replied with all the violence of a sickly man, ' I hate him, and cannot make any concessions.' With me, on the contrary, he entered into the most intimate understanding, as he had so perfect an appreciation of me and my art that our intercourse became almost one of mere pleasantry, for on all serious points we were in entire agreement. Nothing could equal the care with which he sought to help me at every opportunity. He provided the necessary translation into Russian, both of the songs contained in the selections taken from my operas and of my explanatory programme for the concerts. He also displayed the utmost judgment in choosing the most suitable singers for me, and for this he appeared to find abundant recompense in attending the rehearsals and performances. His radiant face beamed every-where upon me with encouragement and fresh inspiration. I was eminently satisfied with the orchestra which I managed to gather around me in the large and handsome hall of the Society of Nobles. It contained one hundred and twenty picked players from the Imperial orchestras, who were for the most part excellent musicians, usually employed in accompanying Italian opera and ballets. They now seemed delighted to be allowed to breathe more freely in thus occupying themselves with nobler music under a method of conducting which I had made peculiarly my own.

After the great success of my first concert advances were made to me from those circles to which, as I could very well understand, I had been secretly but influentially recommended by Mme. Kalergis. With great circumspection my unseen protectress had prepared the way for my presentation to the Grand Duchess Helène. I was instructed, in the first place, to make use of a recommendation from Standhartner to Dr. Arneth, the Grand Duchess's private physician, whom he had known in Vienna, in order through him to be introduced to Fräulein von Rhaden, her most confidential lady-in-waiting. I should have been well content with the acquaintance of this lady alone, for in her I learned to know a woman of wide culture, great intelligence, and noble bearing, whose ever-growing interest in me I perceived to be mingled with a certain timidity, apparently concerned chiefly with the Grand Duchess. She gave me the impression that she felt something more important ought to happen for me than, from the spirit and character of her mistress, she could expect. I was, however, not taken to pay my respects to the Grand Duchess at once, but received first of all an invitation to an evening party in the apartments of the lady-in-waiting, at which, among others, the Grand Duchess herself was to be present. Here Anton Rubinstein did the musical honours, and after the hostess had introduced me to him, she ventured to present me to the Grand Duchess herself. The ceremony went off fairly well, and, as a result, I shortly afterwards received a direct invitation to a friendly evening tea-party at the Grand Duchess's house. Here, in addition to Fräulein von Rhaden, I met the lady next to her in rank, Fräulein von Stahl, as well as a genial old gentleman, who was introduced to me as General von Brebern, for many years one of the Grand Duchess's closest friends. Fräulein von Rhaden appeared to have made extraordinary efforts on my behalf, which for the present resulted in the Grand Duchess expressing a wish that I should make her better acquainted with the text of my *Nibelungen Ring*. As I had no copy of the work with me, although Weber of Leipzig ought by this time to have finished printing it, they insisted that I should at once telegraph to him in Leipzig to send the finished sheets with the utmost despatch to the Grand Duchess's address. Meanwhile my patrons had to be content with hearing me read the *Meistersinger*. To this reading the Grand Duchess Marie was also induced to come — a very stately and still beautiful daughter of the Tsar Nicholas, who was notorious for the passion she had shown throughout her life. As to the impression made upon this lady by my poem, Fräulein von Rhaden only told me that she had been seriously alarmed lest Hans Sachs might end by marrying Eva.

In the course of a few days the loose proof-sheets of my *Nibelungen* work duly arrived, and the Grand Duchess's intimates met at four tea-parties to hear me read it, and listened with sympathetic attention. General von Brebern was present at them all, but only, as Fräulein von Rhaden said, ' to blush like the rose ' in profoundest slumber, a habit which always afforded a subject for merriment to Fräulein von Stahl, a very lively and beautiful woman, when each night I accompanied the two court ladies from the spacious salons along endless corridors and staircases to their distant apartments.

The only other person in the great world whom I learned to know here was Count Wilohorsky, who occupied a high position of trust at the Imperial court, and was chiefly esteemed as a patron of music, and considered himself a distinguished violoncello-player. The old gentleman appeared well disposed towards me, and altogether satisfied with my musical performances. Indeed, he assured me that he had first learned to understand Beethoven's Eighth Symphony (in F major) through my interpretation. He also considered that he had fully grasped my overture to the *Meistersinger,* and said the Grand Duchess Marie was affected because she had found this piece incomprehensible, but had expressed herself enraptured by the overture to *Tristan,* which he himself only managed to understand by the exertion of all his musical knowledge. When I told Séroff of this, he exclaimed enthusiastically, ' Ah, that beast of a Count! That woman knows what love is! '

The Count arranged a splendid dinner in my honour, at which both Anton Rubinstein and Mme. Abaza were present. As I begged Rubinstein to play something after dinner, Mme. Abaza insisted on singing his Persian songs, which seemed greatly to annoy the composer, as he knew very well that he had produced much finer work. Nevertheless both the composition and its execution gave me a very favourable opinion of the talents of both artists. Through this singer, who had originally had a professional engagement in the Grand Duchess's household, and was now married to a wealthy and cultured Russian gentleman of rank, I obtained an entry into the house of M. Abaza, who received me with great ceremony. About the same time a certain Baron Vittinghof had also made himself known to me as an enthusiastic lover of music, and honoured me with an invitation to his house, where I met once more with Ingeborg Stark, the beautiful Swedish pianist and composer of sonatas, whom I had formerly known in Paris. She amazed me by the impertinent outburst of laughter with which she accompanied the performance of one of the Baron's compositions. On the other hand, she assumed a more serious air when she informed me that she was engaged to Hans von Bronsart.

Rubinstein, with whom I exchanged friendly visits, behaved very creditably, although, as I had expected, he felt himself somewhat injured by me. He told me that he was thinking of resigning his position in St. Petersburg, as it had been made difficult by Séroff's antagonism. It was also thought advisable to introduce me to the commercial circles of St. Petersburg, with a view to my coming benefit concert, and a visit was consequently arranged to a concert in the hall of the Merchants' Guild. Here I was met on the staircase by a drunken Russian, who announced himself as the conductor. With a small selection of Imperial musicians and others he conducted the overtures of Rossini's *Tell* and Weber's *Oberon*, in which the kettledrums were replaced by a small military drum, which produced a wonderful effect, especially in the lovely transfiguration part of the *Oberon* Overture.

Although I was admirably equipped for my own concerts as far as the orchestra was concerned, yet I had much trouble in procuring the requisite singers. The soprano was very passably represented by Mlle. Bianchi; but for the tenor parts I had to make shift with a M. Setoff, who, although possessing plenty of courage, had very little voice. But he managed to help me through the ' Schmiede-Lieder ' in *Siegfried,* for his presence at least gave an appearance of song, while the orchestra alone undertook the effective reality. On the conclusion of my two concerts for the Philharmonic Society, I set seriously to work on my own concert, which was to be held in the Imperial Opera House, in the material arrangements for which I was helped by a retired musician. This man often spent hours with Séroff in my well-heated rooms without laying aside his enormous fur coat, and as his incapacity gave us a great deal of trouble, we agreed that he was like ' the sheep in wolf's clothing.' The concert, however, succeeded beyond all my expectations, and I do not think I was ever so enthusiastically received by any audience as on this occasion. Indeed, their greeting when I first appeared was so loudly prolonged that I felt quite touched, a rare occurrence with me. To this wild abandonment on the part of the audience the ardent devotion of my orchestra naturally contributed, as my one hundred and twenty musicians renewed the frantic acclamations again and again, a procedure which appeared to be quite novel in St. Petersburg. From some of them I heard such exclamations as, ' We must admit we have never known what music is till now.'

Conductor Schuberth, who, with a certain amount of condescension, had helped me with advice on business matters, now utilised this favourable turn of affairs to ask for my co-operation at a concert to be given shortly for his own benefit. Although I was fully aware that by this means he reckoned on conjuring a handsome profit out of my pocket into his own, yet on the advice of my friends I thought it best to comply with his request, albeit much against the grain. So a week later I repeated the most popular items of my programme before an equally numerous audience and with the same success, but this time the handsome receipts of three thousand roubles were destined for an invalid man, who as a retribution for this encroachment on my rights was suddenly summoned to another world in the same year.

To balance this, I now had a prospect of further artistic and material successes from a contract concluded with General Lwoff, the manager of the Moscow theatre. I was to give

three concerts in the Grand Theatre, of which I was to have
half the receipts, guaranteed in each case at a minimum of
one thousand roubles. I arrived there suffering from a cold,
miserable and ill at ease, in weather which was a mixture of
frost and thaw, and put up at a badly situated German boarding-house. My preliminary arrangements were made with the
manager, who, in spite of the orders hanging from his neck,
looked a very insignificant person, and the difficult selection of
the vocal items had to be arranged with a Russian tenor and a
superannuated Italian lady-singer. Having settled these, I
entered upon the task of orchestral rehearsals. It was here
that I first met the younger Rubinstein, Anton's brother
Nicholas, who, as director of the Russian Musical Society, was
the leading authority in his profession in Moscow; his demeanour towards me was characterised throughout by modesty and
consideration. The orchestra consisted of the hundred musicians who provided the Imperial household with Italian opera
and ballet. It was, on the whole, far inferior to that of
St. Petersburg, yet among them I found a small number of
excellent quartette players, all devotedly attached to me.
Among these was one of my old Riga acquaintances, the
'cellist von Lutzau, who in those days had a great reputation as a wag. But I was particularly pleased with a certain
Herr Albrecht, a violinist, a brother of the Albrecht who was
one of the party whose Russian fur caps had so scared me on
my way to St. Petersburg. But even these men could not dispel
my feeling that in dealing with this Moscow orchestra I had
descended in the artistic scale. I gave myself a great deal of
trouble without deriving any compensating satisfaction, and my
bile was not a little stirred by the Russian tenor, who came to
rehearsal in a red shirt, to show his patriotic aversion from my
music, and sang the 'Schmiede-Lieder' of *Siegfried* in the insipid
style acquired from the Italians. On the very morning of the
first concert I was obliged to cancel it, and declare myself
on the sick-list, with a bad, feverish cold. In the slush and
snow which inundated the streets of Moscow it seems to have
been impossible to announce this fact to the public, and I heard
that angry disturbances resulted when many splendid equipages
arrived on a fruitless errand and had to be turned away. After

three days' rest I insisted on giving the three concerts I had contracted for within six days, an exertion to which I was spurred by a desire to have done with an undertaking I felt was not worthy of me. Although the Grand Theatre was filled on each occasion with a brilliant audience such as I had never before seen, yet, according to the calculations of the Imperial manager, the receipts did not exceed the amount of the guarantee. With this, however, I was content, considering the magnificent reception accorded to my efforts, and above all the fervid enthusiasm of the orchestra, which was expressed here as it had been in St. Petersburg. A deputation of members of the orchestra begged me to give a fourth concert, and on my refusal, they tried to persuade me to remain for another 'rehearsal,' but this too I was compelled to decline with a smile. However, the orchestra honoured me with a banquet, at which, after N. Rubinstein had made a very enthusiastic and appropriate speech, which was greeted with hearty and tumultuous applause, one of the company hoisted me on to his shoulders and carried me round the hall; whereupon there was a great outcry, and every one wanted to render me the same kindly service. I was presented on this occasion with a gold snuff-box from the members of the orchestra, on which was engraved the words '*Doch Einer kam*,' from Siegmund's song in the *Walküre*. I returned the compliment by presenting to the orchestra a large photograph of myself, on which I wrote the words '*Keiner ging*,' from the same song.

In addition to these musical circles I also became acquainted with Prince Odoiewsky, as the result of an introduction and strong recommendation by Mme. Kalergis. She had told me that in the Prince I should meet one of the noblest of men, who would fully understand me. After a most arduous drive of many hours, I reached his modest dwelling, and was received with patriarchal simplicity at his family mid-day dinner, but I found it exceedingly difficult to convey to him any particulars as to myself and my plans. With regard to any impressions I might be expected to gather respecting himself, he seemed to rely on the effect produced by the contemplation of a large instrument resembling an organ, which he had had designed and erected in one of his principal rooms. Unluckily there was no one there who could play it; but I could not help thinking it must have been intended for some specially devised form of divine worship, which he held there on Sundays for the benefit of his household, relatives and acquaintances. Ever mindful of my kindly patroness, I attempted to give the genial Prince some idea of my position and my aspirations. With apparent emotion he exclaimed, '*J'ai ce qu'il vous faut; parlez à Wolffsohn.*' On further inquiry I learned that the guardian spirit thus commended to me was not a banker, but a Russian Jew who wrote romances.

All these events seemed to justify the conclusion that my receipts, especially if I included what I might still derive from St. Petersburg, would amply suffice to carry out my project of building a house at Biebrich. I therefore sent a telegram about it to my authorised agent in Wiesbaden from Moscow, and left there after a stay of only ten days. I also forwarded one thousand roubles to Minna, who was complaining that her expenses for settling down in Dresden were very heavy.

But, unfortunately, on reaching St. Petersburg I met with serious disappointments. Every one advised me to relinquish the idea of giving my second concert on Easter Monday, the date I had fixed, as it was the general custom in Russian society to reserve that day for private gatherings. On the other hand, I could not well refuse to give a concert, on the third day after the date announced for my own, on behalf of those imprisoned for debt in St. Petersburg, seeing that this was to be given at the urgent request of the Grand Duchess Helène herself. In this latter function all St. Petersburg was already interested for the sake of their own credit, as it was under the most distinguished patronage; so that, while every seat was sold in advance for this function, I had to be content with a very empty house at the Nobles' Casino, and with proceeds which luckily did at least cover expenses. By way of contrast, the debtors' concert went off with the greatest success, and General Suwarof, the governor of the city, a strikingly handsome man, handed me a very beautifully wrought silver drinking-horn as a thank-offering from the imprisoned debtors.

I now set about paying my farewell calls, one of which was on Fräulein von Rhaden, who distinguished herself by the warmth of her sympathy and interest. By way of compensating me for the loss of the receipts I had reckoned upon, the Grand Duchess sent me through this lady the sum of one thousand roubles, coupled with a promise that, until my circumstances improved, she would repeat the gift annually. On discovering this friendly interest, I could not help regretting that the connection thus formed was not likely to have more stable and profitable results. I addressed a petition through Fräulein von Rhaden to the Grand Duchess, praying that she would permit me to come to St. Petersburg for a few months every year, to place my talents at her disposal, both for concerts and theatrical performances, in return for which she would only have to pay me a suitable yearly salary. To this I received an evasive reply. On the day before my departure I informed my amiable guardian of my plan for settling at Biebrich, and in doing so I made no secret of my fear that after spending the money I had earned here in carrying out my building plan, my condition might be very much the same as of yore, a fear which made me wonder whether it would not be better to abandon it altogether. Whereupon I received the spirited reply: 'Build and hope!' At the last moment before starting I gratefully answered her in the same manner, and said that I now knew what to do. Thus at the end of April I departed, carrying with me the hearty good wishes of Séroff and the enthusiastic members of the orchestra, and steamed away across the Russian wilderness without calling at Riga, where I had been invited to give a concert. The long and weary road brought me at last to the frontier station of Wirballen, where I received a telegram from Fräulein von Rhaden: 'Not too rash.' This was in reference to a few lines I had left behind for her, and it conveyed quite enough to revive my doubts as to the wisdom of carrying out my house-building plans.

I reached Berlin without further delay, and at once made for Bülow's house. During the last few months I had heard no news of Cosima's condition, and it was, therefore, with some trepidation that I stood at the door, through which the maid did not seem disposed to let me pass, saying that 'her mistress was not well.' 'Is she seriously ill?' I asked, and receiving a smilingly evasive reply, at once realised to my joy the true situation, and hastened in to greet Cosima. She had been some time delivered of her daughter Blandine, and was now on the highroad to complete recovery. It was only from casual callers that she remained secluded. Everything seemed well, and Hans was quite gay, the more so that he now thought me freed from all care for some time to come, owing to the success of my Russian trip. But I could not regard this assumption as justified, unless my wish to be invited for some months every year to St. Petersburg for renewed activity there met with a ready response. On this point I was enlightened in a more detailed letter from Fräulein von Rhaden following the above telegram, in which she told me on no account to rely upon this invitation. This distinct statement compelled me to reckon up the balance of my Russian receipts very seriously, and after deducting hotel and travelling expenses, the money sent to Minna, and certain payments to the furniture dealer at Wiesbaden, I found I had very little more than twelve thousand marks left. So the scheme of buying land and building a house had to be relinquished. But Cosima's excellent health and high spirits dispelled all anxious thought for the present. We drove out again in a splendid carriage, and in the most extravagant of good humours, through the avenues of the Tiergarten, dined to our hearts' content at the Hôtel de Russie, and made up our minds that bad times had fled for ever.

For the immediate present my plans were directed towards Vienna. I had recently heard that *Tristan* had once more been abandoned, this time owing to the indisposition of Frau Dustmann. In order to have this important matter more directly under my own supervision, and also because I had formed no such intimate artistic ties with any other German city as with Vienna, I clung to this as the most suitable place in which to settle. Tausig, whom I now met there in excellent health and spirits, entirely confirmed me in this opinion, and still further strengthened it by undertaking to find me precisely the pleasant and quiet dwelling in the neighbourhood of Vienna that I had set my mind upon, and through his own landlord he succeeded in getting something exactly to my taste. In what had been the pleasant abode of old Baron von Rackowitz at Penzing, I was offered the most delightful accommodation for a yearly rent of two thousand four hundred marks. I could have the entire upper part of the house and the exclusive use of a shady and fairly large garden. In the housekeeper, Franz Mrazek, I found a very obliging man, whom I at once took into my service, together with his wife Anna, an exceedingly gifted and obliging woman. For many years, amid ever-changing fortunes, this couple remained faithful to me. I now had to begin spending money in order to make my long-desired asylum fit and cosy both for rest and work. The remnant of my household belongings, including my Erard grand, was sent on from Biebrich, as well as the new furniture I had found it necessary to buy. On the 12th of May, in lovely spring weather, I took possession of my pleasant home, and for a while wasted much time over the exciting cares connected with the fitting up of my comfortable apartments. It was at this period that my connection with Phillip Haas and Sons was first established, which was destined with the lapse of time to give me some cause for anxiety. For the moment every exertion expended on a domicile associated with so many hopes only helped to put me into the best of spirits. The grand-piano arrived in due course, and with the addition of various engravings after Raphael, which had fallen to my lot in the Biebrich division, my music-room was completely furnished in readiness for the 22nd of May, when I celebrated my fiftieth birthday. In honour of the occasion the Merchants' Choral Society gave me an evening serenade with Chinese-lantern illuminations, in which a deputation of students also joined and greeted me with an enthusiastic oration. I had laid in a supply of wine, and everything passed off excellently. The Mrazeks looked after my housekeeping fairly well, and thanks to the culinary arts of Anna, I was able to invite Tausig and Cornelius to dine with me pretty frequently.

But I was soon in great trouble again, on account of Minna, who bitterly reproached me for everything I did. Having made up my mind never to answer her again, I wrote this time to her daughter Nathalie — who was still in ignorance of the relationship between them — referring her to my decision of the previous year.

On the other hand, the fact that I sadly stood in need just now of some womanly attentions and care in the management of the household became abundantly clear to me when I expressed to Mathilde Maier of Mayence the ingenuous wish that she would come and supply the deficiency.

I had certainly thought that my good friend was sensible enough to interpret my meaning correctly without feeling put to the blush, and I was very likely right, but I had not made sufficient allowance for her mother and her bourgeois surroundings generally. She appears to have been thrown into the greatest excitement by my proposal, while her friend Louise Wagner was in the end so powerfully influenced that she frankly advised me, with homely shrewdness and precision, to obtain a legal separation from my wife first of all, after which everything else would be easily arranged. Grievously shocked, I at once withdrew my offer, as having been made without due deliberation, and strove as far as possible to allay the excitement thus produced. On the other hand, Friederike Meyer's inexplicable fate still caused me much involuntary anxiety. After she had spent several months of the previous winter in Venice, apparently to her benefit, I had written to her from St. Petersburg suggesting that she should meet me at the Bülows' in Berlin. I had taken into mature consideration the kindly interest which Cosima had conceived for her, with a view to discussing what steps we could take to bring order into our friend's flagrantly disorganised circumstances. She did not appear, however, but wrote instead to inform me that she had taken up her abode with a lady friend at Coburg, as her very delicate state of health seriously interfered with her theatrical career, and was endeavouring to maintain herself by occasional appearances at the small theatre there. It was obvious that for many reasons I could not send her an invitation such as that sent to Mathilde Maier, though she expressed a violent desire to see me once more for a short time, assuring me that afterwards she would for ever leave me in peace. I could only regard it as purposeless and risky to accede to this wish just then, though I kept the idea in reserve for the future. During the course of the summer she repeated the same request from several places, until, as I was engaged late in the autumn for a concert at Karlsruhe, I at last appointed that time and place for the desired meeting. From that time forth I never received the slightest communication from this most singular and attractive friend of mine, and as, moreover, I did not know where she was, I looked upon our connection as severed. Not until many years later was the secret of her position — certainly a very difficult one — revealed to me, and from the facts then stated I could only conclude that she shrank from telling me the truth concerning her connection with Herr von Guaita. It appeared that this man had much more serious claims upon her than I had suspected, and she had apparently been compelled by the necessities of her situation to accept his protection, as he was the only friend left to her, while his devotion was undeniably genuine. I heard that she was then living in complete retirement both from the stage and from society on a tiny estate on the Rhine with her two children, being, it was believed, secretly married to Herr von Guaita.

But my careful and elaborate preparations for a quiet spell of work had not yet been successful. A burglary in the house, which robbed me of the golden snuff-box presented by the Moscow musicians, renewed my old longing to have a dog. My kind old landlord consequently handed over to me an old and somewhat neglected hound named Pohl, one of the most affectionate and excellent animals that ever attached itself to me. In his company I daily undertook long excursions on foot, for which the very pleasant neighbourhood afforded admirable opportunities. Nevertheless I was still rather lonely, as Tausig was confined to bed for a long time by severe illness, while Cornelius was suffering from an injured foot, the result of a careless descent from an omnibus when visiting Penzing. Meanwhile I was in constant friendly intercourse with Standhartner and his family. Fritz, the younger brother of Heinrich Porges, had also begun to visit me. He was a doctor who had just set up practice, a really nice fellow, whose acquaintance with me dated from the serenade of the Merchants' Glee Club, of which he had been the originator.

I was now convinced that there was no longer any chance of having *Tristan* produced at the Opera, as I had found out that Frau Dustmann's indisposition was merely a feint, Herr

Ander's complete loss of voice having been the real cause of the last interruption. Good old Conductor Esser tried hard to persuade me to assign the part of Tristan to another tenor of the theatre named Walter, but the very idea of him was so odious to me that I could not even bring myself to hear him in *Lohengrin*. I therefore let the matter sink into oblivion, and concentrated myself exclusively on getting into touch with the *Meistersinger* again. I first set to work on the instrumentation of the completed portion of the first act, of which I had only arranged detached fragments as yet. But as summer approached, the old anxiety as to my future subsistence began to pervade all my thoughts and sensations in the present. It was clear that, if I were to fulfil all my responsibilities, particularly with regard to Minna, I should soon have to think of undertaking some lucrative enterprise again.

It was therefore most opportune when a quite unexpected invitation from the management of the National Theatre in Buda-Pesth reached me to give two concerts there, in compliance with which I went at the end of July to the Hungarian capital, and was received by the manager Radnodfay. There I met a really very talented violinist named Réményi, who at one time had been a protégé of Liszt, and showed boundless admiration for me, even declaring that the invitation to me had been given entirely on his initiative. Although there was no prospect of large earnings here, as I had professed myself content to accept a thousand marks for each of the two concerts, I had reason to be pleased both with their success and with the great interest manifested by the audience. In this city, where the Magyar opposition to Austria was still at its strongest, I made the acquaintance of some exceedingly gifted and distinguished-looking young men, among them Herr Rosti, of whom I have a pleasant recollection. They organised a truly idyllic festivity for me, in the form of a feast, held by a few intimates on an island in the Danube, where we gathered under an ancient oak tree, as though for a patriarchal ceremony. A young lawyer, whose name I have unfortunately forgotten, had undertaken to propose the toast of the evening, and filled me with amazement and deep emotion, not only by the fire of his delivery, but also by the truly noble earnestness of his ideas, which he based upon a perfect knowledge of all my works and under-takings. We returned home down the Danube in the small boats of the Rowing Club, of which my hosts were members, and on our way had to face a hurricane, which lashed the mighty stream into the wildest tumult. There was only one lady in our party, Countess Bethlen-Gabor, who was seated with me in a narrow boat. Rosti and a friend of his who had the oars were concerned solely with the fear that our boat would be shivered against one of the timber-rafts, towards which the flood was carrying us, and therefore exerted them-selves to the utmost to avoid them; whereas I could see no other way of escape, especially for the lady sitting beside me, than by boarding one of these very rafts. In order to effect this (against the wish of our two oarsmen) I seized with one hand a projecting peg on a raft we were passing and held our little vessel fast, and, while the two rowers screamed that the *Ellida* would be lost, quickly hoisted the lady out of the skiff on to the raft, across which we walked to the shore, calmly leaving our friends to save the *Ellida* as best they could. We two then continued our way along the bank through a terrific storm of rain, but yet on safe and sure ground, towards the city. My conduct in presence of this danger did not fail to increase the respect in which my friends held me, as was proved by a banquet given in a public garden at which a great number of my admirers were present. Here they treated me quite in Hungarian style. An enormous band of gipsy musicians was drawn up, and greeted me with the *Rakoczy* March as I approached, while the assembled guests joined in with impet-uous shouts of ' *Eljen!* ' There were also fiery orations with appreciative allusions to myself and my influence which ex-tended far and wide throughout Germany. The introductory parts of these speeches were always in Hungarian, and were meant to excuse the fact that the main oration would be delivered in German for the sake of their guest. Here I noticed that they never spoke of me as ' Richard Wagner,' but as ' Wagner Richard.'

Even the highest military officials were not behindhand in offering me their homage, through the medium of Field-Marshal Coronini. The Count invited me to a performance by the military bands in the castle at Ofen, where I was graciously received by him and his family, treated to ices, and then conducted to a balcony whence I listened to a concert given by the massed bands. The effect of all these demonstrations was exceedingly refreshing, and I almost regretted having to leave the rejuvenating atmosphere of Buda-Pesth, and return to my dull and musty Viennese asylum.

On the homeward journey, in the beginning of August, I travelled part of the way with Herr von Seebach, the amiable Saxon Ambassador, whom I had known in Paris. He complained of the enormous losses he had incurred through the difficulty of administering the South Russian estates he had acquired by marriage, and from which he was just returning. On the other hand, I was able to reassure him as to my own position, which seemed to give him genuine pleasure.

The small receipts from my Buda-Pesth concerts, of which, moreover, I had only been able to carry away half, were not calculated to afford me any effectual relief as to the future. Having now staked my all on what I trusted might be a permanent establishment, the first question was how best to secure a salary, which should at least be certain though not necessarily over-large. Meanwhile I did not consider myself bound to abandon my St. Petersburg connection, nor the plans I had founded upon it. Nor did I entirely disbelieve the assurances of Réményi, who boasted that he had great influence with the Magyar magnates, and assured me it would be no great matter to obtain a pension in Buda-Pesth, such as I had thought of securing in St. Petersburg and involving similar obligations. He did, in fact, visit me soon after my return to Penzing, accompanied by his adopted son, young Plotenyi, whose extraordinary good looks and amiability made a very favourable impression on me. As for the father himself, although he won my warm approbation by his brilliant performance of the *Rakoczy* March on the violin, yet I quickly perceived that his glowing promises had been meant rather to create an immediate impression on me than to ensure any permanent result. In accordance with his own desire, I very soon afterwards lost sight of him altogether.

While still obliged to busy myself with plans for concert tours,

I was able meantime to enjoy the pleasant shade of my garden during the intense heat, and I used to go for long rambles every evening with my faithful dog Pohl, the most refreshing of these being by way of the dairy-farm at St. Veit, where delicious milk was available. My small social circle was still restricted to Cornelius and Tausig, who was at last restored to health, although he disappeared from my sight for some time owing to his intercourse with wealthy Austrian officers. But I was frequently joined on my excursions by the younger Porges, and for a time by the elder also. My niece Ottilie Brockhaus too, who was living with the family of her mother's friend Heinrich Laube, occasionally delighted me with a visit.

But whenever I settled down seriously to work, I was goaded afresh by an uneasy apprehension as to the means of subsistence. As another journey to Russia was out of the question until the following Easter, only German towns could serve my purpose for the present. From many quarters, as for instance from Darmstadt, I received unfavourable replies; and from Karlsruhe, where I had applied direct to the Grand Duke, the answer was indefinite. But the severest blow to my confidence was a direct refusal which came in response to the application I had at last made to St. Petersburg, the acceptance of which would have ensured a regular salary. This time the excuse made was that the Polish revolution of that summer had paralysed the spirit of artistic enterprise.

Pleasanter news, however, came from Moscow, where they held out prospects of some good concerts for the coming year. I next bethought me of a very sound suggestion about Kieff made to me by Setoff the singer, who thought there was a prospect of a highly profitable engagement there. I entered into correspondence on the matter, and was again put off until the following Easter, when all the smaller Russian nobility congregated at Kieff. These were all plans for the future which, if I then had considered them in detail at that time, would have been enough to rob me of all peace of mind for my work. In any case there was a long interval during which I must provide, not only for myself, but also for Minna. Any prospect of a position in Vienna had to be handled most warily, so that, with the approach of autumn, there was nothing left me but to raise money on loan, a business in which Tausig was able to help me, as he possessed extraordinary experience in such matters.

I could not help wondering whether I should have to give up my Penzing establishment, but, on the other hand, what alternative was open to me? Every time I was seized with the desire to compose, these cares obtruded themselves on my mind, until, seeing that it was only a question of putting things off from day to day, I was driven to take up the study of Dunker's *Geschichte des Alterthums*. In the end my correspondence about concerts swallowed up the whole of my time. I first asked Heinrich Porges to see what he could arrange in Prague. He also held out a reasonable prospect of a concert at Löwenberg, relying upon the favourable disposition of the Prince of Hohenzollern, who lived there. I was also advised to apply to Hans von Bronsart, who at this time was conductor to a private orchestral society in Dresden. He responded loyally to my proposition, and between us we settled the date and programme of a concert to be conducted by me in Dresden. As the Grand Duke of Baden had also placed his theatre at Karlsruhe at my disposal for a concert to be given in November, I thought I had now done enough in this direction to be entitled to take up something different. I therefore wrote a fairly long article for Uhl-Fröbel's paper *Der Botschafter* on the Imperial Grand Opera House in Vienna, in which I made suggestions for a thorough reform of this very badly managed institution. The excellence of this article was at once acknowledged on all sides, even by the press; and I appear to have made some impression in the highest administrative circles, for I shortly afterwards heard from my friend Rudolf Liechtenstein, that tentative advances had been made to him with a view to his accepting the position of manager, associated with which there was certainly an idea of asking me to become conductor of the Grand Opera. Among the reasons which caused this proposal to fall through was the fear, Liechtenstein informed me, that under his direction people would hear nothing but ' Wagner operas.'

In the end it was a relief to escape from the anxieties of my position by starting on my concert tour. First I went to

Prague, in the beginning of November, to try my luck again in the matter of big receipts. Unfortunately Heinrich Porges had not been able to take the arrangements in hand this time, and his deputies, who were very busy schoolmasters, were not at all his equals for the task. Expenses were increased, while receipts diminished, for they had not ventured to ask such high prices as before. I wished to repair this deficiency by a second concert a few days later, and insisted on the point, although my friends urgently dissuaded me, and, as the event proved, they were quite right. This time the receipts hardly covered the costs, and as I had been obliged to send away the proceeds of the first concert to redeem an old bill in Vienna, I had no other means of paying my hotel expenses and my fare home than by accepting the offer of a banker, who posed as a patron, to help me out of my embarrassment.

In the chastened mood induced by these occurrences I pursued my journey to Karlsruhe, via Nuremberg and Stuttgart, under wretched conditions of severe cold and constant delays. At Karlsruhe I was at once surrounded by various friends, who had come there on hearing of my project. Richard Pohl from Baden, who never failed me, Mathilde Maier, Frau Betty Schott, the wife of my publisher; even Raff from Wiesbaden and Emilie Genast were there, as well as Karl Eckert, who had recently been appointed conductor at Stuttgart. Trouble began at once with the vocalists for my first concert, fixed for 14th November, as the baritone, Hauser, who was to sing 'Wotan's Farewell' and Hans Sachs's 'Cobbler Song,' was ill and had to be replaced by a voiceless though well-drilled vaudeville singer. In Eduard Devrient's opinion this made no difference. My relations with him were strictly official, but he certainly carried out my instructions for the arrangement of the orchestra very correctly. From an orchestral point of view the concert went off so well that the Grand Duke, who received me very graciously in his box, desired a repetition in a week's time. To this proposal I raised serious objections, having learned by experience that the large attendances at such concerts, particularly at special prices, were mainly accounted for by the curiosity of the hearers, who often came from long distances; whereas the number of genuine students of art,

whose interest was chiefly in the music, was but small. But
the Grand Duke insisted, as he wished to give his mother-in-
law, Queen Augusta, whose arrival was expected within a few
days, the pleasure of hearing my production. I should have
found it dreadfully wearisome to have to spend the intervening
time in the solitude of my Karlsruhe hotel, but I received a
kind invitation to Baden-Baden from Mme. Kalergis, who had
just become Mme. Moukhanoff, and had gone to live there.
She had, to my delight, been one of those who came over for
the concert, and was now on the station to meet me when I
arrived. I felt I ought to decline her proffered escort into
the town, not considering myself sufficiently smart in my
'brigand-hat,' but with the assurance, 'We all wear these
brigand-hats here,' she took my arm, and thus we reached
Pauline Viardot's villa, where we were to dine, as my friend's
own house was not yet quite ready. Seated by my old acquaintance, I was now introduced to the Russian poet Tur-
genieff. Mme. Moukhanoff presented me to her husband with
some hesitation, wondering what I should think of her marriage. Supported by her companions, who were all society
people, she exerted herself to maintain a fairly lively conversation during the time we were together. Well satisfied by
the admirable intention of my friend and benefactress, I again
left Baden to fill up my time by a little trip to Zürich, where
I again tried to get a few days' rest in the house of the Wesendonck family. The idea of assisting me did not seem even to
dawn on these friends of mine, although I frankly informed
them of my position. I therefore returned to Karlsruhe, where,
on the 22nd of November, as I had foreseen, I gave my second
concert to a poorly filled house. But, in the opinion of the
Grand Duke and his wife, Queen Augusta's appreciation should
have dispelled any unpleasant impressions I might have received. I was again summoned to the royal box, where I
found all the court gathered round the Queen, who wore a blue
rose on her forehead as an ornament. The few complimentary
observations she had to offer were listened to by the members
of the court with breathless attention; but when the royal
lady had made a few general remarks, and was about to enter
into details, she left all further demonstration to her daughter,

who, as she said, knew more about it. The next day I received my share of the takings, half the net profits, which amounted to two hundred marks, and with this I at once bought myself a fur coat. The sum asked for it was two hundred and twenty marks, but when I explained that my receipts had only been two hundred marks, I managed to get the extra twenty knocked off the price. There was still the Grand Duke's private gift, consisting of a gold snuff-box with fifteen louis d'or, for which I, of course, returned my thanks in writing. I next had to face the question whether, after the toilsome fatigue of the past weeks, I would add to my disappointments by attempting to give the proposed concert in Dresden. Many considerations, practically everything indeed that I had to weigh in connection with a visit to Dresden, moved me to have the courage to write and tell Hans von Bronsart at the last moment to cancel all arrangements and not expect me there, a decision which, although it must have caused him much inconvenience after all the preparations he had kindly made, he accepted with a very good grace.

I still wanted to see what I could do with the firm of Schott, and travelled by night to Mayence, where Mathilde Maier's family insisted on my spending the day at their little house, where I was entertained in a simple and friendly fashion. During the day and night I spent here in the narrow Karthäusergasse, I was waited upon with the greatest care, and from this outpost I assaulted the publishing house of Schott, though without securing much booty. This was because I refused my consent to a separate issue of the various selections from my new works which had been picked out and prepared for concert use.

As my only remaining source of profit now seemed to be the concert at Löwenberg, I turned my face thither; but, in order to avoid passing Dresden, I made a short détour by way of Berlin, where, after travelling all night, I arrived, very tired, early on the 28th of November. In compliance with my request the Bülows took me in, and at once began urging me to break my intended journey to Silesia by giving them a day in Berlin. Hans was particularly anxious for me to be present at a concert to be given that evening under his direction, a fact which finally decided me to remain. In defiance of the cold, raw and gloomy weather, we discussed as cheerfully as we could my unfortunate position. By way of increasing my capital, it was resolved to hand over the Grand Duke of Baden's gold snuff-box to our good old friend Weitzmann for sale. The sum of two hundred and seventy marks realised by this was brought to me at the Hôtel Brandenburg, where I was dining with the Bülows, and was an addition to my reserves that furnished us with many a jest. As Bülow had to complete the preparations for his concert, I drove out alone with Cosima on the promenade, as before, in a fine carriage. This time all our jocularity died away into silence. We gazed speechless into each other's eyes; an intense longing for an avowal of the truth mastered us and led to a confession — which needed no words — of the boundless unhappiness which oppressed us. The experience brought relief to us both, and the profound tranquillity which ensued enabled us to attend the concert in a cheerful, unembarrassed mood. I was actually able to fix my attention clearly on an exquisitely refined and elevated performance of Beethoven's smaller Concert Overture (in C major), and likewise on Hans's very clever arrangement of Gluck's overture to *Paris and Helen.* We noticed Alwine Frommann in the audience, and during the interval met her on the grand staircase of the concert-hall. After the second part had begun and the stairs were empty, we sat for some time on one of the steps chatting gaily with our old friend. After the concert we were due at my friend Weitzmann's for supper, the length and abundance of which reduced us, whose hearts yearned for profound peace, to almost frantic despair. But the day came to an end at last, and after a night spent under Bülow's roof, I continued my journey. Our farewell reminded me so vividly of that first exquisitely pathetic parting from Cosima at Zürich, that all the intervening years vanished like a dream of desolation separating two days of lifelong moment and decision. If on the first occasion our presentiment of something mysterious and inexplicable had compelled silence, it was now no less impossible to give words to that which we silently acknowledged.

I was met at one of the stations in Silesia by Conductor Seifriz, who accompanied me in one of the Prince's carriages to

Löwenberg. The old Prince of Hohenzollern-Hechingen was already very well disposed towards me on account of his great friendship for Liszt, and had, moreover, been fully informed of my position by Heinrich Porges, who had been engaged by him for a short time. He had invited me to give a concert in his small castle to an audience composed exclusively of invited guests. I was very comfortably accommodated in apartments on the ground floor of his house, whither he frequently came on his wheeled chair from his own rooms directly opposite. Here I could not only feel at ease, but be to some extent hopeful. I at once began rehearsing the pieces I had chosen from my operas with the Prince's by no means ill-equipped private orchestra, during which my host was invariably present and seemed well satisfied. Meals were all taken very sociably in common; but on the day of the concert there was a kind of gala-dinner, at which I was astonished to meet Henriette von Bissing, the sister of Mme. Wille of Marienbad, with whom I had been intimate at Zürich. As she had an estate near Löwenberg, she had also been invited by the Prince, and now gave me proof of her faithful and enthusiastic devotion. Being both intelligent and witty, she at once became my favourite companion. After the concert had passed off with reasonable success, I had to fulfil another wish of the Prince's next day, by privately playing to him Beethoven's Symphony in C minor, when Frau von Bissing was also present. She had now been for some time a widow. She promised to come to Breslau, when I gave my concert there. Before my departure Conductor Seifriz brought me a fee of four thousand two hundred marks from the Prince, with an expression of regret that for the present it was impossible for him to be more liberal. After all my previous experiences I was truly astonished and contented, and it was with pleasure I returned the gallant Prince my heartfelt thanks with all the eloquence at my command.

Thence I travelled to Breslau, where the concert director, Damrosch, had arranged a concert for me. I had made his acquaintance on my last visit to Weimar, and had also heard of him through Liszt. Unfortunately the conditions here struck me as extraordinarily dismal and desperate. The whole affair had been planned on the meanest scale, as indeed

I might have expected. A perfectly horrible concert-room, which usually served as a beer-restaurant, had been engaged. At the rear of this, and separated from it by a dreadfully vulgar curtain, was a small 'Tivoli' theatre, for which I was obliged to procure an elevated plank-floor for the orchestra, and the whole concern so disgusted me that my first impulse was to dismiss the seedy-looking musicians on the spot. My friend Damrosch, who was very much upset, had to promise me that at least he would have the horrible reek of tobacco in the place neutralised. As he could offer no guarantee as to the amount of the receipts, I was only induced in the end to go on with the enterprise by my desire not to compromise him too severely. To my amazement I found almost the entire room, at all events the front seats, filled with Jews, and in fact I owed such success as I obtained to the interest excited in this section of the population, as I learned the next day, when I attended a mid-day dinner arranged in my honour by Damrosch, at which again only Jews were present.

It was like a ray of light from a better world when, on leaving the concert-hall, I perceived Fräulein Marie von Buch, who had hurried hither with her grandmother from the Hatzfeld estate to be present at my concert, and was waiting in a boarded compartment dignified by the name of box, for me to come out after the audience had left; the young lady came up to me once more in travelling costume after Damrosch's dinner and attempted by kindly and sympathetic assurances somewhat to assuage my evident anxiety respecting the future. I thanked her once more by letter for her sympathy after my return to Vienna, to which she replied by a request for a contribution to her album. In memory of the emotions which had convulsed me on leaving Berlin, and also as an indication of my mental mood to one worthy of the confidence, I added Calderon's words, 'Things impossible to conceal, yet impossible of utter-ance.' By this I felt I had conveyed to a kindly disposed person, though with a happy vagueness, some idea of the secret knowl-edge which was my sole inspiration.

But the results of my meeting with Henriette von Bissing in Breslau were very different. She had followed me thither, and put up at the same hotel. Influenced, no doubt, by my sickly appearance, she seemed to give her sympathy for myself and my situation full play. I placed the latter before her without reserve, telling her how, ever since the upset following on my departure from Zürich in 1858, I had been unable to secure the regular income necessary for the steady pursuit of my calling; and also of my invariably vain attempts to bring my affairs into any settled and definite order. My friend did not shrink from attributing some blame to the relationship between Frau Wesendonck and my wife, and declared that she felt it her mission to conciliate them. She approved my settling down at Penzing, and only hoped that I might not spoil its beneficial effect upon me by distant enterprises. She would not listen to my plan of touring in Russia, in the coming winter, in order to earn money for my absolute necessities, and herself undertook to provide from her own very considerable fortune the not unimportant sum requisite to maintain me in independence for some time to come. But she explained to me that for a short while longer I was to try and get along through thick and thin, as she would have some difficulty — possibly a good deal — in placing the promised money at my disposal.

Greatly cheered by the impressions of this meeting I returned to Vienna on the 9th December. At Löwenberg I had been obliged to remit to Vienna the greater portion of the Prince's gift, part of it for Minna, and part for the payment of debts. Though I had but little cash I felt thoroughly sanguine; I could now greet my few friends with tolerable good-humour, and among them Peter Cornelius, who looked in on me every evening. As Heinrich Porges and Gustav Schönaich sometimes joined us, we founded an intimate little circle and met regularly. On Christmas Eve I invited them all to my house, where I had the Christmas tree lighted up, and gave each one an appropriate trifle. Some work also came my way again, for Tausig asked me to help him with a concert which he was to give in the great Redouten-Saal. In addition to a few selections from my new operas, I also conducted the *Freischütz* Overture, for my own particular satisfaction and entirely according to my own interpretation. Its effect, even upon the orchestra, was truly startling.

But there did not seem the slightest prospect of any official recognition of my abilities; I was, and continued to be, ignored by the great. Frau von Bissing's communications revealed by degrees the difficulties which she had encountered in the fulfilment of her promise; but as they were still hopeful in tone, I was able to spend New Year's Eve at the Standhartner's in good spirits, and to enjoy a poem specially written by Cornelius for the occasion, which was as humorous as it was solemnly appropriate.

The new year 1864 assumed for me an aspect of gravity which soon became intensified. I fell ill with a painful and increasing malady due to a chill, which often made demands on Standhartner's care. But I was yet more seriously threatened by the turn of Frau von Bissing's communications. It seemed she could only raise the promised money with the help of her family, the Slomans, who were shipowners in Hamburg, and from them she was meeting with violent opposition, mingled, as it seemed, with slanderous charges against me. These circumstances upset me so much that I wished I could renounce all help from this friend, and I began once more to turn my serious attention to Russia. Fräulein von Rhaden, to whom I again applied, felt she must vigorously dissuade me from any attempt to visit St. Petersburg, in the first place because, owing to the military disturbances in the Polish provinces, I should find the route blocked, and secondly because, roughly speaking, I should attract no notice in the Russian capital. On the other hand, a visit to Kieff, with a chance of five thousand roubles profit, was represented as undoubtedly feasible. Keeping my thoughts fixed on this, I arranged with Cornelius, who was to accompany me, a plan for crossing the Black Sea to Odessa, and going from there to Kieff, with a view to which we both resolved to procure the indispensable fur coats at once. Meanwhile, the only course open to me was to see about raising money by fresh bills at short dates, wherewith to pay all my other bills, which were also short-dated. Thus I became launched upon a business system which, leading, as it did, to obvious and inevitable ruin, could only be finally resolved by the acceptance of prompt and effectual help. In these straits I was at last compelled to request a clear declaration from my friend, not as to whether she *could* help me at once, but whether she really *wished* to help me at all, as I could no longer stave off ruin. She must have been in the highest degree wounded by some notion or other, of which I was ignorant, before bringing herself to reply in the following tone: 'You wish to know finally whether I *will* or not? Well, then, in God's name, *No!*' Not long after this I received from her sister, Mme. Wille, a very surprising explanation of her conduct, which seemed at the time perfectly inexplicable, and only to be accounted for by the weakness of her not very reliable character.

Amid all these vacillations the month of February had run to an end, and while Cornelius and I were busy on our Russian plans, I received news from Kieff and Odessa that it would be unwise to attempt any artistic enterprises there during the present year. By this time it had become clear that, under the conditions thus developed, I could no longer reckon on maintaining my position in Vienna, or my establishment at Penzing. Not only did there seem no prospect of even a temporary nature of earning money, but my debts had mounted up, in the usual style of such usury, to so great a sum, and assumed so threatening an aspect, that, failing some extraordinary relief, my very person was in danger. In this perplexity I addressed myself with perfect frankness — at first only for advice — to the judge of the Imperial Provincial Court, Eduard Liszt, the youthful uncle of my old friend Franz. During my first stay in Vienna this man had shown himself a warmly devoted friend, always ready to help me. For the discharge of my bill-debts he could naturally suggest no other method than the intervention of some wealthy patron, who should settle with my creditors. For some time he believed that a certain Mme. Schöller, the wife of a rich merchant and one of my admirers, not only possessed the means, but was willing to use them on my behalf. Standhartner also, with whom I made no pretence of secrecy, thought he could do something for me in this way. Thus my position was for some weeks again most uncertain, until at last it became clear that all my friends could procure me was the means for flight to Switzerland — which was now deemed absolutely necessary — where, having saved my skin so far, I should have to raise money for my bills. To the lawyer, Eduard Liszt, this way of escape seemed specially desirable, because he would then be in a position to punish the outrageous usury practised against me.

During the anxious time of the last few months, through which, nevertheless, there had run an undercurrent of indefinite hope, I had kept up a lively intercourse with my few friends. Cornelius turned up regularly every evening, and was joined by O. Bach, little Count Laurencin, and, on one occasion, by Rudolph Liechtenstein. With Cornelius alone I began reading the *Iliad*. When we reached the catalogue of ships I wished to skip it; but Peter protested, and offered to read it out himself; but whether we ever came to the end of it I forget. My reading by myself consisted of Chateaubriand's *La Vie de Rancé*, which Tausig had brought me. Meanwhile, he himself vanished without leaving any trace, until after some time he reappeared engaged to a Hungarian pianist. During the whole of this time I was very ill and suffered exceedingly from a violent catarrh. The thought of death took such hold on me that I at last lost all desire to shake it off, and even set about bequeathing my books and manuscripts, of which a portion fell to the lot of Cornelius.

I had taken the precaution some time before of commending into Standhartner's keeping my remaining — and now, alas! exceedingly doubtful — assets which were in the house at Penzing. As my friends were most positive in recommending preparation for immediate flight, I had written to Otto Wesendonck requesting to be taken into his house, as Switzerland was to be my destination. He refused point-blank, and I could not resist sending him a reply to prove the injustice of this. The next thing was to make my absence from home a short one and to count upon a speedy return. Standhartner made me go and dine at his house in his great anxiety to cover up my departure, and my servant Franz Mrazek brought my trunk there too. My farewell to Standhartner, his wife Anna, and the good dog Pohl was very depressing. Standhartner's stepson Karl Schönaich and Cornelius accompanied me to the station, the one in grief and tears, the other inclining to a frivolous mood. It was on the afternoon of 23rd March that I left for Munich, my first stopping-place, where I hoped to rest for two days after the terrible disturbances I had gone through, without attracting any notice. I stayed at the 'Bayerischer Hof' and took a few walks through the city at my leisure. It was Good Friday and the weather was bitterly cold. The mood proper to the day seemed to possess the whole population, whom I saw going from one church to another dressed in deepest mourning. King Maximilian II. — of whom the Bavarians had become so fond — had died a few days before, leaving as heir to the throne a son aged eighteen and a half, whose extreme youth was no bar to his accession. I saw a portrait of the young king, Ludwig II., in a shop window, and experienced the peculiar emotion which is aroused by the sight of youth and beauty placed in a position presumed to be unusually trying. After writing a humorous epitaph for myself, I crossed Lake Constance unmolested and reached Zürich — once more a refugee in need of an asylum — where I at once betook myself to Dr. Wille's estate at Mariafeld.

I had already written to my friend's wife to ask her to put me up for a few days, which she very kindly agreed to do. I had got to know her very well during my last stay at Zürich, while my friendship with him had somewhat cooled. I wanted to have time to find what seemed suitable quarters in one of the places bordering on Lake Zürich. Dr. Wille himself was not there, as he had gone to Constantinople on a pleasure trip. I had no difficulty in making my friend understand my situation, which I found her most willing to relieve. First of all she cleared one or two living rooms in Frau von Bissing's old house next door, from which, however, the fairly comfortable furniture had been removed. I wanted to cater for myself, but had to yield to her request to take over that responsibility. Only furniture was lacking, and for this she ventured to apply to Frau Wesendonck, who immediately sent all she could spare of her household goods, as well as a cottage piano. The good woman was also anxious that I should visit my old friends at Zürich to avoid any appearance of unpleasantness, but I was prevented from doing so by serious indisposition, which was increased by the badly heated rooms, and finally Otto and Mathilde Wesendonck came over to us at Mariafeld. The very uncertain and strained attitude apparent in these two was not entirely incomprehensible to me, but I behaved as if

I did not notice it. My cold, which rendered me incapable of looking about for a house in the neighbouring districts, was continually aggravated by the bad weather and my own deep depression. I spent these dreadful days sitting huddled in my Karlsruhe fur coat from morning till night, and addled my brain with reading one after another of the volumes which Mme. Wille sent me in my seclusion. I read Jean Paul's *Siebenkäs*, Frederick the Great's *Tagebuch*, Tauser, George Sand's novels and Walter Scott's, and finally *Felicitas*, a work from my sympathetic hostess's own pen. Nothing reached me from the outside world except a passionate lament from Mathilde Maier, and a most pleasant surprise in the shape of royalties (seventy-five francs), which Truinet sent from Paris. This led to a conversation with Mme. Wille, half in anger and half with condemned-cell cynicism, as to what I could do to obtain complete release from my wretched situation. Among other things we touched upon the necessity of obtaining a divorce from my wife in order to contract a rich marriage. As everything seemed right and nothing inexpedient in my eyes, I actually wrote and asked my sister Luise Brockhaus whether she could not, by talking sensibly to Minna, persuade her to depend on her settled yearly allowance without making any claims on my person in future. In reply I received a deeply pathetic letter advising me first to think of establishing my reputation and to create for myself an unassailable position by some new work. In this way I might very probably reap some benefit without taking any foolish step; and in any case I should do well to apply for the post of conductor which was now vacant in Darmstadt.

I had very bad news from Vienna. Standhartner, to make sure of the furniture I had left in the house, sold it to a Viennese agent, with the option of re-purchase. I wrote back in great indignation, particularly as I realised the prejudicial effect of this on my landlord, to whom I had to pay rent within the next few days. Through Mme. Wille I succeeded in getting placed at my disposal the money required for the rent, which I forwarded at once to Baron Rackowitz. Unfortunately, however, I found that Standhartner had already cleared up everything with Eduard Liszt, paying the rent with the proceeds from the furniture, and thereby cutting off my return to Vienna, which they both considered would be positive ruin to me. But when I heard at the same time from Cornelius that Tausig, who was then in Hungary and who had added his signature to one of the bills of exchange, felt himself prevented by me from returning to Vienna as he desired, I was so sensibly wounded that I decided to go back on the spot, however great the danger might be. I announced my intention to my friends there immediately, but decided first to try and provide myself with enough money to be in a position to suggest a composition with my creditors. To this end I had written most urgently to Schott at Mayence, and did not refrain from reproaching him bitterly for his behaviour to me. I now decided to leave Mariafeld for Stuttgart to await the result of these efforts, and to prosecute them from a nearer vantage-ground. But I was also, as will be seen, moved to carry out this change by other motives.

Dr. Wille had returned, and I could see at once that my stay at Mariafeld alarmed him. He probably feared I might rely on his help also. In some confusion, occasioned by the attitude I had adopted in consequence, he made this confession to me in a moment of agitation. He was, he said, overpowered by a sentiment with regard to me which amounted to this — that a man wanted, after all, to be something more than a cipher in his own house, where, if anywhere, it is not pleasant to serve as a mere foil to some one else. This sentiment was merely excusable, he thought, in a man who, though he might reasonably suppose himself of some account among his fellows, had been brought into close contact with another to whom he felt himself in the strangest manner subordinate. Mme. Wille, foreseeing her husband's frame of mind, had come to an agreement with the Wesendonck family by which they were to provide me with one hundred francs a month during my stay at Mariafeld. When this came to my knowledge, I could do nothing but announce to Frau Wesendonck my immediate departure from Switzerland, and request her in the kindest possible way to consider herself relieved of all anxiety about me, as I had arranged my affairs quite in accordance with my wishes. I heard later that she had returned this letter — which, possibly, she considered compromising — to Mme. Wille unopened.

My next move was to go to Stuttgart on 30th April. I knew that Karl Eckert had been settled there some time as conductor at the Royal Court Theatre, and I had reason to believe the good-natured fellow to be unprejudiced and well disposed towards me, judging by his admirable behaviour when he had been director of the opera in Vienna, and also by the enthusiasm he exhibited in coming to my concert at Karlsruhe the year before. I expected nothing further of him than a little assistance in looking for a quiet lodging for the coming summer at Cannstadt or some such place near Stuttgart. I wanted, above all, to finish the first act of the *Meistersinger* with all possible despatch, so as to send Schott part of the manuscript at last. I had told him that I was going to send it to him almost immediately when I attacked him about the advances which had so long been withheld from me. I then intended to collect the means wherewith to meet my obligations in Vienna, while living in complete retirement and, as I hoped, in concealment. Eckert welcomed me most kindly. His wife — one of the greatest beauties in Vienna — had, in her fantastic desire to marry an artist, given up a very profitable post, but was still rich enough for the conductor to live comfortably and show hospitality, and the impression I now received was very pleasant. Eckert felt himself absolutely bound to take me to see Baron von Gall, the manager of the court theatre, who alluded sensibly and kindly to my difficult position in Germany, where everything was likely to remain closed to me as long as the Saxon ambassadors and agents — who were scattered everywhere — were allowed to attempt to injure me by all kinds of suspicions. After getting to know me better, he considered himself authorised to act on my behalf through the medium of the court of Würtemberg. As I was talking over these matters rather late on the evening of 3rd May at the Eckerts', a gentleman's card with the inscription 'Secretary to the King of Bavaria' was handed to me. I was disagreeably surprised that my presence in Stuttgart should be known to passing travellers, and sent word that I was not there, after which I retired to my hotel, only to be again informed by the landlord that a gentleman from Munich desired to see me on urgent business. I made an appointment for the morning at ten o'clock, and passed a disturbed night in my constant anticipation of misfortune. I received Herr Pfistermeister, the private secretary of H.M. the King of Bavaria, in my room. He first expressed great pleasure at having found me at last, thanks to receiving some happy directions, after vainly seeking me in Vienna and even at Mariafeld on Lake Zürich. He was charged with a note for me from the young King of Bavaria, together with a portrait and a ring as a present. In words which, though few, penetrated to the very core of my being, the youthful monarch confessed his great partiality for my work, and announced his firm resolve to keep me near him as his friend, so that I might escape any malignant stroke of fate. Herr Pfistermeister informed me at the same time that he was instructed to conduct me to Munich at once to see the King, and begged my permission to inform his master by telegram that I would come on the following day. I was invited to dine with the Eckerts, but Herr Pfistermeister was obliged to decline to accompany me. My friends, who had been joined by young Weisheimer from Osthofen, were very naturally amazed and delighted at the news I brought them. While we were at table Eckert was informed by telegram of Meyerbeer's death in Paris, and Weisheimer burst out in boorish laughter to think that the master of opera, who had done me so much harm, had by a strange coincidence not lived to see this day. Herr von Gall also made his appearance, and had to admit in friendly surprise that I certainly did not need his good services any more. He had already given the order for *Lohengrin*, and now paid me the stipulated sum on the spot. At five o'clock that afternoon I met Herr Pfistermeister at the station to travel with him to Munich, where my visit to the King was announced for the following morning.

On the same day I had received the most urgent warnings against returning to Vienna. But my life was to have no more of these alarms; the dangerous road along which fate beckoned me to such great ends was not destined to be clear of troubles and anxieties of a kind unknown to me heretofore, but I was never again to feel the weight of the everyday hardships of existence under the protection of my exalted friend.

INDEX

CPSIA information can be obtained
at www.ICGtesting.com
Printed in the USA
BVHW081118160919
558546BV00017B/1399